FOUNDATIONS OF INDIRECT DISCRIMINATION LAW

Indirect discrimination (or disparate impact) concerns the application of the same rule to everyone, even though that rule significantly disadvantages one particular group in society. Ever since its recognition by the Supreme Court of the United States in 1971, liberal democracies around the world have grappled with the puzzle that it can sometimes be unfair and wrong to treat everyone equally. The law's regulation of private acts that unintentionally (but disproportionately) harm vulnerable groups has remained extremely controversial, especially in the United States and the United Kingdom. In original essays in this volume, leading scholars of discrimination law from North America and Europe explore the various facets of the law on indirect discrimination, interrogating its foundations, history, legitimacy, purpose, structure, and relationship with other legal concepts. The collection provides the first international work devoted to this vital area of the law that seeks both to prevent unfair treatment and to transform societies.

Foundations of Indirect Discrimination Law

Edited by
Hugh Collins and Tarunabh Khaitan

HART
PUBLISHING
OXFORD AND PORTLAND, OREGON
2018

Hart Publishing
An imprint of Bloomsbury Publishing Plc

Hart Publishing Ltd
Kemp House
Chawley Park
Cumnor Hill
Oxford OX2 9PH
UK

Bloomsbury Publishing Plc
50 Bedford Square
London
WC1B 3DP
UK

www.hartpub.co.uk
www.bloomsbury.com

Published in North America (US and Canada) by
Hart Publishing
c/o International Specialized Book Services
920 NE 58th Avenue, Suite 300
Portland, OR 97213-3786
USA

www.isbs.com

HART PUBLISHING, the Hart/Stag logo, BLOOMSBURY and the Diana logo are trademarks of Bloomsbury Publishing Plc

First published 2018

British Library Cataloguing-in-Publication Data
A catalogue record for this book is available from the British Library.

ISBN: HB: 978-1-50991-254-4
ePDF: 978-1-50991-256-8
ePub: 978-1-50991-253-7

Library of Congress Cataloging-in-Publication Data

Names: Collins, Hugh, 1953- editor. | Khaitan, Tarunabh, 1981- editor.

Title: Foundations of indirect discrimination law / edited by Hugh Collins and Tarunabh Khaitan.

Description: Oxford ; Portland, Oregon : Hart Publishing, an imprint of Bloomsbury Publishing Plc, 2018. | Includes papers presented at a "lively workshop held in All Souls College and Wadham College, Oxford in March 2016."—Acknowledgements. | Includes bibliographical references and index.

Identifiers: LCCN 2017050498 (print) | LCCN 2017055563 (ebook) | ISBN 9781509912537 (Epub) | ISBN 9781509912544 (hardback : alk. paper)

Subjects: LCSH: Disparate impact (Law)—Congresses.

Classification: LCC K3239.8 (ebook) | LCC K3239.8 .F68 2018 (print) | DDC 342.08/5—dc23

LC record available at https://lccn.loc.gov/2017050498

Typeset by Compuscript Ltd, Shannon

Acknowledgements

We would like to thank Wadham College, All Souls College, and the Faculty of Law, University Oxford, for their generous support for the organisation of the lively workshop held in All Souls College and Wadham College, Oxford in March 2016, from which these papers emerged.

We owe a great debt of gratitude to everyone who made the workshop a success, as authors, discussants, chairs, participants and volunteers. They include Aaron Baker, Allan Manson, Amba Kak, Amit Pundik, Anne Davies, Anne Lofaso, Barbara Havelkova, Benjamin Eidelson, Caroline Greenfield, Catherine Briddick, Cathryn Costello, Colm O'Cinneide, David Edmonds, Deborah Hellman, Denise Réaume, Fadzai Madzingira, Geoffrey Yeung, Gitanjali Kesheva, Iyiola Solanke, James Rooney, Joanne Conaghan, John Bowers, Julie Suk, Karon Monaghan, Kasper Lippert-Rasmussen, Kate O'Regan, Laura Carlson, Leslie Green, Lucy Vickers, Marlena Valles, Max Harris, Meghan Campbell, Nicholas Bamforth, Nomfundo Ramalekana, Philippa Collins, Raag Yadava, Robert Wintemute, Robin Allen, Roisin Swords-Kieley, Ronan McCrea, Sandra Fredman, Sandy Steel, Sanya Samtani, Sophia Moreau, Stephen Sedley, Thiago Amparo and Virginia Mantouvalou.

We are particularly grateful to Philippa Collins for her excellent organisational support for the workshop, and efficient editorial assistance for this volume. Special thanks to Hart Publishing for their patience while we put this volume together.

Finally, we thank Alex for supporting Tarun when it mattered.

Hugh Collins
Tarunabh Khaitan
Oxford, August 2017

Contents

List of Contributors

Nicholas Bamforth, Fellow in Law, The Queen's College, University of Oxford.

Hugh Collins, Vinerian Professor of English Law, All Souls College, University of Oxford.

Sandra Fredman, Rhodes Professor of the Laws of the British Commonwealth and the United States, Pembroke College, University of Oxford.

Barbara Havekelová, Shaw Foundation Fellow in Law at Lincoln College and Faculty of Law, University of Oxford.

Deborah Hellman, David Lurton Massee, Jr, Professor of Law, University of Virginia.

Tarunabh Khaitan, Fellow in Law, Wadham College and Associate Professor of Law, University of Oxford and University of Melbourne.

Kaspar Lippert-Rasmussen, Professor, Department of Political Science, University of Aarhus.

Ronan McCrea, Senior Lecturer in Law, University College London.

Sophia Moreau, Professor of Law and Philosophy, University of Toronto.

Sandy Steel, Fellow in Law, Wadham College and Associate Professor of Law, University of Oxford.

Julie C Suk, Professor of Law, Cardozo School of Law—Yeshiva University.

1

Indirect Discrimination Law: Controversies and Critical Questions

HUGH COLLINS AND TARUNABH KHAITAN

I. THE FOX AND THE STORK

AESOP'S FABLE OF the fox and the stork invokes the idea of indirect discrimination. The story tells how the fox invited the stork for a meal. For a mean joke, the fox served soup in a shallow dish, which the fox could lap up easily, but the stork could only wet the end of her long bill on the plate and departed still hungry. The stork invited the fox for a return visit and served soup in a long-necked jar with a narrow mouth, into which the fox could not insert his snout. Whilst several moral lessons might be drawn from this tale, it is often regarded as supporting the principle that one should have regard to the needs of others, so that everyone may be given fair opportunities in life. Though formally giving each animal an equal opportunity to enjoy the dinner, in practice the vessels for the serving of the soup inevitably excluded the guest on account of their particular characteristics.

Chief Justice Burger invoked this fable of the fox and the stork in the decision of the United States Supreme Court in *Griggs v Duke Power Co*.[1] This famous case introduced the idea of indirect discrimination or disparate impact into the emerging law of discrimination. The issue concerned an employer's requirement that job applicants should pass a particular written test. The use of the test was challenged on the ground of race discrimination. The test could be taken by everyone and there was no explicit disadvantage applied to racial minorities. In practice, however, black applicants performed worse than white applicants on the test, a disparity that almost certainly reflected their different educational opportunities within a segregated school system. Moreover, it was found that good performance in the test seemed to be unrelated to good performance of the job. Speaking

[1] *Griggs v Duke Power Co* 401 US 424 (1971).

for the Court, Chief Justice Burger declared that discrimination could be established on such facts.

> Congress has now provided that tests or criteria for employment or promotion may not provide equality of opportunity merely in the sense of the fabled offer of milk to the stork and the fox. On the contrary, Congress has now required that the posture and condition of the job seeker be taken into account. It has—to resort again to the fable—provided that the vessel in which the milk is proffered be one all seekers can use. The Act proscribes not only overt discrimination, but also practices that are fair in form, but discriminatory in operation. The touchstone is business necessity. If an employment practice which operates to exclude Negroes cannot be shown to be related to job performance, the practice is prohibited.[2]

The case decided that a rule or practice that is apparently neutral between racial groups may be found to be discriminatory if there is a disparate adverse impact on one group in comparison to another group and the need for the rule cannot be justified. Unlike in the fable, where the fox had a malign intention, according to the Court the wrong of what we now call disparate impact or indirect discrimination can be established without reference to intention or motive; instead, proof of the disparate adverse impact on a protected group such as racial minorities or women of an unjustified rule was sufficient in law to count as discrimination.

Many jurisdictions have imitated this idea of indirect discrimination in their laws governing discrimination.[3] As well as including a prohibition against deliberate or intentional discrimination on grounds such as race and sex, which is called direct discrimination, or disparate treatment in the USA, their anti-discrimination legislation also tackles the disproportionate adverse effects of rules that are neutral on their face and may not harbour any discriminatory intent or unconscious bias. For instance, the law of the European Union (EU) provides that

> indirect discrimination shall be taken to occur where an apparently neutral provision, criterion or practice would put persons of a racial or ethnic origin at a particular disadvantage compared with other persons, unless that provision, criterion or practice is objectively justified by a legitimate aim and the means of achieving that aim are appropriate and necessary.[4]

In almost identical terms, the Equality Act 2000 of the United Kingdom (UK) provides in section 19 that:

> (1) A person (A) discriminates against another (B) if A applies to B a provision, criterion or practice which is discriminatory in relation to a relevant protected characteristic of B's.

[2] ibid 431.

[3] As well as the USA and the EU, indirect discrimination laws apply, for instance, in Australia, Canada, Hong Kong and South Africa.

[4] Council Directive 2000/43/EC of 29 June 2000 implementing the principle of equal treatment between persons irrespective of racial or ethnic origin [2000] OJ L180/22, Art 2.2 (b).

(2) For the purposes of subsection (1), a provision, criterion or practice is discriminatory in relation to a relevant protected characteristic of B's if—

(a) A applies, or would apply, it to persons with whom B does not share the characteristic,
(b) it puts, or would put, persons with whom B shares the characteristic at a particular disadvantage when compared with persons with whom B does not share it,
(c) it puts, or would put, B at that disadvantage, and
(d) A cannot show it to be a proportionate means of achieving a legitimate aim.

Using this terminology, facts similar to those in *Griggs v Duke Power* could be described as indirect discrimination in EU and UK law. The employer's requirement of a written test would count as a 'provision, criterion or practice'. The employer (A) applies the requirement both to white and black applicants, but the test puts the group of black applicants at a particular disadvantage compared to white applicants. An individual black claimant (B) suffers that disadvantage. And finally, the employer (A) is unable to demonstrate that the written test is a proportionate means of achieving a legitimate aim such as hiring those employees best suited for the job, so the employer will be found to have discriminated indirectly against B.

A wide range of examples may fit within this legal prohibition against indirect discrimination. In the USA, disparate impact was found when a woman challenged a requirement in Alabama that prison guards should possess a minimum weight of 120 pounds and a minimum height of 5 feet 2 inches in circumstances where about 33 per cent of women were excluded by the former requirement and 22 per cent by the latter, whereas only about one per cent of men fell below those threshold requirements.[5] Indirect discrimination on grounds of sex was applied to invalidate a rule controlling access to a post in the UK civil service to those aged between 17.5 and 28 years on the ground that the proportion of women who could comply with the rule was considerably smaller than the proportion of men who could because many women were engaged with child-rearing within that age range.[6] In another example, indirect discrimination on grounds of ethnic group was applied to prevent a private school using its school uniform policy to exclude boys who wore a turban in line with their practices in the Sikh community.[7] In these cases and many others, the predominant pattern is established of an apparently neutral rule that has a disproportionate adverse effect on a protected group such as women and minorities being invalidated even without proof of a discriminatory intent, unless it can be

[5] *Dothard v Rawlinson* 433 US 321 (1977).
[6] *Price v Civil Service Commission* [1978] ICR 212 (EAT).
[7] *Mandla v Dowell Lee* [1983] 2 AC 548.

justified as necessary for performance of the job or other kind of valuable opportunity.

II. THE PARADOX OF INDIRECT DISCRIMINATION

Evidently, the law of indirect discrimination has become firmly established as part of the law of discrimination in many legal systems. Yet this aspect of the law of discrimination continues to provoke controversies and debates about its moral and political foundations. Few would openly advocate or condone breaches of the law of direct discrimination by favouring explicit sex or race discrimination. Today the moral wrong of treating someone adversely simply by reason of gender or race is widely acknowledged and forms part of a consensus of values that bind a liberal society together. In line with that moral consensus, in recent years, that shared moral condemnation of conduct involving treating people unequally and with disrespect has been extended to other protected characteristics such as sexual orientation, disability, and age. Whilst the law against intentional discrimination has become an accepted foundation of the legal order in many societies, the law of indirect discrimination continues to provoke controversy about its existence, its scope, and its justification. The source of the controversy is not hard to find. The law of indirect discrimination presents an apparent paradox in our moral reasoning.

The central philosophical puzzle raised by the law of indirect discrimination is how can a rule or practice that treats people equally be regarded as an instance of discrimination or unequal treatment? How can equal treatment be labelled by the law as unequal treatment and therefore discrimination? Is there confusion in a law that, in the name of requiring equal treatment and opportunities for all, prohibits the use of rules or practices that offer equal treatment for all? The fable of the fox and the stork tells us that formally equal rules can in practice entail the denial of equal opportunities. But does that disadvantageous practical effect of the rule justify a condemnation of the rule that on its face has no discriminatory purpose at all but rather treats everyone the same?

This paradox can be resolved by insisting that the law of discrimination is seeking something more than formally equal treatment. The law is not simply concerned to uphold the principle of the equality of citizens before the law. The fable of the fox and the stork teaches us that sometimes the valuable moral principle that in general others should be treated equally or as an equal must be qualified by another principle that is concerned not just with the process of equal treatment but is oriented towards the substance of actual outcomes.

That resolution of the paradox by reference to another and partly competing moral principle leads us to ask a number of questions. What is this other substantive principle that seems to underpin the law of indirect discrimination? Is it a principle of equal opportunity, or fair opportunity, or one that seeks to impose substantively equal outcomes? Or perhaps the law of indirect discrimination is best understood as not relying at all upon a moral foundation that is comprised of a conception of equality. If so, the law of indirect discrimination might be explained by a range of alternative moral principles, such as those concerned with the welfare of disadvantaged groups or other principles concerned with the rights or liberties of individuals. It might be argued, for instance, that the law of indirect discrimination tackles problems of social integration and social inclusion by ensuring that disadvantaged groups in society do not encounter nearly insuperable obstacles in becoming integrated through education, work and participation in social life.[8] For instance, Julie Suk in this volume argues that the European Court of Human Rights (ECtHR) has used the idea of indirect discrimination to compel the integration of disadvantaged minorities into the regular public school system. Or it might be argued that in order to protect and enhance the autonomy of individuals in a liberal society, they should have access to many valuable opportunities such as education and work, and so the task of the law of indirect discrimination is to remove unjustifiable barriers to the enjoyment of such a degree of autonomy.[9] Numerous possible formulations of this alternative substantive principle have been articulated. Many of them will be examined further in many of the chapters in this book.

III. THE PUZZLES IN INDIRECT DISCRIMINATION LAW

Yet even if we can identify more clearly the moral principle or principles that underpin and justify the development of the law of indirect discrimination, we are then left with several further puzzles. Three need to be highlighted at this stage.

A. The Unity of the Law of Discrimination

In the light of the preceding suggestion that indirect discrimination may rest on different foundations to that of direct discrimination, does it make sense to describe both as comprising a unified field of law, namely the law of

[8] For the relation of discrimination law to social inclusion: H Collins, 'Discrimination, Equality, and Social Inclusion' (2003) 66 *MLR* 16.

[9] T Khaitan, *A Theory of Discrimination Law* (Oxford, Oxford University Press, 2015); S Moreau, 'In Defense of a Liberty-based Account of Discrimination' in D Hellman and S Moreau (eds), *Philosophical Foundations of Discrimination Law* (Oxford, Oxford University Press, 213) 71.

discrimination? Most people tend to think that the two branches of the law pursue the same or a similar aim, such as making our society more equal or fairer, which makes it possible to link them together. That view leads us to ask whether it really is the case that these two branches of the law of discrimination are founded on different moral and political principles? If they are based on different moral principles, as was suggested above, the question becomes how can it be coherent to speak of them as forming a unified category of the law? Surely, it may be asked, there must be more that unites these laws about direct and indirect discrimination than a similarity of name and that they both concern making differentiations between people?

One route that may permit the conclusion that the law of discrimination is unified is to question the standard view that the law of direct discrimination is founded on the moral and political principle that individuals should receive equal treatment or be treated as an equal, without demeaning adverse stereotypes being applied.[10] If there is a common moral framework that justifies both parts of the law, but we conclude that indirect discrimination cannot be explained in any straightforward way as an example of the principle of equal treatment, we may begin to doubt the correctness of the conventional understanding of the moral underpinnings of direct discrimination law (or disparate treatment law). Our investigation of the moral and political foundations of the law of indirect discrimination may therefore result in the unexpected need for a reassessment of the foundations of direct discrimination law with a view to perceiving an underlying unity of the field.

A different kind of answer to this puzzle about the unity of the law accepts the logic of the argument that if the two branches of the law rest on different principles, they are not closely related. On this view, if the law of indirect discrimination is not really about treating people as equals but rests on some other principles, perhaps the law ought to classify it as a different category from discrimination. Indirect discrimination might more accurately be called, for instance, social mobility law or social inclusion law, where its purpose is to redistribute access to opportunities.[11] Although some legal categories and classifications may lack any clear moral justification and serve purely pragmatic purposes, this issue of whether indirect discrimination is properly classified as discrimination law at all does perplex lawyers and encourages reflections on the moral foundations of the law of indirect discrimination.

[10] eg L Alexander, 'What makes Wrongful Discrimination Wrong? Biases, Preferences, Stereotypes, and Proxies' (1992) 141 *University of Pennsylvania Law Review* 149; D Hellman, *When is Discrimination Wrong?* (Cambridge MA, Harvard University Press, 2008).

[11] B Eidelson, *Discrimination and Disrespect* (Oxford, Oxford University Press, 2015) Ch 2; C McCrudden, 'Institutional Discrimination' (1982) 2 *OJLS* 303.

There is a third way of confirming the unity of the law of discrimination. Instead of finding a different moral wrong embedded in the law of indirect discrimination, it is possible to regard it as merely a technical and pragmatic extension of the law of direct discrimination, without any independent moral value of its own. It might be argued, for instance, that the law of indirect discrimination helps to overcome problems of proving direct discrimination. Or it might be argued that it has been tacked on to the law of direct discrimination in order to enable the selective protection of other groups under the guise of discrimination law. For instance, the law of indirect discrimination was used extensively to protect part-time workers before specific legislation was introduced in Europe. Similarly, the law of indirect discrimination was used to challenge age discrimination at a time when it had not yet been made unlawful. These kinds of explanations of indirect discrimination solve the problem of explaining why it should be classified as part of discrimination law by treating it as a purely instrumental device that assists in the enforcement and expands the scope of the law of direct discrimination. Though solving the puzzle of the unity of the law of discrimination, these instrumental accounts of the law of indirect discrimination raise questions about the legitimacy of the use of this device for these ulterior purposes.

B. The Seriousness of the Moral Wrong of Indirect Discrimination

If it is correct that the paradox of indirect discrimination must be resolved by perceiving indirect discrimination to rest on a different moral principle from that of equality before the law or a requirement of being treated with respect or as an equal, we may then encounter the potential problem that the law of indirect discrimination will be regarded as having moved outside the moral consensus that supports a strong moral condemnation of direct discrimination. It may be asserted, for instance, that indirect discrimination does not amount to a moral wrong in the same way or to the same extent as direct discrimination. Some may doubt whether it amounts to a moral wrong at all. In either case, the legitimacy of the law of indirect discrimination may be called into question.

Indeed, many commentators are tempted to draw a sharp distinction between those found guilty of the wrong of prejudice or disrespect for others and those who simply follow a neutral rule or practice that may turn out to have some unintended, unforeseen, and perhaps unforeseeable disproportionate adverse effects on particular groups. Those who act from prejudice or bias are regarded as guilty of a moral wrong that deserves a legal sanction for discrimination, whereas the moral condemnation of the latter group who follow a neutral rule is probably weaker, if it exists at all. Consider, for instance, a case where a university sets a minimum admissions standard in terms of test scores or results in public exams. It may turn out to be the case that disproportionately fewer men than women can comply with that admissions standard. Although the university may have no desire or intention to discriminate against men, if its rule about test scores or results in public examinations has that disproportionate adverse impact on men as a group when the statistics are examined, the university will be held in law to have indirectly discriminated against men unless it is able to justify the requirement of particular test scores as appropriate and necessary. There is a concern that persons who are innocent of any intention to discriminate might be swept up by the prohibition of indirect discrimination and as a consequence suffer from the application of an undeserved stigma. It is true, of course, that the university admissions standard might be demonstrated to be appropriate and necessary as a tool for selecting the best applicants, and therefore any preliminary finding of indirect discrimination would eventually be rebutted by the justification for the rule as necessary in the pursuit of a legitimate aim. Even so, some may feel tainted by the initial suggestion of discrimination and the need to rebut it. Given that the justification analysis employs a vague standard rather than a clear rule, alleged discriminators may also not be entirely confident that the courts will uphold their view that the justification for using the rule is adequate. These concerns about potentially unsustainable but nonetheless damaging allegations of discrimination often seem to lead to a hesitation to classify indirect discrimination in the same category as direct discrimination because the moral wrong, if there is one, is regarded as significantly different.

It may not seem convincing to equate in law the wrongfulness of a university that, for instance, deliberately excludes black applicants with the wrongfulness of a university that is liable for indirect discrimination because it uses a test score produced by public exams that disadvantages men, but is unable to demonstrate to the satisfaction of a court or tribunal that the exams are a good predictor of performance at university or are in some other way a necessary and appropriate standard for admissions. Those doubts about whether indirect discrimination amounts to the same kind of moral wrong as direct discrimination or whether it is the same wrong but to a lesser degree of wrongfulness raise some profound questions about the law of indirect discrimination that are addressed in many of the essays in this volume.

Some support for the idea that the moral wrong of indirect discrimination is less severe can be found in the difference that is commonly drawn by the law between the remedies for direct and indirect discrimination. If indirect discrimination is a lesser wrong, one might expect that it would attract less severe sanctions. It might be argued, for instance, that instead of an award of compensation, the remedy should merely be to enjoin the discriminator to refrain from the impugned conduct by, for instance, withdrawing its reliance on test scores. In most countries, the law of indirect discrimination does have different (and less harsh) remedies from those applied to direct discrimination. That difference may be based on the acceptance that there is no moral wrong in cases of indirect discrimination or a lesser wrong. Alternatively, that difference might be explained by the point that the law of indirect discrimination rests upon different moral principles from those that underpin direct discrimination, so it is likely that the remedies will reflect those differences in some respects. The difference in the applicable remedies for direct and indirect discrimination tends to support the view that they rest on different moral foundations and that the foundations for indirect discrimination are weaker than those that justify a law of direct discrimination.

C. Interference with Liberty

This puzzle about whether indirect discrimination is based upon a lesser moral wrong or any moral wrong at all can be seized upon by the targets of claims about discrimination such as employers, who may argue that the law of indirect discrimination amounts to a wrong itself owing to its excessive interference with their autonomy and freedom. For instance, the law creates opportunities to challenge behaviour that many employers and other subjects of the law of discrimination regard as normal practice and their own private business. Disallowing and sanctioning the use of formally neutral rules may be viewed as interfering too much with business autonomy or freedom to run a business. Furthermore, it may also impose considerable costs on employers if they are required to justify their rules and practices and to demonstrate not only their effectiveness but also to prove that no other rule or practice would be equally effective. This combination of constraints on liberty and reduction of efficiency in business gives rise to criticisms of indirect discrimination laws and indeed any discrimination laws at all.[12]

In the name of liberty it might be argued that, if a private employer wants to require all its employees to be capable of achieving a good score in a particular test, in order to raise the general level of educational attainment of its workforce even though not all jobs may require such qualification, the state should not be entitled to prohibit that business practice of the employer.[13] Once it is accepted that indirect discrimination, unlike direct discrimination, rests on a weak moral principle, those who resist the law can insist that it should give way to other more important values, or at least values that they

[12] Richard A Epstein, *Forbidden Grounds: The Case Against Employment Discrimination Laws* (Cambridge MA, Harvard University Press, 1992).

[13] eg *Albemarle Paper Co v Moody* 422 US 405 (1975).

regard as more important, such as freedom to conduct their own affairs without interference by the government.

IV. LEGAL DISAGREEMENTS AND MORAL FOUNDATIONS

These puzzles about the foundations of the law of indirect discrimination or disparate impact constantly resurface throughout the contributions to this book. Whilst some authors try to tackle these broad issues head on, others focus on a particular feature of the current law of indirect discrimination and why it is contested or doubted. Nevertheless, these discrete topics are united in the sense that all of them seem to raise questions about the moral and political principles that underlie and shape the law of indirect discrimination. In this volume, the various authors all contribute to the endeavour of seeking to understand the moral and political principles that justify the scope and application of the law of indirect discrimination. They throw light on the foundations of the law of indirect discrimination.

In the remainder of this introduction, we will provide a brief overview of the contested aspects of the law of indirect discrimination and indicate how these issues can be linked to deeper principles of political philosophy. From the outset, it is important to note that in our view disagreements about these particular topics in the law always operate at two levels.

On one level there may be what looks like a purely legal disagreement. For instance, the interpretation of the meaning of the provisions in the legislation governing indirect discrimination may be contested in litigation. A defendant may argue that the law, when properly interpreted and understood, does not apply to the conduct in question. Such a defence may win the case. In the formal legal reasoning, it may succeed on some pernickety textual ground such as the meaning of a particular word used in the legislation. For example, it might be argued that a decision was made not 'because of' a person's race but 'on the ground of' a person's race (or vice versa) in order to circumvent the current statutory formula that defines discrimination. Or it might be argued that the provision, criterion or practice was not 'applied' to the protected group because frequently or sometimes exceptions were made. This casuistry has been a persistent feature of litigation in relation to UK discrimination law.

Debates about the meaning of words, however, often mask deeper disagreements about whether this kind of conduct should be prohibited or should be made vulnerable to critical assessment by the legal system. These deeper disagreements at a second level may be expressed by lawyers and judges in the courts by proposals for rival interpretations of the meaning of statutory provisions. The choice between these interpretations of the law is likely to reflect deeper understandings of the purposes of the law and constitutive elements of the moral wrong that underlies the law of indirect discrimination. This second level of debates about philosophical principles, though not always explicitly acknowledged in the legal arguments, seems to provide the fuel that feeds the legal disagreement.

Our objective in this book is to bring to the fore the often-buried, deeper disagreements about the moral and political foundations of the law of indirect discrimination. This exploration of underlying principles should throw light on the essentials of the legal disagreements and in the long run help to resolve them.

V. THE SCOPE OF THE LAW OF INDIRECT DISCRIMINATION

It is clear from our brief description of the relevant statutes and cases above that the law of indirect discrimination or disparate impact does not require evidence of a malign discriminatory purpose, motive or intention. Of course, the law is likely to catch persons who seek to hide their discriminatory motives or purposes behind deceptive neutral rules. But proof of bias, a discriminatory state of mind or malign purpose is unnecessary to establish a claim for indirect discrimination. Nor is proof of the absence of such an intention some kind of defence or excuse for the conduct that amounts to indirect discrimination. The possibility of a judicial finding of indirect discrimination without there being any intention to discriminate at all often provokes considerable push-back against the law. Because in the lay view the concept of discrimination is normally associated with bias and prejudice, many people are unable to accept that the law may reach a finding of discrimination without proof of a discriminatory purpose of intention. Furthermore, the broad scope of the law of indirect discrimination can permit protected groups to challenge the validity of key elements in businesses' organisational structures and established labour market institutions. Taken-for-granted rules and practices may be criticised for their disparate impact, and if the claim is successful, organisations will have to rethink some of their basic operating procedures.

In the courts, this resistance to the broad scope of the law of indirect discrimination often appears as legal arguments that seek to cut down the potential reach of the law in order to remove from its scope defendants who deny any discriminatory motive. In this volume, Barbara Havelková considers how governments and judges have sought to resist the development of a law of indirect discrimination under article 14 of the European Convention on Human Rights (ECHR). Reading her study it is clear that some members of the ECtHR are unwilling to develop a law of indirect discrimination because it seems to be based on broad policies of social welfare and distributive justice between groups, which might be thought to be outside the scope of the court's mandate. In courts where a law of indirect discrimination is firmly established, to avoid the finding of indirect discrimination, defendants or respondents often generate technical legal arguments in order to avoid liability. For example, the English Court of Appeal accepted in *Essop v Home Office* an argument from the respondent employer that proof of indirect discrimination required not only statistical evidence that a particular test put a protected group (in this instance defined both by age and race) at a disproportionate disadvantage, but also an explanation of the reason why the test had such an effect on these groups.[14] The respondent argued successfully before the Court of Appeal that in the definition of indirect discrimination, the reference in the Equality Act 2010 section 19(2)(c) to 'that disadvantage' could only be understood if one could understand the reason for the disadvantage or why the apparently neutral test resulted in a particular disadvantage to a minority. On appeal, the Supreme Court rejected that argument on the basis of the statutory text that made no reference to the reason for the disadvantage, but instead provided simply for a particular disadvantage for the group that could be established by mere statistical (or even rule of thumb) evidence.[15] The judicial resolution of these legal arguments about the meaning of phrases such as 'that disadvantage' is likely to involve taking positions with respect to views about the moral and political foundations of the law and its purpose as well as the literal meaning of the text. Indeed, the reasoning of the Supreme Court was framed within an explicit discussion of the aims of the law and how the Court of Appeal's decision did not fit that purpose.

> Indirect discrimination assumes equality of treatment—the PCP [provision, criterion or practice] is applied indiscriminately to all—but aims to achieve a level playing field, where people sharing a particular protected characteristic are not subjected to requirements which many of them cannot meet but which cannot be shown to be justified. The prohibition of indirect discrimination thus aims to achieve equality of results in the absence of such justification.[16]

In order to appreciate how far the law of indirect discrimination extends beyond a lay view of the meaning of discrimination and how it frequently provokes closely fought litigation by respondents who regard themselves as unjustly accused of discrimination, consider the following hypothetical instance of its application to a taken-for-granted business organisational structure. Suppose an employer advertises a job that is specified to be a full-time job. Should this advertisement be the subject of an investigation into its breach of the law of discrimination? A lay view might not spot any possible discrimination in such a commonplace advertisement. Nevertheless, it may be possible to bring it within the scope of the law. There must be a group of potential applicants for work of the kind offered by the employer who

[14] *Home Office (UK Border Agency) v Essop* [2015] EWCA Civ 609, [2016] 3 All ER 137.
[15] *Essop v Home Office (UK Border Agency)* [2017] UKSC 27, [2017] 1 WLR 1343.
[16] ibid, per Baroness Hale for a unanimous court, [25].

are only searching for a part-time job. This group is therefore excluded in practice from applying for the job by this criterion of it being a full-time job. Once it is established further that women disproportionately make up the membership of that group of seekers for part-time work, the question is raised whether the requirement for a full-time position indirectly discriminates against women by putting them as a group at a disproportionate disadvantage in comparison with a cognate group such as men with respect to this particular job advertisement.

Although the issue of indirect discrimination would only be finally determined once the employer's justification for offering only a full-time position was assessed under the test of proportionality or business necessity, it is clear that the main elements of a typical claim for indirect discrimination are already in place for this commonplace activity of advertising a full-time job. Some judges and respondents object to such expansive realm for the law of indirect discrimination by contesting whether all the elements of the law have been satisfied.

A. Provision, Criterion or Practice

For instance, it may be questioned what should count as a relevant 'provision, criterion or practice' (or PCP) for the purpose of the law of indirect discrimination. A respondent might seek to distinguish, for instance, informal practices from hard and fast rules, with only the latter being subject to legal review. Or it might be contended that rules that constitute the job description such as a full-time work requirement for a vacancy for a job are not subject to legal regulation. On this latter view, the law of indirect discrimination should be targeted only at rules that control access to applications for the job such as rules about formal educational qualifications rather than rules that describe the core features of the job itself.

That contrast in views about the scope of the law of indirect discrimination indicates a deeper disagreement about the aims of the law. One view imagines the target of the law to be unnecessary and irrelevant formal tests and educational requirements that impede equality of opportunity; another view holds that the aim of the law is to question the structures of organisations in terms of their preferences for full-time jobs and hierarchies based on seniority and long hours of work in order to reduce these structural barriers against women in the labour market. The law of indirect discrimination permits women to challenge the male norm that jobs should be full-time in order to question whether this requirement is necessary for every kind of job or indeed any job.[17]

[17] S Fredman, *Women and the Law* (Oxford, Oxford University Press, 1997) 287.

B. Choice of Comparator Group

Another ground for contesting the scope of the law is to challenge how it should be determined whether there is a legally significant comparative group disadvantage as a result of the application of the rule or practice. In the case of full-time work, for instance, should the comparator group be the working population as a whole or merely those who are qualified for the job and suitably geographically located to be in a position to apply for the job? Assuming that reliable statistics may be available, differences between the groups that are being compared may be accentuated or reduced according to the choice of comparator. For instance, though it is true that in the labour market as a whole women disproportionately constitute the group of part-time workers, that statistic may not hold true for a smaller comparator group, such as those who have the correct formal qualifications to apply for that particular vacancy or meet all the other requirements for the job. Narrowing down the comparator group will often diminish the apparent disproportionate disadvantage. In the United States, such a narrow approach to the identification of a comparator group was at the heart of the controversial decision of the Supreme Court in *Wards Cove Packing Co v Atonio*,[18] an approach that was subsequently reversed by legislation.[19]

In practice, the relevant statistics about the composition of the actual local labour market will usually not be available, so the legal assessment of disproportionate disadvantage may have to rely on various kinds of proxies and inferences from known facts. As a consequence of the lack of precise statistics, the question becomes whether or not it is legitimate to infer from the known national level labour market statistics that are collected by the government something about the conditions in the local labour market applicable to that job. If the national statistics demonstrate that women are disproportionately found in part-time work, can we infer from that some relevant information about the composition of the group seeking part-time work who could satisfy all the other requirements for the job?

The choice between these comparator groups and views about the permissibility of inferences from proxy statistics are likely to reflect different ideas about the purpose of the law of indirect discrimination. For instance, some may think that the law should only be targeted at actual proven barriers to applications for a particular job, whereas others may want the law to try to shape the whole labour market, by, for instance, making part-time jobs or more flexible working hours a normal practice in all sectors of the economy and at all levels of organisations.

[18] *Wards Cove Packing v Atonio* 490 US 642 (1989).
[19] Civil Rights Act 1991.

C. The Cause of Disadvantage

Another ground on which the legal framework of rules may be used to challenge the broad scope of the law of indirect discrimination is to deny that a particular individual suffered from the group disadvantage rather than some other piece of bad luck. An employer might argue, for instance, that a particular claimant was not excluded from the full-time job offer because she was a woman, but simply because she failed to satisfy some other criterion for the job such as a post-graduate qualification that the successful candidate possessed though it had not been mentioned as a requirement for the job. How important is it that this particular claimant should be able to prove that she suffered the disadvantage because of the operation of the rule rather than some particular contingent fact in her case? If it is thought that the law serves the goal of compensating those who have suffered disadvantage because of discrimination, this requirement of proof that a discriminatory rule in fact caused the harm is plainly essential (although it is worth noting that most jurisdictions tend not to allow compensation for the standard cases of indirect discrimination). In contrast, if the aim of the law is seen rather as one of dismantling unjustified rules that have a disproportionate adverse impact on a particular vulnerable group, proof that the particular claimant did or did not suffer a disadvantage caused by the rule in the same way as most of the group does not seem to be especially relevant, for the point is to eliminate the rule that has an adverse disproportionate impact, not to compensate the particular claimant. The latter view was endorsed by the Supreme Court in *Essop v Home Office*, overruling the contrary view that had been preferred by the Court of Appeal.[20]

A similar ground on which to confine the scope of the law of indirect discrimination is to contest whether the provision or practice has caused the disadvantage. It may be argued that the disadvantage is the product of a choice made by the claimant that makes it impossible to comply with the rule or practice. In this case, the legal argument would be that it is not the provision that puts the claimant at a disadvantage, but rather the claimant's choice not to take steps to satisfy the criterion. For instance, an employer may refuse to permit job-shares in its organisation. Such a rule is likely to disproportionately adversely affect women in comparison to men, since women more frequently occupy part-time job-sharing positions as a way of reconciling work with child care. But has the employer's rule against job-shares caused the claimant's disadvantage or was it caused by the woman's choice to want to work part-time? Assuming that she could manage to arrange and pay for child care so that she could work full-time if she so desired, a court might decide that it was not the employer's rule or practice

[20] *Essop* (n 15).

that harmed her but her own choice about how to care for her child.[21] That interpretation of the law might be challenged by various contrary moral arguments. One might be that an employer should respect and facilitate the choice of a mother to try to balance work and child care responsibilities as an exercise of her personal autonomy with respect to two extremely valuable parts of her life, namely her career and raising a family. Another contrary moral argument might be that the public policy designed to support family friendly measures on the ground of improving the quality of our lives and heightening the competitiveness of business should be buttressed by the law of indirect discrimination, which can be used to dismantle unnecessary barriers to flexible working presented by monolithic organisations.

D. Justification

Many of these challenges to the broad scope of the law of indirect discrimination are raised during litigation in an attempt to avoid letting a court consider the hardest and most complex legal issue of whether or not the rule or criterion is justifiable despite its discriminatory adverse effects on a particular group. Certainly, it is not straightforward to determine whether or not the rule or practice serves a legitimate aim in a proportionate way. An employer's objective in hiring only a full-time employee may serve a legitimate aim such as the provision of continuity of service throughout the week, but is this rule really necessary? Could there be a job share, for instance, where the continuous service is provided by two persons, each working part-time? To rebut any suggestion that the rule of full-time work was not necessary, an employer would have to demonstrate either that such a pairing of workers was ineffective in the performance of the job or not practicable on some ground such as a dearth of applicants. Employers often seek to avoid that heavy burden of proof by raising the various points described above about the proper scope of the law and the interpretation of its other provisions. But if the question of justification cannot be avoided, it raises deeper questions about the aims of the law of indirect discrimination.

In assessing the validity of a purported justification or claim of 'business necessity', we would need to consider, for instance, what kinds of aims can be regarded as legitimate aims that support a rule once it is known that a rule has disproportionate adverse effects on a protected group. Is the efficiency of the business a good enough reason to continue to use a rule with disparate adverse impact on a particular group such as women? If an employer could show that a job-share of two part-time workers was 30 per cent more expensive than the employment of a single, full-time employee, the

[21] eg *Clymo v Wandsworth London Borough Council* [1989] IRLR 241 (EAT).

saving of costs might be a legitimate aim, but how would we determine whether it was disproportionate or strictly necessary? How should we balance an employer's interest in efficiency and profits against completely different values such as fair equality of opportunity for women, the benefit in the shattering of glass ceilings inside organisations, or the restructuring of labour markets? Is the avoidance of a rule that would have discriminatory impact against one protected group such as black workers a good justification to continue to use a rule that has an adverse impact on another group such as women? These are very difficult questions and their answers seem likely to appeal to moral principles that support the law of indirect discrimination. In particular, what will be required to resolve legal disputes is a refined understanding of the moral justification and function of the legal possibility for justifying indirect discrimination. Hugh Collins begins such an enquiry in his contribution by asking, in particular, whether the element of justification found in the law of indirect discrimination derives, on the one hand, from the moral principles that underpin the law of indirect discrimination as a whole, such as fair equality of opportunity or social inclusion, or, on the other hand, does this element of justification rest upon an independent moral principle, and if so, what principle?

In the courts and the legal system, the determination of such vexed issues will no doubt partly depend on pragmatic considerations about how the legal process functions, how cases might be proven in courts and tribunals, and how best to make the law effective. To answer those questions properly, however, in our view what is needed is a principled understanding of the aims of the law. These principles should also indicate who should be held responsible for implementing those aims and under what conditions. As part of determining those conditions, we need to ask how great a burden we should place on actors in the private sector such as employers, shopkeepers and landlords to give effect to the law and the benefits that it hopes to confer on society. Having established that many, perhaps all, legal disputes surrounding the law of indirect discrimination have identifiable roots in conflicting visions of the aims and moral justifications for the law, we should now turn to introduce more fully the debates about the content and identity of those aims and justifications.

VI. THE DISTINCTION BETWEEN DIRECT AND INDIRECT DISCRIMINATION

One way to examine the foundations of the law of indirect discrimination in terms of principles and philosophy is to return to a nagging concern mentioned earlier. This is the worry about whether the legal prohibition against indirect discrimination or disparate impact should even be included as part of the law of discrimination. Unless this classification is explicable on purely pragmatic grounds, a principled basis for the distinction must depend on how one understands the wrong or purpose of the law of direct discrimination, how one understands the wrong or purpose of prohibitions against indirect discrimination, and how they are conceived to be related. In turn this raises the vexed question of what exactly the difference may be between direct and indirect discrimination. For instance, is the fable of the fox and the stork really about direct or indirect discrimination? There was certainly an apparently neutral practice such as serving soup in a flat plate to guests, which seems to fit the classification of indirect discrimination. Yet at the same time it might be described as a case of direct discrimination, because undoubtedly the fox in the tale was acting from malicious and disrespectful motives to poke fun at the stork. Developing more fully the contrast between direct and indirect discrimination may help us to sharpen our focus on the moral and political principles that justify the existence and application of the law of indirect discrimination.

Unfortunately, this distinction between direct and indirect discrimination is hard to draw on a conceptual level. Moreover, insofar as a similar distinction is drawn in different legal systems, the distinction is not always exactly the same, and therefore different jurisdictions may reach different results. The chapter in this volume by Sandy Fredman analyses the divergence in the case law between the USA, Europe and Canada in how the division between direct and indirect discrimination has evolved. In his contribution to this book, Nicholas Bamforth examines the use by leading theorists of discrimination of different blends of conceptual arguments, moral justifications and public policy arguments in order to explain the foundations of discrimination law in general and, in particular, how the distinction between direct and indirect discrimination can and should be drawn.

The fundamental reason why it is hard to draw a clear conceptual distinction between direct and indirect discrimination is that any differentiation will depend upon not one difference but at least two or more differences. This is less than ideal, as Lippert-Rasmussen observes in the course of criticising this feature of most definitions of direct and indirect discrimination.

> First, ideally, one would like: (1) the distinction between direct and indirect discrimination to be clearly drawn along one dimension; (2) direct and indirect discrimination to be mutually exclusive—such that a case cannot amount to direct as well as indirect discrimination against the very same group, at least not when one's act as well as the discriminatee are identified under the same descriptions; and (3) that the distinction is exhaustive—such that there are no cases of discrimination that are neither direct, nor indirect, discrimination.[22]

[22] K Lippert-Rasmussen, *Born Free and Equal: A Philosophical Inquiry into the Nature of Discrimination* (Oxford, Oxford University Press, 2013) 65. This paper offers different suggestions as to the dimensions on which the distinction is drawn in law, following more closely T Khaitan, 'Indirect Discrimination' in K Lippert-Rasmussen (ed), *Routledge Handbook of Discrimination* (Abingdon, Routledge, 2017) ch 2.

With respect to legal definitions of the concepts of direct and indirect discrimination, none of these ideal conditions appear to be satisfied (except by resort to a technical closure rule that deems a case that could be characterised as either a case of direct or of indirect discrimination as one only involving direct discrimination). It is therefore not possible to provide a consistent and precise division between the legal categories of direct or indirect discrimination.

A. Individual or Group Complaint

One of those differences by which the distinction is drawn concerns the perspective on discrimination. Direct discrimination is normally (although not necessarily) concerned with a particular action of one individual against another individual, such as where an employer decides not to hire a woman for a job. In contrast, indirect discrimination is always about groups: the question is whether a protected group is disproportionately disadvantaged by an action (or rule or practice) in comparison with a cognate comparator group. Because the two branches of discrimination law are typically viewing the situation from different perspectives, it is possible that the facts in a particular case could be classified as either direct or indirect discrimination. On the facts of *Griggs v Duke Power*, for instance, there was probably enough evidence to support an inference of deliberate though covert discrimination on the part of the employer amounting to direct discrimination,[23] whilst at the same time to use the evidence of comparative group disadvantage to advance a claim for indirect discrimination. So, on the first criterion, the difference between direct and indirect discrimination can be just a matter of perspective and presentation. It depends whether the case is primarily built on an assertion of individual disadvantage or group disadvantage.

A further complexity arises in the case of religious discrimination, as discussed by Ronan McCrea in this volume. Indirect discrimination on the ground of religion concerns the disproportionate disadvantage imposed on a particular religious group. But the same conduct may be regarded as an unjustified interference with a person's right to manifest a religion, as protected in many constitutions and article 9 ECHR. It is possible that there may be no identifiable religious group that suffers a relative disadvantage as a result of an apparently neutral rule or practice, but nevertheless the conduct will be judged unlawful as an unjustified interference with the human right to manifest a religion.[24]

[23] Michael Selmi, 'Indirect Discrimination and the Anti-discrimination Mandate' in Hellman and Moreau (n 9) 250, 252.

[24] eg *Eweida v United Kingdom* (App no 48420/10) (2013) 57 EHRR 8.

B. Intention or Effects?

The difference between direct and indirect discrimination also invariably turns on a second axis or criterion of differentiation, though legal systems differ as to the content of that criterion. In the United States, this second criterion is usually understood to be constituted by an intention to discriminate by the use of a protected characteristic such as sex or race as a stated ground for the decision, though intent can be proven without any necessity to prove a malevolent motive and or desire to denigrate the protected group.[25] In the absence of such clear evidence of intention to discriminate on the ground of membership of a protected group or a 'suspect classification', a legal claim must be presented as one of disparate impact on the group.

In contrast, the usual approach to the definition of direct discrimination adopted in the United Kingdom does not require proof of an intention to discriminate. Rather, direct discrimination is usually defined as the adoption of a ground for decision that will exclude 100 per cent of the protected group, but none of its cognate and comparative group. It follows that indirect discrimination applies where the exclusionary effect of the practice or rule is less than 100 per cent, but is disproportionate in comparison to cognate groups. That conception of direct discrimination permits the finding of direct discrimination when the ground for the decision makes no reference to the protected characteristic. In *Bull v Hall*, for instance, a majority of the court found that a rule of a hotel that denied the sharing of a double-bedded room to all guests except those who were married constituted direct discrimination against gays and lesbians because at that time those protected groups could not marry but only enter into 'civil partnerships', so the rule excluded 100 per cent of those in civil partnerships, all of whom were in the protected group. At the same time, the hotel's rule constituted indirect discrimination against gays and lesbians because they were disproportionately adversely affected as a group in comparison with heterosexuals who had the opportunity to marry even if not all of them were married. This approach that looks at effects rather than intentions can produce results that seem to be surprising where, in the absence of any discriminatory intention or motive, a neutral rule happens to have the effect in practice of excluding 100 per cent of a protected group and therefore must be classified as direct discrimination.[26]

[25] eg *Tax Deferred Annuity & Deferred Comp Plans v Norris* 463 U.S. 1073, 1084 (1983). This is the position under Title VII of the Civil Rights Act. Under the equal protection clause of the Constitution, not only is there no claim for indirect discrimination available, but disparate treatment appears to require proof of lack of equal regard or prejudice (*City of Cleburne v Cleburne Living Ctr* 473 US 432, 450 (1985)) though the grounds of discrimination are not confined to a particular list of protected characteristics.

[26] *James v Eastleigh Borough Council* [1990] 2 AC 751.

These legal definitions of the second criterion of differentiation between direct and indirect discrimination make it clear that neither ground requires proof of a hostile or disrespectful motive. The popular lay view that direct discrimination, unlike indirect discrimination, is concerned with deliberate prejudice is not strictly true. Whilst the law of direct discrimination undoubtedly prohibits deliberate prejudicial actions, it is broader in scope. In the USA, for disparate treatment it is sufficient that the rule or decision is made by reference to a suspect classification such as race or sex. In the UK, it is not even necessary for proof of direct discrimination that a ground for the decision is a protected characteristic such as sex and race. Provided the ground for the decision is 100 per cent correlated with an adverse effect on a protected group, direct discrimination is established.

This approach to drawing the distinction between direct and indirect discrimination without reference to motive, but rather with a suspect ground for a decision, seems to make it easier to imagine that both branches of the law of discrimination share some common principles. In the United Kingdom, for instance, the law focusses on the adverse effects of a rule or practice for both direct and indirect discrimination. This emphasis on adverse effects may support an interpretation of the aims of the law that perceives a unity of purpose between the two branches of the law. That common aim may be discovered in the prevention and reversal of those adverse effects on the protected groups. On this view, both direct and indirect discrimination are promoting social goals such as fair equality of opportunity or social inclusion, though the law may also provide compensation for victims of prejudice. At the same time, of course, this line of argument has the potential to diminish the distinction between direct and indirect discrimination to vanishing point. If a crucial ground of differentiation is that direct discrimination is limited to rules or practices that have an adverse impact on 100 per cent of the protected group, whereas indirect discrimination must be used if the adverse impact is on 99 per cent or less of the protected group, there does not seem to be much of a principled distinction.[27]

C. Justification as a Third Distinguishing Criterion?

Although it produces some clarity to adopt this analysis of the distinction between direct and indirect discrimination based upon the two criteria of group versus individual claims and another axis based on intention or effects, these may not be the only grounds for differentiation or even

[27] See, for example, *Rodriguez v Minister of Housing* [2009] UKPC 52, [2010] UKHRR 144 [19]: if all members of the disadvantaged group fail, but so do some members of its comparator group, the discrimination is still indirect, albeit 'a form of indirect discrimination which comes as close as it can to direct discrimination'.

the most important ones. For instance, it is often pointed out that one of the most significant differences in the legal framework between direct and indirect discrimination is that in general the opportunity for a defendant to rebut the charge by justifying its actions is only available in relation to indirect discrimination.

> The main difference between them [ie direct and indirect discrimination] is that direct discrimination cannot be justified. Indirect discrimination can be justified if it is a proportionate means of achieving a legitimate aim. …[28]

The availability of a justification or business necessity defence therefore provides an apparently clear legal difference between the categories of discrimination. But that apparently sharp distinction can be questioned as a matter of fact: for instance, direct discrimination can be justified in relation to some protected characteristics such as age and disability. It can be argued, as is suggested by Sandy Fredman and Hugh Collins in their contributions to this volume, that the availability of the possibility of justification may be more a matter of degree than pointing to a difference in kind.

Nevertheless, it is correct that most legal systems also render it much harder to justify or find exceptions to instances of direct discrimination than instances of indirect discrimination. In particular, the 'business necessity' test or the proportionality test of justification will not generally apply to claims for direct discrimination. Justifications and exemptions from claims for direct discrimination are normally strictly confined or in some instances rejected altogether. This difference can be illustrated by cases where employers ban headscarves from the workplace. The ban might refer explicitly to headscarves, or more neutrally to any head-covering. If the employer's rule is found to be direct discrimination on the ground of religion, the employer will have little chance of justifying the rule.[29] The main exception for direct discrimination concerns a genuine occupational requirement to perform the job. Leaving aside the possibility that scarves and caps might be a safety hazard, the more typical argument put forward by employers that customers of the employer's business prefer to deal with people without headscarves is unlikely to count as a genuine occupational requirement.[30] In contrast, if the case is analysed as an instance of indirect discrimination because the rule against any kind of head covering does not directly target any religion, it will be open to the employer to argue that it has a legitimate aim such as projecting a neutral image and that its rule against caps and scarves is a

[28] *R (E) v Governing Body of JFS and another (United Synagogue and others intervening)* [2010] 2 AC 728, [57] (Baroness Hale).

[29] *EEOC v Abercrombie & Fitch Stores, Inc* 135 S Ct 2028 (2015). MC Harper, 'Confusion on the Court: Distinguising Disparate Treatment from Disparate Impact in Young v UPS and EEOC v Abercombie & Fitch, Inc' (2016) 96 *Boston University Law Review* 543.

[30] Case C-188/15 *Asma Bougnaoui and ADDH v Micropole* [2017] IRLR 447.

proportionate way of achieving that aim.[31] The law of indirect discrimination typically provides defendants with greater opportunities to defend their business rules and practices.

This difference with regard to the availability of a justification for a rule or practice seems likely to reflect different views about the purpose of the law. The exceptional difficulty of justifying direct discrimination makes sense where direct discrimination is conceptually linked to prejudicial or disrespectful action, but seems harder to explain when direct discrimination is defined by reference to the effects of a rule rather than any malicious intention. Moreover, if it is argued that both parts of the law, despite any formal differences, serve the same goal or purpose, it becomes questionable why the ability to justify a practice or a rule is not the same in direct and indirect discrimination, for ultimately the question of compatibility with the purpose may be the same regardless of how the issue is framed. It may seem odd, for instance, that in the cases concerning headscarves, in the absence of health and safety concerns, there is no practical possibility for the employer to justify a ban within the framework of direct discrimination, but if an identical case is analysed as an instance of indirect discrimination the employer will be able to advance a wide range of business considerations in favour of its rule.

D. Remedies

There is a further notable difference between the law governing direct and indirect discrimination that may indicate another axis of differentiation. As we have already noted, the available legal remedies for the two kinds of discrimination often differ. Proof of direct discrimination normally results in an award of financial compensation, whereas the remedy for indirect discrimination might be merely an order to cease to use the apparently neutral rule or practice. For instance, under the UK's Equality Act 2010, section 124, a tribunal is required to consider making a declaration or a recommendation before examining the possibility of a compensatory remedy if the tribunal concludes that the indirect discrimination was unintentional. This difference in remedies might be regarded as a mere consequence of the distinction between direct and indirect discrimination or instead it might be presented as a ground for making the distinction.

The option of making an appropriate recommendation as a remedy applies particularly to cases of indirect discrimination. The tribunal can order an employer to cease to use a PCP that has a disproportionate adverse impact on a protected group. The tribunal might also suggest what alternative PCP

[31] Case C-157/15 *Achbita v G4S Secure Solutions* [2017] IRLR 466.

would be more appropriate in view of the employer's legitimate aim and the need to satisfy a test of proportionality. Such a remedy comes close to an order for affirmative action in favour of a minority group by requiring the employer to establish a PCP that provides fair opportunities for a protected group. This link between affirmative action and indirect discrimination can be detected in discussions of whether PCPs can be justified in view of the alternatives available and in duties to take steps of reasonable accommodation for disabled persons. This fascinating linkage between remedies for indirect discrimination and affirmative action is explored by the chapter by Kaspar Lippert-Rasmussen in this volume.

E. Instrumentalism

As well as encountering these difficulties in developing a clear conception of the difference between direct and indirect discrimination, which might help us to understand the foundations of the law, it has also to be conceded that the categories of the law of discrimination, even if reasonably clearly defined, are frequently liable to be manipulated in different ways by the courts. In EU law, for instance, it seems that a court may infer from the existence of a disproportionate group disadvantage that an apparently neutral rule or practice was probably in fact an example of concealed intentional discrimination, and if so, it will be described as direct discrimination as well as indirect discrimination. Surprisingly, on this approach that regards substantial and persistent group disadvantage as a way of proving direct discrimination, the inference of intention can provide a basis for a claim for direct discrimination even for a person who is not in fact a member of the protected group, but who has suffered also from the particular disadvantage that is disproportionately encountered by the protected group.[32] EU law also accepts, however, the role of indirect discrimination as a completely independent form of discrimination law that can apply regardless of a harmful intention. Indeed, to diminish indirect discrimination to a device for proving direct discrimination would certainly hamper the ambition of many of its advocates, who see in the law of indirect discrimination a legal mechanism that can be used for the purpose of tackling structural inequalities and invisible barriers to fair opportunities for all.

The possibility of blurring the conceptual distinctions between direct and indirect discrimination in the way that it has been done in EU law and other jurisdictions perhaps demonstrates that it is unstable but not necessarily without foundation in distinct moral principles. Nevertheless, the ability to

[32] Case C-83/14 *CHEZ Razpredelenie Bulgaria AD v Komisia za zashtita ot diskriminatsia* [2016] 1 CMLR 14.

manipulate the distinction and apply either category to many fact situations in order to gain procedural, substantive or remedial advantages has led the Canadian courts to conclude that the distinction between direct and indirect discrimination should be abandoned and replaced by a unified law against discrimination.[33] In most legal systems, however, the distinction between direct and indirect discrimination still plays an important role and usually has significant legal consequences. Unfortunately, because the two kinds of discrimination are typically differentiated by reference to two or more criteria, it is hard to draw more than some tentative conclusions about their moral and political foundations and in particular to find strong clues to the foundations of the law of indirect discrimination.

VII. THREE APPROACHES TOWARDS THE FOUNDATIONS OF INDIRECT DISCRIMINATION LAW

Having acknowledged above the uncertainties and difficulties regarding the concept of indirect discrimination and its difference (if any) from direct discrimination, we may be able to draw this general examination to a close by proposing an intellectual framework which suggests that broadly speaking there are three approaches towards understanding the place and purpose of indirect discrimination or disparate impact in a system of discrimination law.

A. The Instrumental Account

The first perspective argues that a law of indirect discrimination is needed for various possible instrumental reasons in support of the law of direct discrimination.[34] Prohibitions against indirect discrimination may overcome a perennial difficulty in establishing a discriminatory intent or purpose. Defendants rarely concede that they were prejudiced and indeed their bias may have been completely unconscious. This instrumental use of indirect discrimination relies upon the disproportionate adverse effects of a rule or practice to infer proof of or at least a presumption of a discriminatory intention or purpose.[35] Another instrumental purpose of the law of indirect discrimination could be to block an easy route around a finding of direct discrimination. Indirect discrimination on this view is not a moral wrong in

[33] *British Columbia (Public Service Employee Relations Commission) v British Columbia Government Service Employees' Union* [1999] 3 SCR 3.

[34] eg J Gardner, 'On the Ground of Her Sex(uality)' (1998) 18 *OJLS* 167.

[35] This is the only permitted use of disparate impact evidence in cases solely involving the equal protection clause of the US Constitution: *Washington v Davis* 426 US 229 (1976).

itself, but rather is a necessary ingredient in an effective law against deliberate discrimination, which constitutes serious wrongdoing. For instance, employers who might want to exclude older workers from their workforce could introduce a requirement or practice that tested physical fitness, with the effect that older workers and workers with some kinds of disabilities would be excluded. By applying this apparently neutral rule about fitness, an employer could avoid the appearance of discrimination and so it would be hard to prove any kind of intention to discriminate on grounds of age. On this view, the law of indirect discrimination is necessary for the instrumental reason of preventing a huge loophole emerging in the law's prohibition against direct discrimination by the calculated use of apparently neutral rules that achieved the desired discriminatory outcome.

That reasoning can be extended to cover accidental or unthinking use of rules and practices that have a disproportionate adverse effect on a protected group, for if such rules were permitted to continue, because they function as proxies for the prohibited grounds of discrimination, they could substantially weaken the beneficial effects of the law of discrimination. On this view, indirect discrimination is regarded as parasitic upon the wrong of deliberate discrimination and serves to buttress the effectiveness of the law of direct discrimination, even though it may sometimes sanction actors who are wholly innocent of either conscious or unconscious bias. This instrumental account of the law of indirect discrimination seems to be supported by the further point that the protected groups are invariably identified by a belief that they have in the past suffered from direct discrimination that resulted in disadvantage, so that the law of indirect discrimination can be regarded instrumentally as a mechanism for weeding out the persistent effects of direct discrimination.

This instrumental account removes the need to discover separate moral and political principles that support a law of indirect discrimination. Instead what is required is a theory of the moral foundations of direct discrimination plus an explanation of why it is necessary on pragmatic grounds to prohibit indirect discrimination in the pursuit of the goal of eradication of the moral wrong of direct discrimination. The framework for such an argument is likely to stress the great harm that direct discrimination has caused in the past and how strong measures are needed to eradicate its presence today and the lingering effects of past discrimination. On that approach it might follow that strong measures that control private business decisions would be warranted in pursuit of the vital goal of the eradication of the moral wrong and its effects. Such strong measures could include permitting claims for indirect discrimination and they could go further to permit or encourage various affirmative action programmes, positive discrimination in favour of disadvantaged groups, and duties to accommodate disabled persons.

Although these views have been described as explaining the extension of the law of direct discrimination into indirect discrimination as pragmatic measures designed to ensure the effectiveness of the former law, it seems possible to argue such measures to ensure the effectiveness of the law of direct discrimination have an independent value on top of their instrumental effects. In this volume, Deborah Hellman presents an account of indirect discrimination that resembles this pragmatic justification, but argues powerfully that in fact there is in addition a moral principle that can justify this extension of the law of direct discrimination. She argues that, at least in some cases of indirect discrimination or disparate impact, the moral wrong that is being addressed by the law is the continuation of the effects of past direct discriminatory acts. She claims that such conduct is morally wrong because it compounds the injustice of earlier intentional discrimination. For instance, if in the past minorities were excluded from good jobs on career ladders, employers who use apparently neutral seniority rules to determine pay or access to promotions will compound the effect of past discrimination that prevented the minorities from access to such jobs from the outset.

B. An Independent Moral Wrong

A second perspective on the aims or purposes of the law of indirect discrimination argues that there is a moral wrong in cases of indirect discrimination, though the wrong differs significantly from the reason for the wrongfulness of direct discrimination. Whereas the latter would normally be regarded as closely linked to the wrong of not treating others with respect and dignity or as an equal, indirect discrimination will be described on this perspective as concerning a different value. That independent value might be described as one of equal opportunity or fair opportunity (taking into account various kinds of handicaps such as poor educational opportunities). Or it might be characterised as the need for reasons of social justice to break down structural barriers of various kinds to valuable opportunities such as jobs, housing and education. On this view, indirect discrimination may serve such goals as maximising general welfare by supporting merit-based criteria for allocating benefits and opportunities, or social inclusion for everyone, or a more equal society.

On these accounts of indirect discrimination as founded on an independent moral wrong, in the pursuit of one or more of these goals concerning equal welfare, fair opportunities, or righting the wrongs of the past, the law places duties on key actors such as employers and university admissions officers who control access to valuable opportunities. These key actors are required to consider whether all their rules and practices avoid disproportionate adverse effects for disadvantaged groups, and if they do not, whether those rules are justifiable as necessary and appropriate.

On this second response to the question of the foundation of the law of indirect discrimination, its underlying moral justification is significantly different from the moral grounds for the law of direct discrimination. Its moral justification is not grounded in ideas of equal respect or equality before the law, but rather by reference to social welfare goals such as a fair distribution of wealth, or the opening of valuable opportunities for everyone, or even the goal of a more egalitarian society in general. Using this second response, we should expect to be able to draw some sharp distinctions between the concepts of direct and indirect discrimination. It is even possible that the two parts of the law of discrimination could in some instances point in opposite directions.

C. A Common Moral Foundation

A third perspective argues that both direct and indirect discrimination share a common moral foundation and that they are closely related. This perspective can take two forms.

One form argues that it is possible to discover the moral wrong that characterises direct discrimination in the category of indirect discrimination, though probably in a slightly weakened or attenuated form. A person found to have applied a rule or practice that is indirectly discriminatory may not have deliberately treated a person with disrespect or in a demeaning way, but the adoption of such a rule is not a wholly innocent act either, because the adverse effect may well be foreseeable or should have been foreseen and the actor may have done nothing to check on the justifications for the rule. In this volume Sophia Moreau develops the argument that there is fault in the sense of a failure to take care to avoid the imposition of a disadvantage on members of a protected group. In our moral thinking, we usually condemn intentional wrongdoing more forcefully than we reproach negligent or careless conduct. In law, following that moral pattern, criminal law is often confined to intentional conduct or conduct that is almost intentional, relegating instances of negligently caused harm either to be classified as minor offences or merely offering a civil remedy in tort. The fault involved in careless discrimination may be less than that involved in the wrong of deliberate discrimination, but that does not mean that a civil remedy for indirect discrimination should not be available. On this view, the moral wrong of treating persons unequally applies to both kinds of discrimination, but the degree of fault is diminished in instances of indirect discrimination.

An alternative form of finding a common moral foundation for both direct and indirect discrimination is to suggest that the moral purpose behind the law of indirect discrimination also justifies the law of direct discrimination. This purpose is likely to be conceived in terms of the purposes mentioned above such as social welfare goals or making valuable opportunities available for everyone for the sake of enhancing personal autonomy. The different legal treatment of direct and indirect discrimination only arises, on this view, as an additional response to the presence of deliberate or intentional discrimination, which deserves a further mark of censure. For instance, if (as Khaitan and others suggest)[36] the justification for indirect discrimination is to make valuable opportunities available to a greater number of people by the removal of unnecessary and inappropriate barriers, that principle can be extended without difficulty to instances of direct discrimination as well. The difference in the way the law handles direct discrimination can be accounted for by the fact that the denial of valuable opportunities to a protected group is flagrant or intentional and so deserves even greater castigation or expressions of disapproval of wrongdoing.[37]

In this volume, the essay by Tarunabh Khaitan and Sandy Steel explores the possibility of combining these two forms of finding a common moral foundation for both branches of the law of discrimination. They argue that indirect discrimination is doubly wrongful because it both tends to exacerbate existing relative disadvantage between groups and it also imposes a particular disadvantage on a victim of indirect discrimination. There is both a failure to promote a desirable social goal such as reducing the relative disadvantage of protected groups and a wrong of imposing a particular disadvantage on an individual victim, albeit not intentionally.

VIII. CONCLUSION

On close examination, indirect discrimination is a protean concept. The various explanations given above of the aims of indirect discrimination and its fundamental moral principles all seem to be valid in some instances, though not in every instance. At times the law of indirect discrimination serves as a tool to reveal and to eliminate disguised intentional discrimination. At other times it may help to overcome difficulties in satisfying the burden of proof for establishing a claim for direct discrimination. It can also provide a tool to challenge institutional structures that consolidate prior unfair distributions of advantages and disadvantages between various groups in society. Yet what seems most distinctive about the law of indirect discrimination is the manner in which it provides a legal mechanism for challenging unfairness in the distribution of benefits in a society between various groups.

In an important respect, the real world is not like the fable of the fox and the stork. Victims of indirect discrimination come from disadvantaged groups in society. As a consequence, they are rarely in a position to engage in the kind of retaliatory action performed by the stork when he served dinner from a bottle with a long neck. In a more realistic fable, the stork would

[36] Khaitan (n 9); Moreau (n 9) 71.
[37] Khaitan (n 9).

remain hungry, unable to access the proferred benefit of a meal. That is why indirect discrimination is so important as a legal mechanism. It permits an interrogation of our practices, conventions and rules to see whether they meet high standards of fairness in the distribution of opportunities and benefits between various groups. We can ask, for instance, whether the decision of a public authority to close a public lending library disproportionately adversely affects certain groups such as the elderly or schoolchildren, and if so, the public authority will be forced by the law of indirect discrimination to justify its decision as a necessary measure to meet a legitimate aim such as the need to balance its budget.[38] Or we can ask whether high fees charged by the Ministry of Justice for bringing discrimination claims before employment tribunals place women at a particular disadvantage compared to men, and if so whether the fees are a proportionate means of carrying out a legitimate aim such as deterred vexatious claims or, as was decided, a disportionate measure because the level of fees effectively deterred nearly all claims including meritorious ones.[39] Similarly, in the private sector, an employer who insists that all positions should be full-time contracts can be challenged using the law of indirect discrimination to justify this rule that is likely to have a disproportionate adverse impact on women. The law of indirect discrimination can be one of the most powerful legal measures available to disadvantaged groups in society to assert their claims to justice.

[38] eg in combination with the public sector equality duty: *R (Green and others) v Gloucestershire County Council & Somerset County Council* [2011] EWHC 2687 (Admin).

[39] *R (on the application of UNISON) v Lord Chancellor* [2017] UKSC 51.

2

Direct and Indirect Discrimination: Is There Still a Divide?

SANDRA FREDMAN

IN PRINCIPLE, THE divide between direct and indirect discrimination is vivid. Direct discrimination, or disparate treatment, deals with unequal treatment. Indirect discrimination or disparate impact, deals with inequality of results. The powerful intuition behind *Griggs v Duke Power* is unassailable.[1] Equal treatment is not in itself sufficient to address inequality in society. Given significant antecedent disadvantage, equal treatment may well lead to unequal results. Selection criteria based on educational qualifications, although equally applicable to all, will exclude those who have been deprived of proper schooling; jobs which require full-time working and mobility will exclude those with primary responsibility for childcare. Yet, recent developments in the jurisprudence of the courts in the US, the UK and Canada make it increasingly difficult to situate the divide.

At first glance, the reasons for this are widely divergent. In the US, those Supreme Court judges who are hostile to disparate impact generally attempt to revert to intention and symmetry as the touchstone of the right to equality. They warn that a disparate impact regime leads inexorably to affirmative action or reverse discrimination, which they regard as anathema to their conception of equality as symmetrical, colour-blind and fault based. The result has been to continually narrow down the principle of disparate impact. Dissenting judges even argue that it is unconstitutional. In the UK, by contrast, there has been a strong sense that allowing intention or motive into even a direct discrimination analysis will open the door to legitimating discrimination on the grounds of ostensibly benign motives. This has had the consequence of turning even direct discrimination into what is in practice an effects-based test, but one which leaves no scope for justification on the grounds that this might reintroduce motive at the justification stage. This means that the divide is instead situated at whether or not a justification defence is available: direct discrimination cannot be justified, on this

[1] *Griggs v Duke Power Co*, 401 US 424 (1971).

view, while indirect discrimination can. On the other hand, the concept of indirect discrimination in UK law remains fragile, with continued attempts to reintroduce equal treatment notions into the framing of the test. This leaves the background rationale for both direct and indirect discrimination unclear, and little or no attention is paid to social context or implications. The Supreme Court of Canada has embarked on a much more conscious process of analysis of the relationship between the two principles. Acknowledging that the divide is often unclear, it has been keen to streamline defences and remedies, so that little hangs on the initial classification. The Court of Justice of the European Union (CJEU), in its recent case law, is similarly flexible about the divide.

This raises the question of why, despite in principle having apparently clearly demarcated boundaries, the interaction between direct and indirect discrimination remains so tense and conflictual. Even more so, why has the UK addressed this tension by moving direct discrimination into an effects-based mould, while the US jurisprudence tends to push disparate impact into a treatment- or intention-based mould? It is argued here that a closer look at the case law reveals some common closely intertwined themes. The first is a strong allegiance to a symmetrical notion of equality and an aversion to affirmative action. Majority judgments reveal a deep discomfort with the basis of an asymmetric approach, which is that we should be able to distinguish between legitimate and illegitimate uses of suspect or protected characteristics. A cause of action based on unequal results requires decision-makers to pay attention to the gender- or colour-based effects of their decisions even if the original decision is not expressly on grounds of race or gender. In adjudicating disparate impact, courts too are also required to make colour- or gender-conscious decisions. The second is a continued attachment to an individualised notion of liability. This entails, on the one hand, an unwillingness to move away from a fault-oriented model, which insists that only those responsible for a social problem should be required to remedy it, to one which is genuinely effects-based, and asks those in a position to change to do so. On the other hand, an individualised approach focuses on individual victims and requires a showing of individual detriment as well as collective impact. Third, there is a problematic ambiguity about the aims of an effects-based test and its relationship to a treatment-based test. Is the aim to redress disparities in outcomes or to augment the equal treatment principle by flushing out illegitimate reasons for decision-making which cannot otherwise be established or proved? Finally, not enough explicit attention is paid to the consequences of a finding of breach, and particularly to remedy, although this clearly influences in an unarticulated way the decision as to whether it is a breach in the first place. Should the individual be accommodated or the practice removed or results-oriented measures such as quotas be expressly put in place?

These points are developed below. It should be noted that this chapter does not aim to develop a theory of discrimination, nor to contribute to debates about the theory of discrimination. Its aim is instead to analyse the legal concepts of discrimination which have been developed by legislatures and courts to explore whether the background assumptions as to the meaning of equality and discrimination underpinning them are coherent and whether they are capable of confronting the real social problems of inequality in society. The paper is agnostic as to whether there can be a 'theory of discrimination law' outside of real legal systems and instead focuses on actual legal systems and their responsiveness to social context.

The paper examines these themes by comparing and contrasting the case law in the US and the UK in relation to three issues which illuminate the themes above: the relationship of intention, justification and pre-emptive action; the role of fault, responsibility and individual harm; and the aims and objectives which can be discerned from these cases. The final section briefly canvasses legal systems which have consciously diluted or moved beyond the distinction.

I. BRIGHT LINE DISTINCTIONS: INTENTION, JUSTIFICATION AND PRE-EMPTIVE ACTION

On the face of it, US and UK jurisprudence draw the distinction between direct and indirect discrimination in very different ways. In US case law, the key difference relates to intention. Whereas disparate treatment is intentional, disparate impact looks to effects. Disparate impact cannot be redeemed by good intentions. UK jurisprudence by contrast has eschewed intention for both direct and indirect discrimination. Instead, the distinction is based on whether or not justification is available. Direct discrimination cannot be justified, whereas indirect discrimination can. A closer look, however, shows that intention and justification are closely related. While of course there may be differences in burden of proof, both intention and justification raise the question of what reasons are legitimate and which are not, and how to draw the balance between impermissible and permissible reasons. This relationship is highlighted when it comes to pre-emptive action. This section considers the initial 'bright line' distinctions while the next section examines how they have become blurred.

Ever since the landmark decision on disparate impact in *Griggs v Duke Power*,[2] US jurisprudence has located the distinction between disparate treatment and disparate impact in the role of intention. The facts of *Griggs* are familiar. The employer, Duke Power, required a high school education

[2] ibid.

and satisfactory scores in an aptitude test as a condition of employment or transfer to the jobs in question, manual work which required no specific level of education. The same test was applied to all candidates, but because African-American applicants had long received inferior education in segregated schools, both requirements operated to disqualify such applicants at a substantially higher rate than whites. Neither standard was shown to be significantly related to successful job performance. The case was litigated under Title VII of the Civil Rights Act, which at that time simply made it unlawful to discriminate against an individual 'because of' that individual's race, colour, sex or national origin.[3] The Court responded by expanding the principle of equality in Title VII to include disparate impact. As Burger CJ, delivering the judgment of the Court, put it: 'The Act proscribes not only overt discrimination but also practices that are fair in form, but discriminatory in operation.'[4] The principle of disparate impact was given statutory force in the Civil Rights Act of 1991.[5]

Importantly, the Court in *Griggs* explicitly struck a different course on the role of intention from that taken by the lower courts in the case. The District Court found no showing of a discriminatory purpose in the adoption of the test requirements, and both that Court and the Court of Appeals concluded on that basis that there was no violation. Crucially, however, the Supreme Court in *Griggs* held that 'good intent or absence of discriminatory intent does not redeem employment procedures or testing mechanisms that operate as "built-in headwinds" for minority groups and are unrelated to measuring job capability.'[6] That meant 'unnecessary barriers to employment' must fall, even if 'neutral on their face' and 'neutral in terms of intent.' This set it apart from the disparate treatment principle. The US Supreme Court has consistently held that to establish disparate treatment, a plaintiff must prove that the defendant had a discriminatory intent or motive.[7]

The lack of a requirement for discriminatory intent almost immediately led a different configuration of the Supreme Court to refuse to extend the disparate impact from the statutory context of Title VII to the constitutional context of the Fourteenth Amendment. *Washington v Davis*,[8] like *Griggs*, constituted a challenge to selection criteria with a disparate impact, here on the representation of minorities in the Washington DC police force. Distancing itself from the statutory standard, the Court held that

> we have not held that a law, neutral on its face and serving ends otherwise within the power of government to pursue, is invalid under the Equal Protection Clause simply because it may affect a greater proportion of one race than of another.[9]

[3] § 2000e-2(a)(1); see also 78 Stat 255.
[4] *Griggs* (n 1) at 431.
[5] 105 Stat 1071 (42 USC § 2000e-2(k)(1)(A)(i)).
[6] *Griggs* (n 1) at 432.
[7] *Watson v Fort Worth Bank & Trust*, 487 US 977 at 986, 108 S Ct 2777 (1988).
[8] *Washington v Davis* 426 US 229, 96 S Ct 2040 (1976).
[9] ibid, 242.

Nevertheless, the US Supreme Court has continued to develop a non-intentional disparate impact liability under statute. Disparate impact was read into the Age Discrimination in Employment Act 1967 (ADEA)[10] in *Smith v City of Jackson* in 2005.[11] In *Smith*, a plurality of the Court interpreted statutory language referring to actions which 'otherwise adversely affect' an employee as requiring an effects-based interpretation. According to the plurality, this wording 'focuses on the *effects* of the action on the employee rather than the motivation for the action of the employer' and therefore entails recognition of disparate-impact liability.[12] Similarly, in 2015, in *Texas Department of Housing*, the Court drew on both *Griggs* and *Smith* to read the Fair Housing Act as likewise including disparate impact. Here too, the Court situated the boundary clearly in the distinction between intention and effects:

> Together, *Griggs* holds and the plurality in *Smith* instructs that antidiscrimination laws must be construed to encompass disparate-impact claims when their text refers to the consequences of actions and not just to the mindset of actors, and where that interpretation is consistent with statutory purpose.[13]

Similarly in *Ricci v DeStefano*, Kennedy J reiterated that: '[Title VII] prohibits both intentional discrimination (known as 'disparate treatment') as well as, in some cases, practices that are not intended to discriminate but in fact have a disproportionately adverse effect on minorities (known as "disparate impact").'[14]

This puts the US jurisprudence in vivid contrast with that of the UK. Although the concept of disparate impact was directly imported from the US and put into statutory form in the Sex Discrimination Act 1975 (SDA) and the Race Relations Act 1976 (RRA), the division was not formulated along the fault line of intention. Indeed, from its early case law on direct discrimination, UK courts firmly set their face against requiring proof of intention in a direct discrimination case. Thus, according to Lord Goff:

> The intention or motive of the defendant to discriminate … is not a necessary condition of liability … [Otherwise] it would be a good defence for an employer to show that he discriminated against women not because he intended to do so but (for example) because of customer preference, or to save money, or even to avoid controversy.[15]

[10] 81 Stat 602 et seq, as amended: see s 4(a).

[11] *Smith v City of Jackson* 544 US 228 (2005).

[12] ibid at 236 (emphasis added).

[13] *Texas Department of Housing and Community Affairs v Inclusive Communities Project, Inc* 135 S Ct 2411, 576 US_—Supreme Court, 2015 per Kennedy J.

[14] *Ricci v DeStefano* 129 S Ct 2658 (2009) (US Supreme Court), 2672.

[15] *R v Birmingham City Council, Ex p Equal Opportunities Commission* [1989] AC 1155 (HL), [175].

For example, in the *Roma* case, immigration officers explained their targeting of Roma on the grounds that Roma were disadvantaged in their country of origin and thus were more likely to claim asylum. To allow such explanations, it has been argued, would amount to an excuse for direct discrimination.[16] For this reason, it is now settled law that the motive of the perpetrator is irrelevant. Rather, UK courts have established a 'but for' test, which founds liability on the simple causative assessment that 'but for' the applicant's protected characteristic, she would not have been treated less favourably.[17] Instead of intention, the key factor distinguishing direct and indirect discrimination has been held to be the possibility of justification. As Baroness Hale has put it:

> Direct and indirect discrimination are mutually exclusive. You cannot have both at once ... The main difference between them is that direct discrimination cannot be justified. Indirect discrimination can be justified if it is a proportionate means of achieving a legitimate aim.[18]

II. BLURRING THE DISTINCTIONS: PRE-EMPTIVE ACTION AND 'INTRINSIC' DISCRIMINATION

Bright line distinctions on both sides of the Atlantic have, however, been blurred in recent cases. From the US perspective, this has been catalysed by the question of whether a respondent is entitled to take pre-emptive action to avoid disparate liability. On the one hand, at least since 1986, the Supreme Court has recognised that Congress intended that 'voluntary compliance' be 'the preferred means of achieving the objectives of Title VII.'[19] On the other hand, pre-emptive action can itself be construed as race-conscious decision-making, depending on the background theory of equality being used. It is the spectre that pre-emptive action in relation to a disparate impact claim will lead to quotas or express race-based preferences that has led shifting majorities of the Court to blur the boundaries between disparate treatment and disparate impact analyses. Behind this is a continued adherence to a symmetrical, equal treatment-based

[16] *R (European Roma Rights Centre) v Immigration Officer at Prague Airport* [2004] UKHL 55, [2005] 2 AC 1.

[17] *James v Eastleigh Borough Council* [1990] 2 AC 751 and *R (on the application of E) v JFS Governing Body* [2009] UKSC 15, [2010] 2 AC 728.

[18] *R v JFS* (n 17) [57]. In *Bull v Hall*, Lady Hale followed some opinions of Advocates General in EU case law suggesting that direct discrimination occurred when there was an exact coincidence between the category suffering a disadvantage and a category defined by applying a prohibited classification: *Bull and Bull v Hall and Preddy* [2013] UKSC 73, [2013] 1 WLR 3741 [189].

[19] *Firefighters v Cleveland* 478 US 501, 515, 106 S Ct 3063, 92 L.Ed.2d 405 (1986); see also *Wygant v Jackson Board of Education*, 476 US 267, 290, 106 S Ct 1842, 90 L.Ed.2d 260 (1986), O'Connor, J, concurring in part and concurring in judgment.

understanding of equality that does not countenance remedial or legitimate uses of race to counter adverse disadvantage.

This can be seen very clearly in the *Ricci v DeStefano* case,[20] which attempted to resolve an apparent conflict between disparate treatment and disparate impact by diluting the intention requirement in disparate treatment cases. In *Ricci*, the selection tests for promotion to New Haven's fire force had a severely disparate impact, with the result that none of the black fire-fighters and only one Hispanic who took the examinations were in the group selected for promotion to lieutenant or captain. Faced with the possibility of a disparate action suit against it, New Haven decided not to certify the results, but to adopt a new test and re-test all the applicants. This was challenged by disappointed white candidates, on the ground that this decision was itself discriminatory against them on grounds of their race. Had it not been for the cancellation of the test, they argued, they would have been promoted. This, they said, constituted a breach of both Title VII and the Equal Protection Clause in the Fourteenth Amendment. In response, the City argued that if they had certified the results, they could have faced liability under Title VII for adopting a practice that had a disparate impact on the minority firefighters. The Supreme Court, in a 5-4 judgment, held that the decision not to certify the results was itself a race-based decision, and therefore in breach of Title VII. This did not wholly mean that it was impermissible to take action to pre-empt a disparate impact. Kennedy J articulated the relationship between equal treatment and disparate impact as follows:

> We conclude that race-based action like the City's in this case is impermissible under Title VII unless the employer can demonstrate a strong basis in evidence that, had it not taken the action, it would have been liable under the disparate-impact statute.[21]

The respondents, however, had not met this standard and had therefore violated Title VII by discarding the tests. The Court did not feel the need to go further and determine the claim under the Equal Protection Clause.

What is startling about this case is the finding that a failure to certify the results was itself a race-based decision. Kennedy J saw this as uncontroversial.

> Our analysis begins with this premise: The City's actions would violate the disparate-treatment prohibition of Title VII absent some valid defence. All the evidence demonstrates that the City chose not to certify the examination results because of the statistical disparity based on race—*ie*, how minority candidates had performed when compared to white candidates ... Without some other justification, this express, race-based decision-making violates Title VII's command that employers cannot take adverse employment actions because of an individual's race. See § 2000e-2(a)(1).[22]

[20] *Ricci* (n 14).
[21] ibid at 2664.
[22] ibid at 2673.

He rejected the District Court's view that the motivation to avoid making promotions based on a test with a racially disparate impact could not constitute discriminatory intent. Similarly, he discarded the City's argument that an intent to comply with Title VII's disparate impact provisions could not constitute prohibited discrimination on the basis of race.

> Whatever the City's ultimate aim—however well-intentioned or benevolent it might have seemed—the City made its employment decision because of race. The City rejected the test results solely because the higher scoring candidates were white. The question is not whether that conduct was discriminatory but whether the City had a lawful justification for its race-based action.[23]

Kennedy J's formulation of the test for disparate treatment is remarkably close to the approach of the UK courts to intention in direct discrimination cases. Where it differs, however, is in leaving open the possibility of justification. Stopping short of precluding all pre-emptive action in relation to disparate impact, Kennedy J rejected the petitioners' 'broad and inflexible' formulation, namely that avoiding unintentional discrimination cannot justify intentional discrimination. This would ignore the fact that Congress had codified both types of discrimination. On the other hand, he also rejected the contention that good faith belief that its actions are necessary to comply with the disparate impact provisions would be enough to justify race-conscious conduct. To achieve a balance he drew on the standard set in relation to the Equal Protection Clause of the Fourteenth Amendment, namely, that 'certain government actions to remedy past racial discrimination—actions that are themselves based on race—are constitutional only where there is a "strong basis in evidence"' that the remedial actions were necessary.[24] It is telling, however, that the Equal Protection standard that he drew on was that set in affirmative action cases, where a symmetrical understanding of equality has led the court to set the standard of justification for remedial race-based decision-making as high as in the context of detrimental racial classifications. While at least leaving some role for justification on the grounds of remedial purpose, this approach to justification in practice sets a very high standard.

As Siegel points out, the finding of disparate treatment in *Ricci* is extremely difficult to reconcile with the purpose test set out in the earlier case of *Washington v Davis*.[25] Neither the exam itself nor its withdrawal and replacement by a new test involved express racial classifications. Nor was any individual applicant singled out for affirmative action

[23] ibid at 2674.

[24] ibid at 2675 citing *Richmond v JA Croson Co*, 488 US 469, 500, 109 S Ct 706, 102 L.Ed.2d 854 (1989) (quoting *Wygant* (n 19) at 277, 106 S Ct 1842 (plurality opinion)).

[25] R Siegel, 'Equality Divided' (2013) 217 *Harvard Law Review* 1.

for promotion.[26] Nevertheless, the Court regarded the withdrawal of the results as racially discriminatory against the white applicants. It therefore applied a test to the pre-emptive duty more akin to that applied under the affirmative action jurisprudence, which since *Adarand v Pena* has required 'strict scrutiny',[27] here expressed as a 'strong basis in evidence.' In the US context, as Siegel vividly shows, this has the paradoxical effect that

> when minorities challenge laws of general application and argue that government has segregated or profiled on the basis of race, plaintiffs must show that government acted for a discriminatory purpose, a standard that doctrine has made extraordinarily difficult to satisfy. ... By contrast, when members of majority groups challenge state action that classifies by race—affirmative action has become the paradigmatic example—plaintiffs do not need to demonstrate, as a predicate for judicial intervention, that government has acted for an illegitimate purpose.[28]

Ginsburg J made a similar point in her dissenting judgment:

> A reasonable endeavour to comply with the law and to ensure that qualified candidates of all races have a fair opportunity to compete is simply not what Congress meant to interdict. I would therefore hold that an employer who jettisons a selection device when its disproportionate racial impact becomes apparent does not violate Title VII's disparate-treatment bar automatically or at all, subject to this key condition: The employer must have good cause to believe the device would not withstand examination for business necessity.[29]

Ginsburg J emphatically rejected the comparison with affirmative action cases, in which race was the decisive factor.

> An employer's effort to avoid Title VII liability by repudiating a suspect selection method scarcely resembles those cases. Race was not merely a relevant consideration in [the affirmative action cases of] *Wygant* and *Croson;* it was the decisive factor. Observance of Title VII's disparate-impact provision, in contrast, calls for no racial preference, absolute or otherwise. The very purpose of the provision is to ensure that individuals are hired and promoted based on qualifications manifestly necessary to successful performance of the job in question, qualifications that do not screen out members of any race.[30]

The blurring of bright line distinctions in the UK jurisprudence has arisen in a different way. From the direct discrimination side, there has been too little attention given to the respondent's real reasons for drawing a distinction. On the other hand, from the indirect discrimination side, courts have begun

[26] ibid, 54.
[27] *Adarand Constructors v Pena* 515 US 200 (1995).
[28] ibid, 3.
[29] *Ricci* (n 14) at 2701.
[30] ibid at 23.

to insert a requirement for proof of the 'reason why' an apparently neutral criterion has an adverse impact. The former is the consequence of the 'but for' standard.[31] The use of the 'but for' standard of causation for direct discrimination, while aiming to avoid having to adjudicate on intention or motive, has meant that there can be no distinction between legitimate and illegitimate reasons for a distinction. Indeed, allied to the absence of a justification defence, the but for test has left no space for the reason for the action to be aired at all. The result has been to elide the distinction between treatment and effects. It is true that the fact that A is not hostile to B should not excuse A's actions. On the other hand, A's action must be *because of* the protected characteristic. If the treatment was for an entirely different reason, but has the effect of discriminating, then it should fall under the indirect discrimination provisions and be capable of justification. Instead of ignoring the perpetrator's real reason, this would allow courts to determine on proportionality grounds whether the real reason should be allowed to outweigh the differential impact. In the examples given by Lord Goff above, the fact that an employer was following customer preference, or saving money, or avoiding controversy, should not be sufficient to outweigh the fact that women have been excluded. On the other hand, if the reason for the treatment was to compensate for past disadvantage, this may well outweigh the exclusionary effect.

This can be seen by considering the cases of *James v Eastleigh*[32] and *JFS*,[33] where the principle that the perpetrator's *motive* is irrelevant has subtly transformed into an assertion of the irrelevance of the perpetrator's *reason* for the less favourable treatment. Courts have held that even if the reason is not on its face based on a protected characteristic, it might nevertheless be 'inherently' sex- or race-based. This severs the notion of direct discrimination from its moral anchor in fault and responsibility of the perpetrator, and instead makes A responsible for putting in motion a series of steps which have a detrimental *effect* on B, thus crossing the border between direct and indirect discrimination.

James v Eastleigh BC concerned a challenge to Eastleigh Borough Council's policy of free access to swimming pools and other council facilities to anyone over pensionable age.[34] The aim of the concessions was to compensate for the drop in income generally accompanying the end of one's working life. The problem arose because State pension ages were set at 60 for women and 65 for men. This meant that although both Mr James and

[31] This discussion draws heavily on S Fredman, *Discrimination Law* 2nd edn (Oxford. Oxford University Press, 2011).
[32] *James* (n 17).
[33] *R v JFS* (n 17).
[34] *James* (n 17).

his wife were 61, she was entitled to free swimming, but he was not. He argued that he had been discriminated against on grounds of his sex. The authority defended the policy by arguing that people living on pensions are almost always less well off than when in employment. The criterion of pensionable age, while a somewhat broad brush, was the most practical way of identifying people living on pensions. The reason for the differentiation was not the sex of the complainant, but the fact that he had not reached pensionable age.

However, the majority of the House of Lords found that the reason why the policy was adopted could not alter the fact that the man would have received the benefits 'but for' his sex. The reason for the difference, namely to give concessions to pensioners to compensate for their loss of income, was irrelevant. Instead, it was held that the criterion of pensionable age '*itself* ... treats women more favourably than men "on the ground of their sex"',[35] and was 'inherently' discriminatory.[36] The result was paradoxical. As Lord Griffiths put it in his dissenting opinion:

> The result of your Lordships' decision will be that either free facilities must be withdrawn from those who can ill afford to pay for them or, alternatively, given free to those who can well afford to pay for them. I consider both alternatives regrettable. I cannot believe that Parliament intended such a result and I do not believe that the words 'on the grounds of sex' compel such a result.[37]

This difficulty arises because the court has focused not on the reason for A's actions, but on its effect. In this case, the court assumed that pensionable age was simply a proxy for sex; whereas in reality the council regarded pensionable age as a proxy for relative disadvantage. It is true that this had a differential impact on men and women; but this was because, for reasons beyond the council's control, the pensionable age was different for men and women. Although the council could foresee this effect, this was not the reason for its actions.[38] If pensionable age were the same for men and women, it would still have used this criterion. Thus it treated Mr James less favourably than his wife because he was not yet of pensionable age, not because he was a man. This appears quintessentially to be an effects-based test, or indirect discrimination. Of course, it might be argued that pensionable age is too crude a mechanism for determining low income and therefore, given its exclusionary effect on men, the choice of pensionable age was not appropriate or necessary to achieve the aim of ameliorating the loss of income post pensionable age. This, however, should be considered separately, in the form of a justification defence.

[35] ibid at 763.
[36] ibid at 769.
[37] ibid at 768.
[38] ibid at 781.

The boundaries between direct and indirect discrimination were further blurred in the *JFS* case,[39] where the notion that a ground can be 'inherently' discriminatory was entrenched within the structure of direct discrimination. Here both Lords Mance and Clarke expressly held that direct discrimination could arise in one of two ways: 'because a decision or action was taken on a ground which was, however worthy or benign the motive, *inherently racial*, or because it was taken or undertaken for a reason which was subjectively racial'.[40] UK legislation permits designated faith schools to discriminate on grounds of religion, but not on grounds of race or ethnicity. In this case, a boy was refused admission to JFS, a designated Jewish faith school, because he was not recognised as Jewish according to the Orthodox religious rule. This rule, as set out by the Orthodox Chief Rabbi, requires Orthodox conversion or descent from a mother who is herself Jewish or has been converted according to the Orthodox faith. Although the boy's mother was a practising Jewess, she had been converted to Judaism according to Masorti rather than Orthodox tenets. Lord Mance's formulation of this problem is revealing. In order to establish a clear divide between the *motivation* for the decision and the *ground* for the decision, he was required to formulate a conception of 'grounds' which could be 'in their nature inherently ethnic.' Did the admissions policy, he asked, 'religiously motivated as it was, involve grounds for admission or refusal of admission which were in their nature inherently ethnic?'[41]

The majority of the court found that although the Chief Rabbi and the governors of the school were entirely free from moral blame, and acted on what must have seemed to them an entirely legitimate religious objective, the religious element was a mere motive, and therefore irrelevant to the outcome. Instead, the ground was his ethnicity: any rule which relies on descent is an ethnic rule, and, 'but for' the fact that his mother was not Jewish by Orthodox standards, he would have been admitted to the school. The result was that the policy was held to be discriminatory on grounds of race. Yet the majority was at pains to stress that a breach of the prohibition of direct race discrimination did not connote that the school or the Chief Rabbi was racist. It was simply a technical application of the law. This disjuncture between a moral condemnation of racism and a breach of race discrimination legislation should itself give pause for thought. As Lord Rodger points out in his dissent: 'The majority's decision leads to such extraordinary results, and produces such manifest discrimination against

[39] *R v JFS* (n 17).

[40] ibid at [78]; and see Lord Clarke at [132] (emphasis added).

[41] ibid at [78].

Jewish schools in comparison with other faith schools, that one can't help feeling that something has gone wrong.'[42]

What then might have gone wrong? Most importantly, the notion that a criterion is 'inherently' discriminatory ignores the structure of direct discrimination, which is to focus on why a person acted in the way she did. A decision or action is only 'inherently' discriminatory because of its effect; it is this which distinguishes it from an action which is, in the words of Lords Mance and Clark, 'subjectively racial'.[43] Focusing on the effect is the province of indirect discrimination. Direct discrimination, by contrast, requires a finding that the reason for the perpetrator's action was based on a protected characteristic. The refusal to contemplate the real reason for the perpetrator's action is particularly problematic in UK anti-discrimination law because by classifying the case as one of direct discrimination, the possibility of a justification defence is precluded. Thus, as in the *James* case, there was no further opportunity to balance the reason for the decision against its outcome.

The relegation of the real reason to a mere motive undercuts any moral rationale which might underpin direct discrimination. Advocate General Maduro in the context of EU law has identified the 'evil' of direct discrimination as the fact that a suspect classification is an 'essential premise' of the discriminator's reasoning; or constitutes grounds on which the person's reasoning is based. It is the perpetrator's reasoning which is in issue. By contrast, in the context of indirect discrimination, the intentions of the perpetrator and the reasons she or he acts are irrelevant.[44] As both Lord Hope and Lord Rodger pointed out in their dissenting opinions in *JFS*, to reduce the religious element to the status of a mere motive entirely misrepresents the position,[45] removing the link between A's actions and the reason for A's actions. The real reason for the Chief Rabbi's action was religious: he recognised some conversions to Judaism but not others. Indeed, the real dispute in the case was between the Orthodox and non-Orthodox understandings of who should be Jewish, a profoundly religious dispute. Yet the impact of the majority decision is not to require recognition of non-Orthodox conversions. It is to prevent the school from basing its selection policy on the Jewish definition of Judaism at all. Instead, it requires a practice-based definition, familiar to Anglicanism but alien to Judaism. Jewish faith schools have now changed their admissions policy to require evidence of practice of the Jewish faith, through attendance at synagogue twice a month on the

42 ibid at [226].

43 ibid at [78]; and see Lord Clarke at [132].

44 C-303/06 *Coleman v Attridge Law* [2008] ECR 1-5603, [2008] IRLR 722.

45 *R v JFS* (n 17) [201].

Sabbath as well as on all holy days. This is a result which profoundly undermines the stated mission of the school, which is to give a Jewish education to children with no knowledge of Judaism as much as to those who already have such a knowledge. As Lord Brown put it, the result is

> a test for admission to an Orthodox Jewish school which is not Judaism's own test and which requires a focus (as Christianity does) on outward acts of religious practice and declarations of faith, ignoring whether the child is or is not Jewish as defined by Orthodox Jewish law.[46]

One way forward is to regard intrinsically discriminatory rules as a species of indirect discrimination and therefore justifiable. This permits the real reason to be scrutinised to determine whether it is proportionate and necessary in the light of its exclusionary effect. For example, Lord Hope held that the admissions policy in the *JFS* case was not directly but indirectly discriminatory, in that it was not proportionate or necessary to insist on Orthodox conversion in the admission criteria. This would also have made it possible to address the disproportionality with an alternative policy which fitted better with the school's ethos. In other words, an exclusionary criterion could have been justified if it was proportionate.

There has been a reluctance to rely on indirect discrimination in such cases, because the act or decision excludes everyone with the relevant protected characteristic. When all members of the group are excluded, it might be thought that there is too much of a coincidence between the criterion applied and the exclusionary effect to regard the criterion as neutral.[47] Indeed, it is this that prompts the conclusion that the criterion is 'intrinsically' discriminatory. However the criterion is neutral for the purposes of indirect discrimination as long as the same criterion is applied to everyone. This is not changed if the criterion excludes significantly more of one group than another, or all of the group. For example, in *Mandla v Lee*[48] the House of Lords held that a school uniform rule which required pupils to go bareheaded was indirectly discriminatory because, although applied to all students, it excluded Sikhs who wore turbans. The fact that all turban-wearing Sikhs were excluded by the rule did not prevent this result.

This argument is strengthened by the new definition of indirect discrimination which requires that the measure subjects B to a particular disadvantage. This formulation originated in the case of *O'Flynn*,[49] in which the European Court of Justice (ECJ) explicitly stated that a provision would be regarded as indirectly discriminatory if it was 'intrinsically liable' to affect migrant workers more than national workers, with the consequent risk that

[46] ibid at [258].
[47] See eg ibid at [71].
[48] *Mandla v Lee* [1983] 2 AC 548 (HL).
[49] Case C-237/94 *O'Flynn v Adjudication Officer* [1996] 3 CMLR 103.

they would be placed at a particular disadvantage.[50] It has made no difference to the ECJ that the apparently neutral criterion in effect excludes all members of a particular group. In *Schnorbus*,[51] a legal training course was mandatory in order to qualify for the higher civil service or the judicial service. Priority for places on this course was given to individuals who had completed national service. Yet only men were eligible for national service. The CJEU held that regardless of statistics, the provisions at issue were themselves evidence of indirect discrimination since, under the relevant national legislation, women were not required to do military or civilian service and therefore could not benefit from the priority. This analysis closely resembles the 'intrinsically discriminatory' class identified by UK courts as directly discriminatory. By classifying it as indirectly discriminatory, however, the CJEU was able to consider the justification for the rule. Since its aim was to compensate for the delay necessitated by military service, and the detriment to others lasted for only 12 months, it was held to be proportionate and justified.

While insisting on the irrelevance of the perpetrator's reason in a direct discrimination case, UK courts paradoxically began to demand a 'reason why' in indirect discrimination cases. This can be seen in the recent case of *Essop*.[52] Like the US selection cases, *Essop* was concerned with the paradigmatic case of indirect discrimination: namely, the disparate impact of apparently neutral selection tests for recruitment, promotion and training. *Essop* concerned the Core Skills Assessment (CSA) which was necessary to pass in order to achieve promotion to the post of Higher Executive Officer (HEO) or above in the Civil Service. In a set of test cases challenging the CSA as indirectly discriminatory, it was asserted that black and minority ethnic (BME) candidates over the age of 35 were systematically less likely to pass than non-BME and younger candidates. This was based on a statistical report commissioned by the Government, which found that BME and older candidates had a proportionately lower CSA pass-rate than white and younger candidates. In the Court of Appeal, Rimer LJ held that the statistical disparity was not sufficient. In addition, the claimant had to establish 'why the PCP disadvantages the group sharing the protected characteristic.'[53] Indeed, he stated, 'it is conceptually impossible to prove a group disadvantage for the purpose of section 19(2)(b) [indirect discrimination] liability without also showing *why* the claimed disadvantage is said to arise.'[54] This was despite the fact he himself acknowledged that no reason had been provided by the expert report for this differential outcome and that it would in

[50] ibid at [20].
[51] Case C-79/99 *Schnorbus v Land Hessen* [2001] 1 CMLR 40.
[52] *Essop v Home Office* [2017] UKSC 27, [2017] 1 WLR 1343.
[53] *Essop and others v Home Office (UK Border Agency)* [2015] EWCA 609 at [59].
[54] ibid.

all likelihood be impossible to prove what the reason for the disparity was. This result is puzzling. To require the complainants to show the 'reason why' the PCP disadvantages the group as a whole is to fundamentally misunderstand the meaning of indirect discrimination. It is the disparate impact on the group of a PCP itself which constitutes the prima facie discrimination: once we identify a PCP and 'particular disadvantage' to the detriment of a protected group, it is indirectly discriminatory unless the respondent can show it to be a proportionate means of achieving a legitimate aim.[55] The focus on the 'reason why' was further endorsed by the Court of Appeal in *Naeem v Secretary of State for Justice*.[56] Indeed, *Naeem* went even further and held that it was not sufficient to show why the disparate impact occurred. In addition, the applicant had to establish that this reason was something peculiar to the protected characteristic in question. This came close to collapsing the boundary between direct and indirect discrimination altogether.

In a welcome development, however, the Supreme Court in the joined cases of *Essop* and *Naeem*,[57] held unequivocally that there was no need for proof of the reason why. Baroness Hale's judgment helpfully reasserts some of the fundamental principles of indirect discrimination. To require that the applicant must show the reason why there is a disparate impact, or that this reason is because of a protected characteristic, she held, misunderstands the role of causation in indirect discrimination. It is only in relation to direct discrimination that it is necessary to show that less favourable treatment is because of a protected characteristic. For indirect discrimination, by contrast, it is sufficient to establish that the PCP has led to the disparate impact. Contrary to the finding in *Naeem*, therefore, there is no need to establish that the reason why the PCP had a disparate impact was because of a protected characteristic. Ultimately,

> the essential element is a causal connection between the PCP and the disadvantage suffered, not only by the group, but also by the individual. This may be easier to prove if the reason for the group disadvantage is known but that is a matter of fact, not law.[58]

Moreover, Baroness Hale held, there can be many and varied reasons why the PCP has such an impact. Indeed, the reason for disadvantage need not be unlawful in itself or be under the control of the employer or provider. Identifying these reasons, while helpful, are not essential to a finding of indirect discrimination. Whereas for direct discrimination, it must be established

[55] See further S Fredman, 'The Reason Why: Unravelling Indirect Discrimination' (2016) 45 *Industrial Law Journal* 231.

[56] *Naeem v Secretary of State for Justice* [2015] EWCA 1264, [2016] ICR 289.

[57] *Essop v Home Office (UK Border Agency)* [2017] UKSC 27, [2017] 1 WLR 1343.

[58] ibid at [33].

that 'but for' the protected characteristic, the person would not have been treated less favourably than a comparator without that characteristic, in indirect discrimination: 'Both the PCP and the reason for the disadvantage are "but for" causes of the disadvantage: removing one or the other would solve the problem.'[59]

III. INDIVIDUALISM: FAULT AND INDIVIDUAL HARM

One of the major challenges of indirect discrimination is that its focus on effects challenges the assumption that only those at 'fault' should be liable to compensate 'victims' of their actions. An effects-based model of liability requires a move away from the need for either a 'perpetrator' or a 'victim'. Yet the jurisprudence easily defaults to a position in which liability is only found if the respondent can be said to be responsible in some way for the outcome. This can be seen both in the *Texas Housing* case in the US and *Essop* in the UK.

In the *Texas Housing* case, although the Court made the significant step of extending the Fair Housing Act (FHA) to include disparate impact liability, it also emphasised the need for clear causation between employers' policies and statistical disparities. Kennedy J stressed that a claim that relies on a statistical disparity 'must fail if the plaintiff cannot point to a defendant's policy or policies causing that disparity. A robust causality requirement … protects defendants from being liable for racial disparities they did not create.'[60] This is true too for the justification standard. Here too, the Court was careful to limit disparate impact liability so that employers and other entities were able to 'make the practical business choices and profit-related decisions that sustain the free-enterprise system.'

The UK statute also demonstrates the uneasy relationship between an effects-oriented understanding of discrimination and the background assumption that only individual 'victims' should have a remedy. The UK statutory provision has always straddled group and individual: requiring a showing not just of disparate impact on the group under section 19(2)(b) of the Equality Act 2010, but also that the individual complainant has suffered that disadvantage (section 19(2)(c)).[61] Similarly, the remedial structure is highly individualised. There is no provision in the statute for requiring the PCP to be removed. At most a tribunal can issue a recommendation that steps be taken by the respondent to obviate or reduce the adverse effect *on the complainant*.[62] The Equality Act 2010 briefly extended this power to

[59] ibid at [26].
[60] *Texas Housing* (n 13) per Kennedy J at 20.
[61] Equality Act 2010, s 19(2)(c).
[62] Equality Act, s 124.

include recommending steps to reduce or obviate the adverse effect on not only the claimant but any others who could be affected by it. But this was repealed in 2015 on the grounds that it was an unnecessary burden on business and was better dealt with through non-statutory guidance.[63] Moreover, the recommendation is not enforceable per se. The statute provides that if the respondent fails to comply without reasonable excuse, the tribunal may either order compensation, or increase the amount of compensation payable.[64] Thus the respondent still has the opportunity to make a reasonable excuse for failure to comply. Even without such an excuse, at most the tribunal has the discretion to order compensation. Therefore the primary remedy is compensation to the individual.

This focus on the individual in the remedial structure gives the impression that the result of a successful claim should be to give the applicant the job or promotion sought. This goes some way to explaining the preoccupation in the Court of Appeal in *Essop* with the prospect that a successful indirect discrimination claim would reward an unmeritorious applicant unless the reason why she had failed the test could be established. In the lower courts' view, it was quite possible that the individual had failed the test for an unrelated reason, such as failing to prepare or coming late.[65]

The focus on the individual is difficult to reconcile with the principle behind indirect discrimination, which is not to benefit specified individuals, but to level the playing field so that everyone has a fair chance to pass the test, if they merit it. Although Baroness Hale in *Essop* reasserted this principle, her judgment still evinces a concern that ways should be found to prevent a successful claim by an unmeritorious applicant. Thus, she suggests that, rather than requiring the applicant to establish the reason why the disparate impact occurred, it should be left open to the respondent to show that the PCP did not cause disadvantage to this individual. This is a better approach than that of Sir Colin Rimer in the Court of Appeal, who in effect put the burden on the candidate to demonstrate that, but for the unfairness of the test, she would have passed. However, it still suggests that the aim is to benefit individual deserving applicants, rather than to remove the obstacles so that there is a level playing ground for all. What the claimant should get is a fair chance through a fair test. The unmeritorious candidate, if genuinely unmeritorious, will fail again. It should therefore be unnecessary to re-introduce the reason why an individual claimant failed, given the risk that the objective of indirect discrimination could be subverted.

[63] Deregulation Act 2015, s 2.
[64] Equality Act, s 124.
[65] *Essop* (n 56) at [65].

IV. AIMS AND OBJECTIVES

The blurring of the boundaries between disparate treatment and disparate impact reopens the question of what the aims of each are. Despite the intuitive appeal of indirect discrimination, or disparate impact, its aims are not entirely clear. Indirect discrimination is often thought of as aiming to achieve equality of results. However, on closer examination of the principle as formulated in both the UK and the US, it can be seen that this is only partially true. Unequal results will not breach the principle of indirect discrimination if the inequality can be justified by reference to business needs or State social policy; or if no exclusionary provision, criterion or practice can be identified.

This can be seen clearly in the *Texas Housing* case in the US Supreme Court. In the *Texas Housing* case, Kennedy J stressed that although disparate impact had an important role to play, its aim was not to achieve equality in distribution of housing opportunities. 'Racial imbalance does not, without more establish a prima facie case of disparate impact.'[66] Without such safeguards, he warned, 'disparate liability might cause race to be used and considered in a pervasive way', which in turn would 'almost inexorably lead' to the use of numerical quotas, in turn raising 'serious constitutional questions.' The result in *Ricci* reinforces this point. As Ginsburg J noted:

> By order of this Court, New Haven, a city in which African-Americans and Hispanics account for nearly 60 percent of the population, must today be served—as it was in the days of undisguised discrimination—by a fire department in which members of racial and ethnic minorities are rarely seen in command positions.[67]

A different approach could be to regard both disparate treatment and disparate impact as furthering equality of opportunities, rather than equality of outcome per se. Thus in her dissent in *Ricci*, Ginsburg J stated: 'Standing on an equal footing, these twin pillars of Title VII advance the same objectives: ending workplace discrimination and promoting genuinely equal opportunity.'[68] She pointed to the same underlying understanding of equality in *Griggs*: '[T]o achieve equality of employment opportunities', the Court comprehended, Congress 'directed the thrust of the Act to the consequences of employment practices, not simply the motivation.'[69] Similarly, Baroness Hale in the UK Supreme Court in *Chief Constable for West Yorkshire Police v Homer* stated, 'The law of indirect discrimination is an attempt to level the playing field by subjecting to scrutiny requirements which look neutral

[66] *Wards Cove Packing Co v Atonio* 490 US 642 (1989).
[67] *Ricci* (n 14) at 2690.
[68] ibid at 2699.
[69] *Griggs* (n 1) at 429, 432.

on their face but in reality work to the comparative disadvantage of people with a particular protected characteristic.'[70]

However, disparate impact or indirect discrimination on its own can only further equality of opportunities in a shallow sense. This is because business-related justifications are sufficient to displace the presumption of liability. Indirectly discriminatory barriers need not be dismantled if they can be justified. Criteria which are job-related remain legitimate even though disadvantaged groups, by virtue of their disadvantage, might find it impossible to comply. Thus, certain qualifications may be necessary for a job, yet an individual may lack those qualifications precisely because of past or ongoing discrimination. Nor does indirect discrimination on its own give rise to any obligation to ensure that applicants are equipped for a job or other benefit; for example, by training or provision of childcare. The benefits and limitations of indirect discrimination are clearly evident in respect of part-time work. In the UK and EU, the indirect discrimination provisions have made significant progress in the removal of specific detriments attached to part-time work.[71] But they do nothing to change the underlying division of power within the family which leaves women with the primary responsibility for childcare. The result is that women part-time workers might find their position at work improved as a result of the prohibition of indirect discrimination. But the fact that the vast majority of part-time workers are women remains unchanged. On the other hand, a robust remedial system, or indeed a requirement of pre-emptive action, might give more substance to the claim that disparate impact is an equal opportunities standard.

Could it be argued then that, instead of constituting the aim of indirect discrimination, results are part of the diagnosis of discrimination, exposing the existence of obstacles to entry rather than the pattern of outcome? The assumption is that, in a non-discriminatory environment, there will be a fair distribution of different men and women, ethnic and religious groups, heterosexuals and homosexuals, able-bodied and disabled people. Under-representation of one of these groups is a sign that there might be a hidden obstacle to entry, which, unless justifiable, should be removed. This is particularly useful where the practice is opaque and informal, such as a pay policy which is characterised by a total lack of transparency,[72] or a recruitment policy based on unwritten and subjective criteria. It is also useful in situations in which the measure itself is not suspect and there is clearly

[70] *Homer v Chief Constable of West Yorkshire Police* [2012] UKSC 15, [2012] 3 All ER 1287 at [17].

[71] Case C-96/80 *Jenkins v Kingsgate* [1981] ECR 911; Case C-170/84 *Bilka-Kaufhaus GmbH v Weber von Hartz* [1986] ECR 1607; Case C-77/02 *Steinicke v Bundesanstalt für Arbeit* [2003] ECR 1-9027 (ECJ); *Ex p EOC* (n 15).

[72] Case C-109/88 *Handels- og KontorfunktionÆRernes Forbund I Danmark (Union of Clerical and Commercial Employees) v Dansk Arbejdsgiverforening (Danish Employers' Association)* [1991] 1 CMLR 8.

no intention on the part of the perpetrator.[73] In the *Texas Housing* case, Kennedy J also saw the purpose of disparate impact as playing an important role in uncovering discriminatory intent: it 'permits plaintiffs to counteract unconscious prejudices and disguised animus that escape easy classification as disparate treatment.'

The difficulty with this approach is that it can quickly dissolve into a disparate treatment standard and undermine disparate impact entirely. Thomas J in his concurring opinion in the *Seattle* case demonstrated how easily this slippage can occur: 'Although a presently observed racial imbalance might result from past [discrimination], racial imbalance can also result from any number of innocent private decisions.'[74] Thomas J was even more stinging in his dissent in the *Texas Housing* case:

> As best I can tell, the reason for this wholesale inversion of our law's usual approach is the unstated—and unsubstantiated—assumption that, in the absence of discrimination, an institution's racial makeup would mirror that of society. But the absence of racial disparities in multi-ethnic societies has been the exception, rather than the rule.[75]

V. RELAXING THE BOUNDARIES: DO WE NEED THE DISTINCTION?

The difficulty in delineating a clear boundary between the principles of liability means that it becomes important that, while both can be tools in detecting discrimination, the precise classification as one or the other should not significantly affect the defences available or the appropriate remedies. This was the conclusion reached in the Supreme Court of Canada. In a case in 1997 (the '*Firefighters*' case),[76] McLachlan J took the opportunity of revisiting the conventional bifurcated approach which categorised discrimination as either 'direct', meaning discriminatory on its face, or 'adverse effect', meaning discriminatory in effect. She recognised that 'the conventional analysis was helpful in the interpretation of the early human rights statutes, and indeed represented a significant step forward in that it recognized for the first time the harm of adverse effect discrimination'.[77] However, it no longer served the purpose of human rights legislation. There were a number of reasons for this. Most important for our purposes was the fact that few cases could be neatly categorised as direct or adverse

[73] O DeSchutter, 'Three Models of Equality and European Anti-Discrimination Law' (2006) 57 *Northern Ireland Legal Quarterly* 1.

[74] *Parents Involved in Community Schools v Seattle School District* 127 S Ct 2738 (2007).

[75] *Texas Department of Housing* (n 13) per Thomas J.

[76] *British Columbia (Public Service Employee Relations Commission) v British Columbia Government Service Employees' Union* [1999] 3 SCR 3.

[77] ibid at [25].

effect discrimination. The example given by McLachlan CJ is particularly instructive. She referred to a rule requiring all workers to appear at work on Fridays or face dismissal. This could be directly discriminatory, in that no workers whose religious beliefs preclude working on Fridays may be employed there. Or it could be characterised as a neutral rule that merely has an adverse effect on a few individuals (those same workers whose religious beliefs prevent them from working on Fridays).[78] The same analysis would work in UK law: the rule would be 'intrinsically' directly discriminatory under the *JFS* test; or indirectly discriminatory because workers whose religious beliefs prevent them from working on Fridays would be subject to a particular disadvantage. She also recognised that the size of the 'affected group' is easily manipulable. The difficulty in classification led McLachlan CJ to conclude that it was not appropriate for the distinction to constitute the basis for diverging remedial or other outcomes. Instead, she established a unified approach. Where a standard is prima facie discriminatory, it can only be justified if the employer can show that the purpose of the standard is rationally connected to the performance of the job, the standard was adopted in a bona fide belief that it was necessary to fulfil a legitimate work-related purpose, and the standard is reasonably necessary to the accomplishment of that purpose.

Other jurisdictions have relaxed the boundary in a different way. The European Court of Human Rights (ECtHR) only adopted an indirect discrimination standard relatively recently, in the *DH* case. But the boundary between the two concepts is less rigid than that of the UK in that it leaves open the possibility of a justification defence in both equal treatment and indirect discrimination claims. By contrast, the ECtHR has preferred to calibrate the strictness of the standard of justification depending on the ground and context. It has also been less concerned than US judges at the prospect of affirmative action. Indeed it has held in some situations, the principle of equality requires different treatment in order to correct factual inequalities. Thus in *Sejdic*, the applicants invited the Court to follow EU jurisprudence and hold that difference in treatment based expressly on race or ethnicity was not capable of justification and amounted to direct discrimination.[79] The Court rejected this approach, largely because of the danger that a blanket refusal to allow justification would also outlaw affirmative action.[80] Instead it held that, 'where a difference in treatment is based on race or

[78] ibid at [27].

[79] *Sejdić and Finci v Bosnia and Herzegovina* (Applications nos 27996/06 and 34836/06) (22 December 2009, ECHR).

[80] US jurisprudence has oscillated widely between accepting affirmative action as a means to achieve (substantive) equality and rejecting it as a breach of (formal) equality: *Ricci v DeStefano*. The EU permits affirmative action as an exception to the equal treatment principle only when it does not disrupt the merit principle, that is in 'tie-break' situations: C-450/93 *Kalanke v Freie Hansestadt Bremen* [1995] IRLR 660.

ethnicity, the notion of objective and reasonable justification must be interpreted as strictly as possible.' Nevertheless,

> Article 14 does not prohibit Contracting Parties from treating groups differently in order to correct 'factual inequalities' between them. Indeed, in certain circumstances a failure to attempt to correct inequality through different treatment may, without an objective and reasonable justification, give rise to a breach of that Article.[81]

At the same time, the Strasbourg court has shown itself to be capable of resisting attempts to use justification to permit invidious direct discrimination, as demonstrated by the recent case of *Emel Boyraz v Turkey*.[82] In this case, the applicant had been denied a position as a security officer in the State-run electricity company because she was a woman. Although she had successfully written the public service examination, she was informed that she could not be appointed as she did not fulfil the criterion of being a man. The State justified this exclusion on the grounds that the job required the incumbent to handle weapons, work day and night and use physical force in case of an attack, for which women were not suitable. The Court took the high standard of justification for sex discrimination seriously, reiterating that, since 'the advancement of gender equality is today a major goal in the member States of the Council of Europe … very weighty reasons would have to be put forward before such a difference of treatment could be regarded as compatible with the Convention.'[83] The Court concluded that 'the mere fact that security officers had to work night shifts and in rural areas and might be required to use physical force and firearms under certain conditions could not in itself justify the difference in treatment between men and women.'[84] The existence of a possible justification defence is not, therefore, problematic. The real challenge is for it to be calibrated in a manner which can discern invidious discrimination and distinguish it from appropriate differentiation.

The EU has also shown signs of moving beyond a rigid boundary between direct and indirect discrimination. In the recent case of *Chez v Nikolova*,[85] the Court found that the same facts could give rise to both direct and indirect discrimination. In this case, all the electricity meters in an urban district predominantly populated by Bulgarian citizens of Romani origin were placed in large silver locked boxes on pylons at a height of between six and seven metres. In other districts, the meters were placed in small boxes on the outer walls of houses. The company claimed that this was to avoid

[81] *Sejdić and Finci* (n 79) at [44].
[82] *Boyraz v Turkey* (App no 61960/08) (2015) 60 EHRR 30.
[83] ibid at [51].
[84] ibid at [54].
[85] Case C-83/14 *CHEZ Razpredelenie Bulgaria AD v Komisia za zashtita ot diskriminatsia* [2016] 1 CMLR 14.

consumers from those areas manipulating meter readings. The Court held that a measure such as that at issue in this case would constitute direct discrimination if it proved to have been introduced and/or maintained for reasons relating to the ethnic origin common to most inhabitants of the district concerned. Importantly, the Court did not require the claimants to establish more than a prima facie case that the policy was on grounds of ethnic origin. Following its established jurisprudence, the burden of proof shifts once facts have been adduced which give rise to a presumption of discrimination. This in turn requires the respondent to rebut the presumption by showing that the practice and its retention are not in any way founded on the fact that it is instituted in predominantly Romani areas but is instead exclusively based on objective facts unrelated to any discrimination on grounds of racial or ethnic origin. Notably, the process of determining whether the discrimination is on grounds of racial or ethnic origin is not one of determining motive or intention. Instead, it is to establish facts from which a presumption of discrimination can be inferred. Notably too, the process of rebutting the presumption is very similar to that of justification in indirect discrimination.

If direct discrimination was not established, in other words, it was not established that the reason for the practice was related to ethnic origin, then the practice could constitute a neutral criterion for the purposes of indirect discrimination. It was common ground that, since the practice was only instituted in predominantly Roma areas, it was liable to affect persons of Roma origin in considerably greater proportions than others, and therefore put them at a particular disadvantage compared with other persons as required by Article 2(2)(b) of the Racial Equality Directive (definition of indirect discrimination).[86] This in turn leads to the difficult question of justification. Here the Court set a relatively high standard of scrutiny. While the measure could, in the right factual situations, be appropriate, to prove necessity required a demonstration that other appropriate and less restrictive measures would not resolve the problems. Even if no other measure could be identified, the referring court will need to decide whether the disadvantages it causes are disproportionate to the aim pursued and whether it unduly prejudices the legitimate interests of the local inhabitants. In doing so, again, the Court will need to be mindful of the legitimate interest of consumers of electricity in having access to electricity supply in conditions which do not have an offensive and stigmatising effect. It will also need to be mindful of the fact that the practice has been in place for 25 years without individual unlawful acts having been proved and the fact that they cannot be held liable for third parties either. Finally, the legitimate interest in monitoring their electricity consumption should be taken into account.

[86] Council Directive 2000/43/EC of 29 June 2000 implementing the principle of equal treatment between persons irrespective of racial or ethnic origin [2000] OJ L180/22.

The Court concluded that it seemed that on the basis of all these issues, the practice could not be justified because the disadvantages it causes seem disproportionate to its objectives. Nevertheless, it was for the referring court to make the final decision on this issue.

VI. CONCLUSION

It has been demonstrated here that courts in the US and the UK have found it difficult to draw a bright line distinction between direct and indirect discrimination, which is coherent and reflects the social issues at which discrimination law is aimed. Although on the surface, the reasons for blurring the distinction have differed widely on each side of the Atlantic, it has been argued that there are some common themes driving these reactions: a strong allegiance to a symmetrical notion of equality and an aversion to affirmative action; a continued attachment to an individualised notion of liability, both in terms of requiring individual liability on behalf of the respondent and individual harm on the part of the complainant; and a problematic ambiguity about the aims of an effects based test. Nevertheless, the insights of disparate impact/indirect discrimination remain as compelling as they were when formulated in the *Griggs* case. To achieve coherence in the notion requires courts to recognise the asymmetric consequences of this test, which requires an ability to distinguish between uses of protected characteristics which further equality against a background of antecedent disadvantage, and those which deepen existing disadvantage. Similarly a genuine effects-based approach would place responsibility on those who are able to bring about change rather than insisting on finding a perpetrator who can be shown to be 'at fault.' Ultimately, an impact-based test needs to be capable of dealing with structural inequalities and this in turn requires greater attention both to pre-emptive action, whether or not this involves quotas, and to remedies which are capable of addressing the underlying problem.

3

Approaching the Indirect–Direct Discrimination Distinction: Concepts, Justifications and Policies

NICHOLAS BAMFORTH*

THE PERSPECTIVE FROM which we understand indirect (or disparate impact) discrimination has practical consequences for our treatment of the location of its boundary with direct (or disparate treatment) discrimination, and of the appropriateness of allowing for proportionality and/or benign motive-based justifications or defences under both headings. With this practical point in mind, the present chapter will explore some of the perspectives—philosophical, constitutional, conceptual and policy-based—which are evident in theoretical accounts of discrimination law. Our concern is with direct and indirect discrimination in the abstract, and in particular with how the wrongdoing involved in prohibited forms of discrimination is categorised, and the basis or bases on which the legal prohibition of discrimination can be justified, in selected theories of discrimination law. However, while discrimination law is no exception to the liberal requirement that law must possess a clear and suitably-tailored justification in order legitimately to impose coercion upon others,[1] discrimination legislation and judicial interpretation of constitutional non-discrimination provisions is often tied (particularly in public debate) to the highly sensitive social policy issues associated with invidious forms of discrimination. It can thus be harder to detach concerns of policy from those of theory in the discrimination law sphere than might be the case in other areas—something which in turn has implications for our approach to the distinction between indirect and direct discrimination.

In the first section of the chapter, the differing perspectives will be outlined, alongside some key issues affecting the theories to be discussed. The theories

* Fellow in Law, The Queen's College, Oxford.

[1] See, generally, TRS Allan, 'Citizenship and Obligation: Civil Disobedience and Civil Dissent' (1996) 55 *CLJ* 89, 93–98.

themselves will be outlined and analysed in the second section, before being applied to the indirect-direct discrimination in the third section.

I. PERSPECTIVES AND ISSUES

The first two perspectives—philosophical and constitutional—can be distinguished if we consider what it means to say that the law must possess a suitable justification in order legitimately to apply coercive power in society.[2] The first, more abstract level at which a justification can come into play might be described as 'philosophical' on the basis that it should be able to show that the exercise of state power is permissible according to a vision of how the state (considered in the abstract) ought legitimately to act, including the interests state action may properly protect and override, and the purposes it should serve. Sir Neil MacCormick categorised arguments at this level as being concerned with:

> [T]he right exercise of the public powers vested in agencies of state—legislators, governments, judges, police, and prosecutors. Whoever attempts to give a general answer to the question about the right exercise of such powers is necessarily committed to stating practical principles for the guidance of those who exercise them. And practical principles of right conduct are moral principles.[3]

In logic, such justifications will entail a theory of justice, concerning rightful and wrongful distributions of entitlements among members of society,[4] and a theory of political morality, concerning the principles which should guide the exercise of power by state institutions (including in the creation and enforcement of laws). The second, more concrete level can be described as 'constitutional', in that the substance or content of an exercise of power must be justifiable by reference to whatever constitutional rules or principles (if any) exist in the society in issue,[5] and the exercise must fall within the legal limits to the powers of the institution or institutions concerned.[6]

[2] A point captured in HLA Hart's defence of the 'general critical principle that the use of legal coercion by any society calls for justification as something *prima facie* objectionable to be tolerated only for the sake of some countervailing good' (*Law, Liberty and Morality* (Oxford, Oxford University Press, 1963) 20).

[3] Neil MacCormick, *Legal Right and Social Democracy: Essays in Legal and Political Philosophy* (Oxford, Oxford University Press, 1982) 18; see also Joseph Raz, *The Morality of Freedom* (Oxford, Oxford University Press, 1986) 2–3.

[4] Such a theory may well be associated with a background political philosophy.

[5] Which, as the UK constitution and the notion of 'constitutional statutes' seemingly demonstrates, need not be in written form: see *R (on the application of HS2 Action Alliance) v Secretary of State for Transport* [2014] UKSC 3, [2014] 1 WLR 324.

[6] Sandra Fredman, *Human Rights Transformed* (Oxford, Oxford University Press, 2008) ch 1.

In practice, arguments from one level are often relevant to analyses conducted at the other: a philosophical analysis of equal treatment may well find it helpful to examine judicial interpretations of the concept, for example, while judicial expositions may seek reinforcement through references to theory.

A perspective on discrimination law can be described as philosophical if it is concerned to examine indirect and direct discrimination, including the nature of the wrongs in play, in abstract moral and/or political terms, even if examples are drawn from the law as illustrations. Such a perspective might also be concerned to explain why it fell within the legitimate remit of the state to prohibit such wrongdoing through law. A constitutional perspective, by contrast, would be in play when identifying and explaining the discrimination-related limitations imposed on government by the constitution of a society, or explaining how constitutional non-discrimination values fed into the interpretation or structure of discrimination legislation applicable between private actors.

A highly visible perspective is that based on policy. This perspective concerns discrimination law's practical goals, and is represented in questions going to the most effective strategy for this branch of law to deploy as a basis (for example) for countering those forms of social and material inequality which its underpinning theory of justice (more exactly, the theory we have identified) deems illegitimate. Much less conspicuous is what might be termed the conceptual perspective, which concerns whether the forms of legal liability in play—here, indirect and direct discrimination—have, as a matter of logic, definite or ideal structures which might *themselves* be sufficient to explain the inclusion or exclusion of particular legal aspects of liability irrespective of policy arguments and arguments of justice. These structures might relate, for example, to the idea of logical correlatives—the notion that a private right *by definition* entails a corresponding obligation on another party—or turn on the logical limits of the words used in the drafting of the relevant legal rule. As we will see, examples of each of the different perspectives are visible in the accounts of discrimination law considered in later sections.[7]

Turning to issues, Denise Réaume has observed that 'A central trend in the development of discrimination law, in every jurisdiction, has been the movement from a requirement of intention to ground a complaint to

[7] The analyses of 'legal borrowing' in Sir Bob Hepple, 'The European Legacy of *Brown v Board of Education*' [2006] *University of Illinois Law Review* 605 and Lord Lester, 'The Overseas Trade in the American Bill of Rights' (1988) 88 *Columbia Law Review* 537, imply that purely philosophical or conceptual perspectives are unlikely to be sufficient to provide a complete explanation of the ambit of prohibited discrimination in a given jurisdiction.

the recognition as actionable of indirect or adverse effect discrimination'.[8] This practical expansion—conducted through legislative development and judicial interpretation—has been echoed at a theoretical level. Whereas some theorists of discrimination law have granted the defendant's mental state (more particularly, their intention) a central place in their justifications of discrimination liability,[9] Sophia Moreau points out that much recent analysis

> has focused on the broader political goals that these laws serve. Because they combat the systemic subordination and stigmatization of groups identified by the prohibited grounds of discrimination, anti-discrimination laws have been seen as a tool for effecting distributive justice between these groups and those that are more privileged.[10]

It is thus important, when exploring individual analyses, to see how far the paradigm example of wrongful discrimination is taken to be *intentional* adverse treatment based on a prohibited ground of discrimination, and how far—by contrast—it is the *effects* of the defendant's conduct, irrespective of their mental state, which occupy centre-stage.

Three related points, relevant throughout the subsequent analysis, can be associated with this. First, as a practical matter the distinctions found in different legal systems between direct and indirect discrimination do not *necessarily* map neatly and exactly onto a division between intention-driven and effects-driven liability. In reality, there are overlaps between these schemes. For example, the difference of treatment required for direct discrimination liability is frequently demonstrated through showing that the claimant was unfavourably treated (ie that the impugned decision's effects were bad for them), while English law following *James v Eastleigh Borough Council* (considered below) was keen to discount a role for intention in direct discrimination.[11] When it comes to intentions and effects, the deep-level debate (notwithstanding the overlap in some cases) is about the relative significance of each for our *overall* understanding of the shape of, rationale behind and justifications for discrimination law, assuming the latter can be viewed as a whole. The subject's contours and internal priorities will look different depending upon the position adopted in this debate. Individual theories of discrimination law seek to locate the boundary between direct

[8] Denise Réaume, 'Harm and Fault in Discrimination Law: The Transition from Intentional to Adverse Effect Discrimination' (2001) 2 *Theoretical Inquiries in Law* 349, 350. See also Tarunabh Khaitan, *A Theory of Discrimination Law* (Oxford, Oxford University Press, 2015) 1–2. For a classic study of developments in the UK, see Christopher McCrudden, 'Institutional Discrimination' (1981) 2 *OJLS* 303.

[9] See, for example (and concerning direct discrimination) John Gardner, 'Liberals and Unlawful Discrimination' (1989) 9 *OJLS* 1.

[10] Sophia Moreau, 'What is Discrimination?' (2010) 38 *Philosophy and Public Affairs* 143, 144–45. See also Colm O'Cinneide, 'Justifying Discrimination Law' (2016) 36 *OJLS* 909.

[11] *James v Eastleigh Borough Council* [1990] 2 AC 751.

and indirect discrimination in particular places, but it is the details of the theory in issue which will determine how far these devices are influenced by and affect the relative priorisation of intentions and effects in discrimination law as a whole.

Second, a distinction is sometimes drawn between theories concerned primarily with securing remedies for individuals and those which aim to address the relative injustice experienced by groups. Depending upon the remedial provisions in force in a given jurisdiction, indirect discrimination liability has often been associated more directly with tackling group disadvantage.[12] However, there is no necessary correlation between the legal classification and theoretical aim in play: there are individual redress-based theories of indirect discrimination, and group disadvantage-based theories of direct discrimination.

Third, it is necessary to keep in mind that one dimension of discrimination law is constitutional, and as such concerned with review of executive action and (in jurisdictions where this is allowed) legislation, while another is concerned with the liability of private employers and service-providers, such liability often being established through national legislation. Since ideas of direct and indirect discrimination can be found in both contexts, theoretical understandings of direct and indirect discrimination need, ideally, to be able to keep both within their contemplation (unless it is thought that constitutional instances of discrimination concepts are somehow wholly distinct from instances in the private sphere). The differing procedures, remedies, and sometimes styles of inquiry involved in actions for damages and in judicial review of executive action can add complexity to this.

II. THEORETICAL APPROACHES TO DISCRIMINATION LAW

In this section, six prominent theories which seek to explain and justify discrimination liability—those of Hugh Collins, John Gardner, Deborah Hellman, Tarunabh Khaitan, Sophia Moreau and Denise Réaume—are examined.[13] By comparing them, some important features of discrimination law, and the ways in which we can approach it, will become evident.

[12] See, for example, Christopher McCrudden (n 8) 311–13; Lord Lester, 'Equality and United Kingdom Law: Past, Present and Future' [2001] *PL* 77, 90.

[13] These theories have been chosen for the reason that they seek to provide sufficiently abstract accounts of discrimination law which are nonetheless capable of direct connection with the indirect–direct discrimination distinction. Other excellent accounts could have been included: for example, those by Sandra Fredman, *Discrimination Law* 2nd edn (Oxford, Oxford University Press, 2011) and Aileen McColgan, *Discrimination, Equality and the Law* (Oxford, Hart, 2014) and, at a more philosophical level, Benjamin Eidelson, *Discrimination and Disrespect* (Oxford, Oxford University Press, 2015) and Kasper Lippert-Rasmussen, *Born Free and Equal? A Philosophical Inquiry into the Nature of Discrimination* (Oxford, Oxford University Press, 2014).

They will, in turn, have implications for our later treatment of the concrete issue of the distinction between indirect and direct discrimination. A key concern will be with what *distinguishes* the theories in terms of methodology, as much as with what they have in common. As we will see, some approach matters at a more openly philosophical level, others at a constitutional level. Conceptual and policy-related factors also make an appearance. Since the theories advanced by Réaume, Hellman and Moreau have a more North American focus, they will be considered together following discussion of Collins, Khaitan and Gardner.

Hugh Collins highlights the importance of social inclusion as a factor additional to equal treatment in our understanding of discrimination law.[14] Equal treatment plays 'an important role' in any interpretation of discrimination law, but

> an explanation of why different treatment is sometimes required or permitted seems to necessitate the inclusion of a distributive aim for the legislation. It is the distributive aim that explains when and why deviations from equal treatment should be required or permitted.[15]

As a justification for current discrimination law, social inclusion—aimed at combating the persistent or absolute disadvantage faced by particular groups rather than relative disadvantage as between groups[16]—in some respects 'provides a more coherent explanation of the legal framework', although not a complete one given 'the influential role that the notion of equality has played in the construction of the legislation'.[17] While equal treatment constitutes the normal rule, as required by respect for individual dignity or equal worth, social inclusion provides 'a theory of distributive justice … which … explains when and why deviations from the normal rule should be required or permitted'.[18] A distributive aim or criterion of fairness is 'understood in the aim of social inclusion',[19] although the 'distributive goal of social inclusion'[20] must sometimes give way to the principle of equal treatment.

An immediate question is how far Collins is thinking of social inclusion as a justification in the sense described above, and how far it plays the role of a political (or other) goal—or whether, indeed, it serves both functions

[14] Hugh Collins, 'Discrimination, Equality and Social Inclusion' (2003) 66 *MLR* 16.
[15] ibid, 20. See also 17.
[16] ibid 22, 29.
[17] ibid 40.
[18] ibid 41. At 40, social inclusion is described as 'a goal for the legislation that supplies a justification in particular instances for departures from the general rule of equal treatment'. For discussion of the agent-relative focus of distributive justice, see John Gardner, 'Discrimination as Injustice' (1996) 16 *OJLS* 353, 357–58.
[19] Collins (n 14) 42.
[20] ibid 42.

in his analysis. On the one hand, it is clear that Collins often views social inclusion as an actual or potential justification. He categorises it as 'an aim or principle of justice' which is 'often mistaken for an egalitarian notion of distributive justice', but is distinct in its concern for the absolute disadvantage faced by some groups.[21] He analyses its operation as a theory of justice concerned with the distribution of social goods, and contrasts it in this regard with contemporary liberal theories of justice.[22] Collins notes that 'in the selection of the nature of the disadvantages that should be addressed by discrimination laws, the notion of social inclusion has played a role as an underlying justification for legal regulation in determining the types of disadvantage that need to be addressed',[23] and he engages in a lengthy analysis of the differing interpretations and assessments (not least, in terms of their desirability or undesirability) of particular aspects of discrimination law which will result from the adoption of an equality or a social inclusion justification.[24] He suggests that the justification in play can help define the nature of the problem to be addressed and the appropriate ambit of discrimination liability.[25]

On the other hand, Collins also frequently talks of equal treatment and social inclusion in looser terms, most often as 'aims' but also as 'goals', 'justifications for the aims', or 'principles', of discrimination law.[26] It may well be that this is mainly a matter of terminology: in many places, 'aim' might easily be replaced by 'justification'. However, in two important regards this is not the case.

First, Collins notes the role of social inclusion in 'current government documents' (at the time he was writing) as an 'explicit political justification' for (then) forthcoming discrimination legislation in the United Kingdom.[27] In doing so, he highlights the term's part (which might also encompass some of his other references to 'aims' and 'goals') not as a justification but as an underpinning *policy goal* of discrimination legislation and discrimination law more generally. As a policy goal, social inclusion (like equality) focuses explicitly on desired political or social outcomes rather than more abstract concerns such as theories of justice—although, obviously, a theory of justice may underpin a policy goal. Collins's account is not unusual in containing this overlap. In the United Kingdom, the Home Office White Paper *Equality for Women*, which preceded and provided justifications for enacting the Sex Discrimination Act 1975, began by stating that it would set out 'what

[21] ibid 22.
[22] ibid 22–26.
[23] ibid 30.
[24] ibid 31–39, 40.
[25] ibid 319.
[26] For particular examples of the variety, see ibid 17, 25, 26, 39, 40, 41.
[27] ibid 21.

needs to be done by legislation to promote equal opportunities for men and women', that the 'policy which it proposes applies to discrimination against either sex', and that 'legislation is essential for an effective policy for equal opportunity'.[28] Meanwhile, writing in the period when the Race Relations Act 1976 was first being applied, Christopher McCrudden categorised anti-discrimination legislation as one of a range of devices, others including financial subventions and the creation of bodies to foster good inter-community relations, which were being deployed to deal with issues raised by the emergence of a multi-racial society.[29] Since discrimination legislation often constitutes a response to what has been officially categorised as a policy problem, it is hardly surprising that policy goals play a strong role in relation to it, alongside justifications.

However, one might plausibly ask whether a significant difference nonetheless exists between policy goals and matters of justice, and at this stage Tarunabh Khaitan's analysis is relevant. The details of Khaitan's theory—in particular, his concern to distinguish the analytical from the normative—will be discussed below, but for the moment it is useful to consider his point that prior to determining *whether* the goals of discrimination law can be justified, it is logically necessary first to be clear about *what* it is seeking to do. This functional inquiry (as he terms it) 'is a question that a legislator asks herself before designing any legislation: what is the mischief that the law should seek to correct?'.[30] For Khaitan, the answer to this 'thin' question will turn on how we identify 'the most salient features' of discrimination law, which 'may relate to the law's subject matter, its mode of operation, or the remedies it provides'.[31] As we will see below, Khaitan derives these features from a largely, but not completely, conceptual analysis of the prevailing *features* of discrimination law. As such, it is clearly a salient question—not least, given the potential for overlap between policy goals and justifications—whether it is preferable to locate our handling of the background question 'what is the law here to do?' purely in policy, purely in legal abstraction, or in some combination of the two.

Second, when talking of 'principles' Collins often has something rather different in mind from justifications. In fact, he frequently uses the term to mean a norm which has a particular weight within the legal system

[28] Home Office, *Equality for Women* (White Paper, 1974, Cmnd. 5724) [1] and [2]. The (then) Special Advisor who devised the White Paper, Lord Lester, has in his own writing distinguished the theory of equality from the more focused purposes of pieces of legislation: Lord Lester (n 12) 81–85.

[29] McCrudden (n 8) 303. For analysis of the differing social problems (and hence differing treatments of legal concepts) associated with racial discrimination in the USA and Europe, see Hepple (n 7) 620–23.

[30] Khaitan (n 8) 118.

[31] ibid.

concerned and which operates as a device or value which may organise cases or influence outcomes (almost or perhaps a Dworkinian notion).[32] This is captured in his characterisation of the role of discrimination legislation in fostering or interacting with values already latent in the legal system:

> A legal system, which has achieved autonomy from the political and economic systems, has its independent demands of fair process, of evidence and proof, of remedial devices, of legal justification, and, in general, of preservation of the integrity of the system. The maxims of 'equal protection of the laws' or 'treat like cases alike' represent fundamental operational principles of these legal systems. The significance of this legal framework is that whatever political goals have to be incorporated into law, the legal system must accommodate them within its own operational principles. The political goal behind anti-discrimination legislation becomes translated in the operations of the legal system as a rule that like cases should be treated alike. In other words, the legal system has its own independent values or communication system, which place constraints on how political goals can be pursued through its mechanisms. Whatever the political aim behind anti-discrimination legislation, whether it comprises equality of results, equality of opportunity, or social inclusion, that aim has to be modified to comply with the principle of equal treatment in order for it to be accommodated with integrity within the legal system.[33]

Here, Collins is using the argument that equal treatment operates as an underpinning value of the legal system to help explain why discrimination laws are so strongly and widely seen as reflecting this value, and to explain how in consequence the role of social inclusion may often seem to take second place to that of equal treatment. His comments also show, however, how equal treatment plays a role in his theory—as, where appropriate, does social inclusion—as an organising device or value of normative weight *within* the legal system, in contrast with the role played by a general principle of justice *underpinning* discrimination laws.[34] Collins's argument draws partly on Gunther Teubner's distinction between political goals and the operational requirements of the legal system, and partly on the Dworkinian notion of integrity and (here) its demand for equal respect.[35] Returning to Khaitan's analysis, Collins's use of systems theory may demonstrate how

[32] Best captured in Ronald Dworkin, *Taking Rights Seriously* (London, Duckworths, 1977) and *A Matter of Principle* (Oxford, Oxford University Press, 1986).

[33] Collins (n 14) 41–42.

[34] In this regard, it might be interesting to speculate how far Collins's notion of 'principles' is akin to Dawn Oliver's notion of values generally underpinning the common law: Dawn Oliver, *Common Values and the Public-Private Divide* (Oxford, Butterworths, 1999); 'Common Values of Public and Private Law' [1997] *PL* 630; 'Public Law Procedures and Remedies—Do We Need Them?' [2002] *PL* 91.

[35] At (n 14) fn 87, Collins draws upon Teubner's *Law as an Autopoietic System* (Oxford, Blackwell, 1993) and on Dworkin's work.

legal rules and the justifications for them can operate at a distinct level from the policy analyses which are also associated with their creation.[36]

The relationship between the actual features of discrimination law and normative analysis gives rise to questions, in turn, concerning Khaitan's approach. Having identified 'what is salient in discrimination law ... at a level of abstraction which is neither too close to, nor too removed from, the practice',[37] in order to identify the features which, analytically, might be associated with the categorisation 'discrimination law', Khaitan proceeds to ask 'what is the *point* of discrimination law, ie what is the general justifying aim?'[38] He is sensibly concerned to separate conceptual from normative analysis.[39] One of the novel features of his account is the further distinction drawn (borrowing from HLA Hart[40]) between the general justifying aim of discrimination law and what he styles the separate distributive questions, which specify which parties must bear the burden of anti-discrimination duties.[41] He argues that the (normative) general justifying aim (point or purpose) of discrimination law is to secure an aspect of individual well-being by reducing and ultimately removing the abiding, pervasive and substantial relative disadvantage faced by members of protected groups (defined by an immutable or valuable ground), the relevant relative disadvantage impeding a person from accessing the basic goods—negative freedom, an adequate range of valuable opportunities, and self-respect—which are necessary to live a good life.[42] This normative argument explains why it is wrongful to breach what Khaitan styles, based on his conceptual analysis of the nature of discrimination law (prior to his consideration of issues of distribution), the 'antidiscrimination duty'.[43] This analysis is freedom- rather than equality-driven, and Khaitan argues that 'it is freedom rather than equality which provides a better foundation for discrimination law'.[44]

For present purposes, it is useful to further consider how far Khaitan succeeds in disentangling analytical from normative factors, not least given that his concern with this issue seemingly demarcates his analysis from that

[36] For a valuable discussion of policy considerations associated with indirect discrimination liability, see McCrudden (n 8).

[37] Khaitan (n 8) 91.

[38] ibid; see also 117, 244.

[39] It is an open question, given the discussion at the end of ch 2, how far Khaitan may be touching on factors which are inevitable in legal scholarship or which have a particular resonance in relation to discrimination law.

[40] HLA Hart, *Punishment and Responsibility: Essays in the Philosophy of Law* (Oxford, Oxford University Press, 1968).

[41] Khaitan (n 8) 91. And clearly, the extent to which such issues are reliably separable will undoubtedly be a matter for further discussion.

[42] ibid 91, 117, 135, 138, 195-6, 244-5. See also 56 on disadvantage, and for a practical illustration see 167–68.

[43] ibid 143–46, 194.

[44] ibid 113. See also 91–92, 117, 130, 244.

offered by Collins. Khaitan suggests that what he categorises as the key *analytical* concepts at the heart of anti-discrimination norms—personal grounds, cognate groups, relative disadvantage and eccentric distribution of benefits[45]—can be deployed in order to discern that the functional objective of discrimination law is the reduction (and ultimate removal) of any significant advantage gap between a protected group and its cognate group (for example, women as opposed to men).[46] Khaitan stipulates that these concepts are distinct from 'full-blown normative' arguments,[47] and simply lay the groundwork for such arguments at a later stage: they are

> meant to be criteria which determine whether an *existing* legal norm ought to be characterized as a norm of discrimination law. They have not been presented as a set of criteria which help us determine which norms of discrimination law *ought* to exist.[48]

The concepts derive from Khaitan's investigation of what he terms the essence of discrimination law: 'the key features that lend an identity and a degree of internal coherence to discrimination law', things 'which share a feature which is not shared by other legal norms' so that 'the practice is therefore right in grouping them together'.[49] Possession of the relevant features, as factors distinct from those prevailing in other areas, enables one to determine that a given norm is a norm of discrimination law.[50] They help to 'describe the structure of the "legal model" of identifying and regulating discrimination'.[51] In a further attempt to separate the analytical from the normative, Khaitan stresses that the four concepts might be compatible with a variety of mutually inconsistent positions concerning what fully fleshed-out discrimination law norms might look like, as is shown by the variety of normative interpretations which might be placed on the notion of relative disadvantage.[52] They are thus 'necessary and sufficient conditions which help distinguish norms of discrimination law from other legal norms', there being no intention 'to resolve controversial disputes by definitional fiat'.[53]

While Khaitan's analytical concepts may stand in strong contrast to Collins's proffered analysis of the background to discrimination law, he nonetheless acknowledges that they can also amount to weak constraints 'for suggestions of practical reform and for theoretical explanations of

[45] ibid 25, 43, 244–45. The details of these concepts are explained in ch 2.
[46] ibid 121.
[47] ibid 25.
[48] ibid 43.
[49] ibid 42.
[50] ibid 24–25.
[51] ibid 46.
[52] ibid 42. See 34 for an example.
[53] ibid 34.

discrimination law'.[54] For, if they constitute necessary and sufficient conditions for distinguishing norms of discrimination law, they are likely to provide some background constraints to discrimination law theory and practice, particularly when it comes to determining whether given norms fit within it. Obviously, the solidity of this distinction turns upon how far one believes it possible to distinguish strict conceptual analysis from normative argument: a topic of vast controversy in legal theory. More particularly, however—and depending on how far we think he succeeds in drawing a distinction between analytical and normative factors—Khaitan's approach seemingly stands in stark contrast to Collins's: conceptual analysis *predetermines* boundaries, within (and by reference to) which normative analysis *then* takes place. It is an interesting question whether the two approaches are talking past one another, or whether they can both form part of a larger picture. A second query generated by Khaitan's analysis is whether the overall 'point' and the 'general *justifying* aim' of a theory need always to be equated. For, as a comparison with Gardner's arguments demonstrates, this may well depend upon how we understand the terms in play.

John Gardner is more consistently focused than Khaitan on providing a normative justification for discrimination law.[55] As such, his account provides a visibly philosophical perspective. He favours Joseph Raz's notion of a single legitimacy doctrine whereby the state must protect and promote a particular conception of valuable freedom. This single and continuous principle mandates the creation of conditions of valuable autonomy.[56] Legal coercion may thus be used to stop actions which would diminish people's autonomy, and to force actions which improve options and opportunities. The right not to suffer intentional discrimination is associated with fostering a public culture in which individuals may have pride in their identity as members of groups, and the right not to suffer indirect discrimination with the generation of an adequate range of options and the opportunities to choose them.[57] Both rights derive from protection of the principle of autonomy, which also allows for the prevention or correction of harm (often described as a variety of corrective justice) and distributive justice to be viewed as concomitants rather than as competing principles.[58] Gardner later emphasised[59] that accounts of what makes legal regulation legitimate (that is, accounts of the normative justifications for laws against discrimination)[60] should not be conflated with underpinning accounts of the different types of

[54] ibid 43. Khaitan thus describes the concepts as a 'prelude' to any normative theory of discrimination law.

[55] Gardner (n 9) 1. See also 3, 21–22.

[56] ibid 17–18, 21.

[57] ibid 18–19.

[58] For analysis of the harm principle and distributive justice, see ibid 1–2, 12, 15–16.

[59] Gardner (n 18) 366.

[60] Emphasised in Gardner (n 9) 1, 2, 5, 12, 15, 16.

wrongdoing involved in discrimination. Different kinds of reasons—reasons of distributive justice, of corrective justice, and 'reasons which are not reasons of justice at all'[61]—can help explain what makes discrimination wrong, and at this level, there is no need to insist on a unified or reductive view:

> [O]ne should not expect the conflicts and discontinuities [between different accounts of wrongdoing] to be ironed out in the structure of the legal (or for that matter moral) duty. One should only expect that, whatever the structure of the moral duty, it should pass into law only so long as it *also* passes the test provided by whichever account of the limits of legal legitimacy in a free society turns out, on closer examination, to be the superior account.[62]

The relevant duties of non-discrimination should be seen as autonomy-based, with the liberal state being able legitimately to enforce only autonomy-based duties.[63] The justification for legislating is thus separate from the wrongdoing involved in discrimination.[64]

Gardner's distinction between wrongdoing and justification is a distinction between two essentially (but perhaps not entirely, given his comment about the reasons for legislating) normative inquiries. In contrast with Khaitan's approach, there is no functional inquiry, in response to which (and referring to the analytical nature of discrimination law) an anti-discrimination duty may arise. Rather, the normative 'point' of discrimination law—namely, acting against a corrective or distributive injustice—is separate from, while playing a central role in, explaining the operation of the justifying aim of legislation, namely the promotion of autonomy. An analytical similarity to Khaitan's approach is the separation of the inquiry into distinct stages, but a key difference is the focus of those stages (almost) entirely on normative matters. Nonetheless, and as one might expect, Gardner is fully aware of the practical context within which discrimination law operates. For example, he notes that

> In order to understand completely the role of legislation against discrimination in our culture, it is necessary to appreciate the creative power which governments in participative democracies necessarily enjoy. The application of forms of institutional control is as much an alteration of the future value-structure of society as it is a response to specific social ills, and the full importance of the discrimination legislation is only understood when its reconstitutive features are recognized.[65]

[61] Gardner (n 18) 366.
[62] ibid 367.
[63] Gardner 'On the Ground of Her Sex(uality)' (1998) 18 *OJLS* 167, 170–74, 179.
[64] For an analogous distinction, see Deborah Hellman, 'Equality and Unconstitutional Discrimination' in Deborah Hellman and Sophia Moreau (eds), *Philosophical Foundations of Discrimination Law* (Oxford, Oxford University Press, 2013) at 69–70.
[65] Gardner (n 9) 19.

This is an important observation, in that Gardner is highlighting the policy consequences of discrimination legislation by drawing attention to its effects on a society's public culture. His comment might indeed be thought to offer a chance to establish a link between the policy consequences or effects of legislation and the importance of finding a clear and exact justification for it—points which, as noted earlier, may sometimes appear to overlap in Collins's analysis.[66] Remaining with policy, it would also be interesting to know how far Gardner might be willing—if at all—to allow policy arguments to feature among the reasons 'which are not reasons of justice at all' for deeming discrimination to be wrongful. Clearly, the answer will have implications for how far we can understand his account to be essentially normative in its *practical* workings.[67]

It is worth summarising some of the divergences of focus and emphasis between the theorists considered so far. Collins is primarily concerned to analyse legislation, in part by reference to current policy, Gardner to justify it, and Khaitan to categorise and to justify. Each theorist subscribes to a particular justification for discrimination law (employing a philosophical perspective in doing so), but Khaitan and Collins appear more committed to associating *specified* goods with non-discrimination or specified wrongs with discrimination than is Gardner, who by the end of his analysis is willing to allow for a variety of wrongs to be associated with discrimination. It also seems fair to say that Collins's reasons are more visibly associated with the language of public policy than are those offered by Khaitan and Gardner, although Gardner's analysis of the wrongs of discrimination—tied to notions of harm and distributive justice—is perhaps more likely to entail a detailed substantive focus than is Khaitan's relatively thin notion of basic goods (in turn allied with conceptual questions concerning the nature of discrimination law).

Clear analogies can be drawn between the work of the three North American theorists—Réaume, Hellman and Moreau—given that each advances a constitutional theory with philosophical underpinnings. First, Denise Réaume suggests—in relation to human rights instruments, including those dealing with discrimination—that a key underpinning value is human dignity, which must be fostered equally among all. The value expresses an individual right to be treated with dignity, but such a concept is vague. There is a degree of intrinsic value to human beings, and dignity is

[66] See also Gardner (n 63)177 in relation to the effects of social change on understandings of wrongfulness.

[67] A point perhaps reinforced by Gardner (n 9) 16–17, where it is noted that members of society have a pre-theoretical understanding of what is going on, and given the continuity of culture we have reason to distrust the radical discontinuity involved in discrimination analyses based on the harm principle and distributive justice.

associated with a sense of identity, the satisfaction of basic material needs, and the importance of being able to make and execute plans. As such, 'The task of a theory of discrimination law … is to sketch the process whereby such abstract concepts are brought down to earth in a sufficiently fine-grained way to help decide cases' concerned with constitutional equality rights.[68] The 'interest in treatment with dignity, a position situated within a larger tradition that claims equal moral status for all human beings' can be identified as the interest 'worthy of constitutional protection' and 'by virtue of which particular distributions [of some benefit or burden] can be declared wrongful'.[69] Equality rights are not inherently comparative and are not ultimately based on the value of equality itself.[70] While the 'equal moral status' principle—which says that each person is entitled to treatment with dignity—is a distributive principle which produces an equal entitlement,

> equality as a distinct value is no more operative here than in the universal principle that each person is entitled not to be tortured. It is not because some others get respect that I am entitled to it, but because it is owed to all humans, and I am human.[71]

Réaume argues that it would be hard to see how equality, if viewed as a distinct value, could explain the good of respect for dignity.

Réaume is keen to associate these (essentially philosophical) arguments with constitutional equality rights, particularly in Canada. She suggests that the features or qualities associated with a life with dignity can be used in equality rights litigation to decide whether a given distribution of a benefit accords with the constitutional guarantee of equality. Such litigation may involve comparisons between the treatment of members of different groups, but this is to illustrate 'whatever common qualities, interests or needs there are between the two groups', revealing the underlying dignity-associated criterion according to which both should be treated.[72] It is thus 'wrong to think that, because some form of comparison is involved, equality is the value that grounds the claim'.[73] (Indeed, Réaume seemingly wishes to treat the role of comparison as an incidental or evidential issue, preventing it from affecting her overall characterisation of discrimination law). The central work in constitutional equality litigation is done by

[68] Denise Réaume, 'Dignity, Equality, and Comparison' in Hellman and Moreau (n 64) 21. These are cases involving 'the existing distribution of some benefit or burden contained in statutory criteria or flowing from administrative practice' (10).

[69] ibid 8; see also 19–20 (in which she argues that Hellman falls within the 'all are entitled to be treated with dignity' tradition even though she treats equality as the 'ground of her account of the right'; note also 26).

[70] ibid 8–13.

[71] ibid 20.

[72] ibid 26.

[73] ibid.

dignity analysis, albeit that this is often very fact-specific. In case law under section 15 of the Canadian Charter of Rights and Freedoms, a 'process of naming dignity as the touchstone of equality analysis'—in other words, as the substantive concept informing equality rights—has been underway at Supreme Court level.[74]

The foundation of Deborah Hellman's theory is the notion—again, philosophical—that all persons are equally morally worthy of concern and respect. The worth or inherent dignity of persons—which does not vary according to any individual's other traits—requires that we treat one other with respect. This in turn requires us to understand when the drawing of distinctions fails to treat those affected as having equal moral worth, equality—rather than respect per se—being the foundational value in play.[75] It is here that what has been styled the 'expressivist' character of Hellman's theory becomes evident.[76] Since traits are inert, what matters is their social significance. Drawing distinctions based on certain traits, generally or in particular contexts, may serve to demean, thereby wrongfully denying the equal moral worth of the person concerned. Whether a distinction demeans depends upon its socially or conventionally understood meaning in the social context in issue.[77] Demeaning a person 'is to treat [them] as not fully human or not of equal moral worth' and is 'therefore ... partly an expressive act',[78] as well as something which inherently involves comparison.[79] The power or social status of the speaker may enable a statement to demean, and social convention helps dictate the meaning of the distinction drawn.[80] Furthermore, a speaker's intent is not determinative of the social meaning of the words used, and the effect on the victim's feelings is irrelevant to our classification of an action as demeaning: 'classification is sometimes wrong because of what one does in classifying and this wrongness is not reducible to the harm that one may inflict'.[81]

Hellman is clear that wrongful discrimination is an individual wrong, and rejects the notion that the key to its wrongfulness lies in unequal treatment

[74] Denise Réaume, 'Discrimination and Dignity' (2002–03) 63 *Louisiana Law Review* 645, 646. See also her 'Of Pigeonholes and Principles: A Reconsideration of Discrimination Law' (2002) 40 *Osgoode Hall Law Journal* 113, 131.

[75] Deborah Hellman, *When is Discrimination Wrong?* (Cambridge MA, Harvard University Press, 2008) 6–7, 48.

[76] This term is used by Sophia Moreau in 'In Defense of a Liberty-based Account of Discrimination' in Hellman and Moreau (n 64).

[77] Hellman (n 75) 27–29. See also 57–58, 63.

[78] ibid 35.

[79] Deborah Hellman describes her equality-based account as 'essentially comparative' (Hellman (n 64) 54) and goes on to suggest that it is better to categorise accounts according to whether they are comparative or non-comparative, rather than whether they are equality- or liberty-based. For Sophia Moreau's critique, see Moreau (n 76) 72–76.

[80] Hellman (n 75) 32, 36. The meaning and operation of social conventions is analysed at 38–47.

[81] ibid 27. See also 26, 30, 35.

of groups.[82] Given the focus of her theory on the social meaning of distinctions, the historical treatment and current social status of a group are instead relevant when assessing whether a given policy or practice treated individuals unfairly. The constitutional element of Hellman's theory comes into play most visibly in relation to the role of courts. She emphasises that a virtue of her equality-based approach is that it avoids the need to posit a particular conception of the good life: a policy or practice is condemned because it demeans, not on the basis of an assessment of its innate value.[83] In a liberal democracy, a constitution will—she argues—ideally contain commitments that people with diverse views can be expected to be able to accept, so that judicial decision-making based on assessments of the social world (via questions such as whether a distinction, in the context concerned, is demeaning) is preferable to the court engaging in value-laden normative assessments of the ideal width of the social institutions, such as education or marriage, to which particular litigants are seeking access via discrimination litigation.[84]

Sophia Moreau is concerned with 'when and why discrimination by governments'[85] and—in a separate piece of writing—'in the private sector'[86] is wrongful to victims. The 'surface structure' of private sector discrimination law suggests that 'the wrong is a personal one, akin to a tort', with the discriminator having interfered with the victim's deliberative freedoms.[87] Such freedoms are also crucial, on Moreau's theory, when the government is involved.[88] In a liberal society, each person may decide for themselves what they value and how they will live in light of their values, and deliberative freedoms are 'freedoms to have our decisions about how to live insulated from the effects of normatively extraneous features of us, such as our skin color or gender'.[89] They require that we have available to us the options we think we have. We believe that 'each person is entitled' to certain deliberative freedoms,[90] and relevant 'extraneous' features or traits include those we believe people should not have to factor into their decisions *as costs* (even if they happen also to be important to the person concerned) in a particular context.[91]

[82] ibid 22–25, 32.
[83] ibid 33, 47.
[84] This argument is developed in Hellman (n 64); for Sophia Moreau's response, see Moreau (n 76) 78–80.
[85] Moreau (n 76) 71.
[86] Moreau (n 10) 143.
[87] ibid 145.
[88] Moreau (n 76) 76–77.
[89] Moreau (n 10) 147.
[90] ibid 152. See also 147.
[91] Sophia Moreau confirms in 'Discrimination as Negligence' (2010) 40 *Canadian Journal of Philosophy*, Supplement 1, 123, 136, that many personal traits will be ones whose costs we have to bear.

While we take deliberative freedoms seriously in day-to-day life, spaces and institutions frequently privilege some people's needs at the expense of others.[92] Rules or practices are thus challenged as discriminatory when, for example, they fail to include or accommodate someone, or deny them opportunities, because of their possession of an extraneous feature or trait (on this view, the features or traits translate into the legally prohibited grounds of discrimination).[93] Moreau suggests that people care not just about having a particular benefit (for example, employment in a chosen career) but about having the freedom to decide for themselves whether to accept it:

> We care about being able to make these choices ourselves, without pressure from certain extraneous considerations ... what matters to us is not that we have the same amount of freedom as others happen to have, but that each of us has the amount to which he is entitled.[94]

While 'no one is entitled to every deliberative freedom, in every context',[95] discrimination law protects our entitlement to deliberative freedoms to an extent roughly equal to others, something derived from our independent entitlement to the freedoms in question—underlining Moreau's description of her theory as liberty-driven (a label which might be applied from both a philosophical and a constitutional standpoint).[96]

Each of the perspectives—philosophical, constitutional, conceptual and policy-based—outlined earlier has made an appearance in this section. While (to different extents) the theories considered have generally been concerned with philosophical and/or constitutional arguments, the extent to which divergent starting-points, end-goals and methodologies have been involved has been self-evident. It is against this background that the different theorists' approaches to the indirect-direct discrimination distinction can now be considered.

III. THE INDIRECT–DIRECT DISCRIMINATION DISTINCTION

In this section, two separate illustrations of the different theorists' approaches to the indirect–direct discrimination distinction will be considered. The first, from the United Kingdom, has formed a focus for debate between Collins, Khaitan and Gardner. The second, at a more general level, has attracted the attention of Réaume, Hellman and Moreau.

[92] For good examples of situations involving costs due to traits, see Moreau (n 76) 82–84.

[93] Moreau (n 10) 155–57; Moreau (n 76) 82.

[94] Moreau (n 10) 151; see also 169–70.

[95] Moreau (n 91) 137.

[96] Moreau (n 10) 174. Contrary to Hellman, Moreau thus believes that a demeaning message sent by discrimination is a matter of secondary rather than primary concern: Moreau (n 10) 177–78 and Moreau (n 76) 84–86.

The well-known United Kingdom case *James v Eastleigh Borough Council* illustrates the practical consequences for our understanding of direct and indirect discrimination liability flowing from each of Collins's, Khaitan's and Gardner's approaches.[97] In this case, the majority of the (then) Judicial Committee of the House of Lords held that a rule granting free admission to swimming facilities for those of state pensionable age constituted direct discrimination, the background being that, at the time, the United Kingdom pensionable age was unequal for men and women. The Council had applied its rule and charged the 61 year-old male claimant, but not his 61 year-old wife, for swimming. In finding against the Council, Lord Goff had specified that 'cases of [direct] discrimination ... can be considered by asking the simple question: would the complainant have received the same treatment., but for his or her sex?'—on the facts of the case, would the claimant otherwise have had to pay in order to swim?[98] This standard did not require proof of an intention to discriminate, and in that regard it is sometimes thought to move direct discrimination closer to its indirect counterpart: under either standard, liability might be found to result from the effects of a rule applied by the defendant (regardless of intent), the key differences being the way in which the relevant effects are measured and the official availability of a general justification defence for indirect discrimination.[99]

Collins advocates the adoption of a full justification defence for direct discrimination, thereby bringing it closer to indirect discrimination. He argues that 'In pursuit of the goal of social inclusion, the elimination of a strict comparative approach to proof of discrimination necessitates the introduction of a justification defence for both direct and indirect discrimination'.[100] The absence of such a defence to direct discrimination may be mandated by the equal treatment principle: for, by requiring consistent treatment, the principle creates a strong presumption against the notion that intentional discrimination can be justified. Furthermore, 'assessed exclusively from the perspective of a comparative equality principle, it seems to be an inescapable conclusion that there is a difference in treatment between the sexes' in *James*.[101] By contrast, under a principle of social inclusion a justification defence might reflect a broader range of considerations, provided that the objective of the rule in issue served the aim or goal of social inclusion.[102]

[97] *James v Eastleigh BC* (n 11).

[98] ibid 774.

[99] This proposition is arguably demonstrated by the majority's handling of the direct/indirect discrimination distinction in *Bull and Bull v Hall and Preddy* [2013] UKSC 73, [2013] 1 WLR 3741.

[100] Collins (n 14) 34.

[101] ibid 35–36.

[102] ibid 34–35, 39. At 34, Collins seemingly treats the availability of a general occupation qualification defence as leading to the 'limited availability' of a justification defence in direct discrimination.

Social inclusion may thus have produced a different result in *James* if the Council's rule could have been interpreted as aimed at protecting a disadvantaged group—namely, those of pensionable age—who might otherwise find it difficult to take advantage of facilities such as swimming due to the cost relative to their pensions and/or savings. Collins is clear that social inclusion 'permits unequal treatment if that measure favours an excluded group, and the excluded group can be defined by reference to the pattern of social exclusion—persons of state pensionable age'.[103] Thus, Collins's preferred policy basis and/or justification for discrimination liability clearly has the capacity to shift outcomes: general social inclusion-driven justification defences might (where appropriate) cut off liability whether a claim is categorised as direct *or* indirect discrimination.

Gardner also disapproves of the majority's reasoning and decision in *James*, but for a different reason, seemingly associated with what was earlier described as a conceptual perspective. He suggests that due to the wording of the discrimination legislation then in issue—the inclusion of terms such as 'on grounds of' and 'by reason of'—we 'properly' focus in the situation of direct sex discrimination 'on the alleged discriminator's reasoning. The key question is: did the sex of the person before him figure in his thinking when he treated her like this?'[104] The wrongfulness of direct discrimination is 'fundamentally linked to the fact that an improper ground of discrimination figures in the *operative* premises of the discriminator's thinking. That is the core or paradigm case of wrongful direct discrimination'.[105] Core or paradigm cases of direct discrimination are, crucially, 'the ones which capture what is fundamentally wrong with it'.[106] The *James* majority lost sight of this point, in consequence undermining the distinction between direct and indirect discrimination.

Khaitan seeks to rebut Gardner's arguments, linking his effects-based conceptualisation of the nature of discrimination liability to the notion that intention is irrelevant. Khaitan advocates 'a conceptually common foundation for direct and indirect discrimination and harassment', leveling his focus—by building on his broader 'group membership' analysis of the working of discrimination law[107]—on their adverse effects.[108] On this basis, discrimination is direct where its victims are constituted entirely by members of the protected group, and indirect when members of the protected

[103] ibid 36. See also 42–43.

[104] Gardner (n 63) 179.

[105] ibid 182. See also 180–81 (where Gardner argues that the 'but for' interpretation entails a confusion between auxiliary or informational premises and operational ones) 183 and 184–86. In Gardner (n 9) 7, Gardner refers to direct discrimination as 'intentional discrimination'.

[106] Gardner (n 63) 183.

[107] Khaitan (n 8) 49–62.

[108] ibid 159. See also 247.

group disproportionately constitute the victims.[109] As Khaitan notes, this stands in stark contrast to what he terms the 'lay' understanding of direct discrimination, according to which the wrongness of direct discrimination is measured by reference to the reasoning (most often the intention) of the discriminator.[110] Cases such as *James* are consistent with Khaitan's analysis, the case law being effects-oriented. He argues that Gardner, by contrast, draws very much upon the 'lay' model in insisting upon reasoning as a fundamental aspect of the wrongfulness of direct discrimination, even though 'In law ... the term "discrimination" has acquired a special, technical, meaning which overlaps with, but is not concurrent with, its ordinary ["lay"] meaning. At best, some courts have retained the lay *form* in which the inquiry is framed'.[111] Given that the emphasis on adverse effects is now too entrenched in case law from around the common law world to be dismissed as a mistake, Khaitan believes that Gardner's view 'no longer reflects the legal doctrine on direct discrimination'.[112]

Leaving to one side matters of precedent, a key question is how far Gardner's and Khaitan's analyses of this boundary-issue concerning direct and indirect discrimination (ie whether one requires proof of particular reasoning/intention whereas the other does not) derive—as, seemingly, does Collins's—from factors deeper in their respective approaches to discrimination law. At this point, a degree of flexibility becomes evident in each theory, but seemingly more so in Gardner's. Khaitan bases his 'anti-discrimination duty' on his analyses of case law and the conceptual nature of discrimination law, but admits that it is also an attempt to clarify rather than merely to restate matters.[113] It is against this partly analytical but also partly *purposive* background that he discerns a common foundation for direct and indirect discrimination liability. Furthermore he admits, as noted above, that his various concepts may be compatible with a variety of positions in terms of what anti-discrimination norms might look like in practice. This, in itself, appears to be relatively flexible, save that his effects-driven conception of direct and indirect discrimination liability appears to be connected more basically with his conception of anti-discrimination norms. This, in itself, appears to limit the range of practical positions, in relation to liability, that his theory is capable of justifying.

Interestingly, Gardner notes that

> there is no inevitable link between the reason-based paradigm of direct discrimination and the assumption of symmetrical protection as between disadvantaged

[109] ibid 160.

[110] ibid 160–61.

[111] ibid 161, building on case law from Canada, South Africa and the United Kingdom. Khaitan explains the 'lay' meaning at length in ch 1.

[112] ibid 162.

[113] ibid 143–46.

> and correspondingly advantaged. There is no reason, in principle, why the most radical quota-based programmes of positive discrimination should not be accommodated within the paradigm of direct discrimination.[114]

Gardner's dissociation of the wrongfulness of discrimination from the justification for its regulation (including its prohibition) clearly opens a space for rather less determinate and case-specific arguments concerning situations in which liability deserves to be and should justifiably be imposed. It is an interesting question whether an equivalent intellectual space might explain the infiltration of the 'lay model' of discrimination—at least, if Khaitan is correct—into Gardner's more general reasoning, which does not in itself appear to mandate the conclusions he advocates concerning the respective roles of direct and indirect discrimination liability. Such a space might tie directly to the apparent switch of perspective—from philosophical to conceptual—in this part of Gardner's analysis.

Finally, while it is clear that each theorist favours a different interpretation of *James*—and, in consequence, of the boundary between direct and indirect discrimination—each does so for a separate reason. An interesting point for present purposes is therefore how far each interpretation is a visibly direct product of its author's more general approach to discrimination liability, and how far additional factors have entered into the assessment. As a practical matter, Collins's premise most likely produces his conclusion concerning a general justification defence, albeit at the cost of accepting that law may be driven by forward-looking considerations such as social inclusion. It is less clear whether the foundational elements of Khaitan's theory have a similar effect, not least given the sometimes uncertain relationship between normative and analytical elements in his reasoning—although it is important to note that, as a committed liberal, he admits at several stages in his argument that his own interpretation may be contested. In Gardner's case, however, it is far from clear that there is a necessary connection between his general account of the wrongfulness of discrimination and the legitimacy of legal intervention, and his view that reasoning/intention is a *required* element of direct discrimination liability. His view concerning reasoning/intention might in logic be explained on a completely distinct basis—including, as Khaitan suggests, as a defence of the 'lay' rather than the 'legal' model of impermissible discrimination (or due to some other policy-based or philosophical factor)—but for the moment we cannot be certain.

Our second illustration entails a comparison between the arguments of the North American theorists. In each case, the underpinning philosophical or constitutional perspectives in play help produce a conclusion concerning the indirect–direct discrimination distinction.

[114] Gardner (n 63) 187. It is interesting to consider how this relates to the discussion in Gardner (n 18) 355.

Denise Réaume has sought to relate dignity analysis to 'the regulation of discrimination in the private context' by using concepts drawn from tort law.[115] Discrimination liability was 'related to tort in *that* it is an extension of the realm of non-voluntary obligation giving rise to a private right of action',[116] and fault-based analysis—as a central ingredient in tort actions—helped clarify (alongside the range of interests which deserved protection) what was in issue in direct and indirect discrimination. With particular reference to the Canadian context, she suggested that early treatment of direct discrimination involved a narrow standard of fault associated with proof of illicit motive or malice,[117] with later expansion in the scope of liability reflecting 'an implicit expansion of the concept of fault appropriate to this social context'.[118] If the (moral) right not to be discriminated against was grounded in 'the fundamental interest in dignity', the shifting intention standard in direct discrimination could be understood as 'an expansion of liability made possible by an expansion of the concept of human dignity'.[119] In turn, 'there may be something about some, even if not all, instances of adverse effect [indirect discrimination] that gives them a social meaning that is demeaning to human dignity'.[120] Implicitly exclusionary rules and policies could infringe human dignity just as could their explicit counterparts: 'the setting of norms implicitly based on the attributes of members of the dominant group that are associated with their dominant status will inevitably tend to exclude or disadvantage those who do not share them', sending a message that those excluded are less worthy than others.[121] Dignity could, in response, support an interest in fair opportunity to participate which was 'sufficiently important to impose obligations on employers to accommodate at least some religious, ethnic, race, and sex differences'.[122]

These arguments have uncertain consequences for the indirect–direct discrimination distinction. Both heads of liability are to be understood in private contexts as safeguarding the moral value of dignity, which also finds its way—on Réaume's view—into constitutional equality litigation. While intention is relevant to both heads of liability, its exact role seemingly varies, reflecting the notion of fault and in turn dignity in play in each context. A distinction thus remains between direct and indirect discrimination, but clearly the acceptability of Réaume's approach will depend upon whether

[115] Réaume (n 8) 351; dignity is discussed in more detail at 357–58, 361–62.
[116] ibid 351.
[117] ibid 352, 358, 385.
[118] ibid 351.
[119] ibid 372.
[120] ibid 375. Interestingly, Réaume argues at 372–73 that the recognition of indirect discrimination in Canadian law was reconcilable with a continuing role for intention: it was merely malice-based definitions of discrimination that were ruled out.
[121] ibid 377.
[122] ibid 381.

we believe she employs an appropriate or unduly loose notion of intention in her analysis (particularly when cases such as *James v Eastleigh BC* appear, by contrast, to discount a role for intention). In this regard, the plausibility of Réaume's conceptual analysis may have important consequences for the ability of her philosophical and/or constitutional arguments concerning dignity to find a place in relation to discrimination liability in cases involving private actors.

Deborah Hellman does not focus squarely on the direct–indirect discrimination distinction, but her arguments rejecting the significance of intention to wrongful discrimination (and seemingly involving a mix of moral and policy perspectives) are clearly relevant in this context. She notes that '[i]t is hard work to change the deeply ingrained social meanings that attach to traits in our culture' and that '[i]f we only take steps in that direction when we have concluded that someone is culpable for acting badly, we set the bar too high'.[123] The focus, when considering whether a remedy is merited, should be on how a person has been treated—that is, on the features of the laws or policies under scrutiny—not on passing moral judgement on the actors who have drawn the distinction concerned. She thus seeks to reject 'the doctrinal focus in equal protection law on a finding of bad intentions by the actor in question'.[124] Taken together, these observations imply that the categorisation of individual instances of discrimination liability as direct or indirect might in an ideal world be a technical or contingent matter for Hellman, even if the distinction between the two heads of liability will be crucial for so long as one—presumably direct discrimination—is associated in practice with intention (or any other mental state) in a given legal system.

Finally, Sophia Moreau suggests that direct discrimination liability ensures that 'extraneous traits will not explicitly be used to *single us out* for unfavorable treatment', while indirect discrimination prevents us from being 'disadvantaged *even indirectly* because we possess these traits'.[125] However, distinctions between the two headings 'are not deep':[126] 'both are wrong because and insofar as they deny equal deliberative freedoms to certain individuals'.[127] Since direct discrimination is aimed in practice at exclusions which are explicit, it often focuses on intentional discrimination.[128] However, since at a deeper level there is 'no deep difference … (the wrong at issue in both types of case is a denial of someone's right to deliberative freedoms),

[123] Hellman (n 75) 168.

[124] ibid 55.

[125] Moreau (n 10) 155. Moreau acknowledges at 159–60 that this involves normative judgement on a case-by-case basis about which connections are direct enough.

[126] ibid, fn 2.

[127] ibid 175. See also Moreau (n 91) 139—where, perhaps curiously, Moreau seeks to interpret both types of discrimination using an extended account of negligence.

[128] Moreau (n 10) 154–55.

my account implies that there should be no difference in the stringency of the standard applied' in the defences available under each heading.[129] Moreau suggests that assuming, by contrast, that there is a deep legal distinction would leave us without an explanation of why we treat the two headings as forms of the same injustice—namely discrimination—requiring us to give up a 'very fundamental intuition' in the process.[130] Interestingly, therefore, Moreau's underpinning philosophical perspective on discrimination as a whole helps eliminate a role, beyond the perhaps technical—effectively, a difference of degree—between indirect and direct discrimination, in particular when the application of defences is in issue.

IV. CONCLUSION

As has become clear, it is possible to approach discrimination law using a variety of perspectives. To differing extents, all the theorists considered have been concerned to provide normative justifications for discrimination law, albeit in different fashions. At a general level, there is an overlap in Collins's case between a philosophical perspective and policy considerations; in Khaitan's case, normative arguments are shaped by but may also be used to criticise the conceptual structures of discrimination law; and in Gardner's case, the justification for legislation sits alongside but is separate from the normative wrongdoing(s) argued to be involved in the practice of discrimination. Meanwhile, Réaume, Hellman and Moreau employ both philosophical and constitutional perspectives, in the latter case concerning constitutional interpretation and (for Hellman) the appropriate constitutional role of the courts. Collins explicitly addresses the policy considerations guiding the legislator (equal treatment and social inclusion), Khaitan—under his functional inquiry—addresses in more neutral terms the types of question we can expect a legislator to ask (particularly about the nature of discrimination law) when deciding whether to create discrimination legislation, and Gardner—while being concerned overwhelmingly with the question of justification—nonetheless understands the importance of the practical context within which discrimination law operates, and its consequences for the social environment. Hellman, meanwhile, is very strongly concerned with the social significance and consequences of particular forms of behaviour—something treated as being of importance by Moreau, but in a secondary sense. At a substantive level, elements of equality analysis are visible in Collins's account and Hellman rests her arguments on equality, but Khaitan, Gardner, Réaume and Moreau employ other normative bases for

[129] ibid 165.
[130] ibid 176.

their theories of discrimination law. We have also seen that approaches to the distinction between indirect and direct discrimination frequently depend upon the stance adopted when tackling these prior issues, although Gardner seemingly shifts from a philosophical to a conceptual perspective when discussing the meaning of direct discrimination.

A key question begged by accounts of discrimination law,[131] including (to differing extents) some of those considered in this chapter, is how far we can *fully* understand the subject without some acknowledgement of relevant background policy considerations, given the strong social sensitivities often generated by prohibited grounds of discrimination and the legal measures relating to them.[132] Theories which justify discrimination law and help to classify its component parts are vital, but—as is perhaps anticipated in Collins's theory—a full account (and basis for distinguishing discrimination liability from the norms of other legal disciplines) may require us to take proper notice of relevant public policy arguments.[133] As such, discrimination law may be an area in which it is harder to detach policy from the types of philosophical and legal analysis we expect to see elsewhere.

[131] Well captured in Christopher McCrudden's analysis (n 8).

[132] A point very well captured by Khaitan (n 8) 1.

[133] I appreciate that this argument immediately takes us to the contested distinction between policy and principle. My motivation in presenting it is to make the point that from just about any perspective, in terms of 'understanding' a subject, some will fit much more closely and immediately with a particular model than will others.

4

Judicial Scepticism of Discrimination at the ECtHR

BARBARA HAVELKOVÁ*

SEVERAL EUROPEAN JUDGES in recent years have made a number of statements in discrimination cases that are striking in their forthright and blatant hostility towards anti-discrimination and equality law. Perhaps the most 'extremely intemperate and disturbingly worded'[1] statement can be found in the dissent by Judges Vucinic and De Gaetano to the ruling of the European Court of Human Rights (ECtHR) (Chamber) in the *Ladele* case.[2] Ms Ladele, a registrar in the Borough of Islington, City of London, refused to officiate civil partnerships on the grounds of her religion and conscience, an action that led to disciplinary proceedings against her and ultimately the loss of her job. The Court ruled that the balancing of anti-discrimination rights (religion versus sexual orientation) undertaken by the Borough and UK courts did not exceed the UK's margin of appreciation.[3] In their dissent, however, Judges Vucinic and De Gaetano noted that the Borough had been 'blinkered [by] political correctness' and 'clearly favoured "gay rights" over fundamental human rights'.[4] Their contrast of anti-discrimination rights with fundamental rights, along with their use of inverted commas, betrays an unusually conspicuous hostility towards gay rights.

Less disturbing, but nonetheless dismissive, statements about discrimination and inequality can be found in other cases too. Resistance

* I would like to thank Meghan Campbell, Sandra Fredman, Tarun Khaitan, Mike Leach, and Robin Allen and other participants of the March 2016 Oxford Workshop *Theorising Indirect Discrimination Law* for their valuable comments on drafts of this article. The mistakes are all mine.

1 Ronan McCrea, 'Strasbourg Judgement in Eweida and Others v United Kingdom' (*UK Constitutional Law Association Blog*, 16 January, 2013) http://ukconstitutionallaw.org/2013/01/16/ronan-mccrea-strasbourg-judgement-in-eweida-and-others-v-united-kingdom.

2 *Eweida v United Kingdom* (App no 48420/10) (2013) 57 EHRR 8.

3 ibid.

4 ibid, dissenting opinion by Judges Vucinic and De Gaetano [5].

to anti-discrimination law,[5] and especially objections to a robust protection from indirect discrimination, have not been uncommon in submissions put forward by governments,[6] but appear also in some Chamber decisions[7] as well as separate opinions of individual ECtHR judges.[8] These statements can be found both before as well as after the ECtHR established its indirect discrimination doctrine[9] in its 2007 Grand Chamber decision in *DH and Others v Czech Republic*, regarding educational segregation of Roma children. This paper identifies, classifies and analyses these sceptical statements, both regarding the social reality of inequality as well as the legal doctrine of indirect discrimination, and the responses to them by the Grand Chamber of the Court. The aim of the chapter is thus not merely to present a doctrinal assessment of the case law, but to offer a more socio-legal reading of governmental and judicial statements about inequality and discrimination.

[5] This resistance often comes from post-communist Central Europe. These states have made up many of the defendants in cases of indirect racial discrimination, although this could arguably be traced back to the high level of activity of international human rights NGOs in this region, such as the European Roma Rights Centre based in Budapest. Beyond this, judges from the region have been significantly represented in the Chamber decisions not finding indirect discrimination. For example, in the first *DH* decision in 2006, *DH and Others v Czech Republic* (App no 57325/00) (2006) 43 EHRR 41 (Chamber), most of the judges behind the majority Chamber judgment which found no violation came from post-communist countries: The Czech, Hungarian, Lithuanian and Ukrainian judge were joined in the majority by a San Marino judge. The French president of the Chamber concurred; the Portuguese judge dissented. Post-communist judges have also been prominent among the dissenters from the Grand Chamber decisions. For example, in the Grand Chamber decision in 2007, *DH and Others v Czech Republic* (App no 57325/00) (2008) 47 EHRR 3, most of the dissenters who insisted that there had been no violation were judges from post-communist countries: Jungwiert (Czech Republic), Župančič (Slovenia), Šikuta (Slovakia), Borrego Borrega (Spain). The same was true of the dissent in Oršuš in 2010: Jungwiert (Czech Republic), Vajić (Croatia), Kovler (Russia), Gyulumyan (Armenia), Jaeger (Germany), Myjer (Netherlands), Berro-Lefèvre (Monaco), Vučinić (Montenegro). Anti-discrimination law has not fared well in the domestic jurisdictions in post-communist Europe either. My research on the difficulties facing anti-discrimination law in the Czech Republic was the original impetus for this chapter—to assess whether they are mirrored at the European level. It goes beyond the scope of this paper to analyse the specific roots of this resistance here; for an analysis, see Barbara Havelková, 'Resistance to Anti-Discrimination Law in Central and Eastern Europe–a Post-Communist Legacy?' (2016) 17 *German Law Journal* 627 and Barbara Havelková, *Gender Equality in Law—Uncovering the Legacies of Czech State Socialism* (Oxford, Bloomsbury/Hart Publishing, 2017).

[6] Notably *DH (Grand Chamber)*, *Oršuš v Croatia* (App no 15766/03) (2009) 49 EHRR 26, 4, 431–35, and *Horváth and Kiss v Hungary* (App no 11146/11) (2013) 57 EHRR 31.

[7] *DH (Chamber)*; *Oršuš and Others v Croatia* (App no 15766/03) (ECHR, 17 July 2008) (Chamber).

[8] Dissent by Judge Jungwiert and others in *DH (Grand Chamber)* and *Oršuš (Grand Chamber)*.

[9] I thank Hugh Collins for raising the question of whether *DH (Grand Chamber)* actually established a 'doctrine'. It is true that the case set forth neither a completely clear test, nor did it explicitly distinguish indirect discrimination from direct. It did, however, emphasise several aspects typically associated with indirect discrimination, which I elaborate below, among them the emphasis on context and effect, and the need to shift the burden of proof once a disparate impact is shown.

Indirect discrimination (or 'disparate impact' in the US terminology) is an effects-oriented and substantive[10] doctrine, which prohibits apparently neutral measures which have a disproportionately negative effect on members of disadvantaged groups, unless they can be justified.[11] The doctrine is seen as an important part of anti-discrimination guarantees in many legal systems,[12] including the EU,[13] and other progressive liberal jurisdictions around the world, notably Canada[14] and South Africa.[15]

Anti-discrimination law, and indirect discrimination especially, perhaps more than other legal doctrines, depends on several acknowledgments about social reality. One is an awareness that discrimination is enabled by socio-cultural and socio-economic structures, which hierarchically organise society to the disadvantage of certain groups[16] and their members. This context means that discrimination often comes from unconscious prejudice or bias.[17] The focus is thus on the effect of actions,[18] because it is recognised that what was in the head of the discriminator matters less than how the disadvantaged group and/or its member are impacted. It is important to recognise that because of the hierarchical set-up, seemingly 'neutral' rules will impact

[10] Substantive equality is based on the realisation that equal treatment of people unequally situated can lead to injustice. It goes beyond the formal requirement of equal treatment and aims at equality of opportunity, resources or results. Hugh Collins, 'Discrimination, Equality and Social Inclusion' (2003) 66 *MLR* 16; Sandra Fredman, *Discrimination Law* (Oxford, Oxford University Press, 2011) 14–19.

[11] First established in *Griggs v Duke Power Co,* 401 US 424 (1971).

[12] For a comparative discussion, see Sandra Fredman, *Comparative Study of Anti-Discrimination and Equality Laws of the US, Canada, South Africa and India* (European Commission Report, 2012); Tarunabh Khaitan, *A Theory of Discrimination Law* (Oxford, Oxford University Press, 2015); Fredman (n 10) 177.

[13] Originally developed by the Court of Justice of the EU in C-170/1984 *Bilka-Kaufhaus* [1986] ECR 1607, it is now enshrined in secondary law. For race, see Art 2(2)(b) Council Directive (EC) 2000/43 implementing the principle of equal treatment between persons irrespective of racial or ethnic origin, [2000] OJ 180 22. For a discussion, see eg Christa Tobler, *Limits and Potential of the Concept of Indirect Discrimination* (European Commission Report, 2008); Olivier DeSchutter, 'Three Models of Equality and European Anti-Discrimination Law' (2006) 57 *Northern Ireland Legal Quarterly* 1, 9.

[14] The so-called 'Meiorin' of 'Firefighters' case *British Columbia (Public Service Employee Relations Commission) v British Columbia Government Service Employees' Union ('Meiorin')* [1999] 3 SCR 3.

[15] See Khaitan (n 12) 161 and references therein.

[16] The group aspect is important: it is not necessary to use individuals as comparators; the impact on groups matters. This can be shown by the use of statistical evidence. For discussion, see eg ibid, 74–75.

[17] There is considerable literature on the role bias plays in practices which have disparate impact. See eg Linda Krieger, 'The Content of Our Categories: A Cognitive Bias Approach to Discrimination and Equal Employment Opportunity' (1995) 47 *Stanford Law Review* 1161; Samuel Bagenstos, 'Implicit Bias, "Science," and Antidiscrimination Law' (2007) 1 *Harvard Law and Policy Review* 477. This is often connected to proposals to conceptualise anti-discrimination law as based on negligence liability, see eg David Oppenheimer, 'Negligent Discrimination' (1993) 141 *University of Pennsylvania Law Review* 899, or even strict liability, see discussion in Tarunabh Khaitan's and Sandy Steel's chapter in this volume.

[18] See eg *Meiorin* (n 14).

the advantaged and the disadvantaged group differently. In other words, the 'same' treatment might not be 'equal treatment'.[19] Finally, although the origin of the discrimination might be diffuse, there is an acknowledgment that it is legitimate that certain institutions[20] be prohibited from replicating and thus exacerbating these structures.[21]

The Grand Chamber decision in *DH*[22] was based on these understandings. The case arose when a group of Roma children from the city of Ostrava challenged a practice of the Czech educational authorities whereby disproportionately high numbers of Roma children were routinely placed in 'special' schools intended for children with mental deficiencies. The Chamber decision of 2006[23] found no violation of Article 14, but the Grand Chamber[24] overruled in 2007, finding indirect discrimination. The Grand Chamber for the first time quite unambiguously stated that intent was not a necessary element of discriminatory behaviour,[25] nor was it necessary to show that the disadvantaged group was specifically targeted: 'a general policy or measure that has disproportionately prejudicial effects on a particular group may be considered discriminatory notwithstanding that it is not specifically aimed at that group'.[26] The Court allowed the use of statistical evidence to suggest a prima facie case of indirect discrimination[27] and, once the applicant showed a difference in treatment, the burden of proof was shifted to the defendant government to justify it.[28] The Court in *DH* considered the wider societal context, and the particular disadvantages of the Roma,[29] as highly relevant. This led the Court to conclude that a breach can originate from a

[19] Such as the requirement of an educational qualification which disproportionately disqualifies Africans-Americans, as was the case in *Griggs* (n 11).

[20] They become the duty-bearers in anti-discrimination law. The term 'institution' is used in a wider sense here, as including not only public institutions but also employers, schools, service providers, etc.

[21] On the shift from targeting 'prejudiced discrimination' to addressing 'institutional or structural' discrimination, see eg Christopher McCrudden, 'Institutional Discrimination' (1982) 2 *OJLS* 303.

[22] For a detailed analysis of the case, see also Jennifer Devroye, 'The Case of DH and Others v the Czech Republic' (2009) 7 *Northwestern Journal of International Human Rights* 81; Helen O'Nions, 'Different and Unequal: the Educational Segregation of Roma Pupils in Europe' (2010) 21 *Intercultural Education* 1; Roberta Medda-Windischer, 'Dismantling Segregating Education and the European Court of Human Rights. DH and Others vs. Czech Republic: Towards an Inclusive Education?' (2007/8) 7 *European Yearbook of Minority Issues* 19.

[23] *DH (Chamber)* (n 5).

[24] *DH (Grand Chamber)* (n 5).

[25] ibid [179], [194].

[26] ibid [175].

[27] ibid [180], [185]–[195].

[28] ibid [177], [196]–[201].

[29] ibid [182].

de facto situation,[30] and it adopted a novel method of inferring violations in individual cases from the finding of disproportionate prejudicial effect of measures on the Roma community as a whole. It stated that 'the applicants as members of that community *necessarily suffered the same* discriminatory treatment.'[31] Accordingly, it did not feel any need to examine their individual cases. It is perhaps worth noting that although the Grand Chamber decision is rightly considered ground-breaking, as it for the first time clearly and firmly stated that the European Convention on Human Rights (ECHR) protects individuals from indirect discrimination, its contribution was evolutionary rather than revolutionary and the Court relied heavily on its previous case law[32] as well as international and comparative sources.[33]

The Grand Chamber decision in *DH* shows an awareness of how indirect discrimination comes about in reality, as a collection of actions based on bias rather than intent, as well as clarity in terms of what are the necessary elements of a legal doctrine meant to address such discrimination. Despite the clarity of these articulations, doubts have continued to be expressed in subsequent cases. This paper looks at these objections and the Court's responses to them. It argues that although the doctrine of indirect discrimination under Article 14 now appears settled, and the Court has not given in to the challenges and critique, the continued objections from its individual

[30] ibid [175].

[31] ibid [207] (emphasis added).

[32] The Grand Chamber drew on and drew together different strands of previous case law to affirm certain principles. For example the fact that the measure does not need to aim at the group in question, but effect is sufficient, was previously elaborated on in *Jordan v United Kingdom (Admissibility)* (App no 22567/02) (2005) 40 EHRR SE10, [154], and *Hoogendijk v Netherlands (Admissibility)* (App no 58641/00) (2005) 40 EHRR SE22. *Hoogendijk*, a decision on admissibility, was also the basis for allowing the use of statistical evidence to suggest a prime facie case of indirect discrimination. In it, the Court clarified that although statistical evidence is not 'automatically sufficient for disclosing a practice which could be classified as discriminatory', it was sufficient to shift the burden of proof onto the defendant. This statement is itself a nod to previous case law on the matter, *Jordan v United Kingdom* [154]. The possibility that a breach can originate from a de facto situation was first stated in *Zarb Adami v Malta* (App no 17209/02) (2007) 44 EHRR 3 [76]. And the shift of burden of proof to the defendant was used in *Chassagnou and Others v France* (App no 25088/94) (1999) 29 EHRR 615 [91]; and *Timishev v Russia* (App no 55762/00) (2007) 44 EHRR 37 [57], among others. Nor was *DH* the first case in which the Court took account of the wider societal context, and the particular disadvantages of the Roma, although the investigation in *DH* (Grand Chamber) was admittedly more extensive and the Court relied on it more heavily. See eg *Chapman v United Kingdom* (App no 27238/95) (2001) 33 EHRR 18 [96]; and *Connors v United Kingdom* (App no 66746/01) (2005) 40 EHRR 9 [84].

[33] Aside from restating or developing its own previous case-law, the Court looked extensively at other Council of Europe sources, EU directives and the case law of the European Court of Justice, international law (such as ICCPR or CERD) and comparative law (citing for example the US case of *Griggs* and various UK House of Lords' decisions), in particular to firmly establish the objective nature of the liability for discrimination.

judges and defendant governments show that there continues to be a disagreement both about the realities of inequality as well as the role the law should play in addressing them.

In order to see how the indirect discrimination doctrine has fared since *DH (Grand Chamber)*, one needs to identify the indirect discrimination cases before the ECtHR. In Section I, I do so, noting, however, that this is not a straightforward task. The Court itself is rarely explicit in its classification, and often applies a generic discrimination test rather than treating cases as either direct or indirect discrimination. Nonetheless, I identify 16 cases of indirect discrimination and note that the Court has never weakened or departed from its *DH* doctrine and that many principles established in *DH* have become a citation staple in subsequent cases.

In Section II, I discuss the challenges to the effects-based and substantive doctrine of indirect discrimination that have been put forward by defendant governments and some ECtHR judges. They are in part a commentary on social reality—they express a scepticism as to the existence of inequality and discrimination, and a denial that policies that lead to it constitute discrimination. In part, they express a normative position on the law—they formulate a refusal to grant legal protection from unintentional, structural discrimination. I distinguish between three objections. First, there is a belief in the existence of a fair world based on a confidence that existing institutional set-ups are fair and neutral. Such beliefs lie at the root of refusals to acknowledge any connection between institutional structures and the disparate impact they can have on members of disadvantaged groups. This leads, second, to the insistence that anti-discrimination law should only target hostile animus and not implicit bias. Third, it leads to putting the burden of overcoming the disadvantage on the discriminated individual.

These challenges have been answered by the Court in *DH (Grand Chamber)*, and, in Section III, I show how. I argue that despite the resistance of some judges and some governments, the Court has so far not backtracked, departed from, nor limited its effects-oriented and substantive indirect discrimination doctrine established in *DH*. The principles guiding the Court's decision-making in cases of indirect discrimination are reasonably clear as well as robust. I note, however, that the case law on indirect discrimination thus seems to have outpaced the ECtHR case law on direct discrimination. In particular, while the Court is willing to infer race-based discrimination from contextual evidence in indirect discrimination, it does not infer racial basis in direct discrimination cases, even when both the general context as well as more concrete behaviours would suggest it. The progress on indirect discrimination can thus feel limited since its insights on the inference of the race element, be it motive or bias, have not been used in the 'neighbouring' cases of direct discrimination in the form of racial violence.

I. ECtHR CASE LAW ON INDIRECT DISCRIMINATION

Since the Grand Chamber judgment in *DH*, as of November 2016,[34] there have been 16 cases of indirect discrimination decided by the ECtHR.[35] This number is both relatively low and somewhat rough. It is relatively low since the Court sometimes decides not to assess the indirect discrimination aspects of cases. For example, in *Eweida and others v UK*,[36] indirect discrimination was not tested despite the fact that it was pled by all four applicants.[37] It was only examined in the *Ladele* case.[38] It is somewhat rough mainly because the Court is not always particularly clear in distinguishing direct from indirect discrimination. For example, in *Sampanis v Greece*,[39] another case of educational segregation of Roma children, both indirect[40] and direct[41] discrimination were mentioned, but it was unclear which test the Court applied.[42] In some cases, one can only infer that indirect discrimination was at stake. For example, in *Opuz v Turkey*,[43] where the passivity of the Turkish law

[34] The ECtHR HUDOC database was searched for Chamber and Grand Chamber judgments (thus excluding admissibility decisions), using the following criteria: engagement of Art 14, the word 'indirect' and 'discrimination' in the text, and citation of 'DH' To capture judgments available only in French, an additional search with the term 'indirecte' was also conducted. The search yielded over 30 results, but not all the cases could be classified as indirect discrimination.

[35] The cases were identified by a search in the HUDOC database (see previous footnote) and further selected on the basis of whether either the Court explicitly or implicitly identified them as indirect discrimination or whether their facts lend themselves to such an interpretation even if the Court applied a more 'generic' test of discrimination. The classification in those cases is mine, based on the definition of indirect discrimination the ECtHR has adopted, as well as that used in the EU (eg Art 2(2)b) of Council Directive (EC) 2000/43 implementing the principle of equal treatment between persons irrespective of racial or ethnic origin, [2000] OJ 180). *Oršuš (Chamber)* (n 7); *Andrejeva v Latvia* (App no 55707/00) (2010) 51 EHRR 28; *Opuz v Turkey* (App no 33401/02) (2010) 50 EHRR 28; *Muñoz Díaz v Spain* (App no 49151/07) (2010) 50 EHRR 49; *Oršuš (Grand Chamber)* (n 6); *Konstantin Markin v Russia* (App no 30078/06) (2013) 56 EHRR 8; *Eweida and Others v United Kingdom* (n 2); *Horváth and Kiss v Hungary* (n 6); *Church of Jesus Christ of Latter-Day Saints v United Kingdom* (App no 7552/09) (2014) 59 EHRR 18; *Biao v Denmark* (App no 38590/10) (2017) 64 EHRR 1; *SAS v France* (App no 43835/11) (2015) 60 EHRR 11; *Di Trizio v Switzerland* (App no 7186/09) (ECHR Chamber, 2 February 2016); *Guberina v Croatia* (App no 23682/13) (ECHR Chamber, 12 September 2016); *Biao v Denmark* (App no 38590/10) (ECHR Grand Chamber, 24 May 2016); *Taddeucci and McCall v Italy* (App no 51362/09) (ECHR Chamber, 30 June 2016); *British Gurkha Welfare Society and other v UK* (App no 44818/11) (ECHR Chamber, 15 September 2016).

[36] *Eweida and Others v United Kingdom* (n 2).

[37] *SAS v France* (n 35) [160].

[38] *Eweida and Others v United Kingdom* (n 2) [104].

[39] *Sampanis and Others v Greece* (App no 32526/05) (ECHR, 5 June 2008).

[40] ibid [78]–[79].

[41] ibid [89].

[42] While Sampanis can on the facts be considered more of a direct discrimination case, *Konstantin Markin v Russia*, another case where the court is not clear on which type of discrimination it examines, would on the facts arguably be indirect.

[43] *Opuz v Turkey* (n 35).

enforcement agencies towards domestic violence was at issue, it could be deduced from the statement that 'the general and discriminatory judicial passivity in Turkey, *albeit unintentional*, *mainly affected women*', which points to an effects-oriented understanding of discrimination.[44] Similarly, in *Muñoz v Spain*, the Court concentrated on harm caused by seemingly neutral practices, finding them discriminatory, but never explicitly stating that they were an instance of indirect discrimination.[45] To summarise, it is hard to identify indirect discrimination cases, sometimes because the Court applies a generic discrimination test,[46] sometimes because although it might have either direct or indirect discrimination in mind, it does not state this explicitly.[47]

One reason why the Court so rarely explicitly identifies indirect discrimination could be the fact that the Court is not obligated to decide between direct and indirect discrimination in order to conduct an Article 14 assessment. Unlike in some other jurisdictions, such as in EU law where for most grounds only indirect discrimination can be justified,[48] the justification test under Article 14 is the same for both direct and indirect discrimination. This statement should perhaps be qualified, since the Court has not been entirely consistent on this point. In *Timishev*, the Court stated that direct discrimination cannot be justified.[49] This statement was reiterated in *DH (Grand Chamber)*:

> The Court has also held that no difference in treatment which is based exclusively or to a decisive extent on a person's ethnic origin is capable of being objectively justified in a contemporary democratic society built on the principles of pluralism and respect for different cultures.[50]

While stating this in the abstract, the Court never appears to apply this rule when assessing the case before it. I thus take the statement to be a hyperbolic comment about the gravity of race discrimination and not a doctrinal statement on justificatory rules.

Another explanation might be that the ECtHR has begun to blur or eliminate any doctrinal distinction between direct and indirect discrimination.

[44] ibid [200] (emphasis added).

[45] *Muñoz Díaz v Spain* (n 35) [61]. Spain did not recognise marriage by Roma rites.

[46] Aside from *Konstantin Markin v Russia* (n 35), see also eg *British Gurkha Welfare* (n 35).

[47] eg *Opuz v Turkey* (n 35); *Muñoz Díaz v Spain* (n 35).

[48] Council Directive (EC) 2000/43 implementing the principle of equal treatment between persons irrespective of racial or ethnic origin [2000] OJ 180 22, Art 2(2)(b). It is exactly this distinction in EU law which has led some to argue for a clearer distinction in the ECtHR jurisprudence. Sina van den Bogaert, 'Roma Segregation in Education: Direct or Indirect Discrimination? An Analysis of the Parallels and Differences between Council Directive 2000/43/EC and Recent ECtHR Case Law on Roma Educational Matters' (2011) 71 *Zeitschrift für ausländisches öffentliches Recht und Völkerrecht* 719.

[49] *Timishev v Russia* (n 32) [58].

[50] *DH (Grand Chamber)* (n 5) [176].

It might be too early to conclude this;[51] however, if it were doing so, it is worth pointing out that it would not be alone in this trend.[52] And it could be argued that a substantive, effects-oriented approach to both direct and indirect discrimination law makes the distinction between them less crucial.[53] As I point out in Section III, however, the Court has yet to apply its insights from indirect discrimination to Article 14 more widely.

As for the role *DH (Grand Chamber)* has played in subsequent cases, several aspects of the decision have been repeatedly cited, both in cases which can be identified as indirect discrimination as well as in cases where this is less clear: the fact that relevantly similar situations need to be compared;[54] that discrimination can result from a de facto situation[55] and no intent or aiming at a particular group is necessary;[56] and/or the need to shift of the burden of proof.[57]

In terms of cases explicitly decided as indirect discrimination where the Court has relied on *DH*, there were two cases with a fact pattern closely related to *DH*. In *Oršuš v Croatia*,[58] Roma children were disproportionately transferred to separate classes on the grounds of their inadequate command of the Croatian language. In *Horváth v Hungary*,[59] Roma children were disproportionately placed in remedial schools based on culturally biased schooling assessments. The Court found indirect discrimination on the basis of ethnic origin in both. More recently, in 2016, three further indirect discrimination cases benefited from insights from *DH (Grand Chamber)*. The case of *di Trizio v Switzerland*[60] concerned Swiss rules under which disability allowance was discontinued to recipients who became parents. The Court considered this to constitute indirect sex discrimination. The assessment mirrored *DH* in emphasis on the disproportionate effect on

[51] The requirement of 'exhaustion of domestic remedies' means that applicants cannot make new pleas before the ECtHR which they did not raise before domestic courts. This has meant, for example, that the discriminatory nature of the tests in *Horváth* could not be assessed by the Court. There will thus always be a delay in using new doctrines before the ECtHR; the analysis and conclusions of my chapter thus need to be seen as somewhat preliminary.

[52] See for example McLachlan J in the *Meiorin* case (n 14) (also known as 'Firefighters'). For a discussion, see Fredman (n 10) 213.

[53] For a critique of the blurring, as relates to the lack of attention to reasons in direct discrimination cases, see Fredman (n 10) 204–05.

[54] eg *Berger-Krall and Others v Slovenia* (App no. 14717/04) (ECHR, 12 June 2014) [293]; *Biao (Grand Chamber)* (n 35) [89]; *Di Trizio* (n 35) [85].

[55] eg *Berger-Krall and Others v Slovenia* (n 54) [295]; *Guberina* (n 35) [71].

[56] eg *SAS v France* (n 35) [161]; *Biao (Grand Chamber)* (n 35) [91]; *Izzetin Dogan and others v Turkey* (App no. 62649/10) (ECHR Grand Chamber, 26 April 2016) ECHR [157]; *Taddeucci and McCall* (n 35) [81].

[57] eg *Berger-Krall and Others v Slovenia* [296]; *Biao (Grand Chamber)* (n 35) [92]; *Di Trizio* (n 35) [84]; *Taddeucci and McCall* (n 35) [90].

[58] *Oršuš (Grand Chamber)* (n 58).

[59] *Horváth and Kiss v Hungary* (n 6).

[60] *Di Trizio* (n 35).

the relevant group (women) and the use of statistics.[61] In *Biao v Denmark*,[62] the Grand Chamber, on appeal, reviewed the Danish family reunification rules which exempted citizens who lived in Denmark for more than 28 years from the otherwise applicable requirement of proving the attachment to Denmark over other countries. Since this impacted disproportionately Danish citizens born outside of Denmark, thus non-ethnic Danes, this rule was found to be indirectly discriminatory on the basis of ethnic origin. Finally, in *Taddeucci and McCall v Italy*,[63] the fact that same-sex couples living in legally recognised civil partnerships were treated the same as different-sex couples who did not formalise their relationship with regards to family reunification, was considered to be indirect discrimination on the basis of sexual orientation.

In the following, I turn to the objections to the indirect discrimination doctrine, raised by defendant governments and ECtHR judges in those cases. From the outset, it should be noted that the resistance seems to plague the race and ethnic origin discrimination cases more than others.

II. OBJECTIONS TO THE INDIRECT DISCRIMINATION DOCTRINE

The Czech Government's submissions in the *DH* case can be somewhat jocularly paraphrased in three basic propositions in the following way: The rules are neutral; we are not racists and we did not intend it; they want it that way and could have overcome it. This position combines a certain understanding of social reality and therefore the legally relevant facts of the case with the interpretation given to the prohibition of discrimination under Article 14. In other words, the two elements come together. First, there is the assessments and interpretation of reality, namely the belief that the societal and institutional set-up is neutral and fair (the descriptive and evaluative element). Second, there is the understanding of the role of anti-discrimination law: that it should only interfere in cases of motivated or intentional discrimination, and that it shouldn't help the disadvantaged if they are not seen to be helping themselves (the normative position).[64] These positions seriously impede the formation and the application of an effects-based and substantive doctrine of indirect discrimination. The descriptive and evaluative exercise, as performed by the dissenters, is problematic because it is an

[61] ibid [89].

[62] *Biao (Grand Chamber)* (n 35).

[63] *Taddeucci and McCall* (n 35).

[64] This resonates with work by gender legal scholars, especially Deborah Rhode's analysis of the '"no problem" problem'. She identified three types of denial: the denial of inequality, the denial of injustice and the denial of responsibility: Deborah Rhode, *Speaking of Sex: Denial of Gender Inequality* (Cambridge MA, Harvard University Press, 1997) 1–20.

inaccurate understanding of how inequality comes about in social terms and how discrimination arises in psychological terms.[65] It can lead to judicial positions that are particularly dismissive of notions of implicit bias, especially when institutional or structural, in discrimination cases. As for the normative aspect, these renderings of social reality have inevitable normative implications as they contribute to a limited understanding of what problems should anti-discrimination law address.

The Czech Government's assessment of the facts, and its interpretation of Article 14, was accepted by the Chamber in the first judgment in *DH*, which found no violation. It also resonated with several dissenting judges who wrote separate opinions to the Grand Chamber decision in *DH* which overturned the Chamber decision. And despite the fact that the Grand Chamber in *DH* showed how these interpretations of social reality and of anti-discrimination law do not exonerate the defendant state, similar arguments have continued to be put forward in the Government submissions in the cases of *Oršuš v Croatia*,[66] and *Horváth v Hungary*.[67] They continued to be accepted by some judges, indeed the majority of the Chamber deciding in the first instance in *Oršuš* (2008),[68] despite the fact that this judgment was decided after the Grand Chamber ruled in *DH*. Finally, they continued to be raised by dissenting judges to the Grand Chamber judgment in *Oršuš*[69] and *Biao*.[70] In the following, I present examples of the three[71] types of objections from these sources.

A. Belief in Neutral, Unbiased Structures and a Fair World

The judges' belief in the neutrality of reality is evident in their discomfort at the use of context to identify pre-existing disadvantage of certain groups.

[65] See esp Krieger (n 17).
[66] *Oršuš (Chamber)* (n 7) and *Oršuš (Grand Chamber)* (n 6).
[67] *Horváth and Kiss v Hungary* (n 6).
[68] *Oršuš (Chamber)* (n 7).
[69] Dissent by Jungwiert et al in *Oršuš (Grand Chamber)* (n 6).
[70] *Biao (Grand Chamber)* (n 35).
[71] Arguably, other types of objections could be identified. One is the reluctance to see that privilege for one group is the functional equivalent of a disadvantage for another. See eg *Biao (Grand Chamber)* (n 35) dissent by Judges Villiger, Mahoney and Kjolbro [10]. Another is the underestimation of the importance of symbolic harm. By suggesting that 'separation [is] not always harmful', the dissenters in *Oršuš* ignored the harm to dignity suffered in cases of segregation. This despite the fact that the recognition that separate cannot be equal in a highly unequal society, has been internationally well established since the US Supreme Court 1954 case of *Brown v Board of Education*. See Jungwiert dissent, *Oršuš (Grand Chamber)* (n 6) [17] and *Brown v Board of Education* 347 US 483 (1957) [494]. I am not discussing these points specifically; partly for reasons of space, partly because they are general to anti-discrimination law rather than being of particular salience in indirect discrimination cases.

The Chamber in *DH* decided that it was not 'its task to assess the overall social context.'[72] The dissenters to the Grand Chamber decision in *Oršuš* reiterated the point:

> [in order to] further develop ... the notion of indirect discrimination, [the majority was] obliged to lean on arguments *outside the concrete facts, referring to the situation of the Roma population in general.* ... As a result, this became in some respects more a judgment on the special position of the Roma population in general than one based on the facts of the case.[73]

It can be said, however, that the recognition of relevance of context is at the core of the doctrine of indirect discrimination, since it is the knowledge of the real situation people find themselves in which allows us to assess whether and how an apparently neutral rule will impact them more than others. Finding indirect discrimination is not a formal, abstract exercise, but a substantive, concrete one.

This goes not only for the assessment of whether seemingly neutral rules have, in fact, disparate impact, but also to the question of whether segregation is neutral. When evidence of pre-existing disadvantage is ignored or not viewed as relevant, segregation can be assessed as neutral and symmetrical for both the advantaged and disadvantaged groups. This was the position of the Chamber judges in *Oršuš* (2008), who tried to distinguish *Oršuš* from the Grand Chamber judgment in *DH*, by pointing out that the Croatian educational policy led merely to 'separation', and not discriminatory segregation.[74] The dissenters in the subsequent Grand Chamber decision in *Oršuš* (2010) maintained this point:

> the majority has not taken into consideration at all that one of the rights of a minority consists in 'preserving diversity' ... and that *separation is therefore not always considered to be harmful*, especially when accompanied—as in the given situation—by various social activities and measures organised in the common school.[75]

Again, for segregation, a sub-type of discriminatory practices, the pre-existing context matters, especially when one is asked to assess dignitary (socio-cultural), not merely material (socio-economic) harms.[76]

The disinterest in context is based in the belief that the societal and institutional set-up is neutral and fair (hence the lack of need to actually assess it). Government submissions as well as some judicial opinions have failed to acknowledge that existing structures, tests or other forms of assessing children might in fact be in effect discriminatory. They assume that the existing structures and norms are neutral and objective. They do not acknowledge

[72] *DH (Chamber)* (n 5) [45].
[73] Jungwiert dissent, *Oršuš (Grand Chamber)* (n 6) [15] (emphasis added).
[74] *Oršuš (Chamber)* (n 7) [60].
[75] Jungwiert dissent, *Oršuš (Grand Chamber)* (n 6) [17] (emphasis added).
[76] See n 71 above.

that when structures and norms are based on the majority characteristics, experiences or needs, they can benefit the majority but exclude or disadvantage a minority. The Chamber judges in *Oršuš*, for instance, tried to distinguish the previously decided *DH (Grand Chamber)* from the case before them by pointing out that while in *DH*, the 'difference in treatment was *based on race*, which required the strictest scrutiny, in the present case the difference in treatment was based *on adequacy of language skills*',[77] disregarding the disparate impact this had on the Roma. In the subsequent Grand Chamber judgment in *Oršuš*, the judges who offered a dissenting opinion upheld this line of argument, declaring that

> it was not shown that the allegedly different treatment of the applicants was *based on their ethnic origin* or any other 'suspect' grounds, but [that it was] rather *exclusively* [based] on their insufficient command of the language, which means on *pedagogical grounds*.[78]

In the most recent of the cases, *Horváth*, the Hungarian Government still did not meaningfully take on board that the tests might not capture the abilities of the minority as well as they do those of the majority and thus be biased:

> The Government were of the opinion that tests and standards *tailored* to the Roma population would have *no sensible meaning* from the point of view of assessing a child's ability to cope with the mainstream education system—which was the purpose of the assessment of learning abilities of children and of the psychometric tests applied in the process.[79]

This shows a refusal to reconsider the majority-based norm in a way that would take into account the cultural, linguistic and educational differences of the Roma and yet make the results generalisable to both, the majority and the minority. This also illustrated a limited normative understanding of what anti-discrimination ought to capture—only acts somehow clearly 'based on' a protected characteristic, rather than acts which have a disparate effect on those with such a characteristic. This position is clearly expressed in the doctrinal insistence on showing motive and intent, to which I now turn.

B. Looking for Hostile Motive, not Unreflective Bias

The Czech Government in *DH* was careful to emphasise that the systemic placement of Roma children into segregated special schools was not done because they were Roma:

> the applicants had not submitted any evidence to show 'beyond reasonable doubt' that the domestic authorities' decisions had been *prompted* by the applicants'

[77] *Oršuš (Chamber)* (n 7) (emphasis added).
[78] Jungwiert dissent, *Oršuš (Grand Chamber)* (n 6) [18].
[79] Government submission in *Horváth and Kiss v Hungary* (n 6) [95] (emphasis added).

> racial origin ... the special schools *had never been intended* as schools for Roma children.[80]

As far as the Government was concerned, this was supported by evidence that 'none of the authorities' decisions *mentioned the applicants' Roma origin*'.[81]

The Chamber in the first *DH* (2006) judgment accepted this reasoning. The judges declared that their analytical role was to 'establish on the basis of the relevant facts whether the *reason* for the applicants' placement in the special schools was their ethnic or racial origin.'[82] As support, again, the fact that 'the rules governing children's placement in special schools *do not refer to the pupils' ethnic origin*' was mentioned.[83] The Chamber concluded that:

> the concrete evidence before the Court in the present case does not enable it to conclude that the applicants' placement or, in some instances, continued placement, in special schools was the result of *racial prejudice*, as they have alleged.[84]

Such a conclusion implies that the Chamber understanding of discrimination was limited to consciously prejudiced action.

The Grand Chamber in the *DH* judgment was unequivocal in stating that intent or motive was not necessary.[85] This has since been reiterated in *Oršuš*,[86] *Horváth*,[87] as well as other cases.[88] However, the agreement on the issue is not complete. As recently as May 2016, dissenting judges in the *Biao v Denmark* (Grand Chamber),[89] who disagreed with the classification of the distinction as 'on the basis of ethnic origin', emphasised that 'there is no basis in the law or the preparatory work for saying that a difference in treatment on the basis of national or ethnic origin is *intended*.'[90] One would have hoped that the fact that intent is not needed for discrimination to be found, and that, conversely, a lack of intent does not mean that discrimination did not take place, would be well established by this point. This statement indicates that this is not universally the case among the ECtHR judges.

80 Government submission in *DH (Chamber)* (n 5) [33] emphasis added. The quote also speaks to its understanding of the burden of proof as lying much more heavily on the applicant.
81 Government submission in ibid [34], emphasis added.
82 ibid, emphasis added.
83 ibid [49], emphasis added.
84 ibid [52], emphasis added.
85 *DH (Grand Chamber)* (n 5) [179].
86 *Oršuš (Grand Chamber)* (n 6) [155].
87 *Horváth and Kiss v Hungary* (n 6) [105]–[106].
88 See discussion in s I above.
89 *Biao (Grand Chamber)* (n 35), dissent by Judges Villiger, Mahoney and Kjolbro.
90 ibid, dissent by Judges Villiger, Mahoney and Kjolbro [11] (emphasis added).

C. Individual Responsibility to Prevent and Overcome Disadvantage

The lack of willingness to look at and recognise contextual markers of disadvantage was connected to a lack of acknowledgement of how much social structures can limit the ability of individuals from disadvantaged backgrounds to avoid being impacted by discrimination or even imagine that they could.[91] This has manifested itself in two ways. First, the defendant governments in several cases attempted to say that all problems could have been averted had only the applicants made different choices. In *Andrejeva v Latvia*,[92] for instance, the Latvian government suggested the applicant should have changed her citizenship,[93] in order to access the pension rights denied her as a non-Latvian citizen. In *Muñoz*, the Spanish government argued that nothing was preventing Ms Muñoz to enter into a formal marriage according to Spanish law,[94] which would have guaranteed her the survivor's pension she was denied under the existing rules. Second, in the educational discrimination cases, the fact that the parents consented under pressure to their children's segregation,[95] was presented by the governments as an exonerating circumstance.

III. THE RESPONSES

As I have already indicated, these objections are currently in the minority at the ECtHR and have been rejected by the Court, from the Grand Chamber decision in *DH* onwards. The ECtHR's current understanding of indirect discrimination can be somewhat jocularly summarised as: 'the disparate effects your policy has on [insert individuals or group defined by a protected characteristic] is highly suspect, please explain yourselves.' I elaborate on the doctrinal expressions of this position, and thus the responses the ECtHR has given to the objections, in this section.

Before I do so, it is perhaps useful to put indirect discrimination into a wider context of Article 14 case law. In particular, the Court has been heavily, and rightly, criticised[96] for its case law on direct discrimination in the

[91] See eg Nussbaum's theory of 'adaptive preferences', which points out the fact that the choices we can imagine might already be limited by our life's circumstances. Martha Nussbaum, *Women and Human Development* (Cambridge, Cambridge University Press, 2000), 111–61.

[92] *Andrejeva v Latvia* (n 35).

[93] ibid [72].

[94] As cited in the Court's assessment in *Muñoz Díaz v Spain* (n 35) [70].

[95] *DH* (Grand Chamber) (n 5) [148]; *Sampanis and Others v Greece* (n 39) [62].

[96] Marie-Benedicte Dembour, 'In the Name of the Rule of Law: the European Court of Human Rights' Silencing of Racism' in GK Bhambra and R Shilliam (eds), *Silencing Human Rights: Critical Engagements with a Contested Project* (Basingstoke, Palgrave MacMillan, 2009) 184; Mathias Möschel, 'Is the European Court of Human Rights Case Law on Anti-Roma Violence 'Beyond Reasonable Doubt'?' (2012) 12 *Human Rights Law Review* 479 481.

form of 'state-sponsored or state-tolerated violence'[97] against the Roma. Since the late 1990s when these cases started to be litigated before the ECtHR, the Court has decided tens of cases, overwhelmingly not finding racial motive and therefore not finding a substantive violation of the prohibition of direct discrimination on the ground of race.[98] Many cases have similar factual pattern, with strong indications of a racist motive related to the violence. A well-known example of this is *Nachova v Bulgaria*, in which two conscripts of Roma origin went absent without leave and were killed by military police in the process of arrest. The racism involved was supported by the un-contradicted witness statement that the Major in charge of the operation shouted 'You damn Gypsies' immediately after the killing.[99] The Court has mostly been reluctant to infer racial motive from factual patterns such as this[100] and has at most found procedural violations of Article 14 for insufficient investigation of the racial motive by the domestic authorities. While *Nachova* itself precedes *DH*, there have been other cases since.[101] And the Court has not extended the indirect discrimination doctrine to them, although the lack of prevention, investigation and punishment for perpetrators on the side of the authorities would tend to have disparate impact on the Roma,[102] which could be classified as substantive indirect discrimination. Neither has it extended the insights from *DH* regarding inference about race as a ground.[103]

The Court thus appears to be doing the seemingly more subtle, advanced thing—inferring structural bias from contextual (often statistical) evidence in indirect discrimination cases. But it is not inferring racial motive in direct discrimination cases, even when both the general context as well as more concrete behaviours relating to the incident would suggest it. A possible reason for indirect discrimination's outpacing of direct discrimination might be that in indirect discrimination cases, racism is never really at the fore. Finding structural bias can be more palatable than finding racist motives.

[97] Möschel, ibid.

[98] Mathias Möschel who analysed ECtHR's rulings on violence against the Roma up to 2012 notes that only in one case out of over 40 did the Court find a substantive violation of Art 14. ibid, table at 484.

[99] *Nachova v Bulgaria* (2004) 39 EHRR 37 (Chamber) [161].

[100] The Court has on occasion been more willing to infer motive, notable in one case of discrimination on the ground of sexual orientation in enjoyment of freedom of assembly: *Baczkowski*. In it, the Court was willing to 'reasonably surmise' discrimination from the homophobic personal opinions of the Mayor of Warsaw who banned an LGBT equality march: *Baczkowski v Poland* (App no 1543/06) (2009) 48 EHRR 19, [100].

[101] For a typology and examples, see Möschel (n 96) 481–82.

[102] Although this would have to be shown by statistical evidence which has admittedly not always been presented to the Court.

[103] The insistence on intent led for example to the failure of the claim of race discrimination in relation to sterilizations of overwhelmingly Roma women, with the Court finding a breach of Art 8, but not of Art 14 in *C v Slovakia* (App no 18968/07) (ECHR, 8 November 2011) [177].

This raises a few questions about discrimination law more generally. Has anti-discrimination law become a victim of its own success in that it has made the notion of discrimination for racist motive so frowned upon that Courts are now reluctant to make a finding to that end? And does this mean we might need to accept indirect discrimination as the paradigmatic case, and speak about 'inferring' the ground even in direct discrimination cases,[104] but not speak about racism or racist motive? It is not the aim of this paper to be normative, nor is answering these questions possible given its limited scope, but these questions, as well as the so far limited effect the indirect discrimination case law has had on Article 14 more generally, needs to be borne in mind in assessing responses by the Court to the objections raised by the opponents of indirect discrimination.

A. Belief in a Fair World and Unbiased Structures

The Court has rejected the opponents' refusal to look at the wider social context and accepted evidence of pre-existing disadvantage as relevant. It has recognised before, and reiterated in the indirect discrimination cases, that the Roma are a 'disadvantaged and vulnerable minority'.[105] This might seem self-explanatory, but it is an important acknowledgment of the difference of starting points, characteristics, experiences and needs. As such, it is crucial for a substantive understanding of equality which recognises that the same treatment of people in different positions might be undesirable. Thus, because of this 'socio-economic disadvantage or cultural differences'[106] of the Roma minority, the Court has created[107] a strong link between positive obligations and indirect discrimination.[108] In *Horváth*, the Court stated:

> In such circumstances—and in light of the *recognised bias* in past placement procedures—the Court considers that the State has specific *positive obligations to avoid the perpetuation of past discrimination or discriminative practices* disguised in allegedly neutral tests.[109]

This approach has arguably the potential of mitigating the quandary of speaking of racism. No one is said to be racist; at most, defendant states

[104] The Court stated that indirect discrimination ought to have 'less strict evidential rules' than direct discrimination in *DH (Grand Chamber)* (n 5) [186], without closer explanation.

[105] ibid [182].

[106] *Horváth and Kiss v Hungary* (n 6) [115].

[107] This principle was first established in *Thlimmenos v Greece* (2001) 31 EHRR 411 [44].

[108] In *DH (Grand Chamber)* (n 5), the Court did not use the idea of positive obligation yet—it examined the case as a pure breach of the prohibition of indirect discrimination. It has since identified the failure to accommodate difference as indirect discrimination in *Guberina* and *Taddeucci and McCall* (n 35).

[109] *Horváth and Kiss v Hungary* (n 6) [116] (emphasis added).

can be said to have been insufficiently anti-racist. But such approach is not without problems. First, it arguably diminishes the educational effect of anti-discrimination law, because it is not clear about how 'merely' biased decision-making is in fact discriminatory. Second, without discussing the racial bias, states can easily perceive the positive obligation as 'social engineering',[110] and discard it thus as an unjustified interference with society.

In response to the opponents' views of a neutral, objective world, the Court in *DH* recognised the potential for bias. It did so, however, cautiously, which chimes with my previous comment of the restrained way in which the Court speaks about racism or racial bias:

> The Court considers that, *at the very least, there is a danger* that the tests were *biased* and that the results were not analysed in the light of the particularities and special characteristics of the Roma children who sat them.[111]

The Court was robust, however, in accepting that the effect on the protected group is the crucial aspect in indirect discrimination and that it can be proven by statistical evidence relating to groups:

> In these circumstances, the Court considers that when it comes to assessing the *impact* of a measure or practice on an individual or group, *statistics* which appear on critical examination to be reliable and significant *will be sufficient* to constitute *the prima facie evidence* the applicant is required to produce.[112]

B. Necessity to Look for Motive or Intent?

The Court has given a simple answer to whether proof of intent or motive is necessary for a finding of discrimination under Article 14: it is not.[113] This is an unsurprising affirmation of an understanding of indirect discrimination as not targeting racial *motive*, but rather disparate *effects* and thus implicit racial *bias*. It is a recognition of the 'well-established fact that subjectivity is a ready vehicle for discriminatory impulses' and the reality that 'individuals are prone to rely on stereotypes in their decision-making and in a way in which they may be honestly unaware of.'[114] It is also a recognition of the difficulties of proving motive. In this sense, this doctrine could be seen as not

[110] This is a popular way to discredit anti-discrimination law in Central and Eastern Europe. Havelková (n 5).

[111] *DH (Grand Chamber)* (n 5) [201] (emphasis added).

[112] ibid [188] (emphasis added).

[113] In all three racial segregation cases: ibid [179]; *Oršuš (Grand Chamber)* (n 6) [155]; *Horváth and Kiss v Hungary* (n 6) [105]–[106].

[114] Michael Selmi, 'Indirect Discrimination and the Anti-discrimination Mandate' in Deborah Hellman and Sophia Moreau (eds), *Philosophical Foundations of Discrimination Law* (Oxford, Oxford University Press, 2013) 258 and references therein.

saying that indirect discrimination 'does not involve' prejudice or motive, but merely that it 'does not require' its proof.[115]

But considering the obvious reluctance of the Court to find racist motive in direct discrimination in the form of violence against the Roma, a possible different reading of *DH* emerges. On its own, *DH* could be seen as a recognition that racism or racial bias is very difficult to prove and should therefore be inferred. However, in the light of the cases on racial violence, one has to—less generously—ask the question whether the Court is merely avoiding the question of racism or racial bias altogether. This analysis is to some extent supported by the fact that in several of the post-*DH* discrimination cases the Court did not merely *not require* a proof of intent, but seemed to reassure the defendant state that their finding of discrimination was not meant to imply the government racist intentions.[116]

C. Individual Responsibility to Prevent and Overcome Disadvantage?

Another challenge identified above spoke to the behaviour of the discriminated. The opponents of indirect discrimination saw the wrong diminished or extinguished in a situation where the discriminated individual could be seen as somehow having contributed to the outcome. The European opponents of indirect discrimination are not alone in this; in the US, 'employee autonomy' can 'remove cases from the indirect discrimination category'.[117] The Court's response has, however, been robust. First, it was unequivocal about the fact that there was no obligation on an individual to prevent or to mitigate the effects of discrimination upon them. In both *Andrejeva* and *Muñoz*, the Court disagreed with the governments' submissions in the strongest terms. In *Andrejeva*, it ruled:

> Lastly, the Court cannot accept the Government's argument that it would be *sufficient for the applicant* to become a naturalised Latvian citizen in order to receive the full amount of the pension claimed. The prohibition of discrimination enshrined in Article 14 of the Convention is meaningful only if, in each particular case, the applicant's personal situation in relation to the criteria listed in that provision *is taken into account exactly as it stands*. To proceed otherwise in dismissing the victim's claims on the ground that *he or she could have avoided* the discrimination by altering one of the factors in question—for example, by acquiring a nationality—would render Article 14 *devoid of substance*.[118]

[115] ibid 253.

[116] *Oršuš (Grand Chamber)* (n 6) [155]; similarly, in relation to religious discrimination, see *SAS v France* (n 35) [161].

[117] Selmi (n 114) 265.

[118] *Andrejeva v Latvia* (n 35) [91]; see, equally, *Muñoz Díaz v Spain* (n 35) [70] (emphasis added).

A similar line has been taken in the educational segregation cases in relation to the consent given by some parents to the discriminatory placement of their children. In *DH (Grand Chamber)*, the Court first reiterated its earlier case law that 'a waiver' of a Convention right is not always permissible, and even when it is, it has to be unequivocal, 'given in full knowledge of the facts' and 'without constraint'.[119] Given the facts of *DH*,

> the Court [wa]s not satisfied that the parents of the Roma children, who were *members of a disadvantaged community* and *often poorly educated*, were *capable of weighing up* all the aspects of the situation and the consequences of giving their consent.[120]

The Court was careful to examine the dilemma of the children's parents in choosing between 'ordinary schools that were ill-equipped to cater for their children's social and cultural differences and in which their children risked isolation and ostracism' on the one hand, and 'special schools where the majority of the pupils were Roma'[121] on the other. The 'choice' between two non-ideal alternatives is often visited upon victims of discrimination. The Court thus concluded that in cases of racial discrimination, 'no waiver of the right not to be subjected to racial discrimination can be accepted, as it would be counter to an important public interest'.[122]

The Court's recognition of the limited ability of the individual to overcome structural discrimination is notable. The Grand Chamber in *DH* did not waver in the face of accusations of paternalism[123] levied at it by the dissenters and rather recognised that assuming full autonomy of individuals whose autonomy is clearly limited by external circumstances would be a move which would weaken the protection from discrimination.

IV. CONCLUSION

When I started this analysis of the indirect discrimination case law of the ECtHR, I expected to find the concept of indirect discrimination challenged and unsettled. It is challenged, but only to a limited extent.[124] I have

[119] *DH (Grand Chamber)* (n 5) [202] and the cases cited therein.

[120] ibid [203] (emphasis added).

[121] ibid [203].

[122] ibid [204].

[123] Dissent by Judge Borrego Borrego in ibid [14]–[18].

[124] While the doctrinal shift can be said to thus have irreversibly occurred at the European level, the resistance from some judges, as well as defendant governments, shows, however, that it might take some time before it trickles to the domestic level. The misunderstandings and objections identified in this paper, relating to a vision of a fair and unbiased world in which people's behaviour is not influenced and limited by socio-cultural or socio-economic structures, will most probably still very much impact implementation of the doctrine of indirect discrimination domestically. This is of course a speculation, but an educated one. For example,

shown that some judges continued to resist indirect discrimination and its application to certain sets of facts even after the *DH (Grand Chamber)* decision (Chamber in *Oršuš*, dissents in *Oršuš,* dissents in *Biao*). On the other hand, several recent indirect discrimination cases have lacked any dissent.[125] The doctrine also appears to be settled. The Court has applied the interpretation given in *DH* in several subsequent educational segregation cases and beyond. Moreover, it has done so flexibly to the benefit of the doctrine. For example, it did not insist on full identity of the facts or types of proof. Thus in *Oršuš*, it found indirect discrimination without having incontrovertible statistical evidence. Nor did it keep indirect discrimination completely circumscribed and isolated from other doctrines. For example, in *Horváth* as well *Taddeucci,* it created a link between indirect discrimination and positive obligation. And in *Guberina*, it combined indirect discrimination with a case of association discrimination.[126]

The real challenge might thus not be that the indirect discrimination case law becomes challenged or limited doctrinally, but rather that the insights it has brought—about the reality of discrimination and how to assess it judicially—might not be used in Article 14 cases more widely. Especially the racial violence cases would benefit either from the application of the newly robust indirect discrimination doctrine to their facts, or from having the insight about inference of racist bias (in indirect discrimination cases) extended to racist motive (in direct discrimination cases). In its indirect discrimination case law, the Court has recognised how societal structures impact behaviours and decisions of members of both the advantaged and disadvantaged groups. The next question arising from the progress made on indirect discrimination might thus be how its insights can be applied more generally in Article 14 cases.

among post-communist Central and Eastern European countries, improvement has been slow even in countries which joined the EU and have therefore been subject to a much more explicit and stricter anti-discrimination regime. For an analysis of what impact the *DH* (Grand Chamber) decision had domestically, see Iulius Rostas, *Ten Years After. A History of Roma School Desegregation in Central and Eastern Europe* (Budapest, CEU Press, 2012) and Hubert Smekal and Katarína Šipulová, 'DH v Czech Republic Six Years Later: On the Power of an International Human Rights Court to Push Through Systemic Change' (2014) 32 *Netherlands Quarterly of Human Rights* 288.

[125] eg *Horváth and Kiss v Hungary* (n 6) and *Guberina* (n 35) were by a unanimous Court. Some cases only had concurring opinions, such as *Taddeucci and McCall* (n 35).

[126] The disability was of a child rather than the adult parent challenging the tax rules.

5

Indirect Discrimination and the Duty to Avoid Compounding Injustice

DEBORAH HELLMAN

> You do not take a person who, for years, has been hobbled by chains and liberate him, bring him up to the starting line of a race and then say, 'you are free to compete with all the others', and still justly believe that you have been completely fair.
>
> President Lyndon B Johnson, Commencement Address at Howard University, 4 June 1964.

I. INTRODUCTION

THE MORAL UNDERPINNINGS of laws forbidding indirect discrimination[1] are controversial. Some believe that indirect discrimination is simply discrimination and that the difference in form between indirect and direct discrimination is overemphasised and unimportant.[2] As a result, both direct and indirect discrimination can be wrong and laws prohibiting wrongful forms of each are justified. Others believe that indirect discrimination isn't really discrimination and thus policies that cause a disparate impact on a protected group without adequate justification don't wrong the individuals affected.[3] Some of the proponents of this latter view also believe

[1] The term 'indirect discrimination' refers to what US readers refer to as 'disparate impact discrimination'.

[2] Tarunabh Khaitan, *A Theory of Discrimination Law* (Oxford, Oxford University Press, 2015) 18, 159–60 (defining discrimination to include direct and indirect discrimination and emphasising that the difference between them is one of degree rather than of kind); Sophia Moreau, 'What is Discrimination?' (2010) 38 *Philosophy & Public Affairs* 143, 175–76 (claiming that direct and indirect discrimination 'are forms of the same thing, the same kind of injustice').

[3] Benjamin Eidelson, *Discrimination and Disrespect* (Oxford, Oxford University Press, 2015) 6, 39–40; John Gardner, 'On the Ground of her Sex(uality)' (1998) 18 *OJLS* 167, 182–83; Larry Alexander, 'What Makes Wrongful Discrimination Wrong? Biases, Preferences, Stereotypes and Proxies' (1992) 141 *University of Pennsylvania Law Review* 149, 212–16.

that legal prohibitions on indirect discrimination are nevertheless justified.[4] However, the reason they believe prohibitions on indirect discrimination are justified is that these prohibitions produce good social consequences rather than because so-called 'indirect discrimination' wrongs its victims.[5]

Both camps are fusing together two distinct questions. First, are direct and indirect discrimination meaningfully different? Second, does indirect discrimination wrong its victims? For example, Tarun Khaitan argues that because both direct and indirect discrimination can exacerbate pervasive disadvantage, both can wrong the people affected because such pervasive disadvantage interferes with the ability of members of protected groups to enjoy genuine freedom.[6] In contrast, scholars who see a real difference between direct and indirect discrimination tend to think that instances of direct discrimination can wrong the victim while indirect discrimination is justifiably prohibited (if it is at all) only on grounds of distributive justice. For example, Benjamin Eidelson argues that indirect discrimination 'can best be understood as redistributive programs that commandeer employers (and others) as partners in an effort to equalize opportunity for members of systemically disadvantaged groups'.[7] Into this terrain, this chapter offers an alternative account. In what follows, I argue that indirect discrimination can wrong its victims but not because the distinction between direct and indirect discrimination breaks down. Instead, I suggest that some indirect discrimination wrongs its victims because it compounds injustice. On this view, the distinction between direct and indirect discrimination retains its moral significance and yet some indirect discrimination constitutes a moral wrong.

The aims of this chapter are to illustrate this third way of understanding indirect discrimination and to show its initial plausibility. The account will surely generate further questions that will require additional consideration. The view that indirect discrimination is sometimes wrong because it compounds injustice animates early disparate impact cases in the United States.[8] For example, in *Local 189, United Papermakers v United States*,[9] a Fifth Circuit case from 1969, the court prohibited the use of a seniority system that effectively kept African-Americans from better paying jobs

[4] Eidelson, ibid 6, 39–40; Gardner, ibid 182–83.

[5] Eidelson, ibid, 6, 67–68 (referring to laws which prohibit indirect discrimination as 'redistributive programs'). Alexander, however, has the contrary view. Alexander (n 3) 212–16.

[6] Khaitan (n 2) 159–60.

[7] Eidelson (n 3) 68.

[8] I use the terms 'indirect discrimination' and 'disparate impact discrimination' interchangeably. They both refer to a claim in which the fact that a law or policy has a negative disparate impact on a protected group shifts the burden to the other party to offer a justification for the negative impact. If one is lacking or insufficient, the law or policy constitutes discrimination. That said, the claim is more robust in some jurisdictions than others. In the United States, in particular, Michael Selmi documents that disparate impact liability has had only marginal impact. See Michael Selmi, 'Was Disparate Impact Theory a Mistake?' (2001) 53 *UCLA Law Review* 701, 704–06.

[9] *Local 189, United Papermakers v United States* 416 F.2d 980 (5th Cir 1969).

within the company by reasoning that '[w]hen an employer adopts a system that necessarily carries forward the incidents of discrimination into the present, his practice constitutes on-going discrimination, unless the incidents are limited to those that safety and efficiency require'.[10] My account develops what I think is a common intuition about the wrong that indirect discrimination laws seek to prohibit. Yet while the intuition may be common, its philosophical examination and defence appear to be absent. This chapter attempts to fill that void.

In what follows, I begin by arguing for a duty to avoid compounding injustice. Next, I turn to indirect discrimination and suggest that some paradigm cases of indirect discrimination involve the wrong of compounding injustice. Finally, I explore whether this account provides a reason to describe the wrong at issue as either 'indirect discrimination' or 'disparate impact discrimination'.

II. THE DUTY TO AVOID COMPOUNDING INJUSTICE

We live in an imperfect world in which people often treat others badly in ways that wrong those affected. When we interact with people who have been the victims of wrongdoing, does the fact that they have been wronged by others affect our obligations to these victims? Our obligations could be affected in (at least) two distinct ways. First, the fact that people have been wronged by others may give us positive obligations to them—obligations over and above what we owe to all people. For example, perhaps the fact that someone is a victim of wrongdoing provides special obligations to aid this person. Relatedly, the fact that a person has been a victim of wrongdoing may provide the government (or community) with an obligation to vindicate her rights by finding and punishing the wrongdoer. Second, the fact that someone has been a victim of wrongdoing may limit our freedom of action when we interact with him or her. Whether this is the case is the question I explore here. In particular, does a person have a duty to refrain from compounding the prior injustice?

What do I mean by 'compounding' the prior injustice? I am thinking here of an action that exacerbates the harm caused by the prior injustice because it entrenches the harm or carries it into another domain. The question is whether a person has an obligation not to do that. We should note, at the outset, that the mere fact that the action we are evaluating will harm someone isn't a sufficient reason to conclude that one ought not to do it. Our actions often harm others and yet are permitted. I hire Adam rather than Beth for a job because Adam has qualifications that Beth does not.

[10] ibid, 984.

This action harms Beth. A law school admits Carol because she has high grades and denies admission to David because his are lower. This action harms David. I open a store across the street from yours and thereby diminish your profits, which harms you. In each of these cases, and myriad others, people take actions which harm the interests of others. The mere fact that someone will be harmed is not enough, in many cases, to constrain the actor's liberty to conduct his or her business as he or she sees fit.

Other times, an action causes harm and is wrong, at least in part, because of the harm it causes. If Edith punches Frank in the nose, she wrongs him. In order to explore whether compounding injustice could make an action wrong, we should focus on those cases in which the actor is otherwise permitted to cause the harm. If we start with these cases and then add to these cases the additional factor that the person who will suffer the harm was a victim of injustice previously, we will be able to isolate whether this factor—that the person harmed is a victim of injustice—makes a moral difference, and if so, when and why.

The intuition behind President Johnson's remarks is that sometimes it does. In what follows, I explore the claim that the actor has a special reason to avoid harming a victim of injustice when her actions would constitute compounding injustice. I begin with two examples that I hope will show the intuitive appeal of the idea.

A. Case 1: *Early Release*

Suppose a state, in an effort to reduce its prison population, decides to release prisoners who have completed at least half of their sentences and who are determined, based on evidence-based, validated criteria, to be at low risk of recidivism. Suppose further that one highly predictive factor of whether the inmate will in fact recidivate is whether he was a victim of child abuse when he was a child. Should the state take into account the fact that these inmates were themselves victims in deciding whether or not to include this factor among the risk factors used to assess whom to release?

My intuition, which I hope the reader shares, is that the state has a strong reason not to disadvantage abuse victims relative to other prisoners when determining whom to release early. Why not? I want to suggest that a state should be reluctant to do so because it would be sufficiently implicated in carrying forward the prior injustice to make the state partially responsible for the latter harms caused by the original injustice. What were merely harms caused by the state's action are thus transformed into wrongs because the state takes on the wrong by carrying it forward in a particular way. To make it the case that the state is responsible for this latter harm and that this latter harm counts as part of the effect of the prior wrong that now is partially attributable to the state, the state must be sufficiently implicated and must carry forward the prior injustice.

I call the duty at issue here the duty not to 'compound' injustice because that word captures the two morally relevant facets of the later actor's involvement with the prior injustice. A 'compound'—understood as a noun, is a mixture or blend.[11] The actor must interact with the injustice or the effects of the injustice to bear some responsibility for it. Second, to 'compound', understood as a verb, is to increase or magnify.[12] In order to satisfy this element, the actor must not only harm the victim, she must amplify the original injustice or translate it into a new sphere. In this preliminary articulation of the idea that actors have a duty not to compound injustice, I hope only to show that there is such a duty. *Early Release* persuades you of that, I hope. And I want to identify the kinds of features that matter. Of course, further clarifying the nature of the involvement of the actor with the victim that is sufficient for compounding as mixing and of what types of augmentation or of carrying the harm into another domain count as compounding as amplification will be necessary to complete this account.

Let's return to *Early Release* and examine each of these features. In this case, the state interacts sufficiently with the victim by using his status as a victim of injustice in setting release policy. It adopts a policy that determines whether the victim will be in prison or out based on the victim's having suffered the prior injustice. In other words, the state takes the fact of the prior abuse, or its effects, as its reason not to release these prisoners early. Second, the state carries that injustice forward because it is the fact that the prisoner was a victim of wrongdoing that makes him likely to recidivate (or so we suppose). The prior injustice not only harmed the child victim, it also damages the adult he later became by making him more prone to aggression than the average person. If this fact about the adult prisoner is what determines whether or not he is released from prison, the state amplifies the prior injustice by making it relevant to the prisoner's treatment today.

Perhaps *Early Release* is an easy case because the state is the actor and one might think that the state has special obligations to victims of crime that private actors do not have. After all, the state asserts the exclusive right to punish crime, and to vindicate the wrong done to the victim. In so doing, it may incur an obligation to acknowledge and recognise the wrong done to the victim in a manner that *Early Release* negates. A release policy based on a prisoner's prior status as a victim of a crime seems to deny the relevant recognition and to trivialise the prior wrongdoing.[13]

To avoid this complication, consider the following case.

[11] 'Compound' in *The New Oxford American Dictionary* 2nd edn (Oxford, Oxford University Press, 2005) ('a thing that is composed of two or more separate elements; a mixture').

[12] ibid ('Make (something bad) worse; intensify the negative aspects of').

[13] This argument is analogous to the argument that scientists today should not use data from morally suspect medical experiments because it denigrates the victims of these experiments and the wrong done to them. See eg Kristine Moe, 'Should the Nazi Research Data Be Cited?' (1984) 14 *Hastings Ctr Rep* 5, 7 (arguing that '[a] decision to use the data should not be made without regret or without acknowledging the incomprehensible horror that produced them. We cannot imply any approval of the methods').

B. Case 2: *Insuring Battered Women*

Life insurers use a variety of factors to determine what price to charge a person applying for life insurance. Age is one important factor but insurers also try to determine whether a particular purchaser is likely to die earlier than the average person of the same age. In doing so, a person's status as a victim of domestic abuse is relevant. Battered women are likely to die earlier than the average women of the same age. This is true whether the woman stays with or leaves the batterer. Should the insurance company take into account the fact that battered women are victims of wrongdoing when determining whether to include this relevant risk factor?

The insurer, in the normal case, is permitted to consider the likelihood that an insured will die early when offering or pricing life insurance, or so I assume. But is *Insuring Battered Women* different? Does the insurer wrong the battered woman if it charges her a premium for life insurance? If the insurer charges the battered woman a higher rate, it uses the fact that domestic abuse victims are likely to be attacked in the future in making its pricing decisions. Just as in *Early Release*, the effects of the wrongdoing are precisely the facts that the insurer relies on in making its decision. As a result, the insurer bears some responsibility for the effects of the original injustice because the insurer takes the injustice or its effects as a reason to charge battered women higher rates. In addition, the insurer amplifies the original injustice because the harms caused by the battery now include not only the physical and mental suffering caused by domestic violence but also the economic loss of high priced insurance. For these reasons, the insurer who charges the abuse victim a premium for life insurance compounds the prior injustice.

Before proceeding, I want to emphasise three features of these two examples. First, in each, I am assuming that the actor (the state, the insurer) is not responsible for the initial wrong that has been done to the victim. Any responsibility that the actor may have not to harm the victim is not the responsibility to fix a problem one created. Second, in each I assume that the actor would be permitted to harm the victim were it not for the possible significance of the fact that person harmed is a victim of prior wrongdoing. So, I assume that the state may adopt criteria governing whom to release early from prison according to which some will benefit while others will not. And, I assume that life insurers may charge potential insurance purchasers different rates depending on their likelihood of dying during the policy period. Third, while some of the cases involve differentiating between people on the basis of some trait (being a victim of abuse), these cases are not offered as examples of discrimination or with the goal of examining when discrimination is wrong. Rather I offer them as examples of instances where there is a duty not to compound injustice.

Having sketched what I hope are plausible examples of cases of compounding injustice, I want to offer some limiting cases that help to further define the two aspects of compounding. These cases are similar to the first two in the following ways. In each, the actor harms someone who is a victim of a prior injustice. Additionally, the actor is under no duty not to harm the victim in the particular way considered, unless the fact that the victim suffered a prior injustice changes the situation in some relevant respect.

C. Case 3: *Trigger Warning*

A college professor of English literature is aware that a small number of her students are likely to have been victims of sexual assault. The professor is planning to assign a book for the class that contains a graphic rape scene. Does the fact that some students are likely to have been the victims of prior wrongdoing provide a reason to alert the students about the content in the book they will read? In particular, is this a reason distinct and additional to any reason that might arise from the mere fact that some students would be upset by the material, even though they are not themselves victims?

If the professor assigns the book containing the rape scene and does not issue a warning, she risks harming a student who was previously a victim of sexual assault, if reading the book without notice causes the victim to relive the experience.[14] As issuing a warning may seem a fairly easy thing to do, with little negative consequence, one might think that a professor should always issue such warnings. The cases I am trying to focus on are ones in which the actor is not required to do the act in question because of the harm the action is likely to cause (so that we can tease out the significance of the fact that the person affected was a victim of prior injustice). For that reason, let's suppose that providing the warning makes the book less effective as a piece of literature. The professor thus has a good reason to avoid giving the warning. Or suppose that the routine provision of such warnings is bad for the mental health of students generally because it cultivates an emotional vulnerability that makes it difficult for them to weather life's challenges. In other words, suppose that the reasons the professor has to refrain from warning students about the rape scene outweigh the reasons to give the warning unless, perhaps, the professor will be compounding injustice. Will she be?

[14] If reliving the experience in a safe environment helps the student to recover from the trauma of the prior assault, then the teacher may be helping the student rather than harming her. In the example, I will simply assume that reading the rape scene unprepared (without a warning) will harm the student.

In this case, the professor's action satisfies the second element of compounding injustice—amplification of the prior injustice. The victim of the prior assault suffers anew when the teacher assigns the material. What is missing however, is sufficient engagement with prior injustice (the mixing element). The victim of the prior assault may well suffer when reading the book as a result of the injustice she suffered originally. But in order for the professor to implicate herself in the prior injustice such that she bears a responsibility for carrying it forward, the fact that the student was a victim of prior injustice must be part of the reason the professor assigns the reading. Because it is not, the professor does not compound the prior injustice.

In *Early Release*, by contrast, the state's release policy sorts prisoners in part on the basis of the fact that some were victims of abuse as children. The prior injustice, or its effects, are part of the reason for the state's action. *Insuring Battered Women* is similar. The insurer charges higher rates to abuse victims. In adopting this policy, the insurer takes the fact that someone has suffered an injustice as a reason to perform an action that will further harm that person. This compounding of injustice converts the harm of higher rates into a wrong.

Consider one more case that helps to clarify this element.

D. Case 4: *Market Competition*

Suppose you are considering opening a craft store on the same street as another craft store. Lately, that store has been poorly stocked, leading to complaints you've heard around town. Upon investigation, you learn that the store has been the victim of a robbery during which most of its merchandise was stolen. The owner of the store has filed an insurance claim and is awaiting payment from his insurance company, but in the meantime does not have the funds to continue to keep the store adequately stocked. This would thus be an opportune time for you to open a competing store. Should you take the fact that the owner of your would-be competitor has been robbed into account in determining whether you should open a new store now?

In *Market Competition*, you would certainly amplify the prior injustice if you open your store now. But would this harm wrong the victim because you would be compounding the prior injustice? The answer depends on whether you take the fact that the owner was robbed as a reason to open your store now. Posing that question in the context of *Market Competition* allows us to see an ambiguity that needs further clarification. In particular, perhaps we could say that you open the store now because your competitor has low stock rather than that you open the store now because the competitor was robbed? Does this make a difference? In fact, one might make a similar move in both *Early Release* and *Insuring Battered Women*. Perhaps the state declines to release the victims of child abuse because they are likely to recidivate not because they are abuse victims. Similarly, the insurer charges higher rates to abuse victims because they are more likely to die during the policy period rather than because they were battered. Admittedly, in these two cases, the state and insurer directly uses the fact of prior victimisation as its sorting device while in *Market Competition*, you take the low stock of the competitor as your reason for action rather than specifically the fact that he was robbed. Nevertheless, in each of these cases, the injustice or its direct effects are the reason each actor acts. In my view, this is enough for the actor to bear responsibility for compounding the injustice.

Compare two versions of *Market Competition*. In the first, you had planned to open the store later but decide instead to open the store now because your competitor has low stock now due to a robbery. In the second, you had planned to open the store now and just as you are about to do so you learn that your competitor has been robbed (and so has low stock). In the second version, you do not compound the injustice (even though the harm of the robbery is amplified) because you do not take either the prior injustice or its effects as reasons for opening the store now. By contrast, in the first version you do. This incorporation of the effects of the injustice into your calculation implicates you in the wrongdoing and makes it in part your own.

Trigger Warning lacks this element. The teacher assigns the book because it has literary value. Her decision to assign it in no way reacts to the effect of the prior injustice. While the prior injustice causes some students to be vulnerable, the teacher's actions make no use of this vulnerability and therefore do not compound it. The suffering of the victim is an unfortunate effect of the teacher's pedagogical choices but it is not a reason for these choices. Because the teacher doesn't use the effect of the prior injustice, she doesn't carry it forward sufficiently for her action to count as compounding injustice.

While readers may react differently to these cases, I hope that my descriptions of them have been adequate to establish the following claims. First, sometimes an actor has a reason to refrain from actions that would compound a prior injustice suffered by a victim of wrongdoing. This reason, when it exists, adds to the balance of reasons an actor should weigh in deciding what she is permitted to do. However, not all actions that an actor takes that harm a victim of prior injustice count as *compounding that injustice*. Which do and which do not is a difficult line to draw. Through the cases discussed above, I have suggested that the actor must amplify the prior injustice either by making the harm caused by the prior injustice worse or by causing it to lead to a new harm in another sphere of life. Second—and this is the key element—the actor must take the prior injustice or its effects as her reason for action. When these elements are satisfied, the actor compounds the prior injustice.

The fact that the actor would compound injustice provides the actor with a reason not to do the proposed action. This is significant because in these cases the actor is not responsible for the original injustice. Nor does she have a special responsibility to remedy it, though she may have obligations as a member of society or of the political community to help the victim and to prosecute and punish the wrongdoer. The argument presented here shows, however, that she does have a responsibility to avoid making the effects of the prior wrongdoing worse when she involves herself in such a way that she participates in carrying that injustice forward.

The claim that one should avoid compounding injustice might seem troubling. If the argument so far presented is correct, the original wrongdoers (the child-abuser and the batterer, for example) not only wrong the original victim, they also constrain the freedom of action of later actors. After all, the cases we have been considering are ones in which the action at issue would have been permissible, all things considered, if those negatively affected were not the victims of injustice (or so I have assumed). As a result, the fact that the wrongdoer wrongs a victim at time T1 affects not only the victim but also later actors. Should this trouble us?

It is unfortunate, to be sure. The wrongdoer succeeds in wronging not only his direct victim but also others by imposing additional obligations on them. However, this is not surprising. Compare the cases we have been discussing to the case in which an assailant attacks someone and injures her in such a way that she requires special care. In such a case, family members will now have additional obligations of care that they did not have previously. Wrongdoing often imposes on a wider circle of people than those most immediately and directly affected.

This section has argued for the plausibility of a duty to avoid compounding injustice. This duty provides a reason to avoid harming someone who has already been victimised. The duty applies only when an actor would compound that injustice by her actions. To compound injustice, an actor must amplify the harm of the prior injustice and must take the fact of victimisation or its effects as her reason for acting. When these two elements are present, the actor compounds the prior injustice. Unless there are countervailing reasons supporting the action, the actor who compounds injustice wrongs the victim.

III. DOES INDIRECT DISCRIMINATION COMPOUND INJUSTICE?

Now that we have a clearer idea when actions compound injustice, I will suggest that some instances of indirect discrimination compound injustice. This fact provides a reason to avoid these actions. The reason isn't decisive, but the fact that an action will compound injustice provides a strong reason to avoid it. While not all instances of indirect discrimination compound injustice, paradigmatic instances of indirect discrimination do so. Moreover, I think the fact that the disputed action compounds injustice captures common intuitions about why such actions should be prohibited.

Consider the following hypothetical case of indirect discrimination which I will term *classic disparate impact*. I use the description 'classic' for this case and the variations on it discussed below because these are the sorts of cases we often have in mind when we think of indirect discrimination.[15]

A. *Classic Disparate Impact*

A company maintained segregated job categories. Some jobs within the company were open to white workers and others to African-American workers. The 'white' jobs were better paid and more skilled than the 'black' jobs. There is a line of progression in each job type. The whites advanced along the progressions in white jobs and the blacks along the progression in black jobs. When this segregation of job categories is no longer legally permitted, the company stops segregating job categories and opens all jobs to people of all races. However, the company maintains its seniority policy which provides that when an opening in a particular job arises, candidates with the most seniority in the particular job type are favoured. The result of maintaining this seniority policy is that black workers with many years at the firm are never considered for anything other than entry level jobs in the previously white job types.[16] The seniority policy produces a disparate impact on black workers because they lack seniority in the more desirable white job categories and thus lose out to white workers with experience in the particular job type.

The decision of the company to maintain its seniority policy compounds the prior race discrimination. The black workers have suffered the prior injustice of being excluded from white jobs. As a result, they lack the requisite qualifications for the previously white jobs (except the entry-level position in each job type). The employer compounds the prior injustice by using a policy that carries that prior injustice forward. (Admittedly, the employer itself caused this prior injustice—an exacerbating factor that I will disaggregate below.) This decision to retain the seniority policy counts as compounding injustice because the employer amplifies the harm of prior exclusion from particular jobs by carrying that harm into the current time period and because the employer uses the lack of seniority in job type (which is the

[15] Cases like the classic hypotheticals discussed in the paper are also the sort of cases that gave rise to disparate impact liability in the United States. See *Griggs v Duke Power Co*, 401 US 424 (1971); *United Papermakers* (n 9).

[16] This hypothetical is based on *United Papermakers* (n 9).

effect of the prior injustice) to decide whom to promote. As a result, this policy wrongs those affected.

There are, of course, other bases on which to conclude that maintaining the seniority system wrongs the black workers. For example, one could argue that the decision to keep the seniority system in full awareness of its racially disproportionate impact constitutes intentional direct discrimination.[17] My point here is to suggest that a powerful and intuitive reason to think that the employer's maintenance of the old seniority system, while facially neutral, nevertheless wrongs the black workers disadvantaged by this policy lies in the fact that it compounds the prior injustice they have suffered. Indeed, this is, in large part, how the court that decided the real case on which the hypothetical is constructed understood the case:

> Every time a Negro worker hired under the old segregated system bids against a white worker in his job slot, the old racial classification reasserts itself, and the Negro suffers anew for his employer's previous bias. It is not decisive therefore that a seniority system may appear neutral on its face if the inevitable effect of tying the system to the *past* is to cut into the employees *present* right not to be discriminated against on the ground of race.[18]

According to the court, the fact that the employer adopted a policy which made the black worker 'suffer anew' for the previous injustice led to the conclusion that the policy was unlawful because 'by carrying forward the effects of former discriminatory practices the system results in present and future discrimination'.[19]

In the above example, the employer is especially responsible because the original injustice that the employer carries forward is its own prior discriminatory segregation of job categories. However, as we saw in the prior section, actors have a responsibility not to carry injustice forward even when the original injustice is not of their own making. Actual disparate impact cases often have this structure. Consider the following example.

B. *Classic Disparate Impact (2)*

In the selection process for civil service jobs, a state gives veterans a substantial preference. This procedure is put in place at a time when very few veterans are women because most military positions are not open to women. As a result, almost all civil service jobs are filled by men.[20]

[17] Michael Selmi makes this argument. See Selmi (n 8) 712–14.

[18] *United Papermakers* (n 9) 988.

[19] ibid 983.

[20] This hypothetical is loosely based on *Personnel Administrators of Mass v Feeney* 442 US 256 (1979), 278–81. In *Feeney*, the US Supreme Court held that the disparate impact of this policy on women was insufficient to constitute a violation of the equal protection clause without evidence of a specific intent to exclude women from these jobs. The argument presented in this Chapter suggests that this decision was wrong.

Here the fact that women were excluded from serving in many positions in the military was an injustice, but not an injustice for which the particular state is responsible. Rather the restriction on women serving in most military positions results from national policies. If the distinction between the local and the national arm of the government does not feel distinct enough, imagine instead that a private employer uses the same veteran's preference.

In my view, *Classic Disparate Impact (2)* also compounds injustice. The state or private employer compounds the injustice of the national government's exclusion of women from most military jobs because the state or private employer amplifies the harm of exclusion from military service and because it uses the applicant's status as a veteran or non-veteran to determine, at least in part, whom to hire. For those women who would have been veterans but for the unjust federal policy, the employer carries forward that injustice. While there are surely important reasons to help veterans reenter the civilian job market that count in favour of such a policy, the fact that the policy compounds the original injustice of excluding women from the military is a reason that counts against the adoption of this policy.[21]

However in *Classic Disparate Impact (2)*, not all of those affected by the policy are themselves victims of injustice. Some female non-veteran job seekers would not have chosen to enter the military had more jobs been open to women. The fact that these job-seekers are not veterans thus does not result from injustice. Does this matter? In *Early Release* and *Insuring Battered Women*, the actor used the person's status as an abuse victim to determine who would be denied release or denied insurance/charged higher rates and so everyone negatively affected by the challenged policy was him or herself a victim of prior injustice (or so it seemed). Not so in *Classic Disparate Impact (2)*. In order to sharpen this challenge and consider the sort of case that is more common today, consider the following hypothetical case.

C. *Classic Disparate Impact (3)*

A company uses a standardised test to select employees, alone or in combination with other factors. Members of disadvantaged racial minority groups disproportionately score poorly on the exam. As a result, the employees hired or promoted are disproportionately members of privileged racial or ethnic groups.

Is *Classic Disparate Impact (3)* an example of compounding injustice? I think it is, so long as a few plausible assumptions are made. First, it must be likely that members of the disadvantaged group are victims of prior injustice

[21] The Court in *Feeney* would have been unlikely at that time to treat the exclusion of women from many military roles as itself an injustice and so this line of reasoning would have been unlikely to be successful.

and in particular an injustice that has led them to score less well on the standardised test. These assumptions seems plausible if segregated schools and neighbourhoods lead to poorer education, less social capital, fewer role models, less wealth, etc. Because education is a positional good such that to succeed one must not only be qualified but more qualified than those with whom one competes, the effect of past injustice regarding the acquisition of wealth and education continue to produce disadvantage today.[22] The results of a legacy of discrimination have consequences today and those consequences are that minority job applicants are often less qualified than more advantaged counterparts.

However, not all poorly qualified, minority job-seekers are less qualified because of prior injustice. Some minority applicants who scored poorly may have grown up in integrated neighbourhoods and gone to good schools, etc. Does this lack of a perfect correlation between being a victim of prior injustice and scoring poorly on the standardised test weaken or eviscerate the argument that the employer has an obligation to avoid using the test so as not to compound injustice? While use of the test may compound injustice as to some test-takers, it does not do so for all.

In each of the *Classic Disparate Impact* cases, the group protected by a theory of disparate impact liability (racial minorities and women) is correlated with the group of people likely to have suffered a particular injustice, but the fit between the proxy (race and sex) and the target (victim of injustice) is inexact. In my view, as long as the fit between the proxy and target is relatively strong, the lack of a perfect fit is not a problem. In the real world, we are always dealing with approximations. Those prisoners who are categorised as victims of childhood abuse (in *Early Release*) may include some people who were not really abused as children. The trait—categorised as a victim of sexual abuse—is itself only a proxy for the target trait—actual victim of sexual abuse.[23] Perhaps one person made the story up because he thought it would elicit sympathy from the judge and entitle him to a more lenient sentence. If this prisoner is denied early release in part because he is listed as someone who was abused as a child, this action does not compound injustice *in his case*.

The fact that being a racial minority or a woman is only a proxy for being a victim of injustice is not itself a problem. Being categorised as having

[22] Joseph Fishkin, *Bottlenecks: A New Theory of Economic Opportunity* (Oxford, Oxford University Press, 2014) 142 (discussing education as a positional good). This example raises the question whether the injustice at issue can be a distributive injustice or whether the account is limited to the duty to avoid compounding corrective injustice. This question requires further consideration.

[23] Fred Schauer emphasises the way in which all categories involve generalisations in just this way. Frederick Schauer, *Profiles, Probabilities and Stereotypes* (Cambridge MA, Harvard University Press, 2003) 9–11.

been a victim of injustice is also only a proxy for actually being a victim of injustice too. Proxies are usually all we have. What does matter, however, is the degree of fit between the proxy trait and the target trait. It is likely that most prisoners categorised as having been victims of child sexual abuse really were victims of such abuse. It is likely that most women whom the insurance company determines are victims of domestic battery are actually victims of such battery. If the logic of disparate impact liability is grounded in the moral duty to avoid compounding injustice, race and sex and other protected traits must be reasonably good proxies for actually having been the victim of injustice. The fit is likely less tight in *Classic Disparate Impact (3)* than in *Early Release*, for example. But if not being a perfect fit is not disqualifying—because in the real world in which we assess our moral obligations, we must always operate on the basis of likelihoods—then I think the best answer is that the strength of the reason to avoid the action depends, at least in part, on the likely strength of the correlation between members of the protected group and victims of injustice.

IV. IS INDIRECT DISCRIMINATION A FORM OF DISCRIMINATION?

I have described the wrong of indirect discrimination as the wrong of compounding injustice. I also described cases of compounding injustice that are not instances of indirect discrimination. *Early Release* and *Insuring Battered Women* are good examples, (though *Insuring Battered Women* could also be redescribed to emphasise that the insurer's policy produces a disparate impact on women). If indirect discrimination is wrong when and because it compounds injustice and compounding injustice is a more general category that occurs even when indirect discrimination is nowhere in sight, then perhaps we shouldn't call this wrong 'indirect discrimination' or 'disparate impact discrimination'.[24] What makes such cases instances of *discrimination*?

In my view, the terminology is not as inapt as it first appears. The wrong of compounding injustice includes the wrongs of compounding different forms of injustice. Sometimes the original wrong is child sex abuse; *Early Release* compounds that wrong. Other times the original wrong is discrimination; the *Classic cases* compound that wrong. When the wrong that is compounded is the wrong of discrimination, then describing this wrong using the composite term 'indirect discrimination' or 'disparate impact discrimination' captures something important about what occurs. Moreover, other forms of wrongdoing, like child sex abuse, are individual occurrences

[24] Eidelson argues that is confusing to do so. Eidelson (n 3) 45.

which are unrelated to one another. There is thus no need for a term that captures the wrong of compounding that injustice. While 'indirect sex abuse' may describe what occurs in such a context, there is no social need for an amalgamating term, so it hasn't evolved. But discrimination is different. I must tread carefully here because different theorists have different views about what direct discrimination is and what makes it wrong and the aim of this paper is to say something about indirect discrimination that skirts, to the extent possible, engaging with this debate.[25] Still, we can all agree, I hope, that discrimination has a systemic quality. Race and sex discrimination, to pick out two central examples, are characterised by their linkages to other instances of race and sex discrimination.[26] Because the wrong of discrimination necessarily occurs, or by happenstance simply has occurred (depending on one's view), in this systemic way, it is unsurprising that the wrong of compounding this injustice has been frequent and recognisable enough to generate a particular term to describe it. Whether we call it 'indirect discrimination', 'disparate impact discrimination' or, perhaps, 'compounded discrimination'—to coin a term that captures the account presented here—its connection to the primary wrong of discrimination is close enough to warrant such a descriptor.

The account I have offered describes indirect discrimination as wrong because it compounds the wrong of discrimination. However, not all instances of indirect discrimination often forbidden by statute compound the wrong of discrimination. I have argued that classic instances of indirect discrimination do fit this account. By doing so, I hope to have shown that the heart of indirect discrimination rests on the duty to avoid compounding injustice.

But what should we say about those instances of indirect discrimination that are forbidden by statute but which this account provides no justification for? These legal prohibitions are not justified by the duty to avoid compounding injustice. For example, a prohibition on laws and policies that

[25] For those who see prohibitions on direct discrimination as grounded in protecting the freedom of those groups of people for whom systematic disadvantage has constrained their opportunities, indirect discrimination is grounded in the same way as direct discrimination. See Khaitan (n 2) 18, 159–60. Oran Doyle argues, I think correctly, that on this sort of account, indirect discrimination may well be more central than direct discrimination. Oran Doyle, 'Direct Discrimination, Indirect Discrimination and Autonomy' (2007) 27 *OJLS* 537, 538, 550–53.

[26] My own view makes this fact important and salient. Discrimination is wrong, on my view, when it is demeaning. To demean is to express that the other person is of lower status in a context where the person or entity expressing this message has a degree of actual power. Laws and policies that classify on the basis of race or sex, for example, have more demeaning potential because the history of the mistreatment of racial minorities and women gives a social meaning to such classifications that is lacking in the case of more idiosyncratic distinctions. See Deborah Hellman, *What Makes Discrimination Wrong?* (Cambridge MA, Harvard University Press, 2008).

produce a disparate impact on whites or men is unlikely to be justified by this account. In addition, and more controversially, not all policies that produce a disparate impact on previously disadvantaged groups will compound injustice. This is so because the account presented here requires not only that the group affected have suffered injustice but also that the policy at issue compound *that* injustice. As a result, the account might not justify the application of indirect discrimination law in the case of *Naeem v Secretary of State for Justice*,[27] a companion case to *Essop and others (Appellants) v Home Office*.[28] In *Naeem*, Lady Hale upheld the application of the prohibition on indirect discrimination to a policy of the Prison Service that determined the pay of prison clergy by seniority. This policy disadvantaged Muslim clerics who had less seniority than other clerics because in prior years the 'Prison Service believed that there were not enough Muslim prisoners to justify employing them on a salaried basis.'[29] What is missing from the decision is a finding of whether that belief was accurate. If the Prison Service had not previously hired full time Muslim clerics because there was genuinely little need due to there being few Muslim prisoners (not itself an injustice), then the decision in *Naeem* would not be justified by this account. If, however, the Prison Service did not hire Muslim clerics earlier despite the presence of Muslim prisoners in need of their services, then the pay policy would compound that injustice and thus the decision in *Naeem* would be justified by this account.

I began this chapter by noting that scholars' treatment of indirect discrimination falls into one of two camps. On one side are those who believe that there is no meaningful difference between direct and indirect discrimination and that both types wrong their victims. On the other side are those who believe that direct and indirect discrimination are importantly different and that only direct discrimination constitutes a moral wrong. The account presented here provides a third view. Direct and indirect discrimination are conceptually different but some indirect discrimination wrongs its victims by compounding injustice. Thus, where the account applies, the law is justified by the duty to avoid compounding injustice. However, where the account does not apply, the laws are not justified on this ground but may be justified nevertheless as good social policy.

27 *Essop v Home Office*, (2017) UKSC 27, (2017) 1 WLR 1343.
28 ibid.
29 *Naeem* (n 27) para 12.

6

The Moral Seriousness of Indirect Discrimination

SOPHIA MOREAU*

I. COMMON VIEWS ABOUT DIRECT AND INDIRECT DISCRIMINATION

TWENTY YEARS AGO, Canadian equality rights activists Sheilagh Day and Gwen Brodsky criticised the widespread belief that there are deep moral differences between direct and indirect discrimination. Many people, they noted, assume 'that direct discrimination is more loathsome, more morally repugnant' than indirect discrimination 'because the perpetrator *intends* to discriminate or has discriminated *knowingly*.'[1] By contrast, they suggested, indirect discrimination, even when justifiably prohibited by law, is commonly held to be ''innocent,' unwitting, accidental, and consequently not morally repugnant.' These assumptions about direct and indirect discrimination are still very much a part of our shared moral thought about discrimination; and they also linger within anti-discrimination law itself, purporting to justify certain features of these laws. The aim of this chapter is to question these assumptions about the relative moral seriousness of the two forms of discrimination. I shall argue that indirect discrimination is often just as morally problematic as direct discrimination, and its agents often just as culpable.

But first, we need to look more closely at these assumptions. What is it, exactly, that we commonly assume? We tend to assume that agents involved in acts of wrongful direct discrimination are generally more culpable than those who discriminate indirectly, even in cases where we agree that the

* Earlier drafts of this paper were presented at the *Theory of Indirect Discrimination Law* Conference at Oxford in March, 2016; the 2016 *Politics, Philosophy and Economics* Conference; the Legal Philosophy Colloquium at UC Irvine; the Law and Philosophy Workshop at the University of Chicago, and the Law and Philosophy Workshop at Fordham School of Law. I am grateful to these audiences for helpful comments, and especially grateful to Tarun Khaitan, Debbie Hellman, Colm O'Cinneide, Ben Eidelson, Jeff Helmreich, Tom Christiano, Andrew Williams, Peter Vanderschraaf, Youngjae Lee, Arthur Ripstein and Ben Zipursky.

[1] Sheilagh Day and Gwen Brodsky, 'The Duty to Accommodate: Who Will Benefit?' (1996) 75 *The Canadian Bar Review* 433, both this and the next quotation at 457.

indirect discrimination can justifiably be prohibited by law, and even in cases where we agree that it is morally impermissible. This is a judgement about the *culpability of the agent.* We also assume that acts of direct discrimination are, when wrong, seriously problematic from a moral standpoint. By contrast, we are less certain about the moral status of acts and policies that indirectly discriminate. Even if we agree that a government is justified in legally prohibiting policies that are indirectly discriminatory, we may wonder whether the policies are all morally impermissible; and even when we view them as morally impermissible, we may feel that they are rarely *as bad as* most cases of wrongful direct discrimination. We would probably hesitate before ever calling any indirectly discriminatory policy 'morally repugnant'. This second set of judgements is about the *moral status of acts and policies.*

A set of parallel examples may help both to draw out these assumptions and to clarify the way in which the distinction between direct and indirect discrimination is commonly drawn. First, consider direct discrimination. In the UK, it is defined as an act or rule that treats one individual less favourably than another 'because of' a certain protected characteristic, such as race or sex or sexual orientation.[2] The most common way to demonstrate that such treatment has taken place 'because of' a protected characteristic is to show that the agent *intended* to distinguish between this individual and others using this characteristic; but in cases where intent is difficult to prove or where the agent has something closer to an unconscious bias against members of this group, it suffices under UK law to show that the category of the individuals who are disadvantaged and the category of those who are correlatively advantaged 'coincide exactly with the respective categories of persons distinguished only by applying a prohibited classification'.[3] In other words, direct discrimination seems to involve acts that—either consciously or unconsciously—aim at disadvantaging certain individuals because they possess or are presumed to possess a certain characteristic. It is natural therefore to assume that the agents of direct discrimination are culpable. Consider, for instance, a case of direct discrimination that arose recently in Canadian sports: the Quebec Soccer Federation's explicit ban on turbans on the soccer field. In the wake of this ban, the Federation was accused of racism and insensitivity. Because the ban singled out a particular garment from a particular religion, in circumstances where there were no reasons to think that the garment in any way impeded the game, it is difficult to see how the Federation could have been motivated by anything but a combination

[2] Equality Act 2010. This is admittedly a rather messy definition; but it is the legal definition, and since our concept of discrimination is so deeply shaped by our laws, I think it is appropriate to work with this definition rather than artificially imposing a more simplified one.

[3] As per Lady Hale in *Bull and Bull v Hall and Preddy* [2013] UKSC 73, [2013] 1 WLR 3741, citing with approval the EU interpretation of direct discrimination in Case C-73/08 *Bressol v Gouvernement de la Commaunité Française* [2010] 3 CMLR 559 and Case C-79/99 *Schnorbus v Land Hessen* [2000] ECR I-10997.

of religious and racial prejudice. Their aim was to exclude Sikhs from the soccer field, simply because they disliked them. The Federation therefore seemed morally culpable, and the policy, morally repugnant.

By contrast, policies that are indirectly discriminatory are often adopted in the service of perfectly innocent or even commendable goals, but end up having unfortunate side effects on groups that share a protected characteristic. A practice or a rule is treated as indirect discrimination under the law if it disadvantages those who share a particular protected characteristic, but disadvantages them only in an indirect way—that is, if there is not a complete coincidence between the group disadvantaged by the rule and the group marked out by some protected characteristic, but the rule nevertheless works to disadvantage *more* of those who possess that protected characteristic than it does others. In such cases, the agent may not have deliberately tried to disadvantage the group in question, and may not harbour any unconscious biases against them. And indirect discrimination is only prohibited under the law if it cannot be shown to be otherwise justifiable—that is, as the UK's Equality Act of 2010 states, if it cannot be shown to be 'a proportionate means of achieving a legitimate aim' In other words, there is often a good reason for acting in ways that disadvantage certain groups more than others, and it is only if that disadvantage seems, under the circumstances, to be excessive and unreasonable that the law treats the indirect discrimination as justifiably prohibited by law and potentially morally wrongful. Perhaps because indirect discrimination can occur without any overt or even unconscious prejudice on the part of the agent, and because there is usually some legitimate aim that the agent is acting in furtherance of, we tend to assume that agents who engage in indirect discrimination are less culpable, and their policies, less troubling.

Consider a case of indirect discrimination that is directly parallel to the above example of the Soccer Federation's ban on turbans. In the late 1980s, the Royal Canadian Mounted Police (RCMP) still had in place a policy requiring all officers to wear the 'Stetson hat' as part of their dress uniform. Eventually, members of the Sikh community protested that this prevented Sikhs from becoming RCMP officers. Although this policy had the same exclusionary effect on Sikhs as the soccer ban did, it fell into the category of indirect discrimination. It did not explicitly single out any one group on the basis of their religion or on the basis of some item necessarily associated with that religion. Instead, it had a disproportionately disadvantageous effect on Sikh men because of their religion—and, one might add, a similar effect on other people of both genders and of other races, whose religion or creed required them to wear some other headwear. Unlike the Soccer Federation, the RCMP was not vilified by the public for the Stetson hat policy. There was, to be sure, a heated debate over whether continuing to require the kind of hat that would exclude Sikhs from the RCMP was really a proportionate means of promoting Mountie traditions, and it was eventually decided that it was less important to preserve the image of the rugged Mountie in his cowboy hat and more important to increase accessibility. But no one arguing on the side of accessibility seemed to feel as though the character of the head RCMP officers was questionable or as though the policy was morally repugnant. This may have been in part because we can all recognise the reason-giving force of tradition, even though we differ in our assessments of its relative weight. So it seems plausible to suppose that RCMP officers were not actually motivated by a hatred of Sikhs or a desire to exclude them. They had just accorded greater importance to tradition and hadn't thought so much about the effects of the policy on anyone else, in their single-minded focus on preserving their own traditions. Moreover, although the policy had unfortunate and disadvantageous effects on Sikhs, one might argue that it did not insult or demean them in the way that the explicit ban on turbans by the Soccer Federation did—perhaps because it didn't single out turbans, but rather prevented everyone from wearing any other substantial headwear.

I have tried to shed some light on our moral intuitions about the two different forms of discrimination. But it is not only in our ordinary moral thought that indirect discrimination is regarded as importantly different from direct discrimination. In American law, and to some extent also in British law, cases of indirect discrimination are treated with a wariness that is not present in cases of direct discrimination—as though there is always a risk that indirect discrimination may (to borrow a distinction from Judith Shklar) parade as an 'injustice' when in fact it constitutes a mere 'misfortune', an unfortunate state of affairs in which someone suffers a disadvantage but has not thereby been wronged and has no special claim on anyone to rectify that disadvantage.[4] Under American constitutional law, courts cannot find a violation of the 14th Amendment on the basis of disparate impact: it is only disparate treatment, or direct discrimination, that is treated as violating an individual's right to equal treatment by the state. And although some statutes do prohibit disparate impact by private agents in certain contexts, such as employment and housing, these prohibitions are regarded in some circles with suspicion, as potentially violating the 14th Amendment themselves.[5] In Britain, indirect discrimination is treated as something that can and should be prohibited. But interestingly, the Court of Appeal recently placed

[4] See Judith Shklar, 'Misfortune and Injustice' in her *The Faces of Injustice* (New Haven, Yale University Press, 1990) 51. Shklar distinguished between an 'injustice', or a case in which one person has been wronged and has a claim on another person (or institution) to rectify that wrong, and a mere 'misfortune', or a case in which one person suffers a disadvantage but has no such claim on anyone else that they rectify it. Shklar did not discuss this distinction in the context of discrimination; but I think it captures quite well our worries about indirect discrimination.

[5] See, for instance, Richard Primus, 'The Future of Disparate Impact' (2010) 108 *Michigan Law Review* 1341.

additional explanatory burdens on alleged victims of indirect discrimination and expressed great concern over 'coat-tailers'—members of disadvantaged groups who pretend to be victims of indirect discrimination when in fact they have not suffered disadvantage, such as the childless golfer who complains about an inflexible working hours policy because it upsets her golfing schedule or the no-*kara* wearing Sikh steward who simply dislikes his airline's non-jewellery policy.[6] One might be forgiven for wondering why, given the plethora of women who are genuinely disadvantaged by inflexible working hours and the number of Sikhs who do wear karas, we are so worried about hypothetical pretenders taking advantage of honest employers. I think it is probably the same moral intuitions at work here as we saw in my earlier examples of the direct and indirect exclusion of Sikhs. We tend to view the alleged discriminator in cases of indirect discrimination as essentially well-motivated and free of culpability, contributing to the disadvantage of others only accidentally; we view the policies as not intrinsically insulting or degrading; and we see that the disadvantages accrue to members of the minority groups not just because of the policies but also because of the unusual needs or habits of these minority groups. And so legal prohibitions on indirect discrimination seem to teeter dangerously on the edge of forcing innocent agents to subsidise the idiosyncratic needs or lifestyle choices of others.

As a Canadian, I confess to feeling some puzzlement, both at the depth of the mistrust of indirect discrimination in American and British law, and at the moral intuitions about direct and indirect discrimination that I have just tried to explain to you. In Canada, the idea that we can usefully draw a moral—or, for that matter, a meaningful conceptual—distinction between direct and indirect discrimination was rejected by our Supreme Court a few years after Day and Brodsky wrote the article that I began with.[7] Perhaps for this reason, and perhaps also because our Constitution grants explicit protection to affirmative action measures and our human rights statutes give tribunals quite extensive powers to impose very intrusive measures on private organisations to rectify unintentional disadvantages experienced by minority groups, Canadians are not now so suspicious of attempts to redress indirect discrimination. We are more used to thinking that there *is* something morally troubling about continuing to act in ways that disproportionately disadvantage certain historically stigmatised and underprivileged groups, regardless of the aims or intentions of the agent. I shall try, in the rest of this chapter, to explore what this might be, and to answer some objections that might be made by those of you who think firmly that direct and indirect discrimination should be treated as morally different.

[6] *Home Office (UK Border Agency) v Essop* [2015] EWCA Civ 609, [2016] 3 All ER 137.

[7] See *British Columbia (Public Service Employee Relations Commission) v British Columbia Government Service Employees' Union* [1999] 3 SCR 3.

The argument of the chapter runs as follows. In section II, I will look closely at a number of core cases of indirect discrimination, cases that are commonly prohibited by law. I will try to show that the agents in these cases are not plausibly thought of as lacking in culpability, and that the policies do seem morally problematic. Section III of the chapter considers several general principles that someone might use to try to explain why acts of direct discrimination are generally more troubling from a moral standpoint than acts of indirect discrimination. I shall argue that on closer inspection, each of these principles appears inadequate. In section IV of the paper, I use the analyses of section II and III to suggest that we can see both direct and indirect discrimination as involving a kind of negligence. I hope through these arguments to suggest that the picture we initially began with, of a deep moral difference between these two forms of discrimination, is mistaken.

Before I begin, however, I want to say something about my strategy in this chapter. It might seem that an argument purporting to show that agents of indirect discrimination are negligent is, in a troubling sense, socially and political regressive. After all, one of the great achievements of prohibitions on indirect discrimination is that they focus us, not on the agent's intentions or deliberations, but on the *effects* of her policies on *disadvantaged groups*. It might look as though I am turning the clock back, urging that we focus ourselves once again on the agent's attitudes and ignoring the real moral significance of the various effects of discrimination on protected groups—their social exclusion and relegation to the status of second-class citizens, their lack of freedom or lack of access to important opportunities, the huge difference between their levels of well-being and the levels enjoyed by more privileged individuals. But this is not my aim. The harmful effects of indirect discrimination—both the direct effects on those who are excluded or disadvantaged by certain policies, and the more diffuse, long-term effects on the broader social groups that are defined by these traits—are deeply important, and any adequate account of why discrimination is unfair or wrongful must take them into consideration. In section IV of the chapter, I shall explain how the view that I sketch out in this paper—of agents of indirect discrimination as negligent—could be conjoined with an account of why discrimination is unfair that appeals to these very real effects of indirect discrimination.

If these effects on victims are so important, however, why should we bother to focus on the negligence of the agent at all? Because I think that we can only question the view that direct discrimination is more serious if we focus on the particular features of discrimination that lead people to hold this view—features like the agent, the agent's motivation and the agent's deliberations. We could, to be sure, try to show that indirect discrimination is just as serious as direct discrimination from a moral standpoint by pointing to the depth and pervasiveness of its effects on protected groups. But this would not really address the concerns of those who believe that direct discrimination is more serious and more culpable—because they are focussing not on the effects of discrimination but on the agent of discrimination. That is why, in this chapter, I shall focus primarily on the agent as well.[8]

II. ANALYSING CASES OF INDIRECT DISCRIMINATION

In this section of the chapter, I want to analyse some ordinary cases of indirect discrimination—not, obviously, cases in which nothing seems to be problematic about the act or the policy, but cases of the kind that are commonly prohibited by law and in which we might say that the agent has acted wrongly. I want to look in some detail at the agents. Do they seem culpable? And if so, why? And I want to look at their actions or policies. Do they seem as morally troubling as some cases of obviously and seriously wrongful direct discrimination? I am going to use real examples rather than contrived ones, even though they will be somewhat messier, because I worry that contrived examples may inadvertently edit out some of the facts that make a difference to our moral judgements about these agents and their actions.

Acts of indirect discrimination frequently occur as part of a whole set of policies, practices and assumptions that together form what we call 'systemic discrimination'. So let us start by considering one common instance of systemic discrimination: the culture of sexual harassment within the military. Last year, an External Review of the Canadian Armed Forces revealed an environment in which harassment and assault of women and LGBTQ members have become so commonplace that they are regarded as normal and natural.[9] Some of the worst aspects of this culture involve *direct* discrimination: frequent use of sexualised language and sexual jokes targeting women's body parts; comments and posters proclaiming that a woman enters the army 'to find a man, leave a man, or become a man'; and sexual assaults and date rape of younger women by senior ranking officers. But these acts of direct discrimination have been allowed to continue in large part because they are sustained by a whole set of policies that are *indirectly* discriminatory and that work to silence women and LGBTQ members. These include: a practice of ostracising recruits who speak up about any kind of problem; a complaints process that has no provision for confidentiality; a policy of documenting only serious physical injuries and no 'lesser' injuries; and a training programme that does not focus on appropriate

[8] My own prior work has focussed on the effects of discrimination on protected groups, and my own account of why discrimination is unfair appeals to its effects on victims' freedom: see Sophia Moreau, 'What is Discrimination?' (2010) 38 *Philosophy and Public Affairs* 143.

[9] The Honourable Marie Deschamps, 'External Review into Sexual Misconduct and Sexual Harassment in the Canadian Armed Forces' (National Defence and the Canadian Armed Forces, 27 March 2015) available at www.forces.gc.ca.

behaviour towards others. These policies amount to indirect discrimination because, even though they are neutral on their face, they have a disproportionate impact on women and LGTBQ members in a culture in which these people are the most frequent targets of sexual abuse.

If we look at these cases of indirect discrimination within their context—that is, within the culture of sexual harassment that exists in the military, in which everyone is aware that such acts are occurring even if they think this is normal and natural—it is difficult to view the members of the Armed Forces as less than seriously culpable. They have failed to do certain crucial things to stop the subordination of women and LGBTQ members—such as develop a proper training programme, encourage victims of abuse to come forward, cultivate a culture of openness and honesty, and implement a confidential complaints process.[10] And they have failed to do these things, and failed to see the importance of doing them, presumably because they fail to see women and LGTBQ members *as equals*, as beings whose interests are as important, and deserve as much weight in their deliberations, as the interests of straight men. Surely this is a kind of failing that we regard as quite serious. I think we would also deem the policies themselves to be, under the circumstances, morally unacceptable—regardless of whether we think that it is an act's effects, or underlying intent, or expressive message that determines its moral status. These policies work to perpetuate the lower status of women and LGBTQ members and to encourage continued harassment of them. So they clearly have harmful effects. And occurring as they do within an organisation in which everyone knows that women and LGBTQ members are treated as second-class citizens, these policies implicitly condone the subservient treatment of women and LGBTQ members, and so send a demeaning message. It is true that, if they had occurred within an organisation that lacked a culture of sexual abuse, these same policies would not have amounted to indirect discrimination and might not have been morally

[10] One might object that if this behaviour appears to involve a moral failing on the part of the officers, that is primarily because the officers have what we might call an 'institutional duty of care' to look out for the well-being of women and other minority groups in the Armed Forces—that is, a duty that is quite independent of anything to do with discrimination, and has to do with their role in the Armed Forces— and they have violated this institutional duty. In other words, any moral failing that we see in these officers has less to do with indirect discrimination and more to do with a failure to live up to a quite separate duty of care that they stand under, as senior officers. Although it is true that senior officers stand under separate institutional duties of care to look out for the well-being of younger recruits, I do not think that this explains all of our moral discomfort about this case. Even junior members of the Armed Forces—whom we can suppose have no such institutional obligations—would be behaving unacceptably if they showed such disregard of women and LGBTQ members, and such willingness to perpetuate these groups' subordinate status. Moreover, the moral failing that I am noting here is not just a failure *to look after* women and LGBTQ members: it is a failure *to see and treat them as equals*. That failure is not something we can capture in terms of a failure to fulfil an institutional duty to promote someone else's well-being.

problematic. But this is irrelevant for the purposes of evaluating their moral status in this context.

Indeed, when we look closely at this example, the moral failings involved in the indirectly discriminatory policies do not seem so very different from the moral failings involved in the acts of direct discrimination—the sexual jokes, the assaults and the harassment. Those who engage in such acts of direct discrimination are likely either trying to put victims 'in their place' because they think of them as inferior and want their victims to know it, or they are just having a bit of fun on the assumption that having fun at the expense of these groups is perfectly acceptable because women and LGBTQ members aren't real soldiers anyway. Either way, the agents are failing to see these groups as their equals: they are failing to take the harms suffered by these people as a reason to act differently, and they are failing to treat these people's aims and ambitions as seriously as they treat their own. So both those engaged in direct discrimination and those engaged in indirect discrimination in this case are failing to see others as equals: they are failing to give others the moral significance that they should be given in their deliberations.

Of course, those who engage in direct discrimination must, in addition, know that they are directly causing physical or emotional harm to the people whom they assault or harass. But indirect discrimination also harms these groups, and the members of the Armed Forces who continue to support the indirectly discriminatory policies must be aware that they are contributing to the harm that is suffered by these groups. They are just contributing to it in a less direct way, with the causal chain being somewhat longer and mediated by other factors—such as other policies, and other people's words and actions. Should this fact really make that much of a difference to our moral thought about direct and indirect discrimination?

One might object to this analysis on the grounds that I have failed to mention some important distinctions between the direct and the indirect discrimination in this case. First, one might argue that those who engage in direct discrimination are *aiming at harm* towards women and LGBTQ members, perhaps not as an end in itself, but certainly as a means to securing their power over these people. By contrast, those who enforce or fail to change the otherwise neutral policies are not aiming to harm anyone—they are simply *foreseeing harm as a side-effect* of their action or inaction, given the existing culture in the military. So one might argue that there is actually a deep moral difference between the two. Alternatively, one might object that those who are engaged in direct discrimination are *actively bringing about harm*, whereas those who are failing to change policies and training programmes are simply *allowing harm to occur*, and this is the distinction that really explains the moral difference between direct and indirect discrimination. Third, one might suggest that in all cases of indirect discrimination, the policies are not harmful in and of themselves—they are only harmful *given certain background conditions*. In most cases of indirect discrimination, these background conditions are only tangentially or remotely connected to the agent of indirect discrimination. By contrast, in cases of direct discrimination, the harm that is done by the disadvantage or exclusion of a particular group is more immediate or direct. If the two forms of discrimination seem equally morally serious in this military case, this is only—or so our hypothetical objector might suggest—because we are assuming that the people who enforce the indirectly discriminatory policies are themselves contributing to the culture of sexual abuse and denigration, and so the disadvantage is more closely connected to them. But this is a special feature of this case, and not a general feature of cases of indirect discrimination.

I am going to put these three proposed principled explanations of the difference between direct and indirect discrimination temporarily aside: I will discuss them in section III of the chapter. But there is another objection that one might make to my analysis of discrimination in the Armed Forces, related to the last objection I mentioned above. One might argue that this is an unhelpful type of example to use when trying to assess the moral status of indirect discrimination, because the indirect discrimination in this case is so closely bound up with direct discrimination: the policies that amount to indirect discrimination in this example do so only because they help to condone and so to perpetuate direct discrimination against these same groups. So it might seem that in this type of case, indirect discrimination is morally serious, or as serious as direct discrimination, only because of its connection with direct discrimination. We need to examine some other cases of indirect discrimination if we are to show that this is not true.

What we require is an example of indirect discrimination by agents who are not themselves engaged in direct discrimination, and where the indirectly discriminatory policy works to impose disadvantage by some means other than encouraging or permitting agents to engage in acts of direct discrimination against these groups. So consider the physical fitness tests used for hiring in occupations that require considerable strength and stamina—such as fire fighters, forest fire fighters or security guards. Some of the fitness tests used for these occupations have faced legal challenges in the US and Canada, on the grounds that they hold everyone to standards that were originally based on male aerobic capacity and male fitness targets and are therefore much harder for most women to succeed at.[11] The tests do not amount to direct discrimination: there is no reference to gender in the application of the test, the tests are open to both men and women, and some women do pass them. However, as a group, women find it disproportionately harder to

[11] See, for example, *British Columbia v BCGSEU* (n 7).

pass the tests than men, and it seems that this is because of their physique and aerobic capacities as women.

A second, and similarly structured example of independent indirect discrimination involves written tests for aptitude or intelligence that are used by some employers for purposes of promotion.[12] Some of these tests have been found to be very difficult for certain racial minorities to pass: the percentage of blacks or Hispanics that pass the tests, out of all of those who attempt it, is a much smaller percentage than the percentage of Caucasians who succeed, relative to the number who attempt it. Often, this occurs in part because the questions on the test presuppose knowledge of certain kinds of life experiences and certain sorts of social interactions, of a sort that are more commonly had by Caucasian families than by these racial minorities. (In some cases, the disparity in success rates results also from direct discrimination: white employees are part of a social network from which minority employees are excluded, and senior employees within this network are happy to coach friends and family members but not minority candidates. So that this will remain an example of independent indirect discrimination, let us suppose that this is not occurring).

In both of these cases, the tests would be legally prohibited only if there were alternative tests available that could successfully track aptitude for the job, while at the same time increasing the number of minority candidates who pass the test. For if there were such alternatives available, then the current tests would not amount to a proportionate way of achieving a legitimate aim. In other words, if there were tests that are just as accurate (or more so) at measuring the capacities that are really needed to succeed at the job in question—such as the aerobic capacity that one needs if one is to be able to climb a ladder and lift someone out of a burning building, or the general knowledge of people that one needs in order to motivate the employees under one's supervision—and if these alternative tests gave these groups a better chance of success than the current tests do, then, and only then, would the current tests amount to the kind of indirect discrimination that we regard as justifiably legally prohibited and potentially morally wrongful.

The availability of these alternative tests is important, because it makes a difference to what agents of potentially wrongful indirect discrimination are doing and failing to do when they persist in applying the current tests. They are continuing to use their original tests in circumstances where there are alternatives available that would harm the minority groups less, while disadvantaging the employer in only a relatively small way. In some of these cases, the employer realises that there are alternative tests available but decides not to implement an alternative test, either for reasons of cost or simply out of laziness. In other cases, the employer does not know that

[12] See the facts in *Ricci v DeStefano* 557 US 557 (2009).

there are alternative tests available, but has a vague suspicion that there might be, and avoids looking into this because it is easier to turn a blind eye. And in still other cases, it may never have occurred to the employer that the original test poses difficulties for certain minorities, because the employer doesn't often bother to think about minority employees as the kind of people who deserve to be promoted. Regardless of which particular motivation is involved, these employers' actions seem to manifest exactly the same failure to see others as an equal that we saw in the example of indirect discrimination in the armed forces. Here, it is a failure to see other people's interests as significant enough to outweigh the relatively small trouble or cost that would be involved in looking into a particular test's effects on this group, in searching for a viable alternative, or in changing the test once an alternative is found.[13] It does not matter that the difficulties that women and ethnic minorities have in passing the current tests—because of their physique or cultural and educational background—are not themselves due to the organisations that use the tests. We can be culpable for failing to assign other people's disadvantage enough weight in our deliberations, even if we were not ourselves responsible for the underlying conditions that led these other people to be disadvantaged by our actions.

What this analysis shows, I think, is that in those cases of indirect discrimination where we think it is appropriately prohibited by law and potentially morally wrong, the agents *do* seem culpable, and the tests *do* seem morally problematic. And they seem even more so when we reflect that in many of these cases, part of the reason why the organisation in question has not tried to look for or develop alternative tests has to do with a lingering stereotype. Perhaps it is the stereotype that women don't really belong in rough professions such as fire-fighting: they are too delicate, too emotionally fragile, and too distracting to men. Or the stereotype that racial minorities couldn't really cope with managerial positions: they lack initiative, they don't have their lives together, and anyway, they probably have an enormous extended family at home that would take their attention away from their job. I suggested earlier that the cases of indirect discrimination that we examined all involved a failure to see certain groups as equals. I think we often fail to see these groups as equals precisely because we see them through the lens of a stereotype—perhaps the same stereotypes that were once openly used to try to rationalise direct discrimination. By 'stereotype', I mean a generalisation about a trait—a trait allegedly possessed by, all or almost all members of a particular group—which we use as a justification for seeing members of this group as different from ourselves and often as less than fully capable. There may certainly be circumstances in which reliance on stereotypes is necessary

[13] I've said 'relatively small trouble or cost' because if the cost of altering a policy would be significant, then presumably the current test *would* be a 'proportionate' way of achieving a legitimate aim and the case would therefore not be one of *wrongful* indirect discrimination.

and unproblematic;[14] but it does seem in many circumstances to add to the culpability of the agent.

Of course, if I am right about the way in which stereotypes figure in the motivation of agents of indirect discrimination, then this means that what I have called independent indirect discrimination is not completely independent of direct discrimination: both can be rationalised by stereotypes, and the same stereotypes that were once given as explicit justifications for direct discrimination can be used privately to try to avoid having to search for alternatives to policies that disproportionately disadvantage certain groups. This does not pose a problem for my argument: independent indirect discrimination is still 'independent' in the sense that it does not impose disadvantage on minority groups by encouraging *other* agents to engage in *separate* acts of direct discrimination towards this group. And so my examples of indirect discrimination still serve the purpose of helping to demonstrate that indirect discrimination can be seriously troubling from a moral standpoint.

If we turn back to the RCMP's Stetson hat policy—the example which, at the very start of the chapter, I used to illustrate our common view that indirect discrimination is accidental, unwitting, and not culpable—I think we may now see it in a rather different light. I have tried to argue in this section of the chapter that indirect discrimination, at least where it is prohibited by law and potentially a moral wrong, involves a failure to see others as equals, a failure to give their interests an appropriate weight in your own deliberations. But surely this failure is exactly what occurred when the RCMP single-mindedly focussed on the importance of having all Mounties wear the Stetson hat and gave little or no weight in their deliberations to the plight of Sikhs. When the Stetson hat was first adopted, no doubt there were very few Sikhs in Canada and probably none that aspired to be a Mountie. But once the Sikh community became established and it was brought to the RCMP's attention that their dress code prevented Sikhs from joining, the RCMP chose to turn a blind eye, giving more weight to the continuation of a dress uniform than to the needs of a large group of Canadians. Moreover, it is part of the purpose of this ceremonial unit of the police force to represent all Canadian people. For this reason, the RCMP were arguably under a special duty toward Sikhs, a duty to ensure that the police force was open to them and a duty to give their interests greater weight when thinking about how to balance tradition against accessibility. The RCMP was not in the position of a private club that could choose to value tradition and ignore the impact of its policies on others. Giving more weight to an exclusionary tradition than to an entire sector of the population that it is your job to represent does seem morally troubling. It is also demeaning. It sends the message that Sikhs

[14] See Fredrick Schauer, *Profiles, Probabilities and Stereotypes* (Cambridge MA, Harvard University Press, 2003).

are so unimportant that they are worth less than the macho image of the Mountie, and that they look so strange and different from 'us' that something would be lost if they were allowed to appear in ceremonial parades. And of course, like the indirectly discriminatory fitness or managerial tests that we just considered, the reasoning of the RCMP seems to involve stereotypes in a morally troubling way. For the traditional image of the Mountie wearing his Stetson hat—the image that the RCMP thought it so important to preserve—is not just the image of a man who is strong and brave like a cowboy. It is the image of a man who is strong and brave and *white*.

I have argued in this section of the paper that indirect discrimination is not, as we might think, less morally problematic than direct discrimination. I have suggested that it often involves a failure to see other groups as equals, and I have also suggested that the same failure is found in cases of direct discrimination. But one might object that my analysis omits an important principled difference between direct and indirect discrimination, something that might explain why, even if many cases of indirect discrimination involve a failure to treat others as an equal, and even if the same is true of direct discrimination, nevertheless direct discrimination also involves something *further*, something that makes it *even more serious* from a moral standpoint. So I shall turn in the next section to some attempts to appeal to a single principle that might explain the moral difference between these two forms of discrimination. I shall argue that none of these explanations succeeds.

III. WHY MIGHT DIRECT DISCRIMINATION BE MORE SERIOUS FROM A MORAL STANDPOINT?

There are a number of plausible moral principles to which one might appeal in trying to explain why direct discrimination is generally more serious than indirect discrimination and its agents more culpable. In this section of the chapter, I want to look in some detail at four of these principles. I shall argue that although these principles might have an initial intuitive appeal, each of them invokes a distinction that either does not accurately map onto the distinction between direct and indirect discrimination or does not have the explanatory power that it seems to have. Some of the principles fail for both of these reasons.

Consider first the following principle.

A. Principle (i): It is Morally Worse to Act in Ways that bring about Harm than to Omit to Perform an Action that Might have Averted Harm

One might suggest, using principle (i), that in cases of indirect discrimination, the agent merely omits to perform an action that might have averted harm: he allows harm to occur. But in cases of direct discrimination, he takes positive steps to do something harmful. There is a wide philosophical literature on the moral significance of the distinction between acting and omitting, or doing harm and allowing harm, and some of this literature supports (i). But, even if we help ourselves to the large claim that (i) is sound, there are two problems with its application to direct and indirect discrimination.

First, at least within the law—and in particular the law of interpersonal wrongs, or tort law—we don't commonly assume that omissions as a class are less culpable than harmful actions. What is relevant from a legal standpoint is not whether an agent acted or failed to act, but whether he had a duty to act in a certain way and violated that duty. Omissions that constitute violations of duties are, under the law, treated as wrongful and as culpable as actions that constitute violations of duties. So, for instance, if a doctor fails to diagnose and treat a pregnant woman's illness and her foetus is consequently born with medical problems, he is liable for that failure, because he failed to do something that he had a duty to do. I suspect that if we think the action/omission distinction is helpful in explaining cases of direct and indirect discrimination, this is because we are tacitly assuming *that there is no moral duty* owed in cases of indirect discrimination by the alleged discriminator to the group that his policies happen to disadvantage. In other words, we are assuming that all cases of indirect discrimination are cases of omission where there is no violation of a duty to act. But if this is right, then principle (i) does not explain why direct discrimination is more serious than indirect; rather, it smuggles this conclusion in through the back door by requiring that we assume from the start that the agent of indirect discrimination is not violating any moral duty.

And there is a second, independent problem with the application of (i) to cases of direct and indirect discrimination. This is that the distinction between doing harm and allowing harm simply does not map neatly onto the distinction between direct discrimination and indirect discrimination. Indirect discrimination might look like it involves merely allowing harm, if we think of examples such as failing to change a training programme or failing to adopt an alternative test. But most cases of indirect discrimination also involve the discriminator taking certain positive steps. The same members of the Canadian Armed Forces who failed to change their training programme also consistently *ran* the existing programme, and they *enforced* a policy of silence by *punishing* those who complained of abuse. It was this combination of actions and omissions that condoned and so encouraged acts of abuse. The fire-fighting departments that failed to change their tests also *applied* the current tests based on men's aerobic capacities and used these tests to *deny* some women jobs. Again, it was a combination of actions and omissions that led to the increased disadvantage to women. These cases are not analogous to the cases of allowing harm in the philosophical literature, in which an agent simply stands by and watches while some other agent or some natural force causes harm to another person. Both direct and indirect discrimination each involve a combination of actions and omissions. So whatever the moral use of the distinction between doing harm and allowing harm, it is not, I think, helpful in this context.

A more promising explanation of the moral difference between direct and indirect discrimination might be that it lies in whether the agent intends harm as an end or a means to his end, or whether he merely foresees it as a side-effect of his act. Recall that, when we considered the culture of sexual harassment in the military, we noted that many of the officers who engage in direct discrimination, assaulting or insulting women and LGBTQ members, are harming them as a means to increasing or publicly demonstrating their own power over them. By contrast, the officers who enforce or fail to change the otherwise neutral policies are not aiming to harm anyone—they are simply foreseeing further assaults and insults as a side-effect of their action and inaction, given the existing culture in the military.

So perhaps underlying our moral reactions to direct and indirect discrimination is the following principle.

B. Principle (ii): It is Morally Worse to Intend Harm as an End or a Means to your End than Merely to Foresee Harm as an Unfortunate Side-effect of your Act

One problem with applying (ii) in this context, however, is that relatively few cases of direct discrimination involve an agent who maliciously *aims at harm*, either as an end or as a means to some further end. I think that, in our casual thoughts about discrimination, we think far too much about agents who maliciously desire to harm others. We assume that the typical agent of direct discrimination is deeply prejudiced and aims to harm the group in question, either as an end or as a means. Of course it is true that historically, the most heinous cases of discrimination have involved agents setting out to harm others, sometimes out of a cold hatred that makes harm its end, and sometimes as a means to some other end, such as consolidating one's power or ingratiating oneself in the eyes of others who hate these groups. But I think it is crucially important to note here that it is no part of the definition of direct discrimination that an agent must act out of a desire to harm others, either as an end or as a means. And out of all of the cases of direct discrimination that have been recognised in our legal systems, most have actually not involved agents who aim at the harm of the disadvantaged group. Think, for instance, of the many forms of direct gender discrimination in the workplace. Consider the old American laws restricting women's working hours but not men's: although they were paternalistic, they were intended to protect women, not to harm them. Consider the many employers who hired young men over young women, worrying that the women would likely become pregnant and leave their employment. They were not trying to harm the women whom they did not hire: all that they were aiming to do was hire someone who had a greater chance of staying in their employment, because this was more cost-effective. Consider the businesses that impose a dress code requiring only female staff, but not male staff, to wear make-up and short skirts. They too are not aiming at harm: they simply believe this kind of dress code will make their female staff more attractive to clients and hence garner more clients overall. And we can see the same kind of motivation even in instances of racial discrimination. When youth clubs or sports clubs try posting different opening times for minority communities (eg one time for members of the black community, one time for members of the Latino community), we standardly treat this as legally prohibited direct discrimination, since it is a form of explicit racial segregation. But the clubs' aim is to help, not to harm. If we regard such segregationist policies as morally problematic, the problem must lie in some other fact about them—perhaps that they show a presumptious paternalism, an insensitivity to the perspective of blacks and Latinos, and an ignorance of the history of racial segregation and the sorts of messages that segregationist policies now send, given this history.

All of these cases of direct discrimination that I have just mentioned—and there are many similar examples that could be cited—are poorly explained by the suggestion that the agents were intending harm as an end or as a means to their ends. It is true that in both the United States and the UK direct discrimination is proven as a matter of law by showing that an agent *intended* to draw a distinction based on a protected characteristic. But intending *to draw a distinction* is clearly different from intending *to harm* the group that is disadvantaged by that distinction.

A second problem with principle (ii) is that it invokes one part of the Doctrine of Double Effect (DDE), while omitting to mention another part of the doctrine that is crucial to the DDE's explanatory power. The DDE is supposed to explain why certain acts that cause harm might, under special circumstances, be permissible. It does this not just by appealing to the agent's intent, but also by imposing a requirement of proportionality. In order for it to be morally more acceptable for an agent to bring about certain harms when he simply foresees them as side-effects of his action than when he intends them as an end or as a means to his end, the beneficial effects of the action that the agent aims at must outweigh the action's harmful side-effects. The agent who discriminates indirectly seems—at least in cases where the indirect discrimination is prohibited by law and potentially morally troubling—to *violate* this proportionality condition of the DDE. She has failed to adopt an alternative policy in cases where there is an available alternative that would serve her goal and cause *less* disadvantage to the protected group. So she is not acting with a view to bringing about some good that could outweigh the harmful side-effects of her action upon these other groups.

This means that, once we invoke the complete DDE, we are left without a good explanation of why the agent of indirect discrimination is less culpable than the agent of direct discrimination. In fact, far from exonerating the agent of indirect discrimination, the proportionality condition of the DDE may help to explain how she fails.[15] The members of the Armed Forces who continue to enforce a policy of silence within a culture of sexual harassment, and the RCMP officers who insist on preserving a traditional hat and turn a blind eye to the needs of Sikhs, and the companies that choose not to look for alternative tests in the sorts of circumstances we have discussed—all of them have, we might say, made a culpable mistake in their judgements about how much moral weight to give to the interests of others. They have accorded far too little weight to the harms that will be suffered by members of a particular disadvantaged group as a result of their policies, in a situation where these harms are not outweighed by the particular good that the agent is trying to bring about. These agents may indeed be trying to bring about some good—such as preserving tradition, or finding good fire-fighters or promoting the sorts of people who will make efficient managers—and for this reason they may seem innocent. But they do not give enough weight in their deliberations to the harmful effects of their policies on others, in circumstances where they ought to have known better. Is this really so much better from a moral standpoint than aiming at these people's harms? Or are these just different ways of failing to value other people appropriately? I am not sure that we can say that one is morally worse than the other. So *even if* direct discrimination were defined in such a way that all of its agents aimed at harm—which, as I have explained, it is not—it is unclear that principle (ii) would successfully explain why it is worse than the kinds of indirect discrimination that we prohibit by law and that we think are potentially wrongful.

A final difficulty with principle (ii) is that it seems to confuse a lack of absoluteness with a lack of moral seriousness. At least if we agree with Anscombe's interpretation of the DDE,[16] the difference between aiming at

[15] Seana Shiffrin has a very illuminating discussion of how the *negligent* actor fails to meet the proportionality condition of the DDE in her paper, 'The Moral Neglect of Negligence' in David Sobel, Peter Vallentyne, and Steven Wall (eds), *Oxford Studies in Political Philosophy* Vol 3 (Oxford, Oxford University Press, 2016). I think that the agent of indirect discrimination is one sort of negligent actor, and my discussion of how he fails to meet this proportionality condition is indebted to Shiffrin's discussion of negligence. (For a brief defence of my view that indirect discrimination is a form of negligence, see s IV of the chapter; for a longer defence, see my paper, 'Discrimination as Negligence' (2012) in Colin MacLeod (ed), Supplementary Volume 36: 'Justice and Equality' in *Canadian Journal of Philosophy* 123.

[16] See GEM Anscombe, 'War and Murder' in GEM Anscombe *Ethics, Religion and Politics: Collected Philosophical Papers* Vol 3 (Oxford, Basil Blackwell, 1981) 51.

or intending a harm and acting in a way that one foresees will cause harm lies in the *absoluteness* of the prohibition: there is an absolute prohibition on making harm the object or purpose of your action, whereas there is only a relative prohibition on acting in ways that one foresees will bring about harm (because whether an act that foreseeably causes harm actually amounts to a moral wrong in a particular case is contingent on the circumstances—and in particular, as I noted above, on whether the beneficial consequences of the act outweigh its harmful ones). But absoluteness and moral seriousness are not the same thing. Even if we accept that there is only a relative prohibition on acting in ways that foreseeably cause harm, this does not commit us to any view at all about *how bad* or *how culpable* it is to act in ways that foreseeably cause harm *in those cases where such acts are wrong*. So although the DDE gives us a way to distinguish absolute from relative prohibitions, it is not clear that it can do the kind of work that principle (ii) needs to do, which is to explain a difference in moral seriousness.

Perhaps, though, the real moral difference between direct and indirect discrimination lies in the extent to which the harm is closely or directly connected to the agent. Although it is not true that all agents of direct discrimination aim at harm, it is true that because they draw explicit distinctions on the basis of a protected characteristic (or on the basis of a characteristic that is very tightly connected to a protected characteristic), the harm to the disadvantaged group usually results more directly or immediately from the agent's action. By contrast, cases of indirect discrimination usually involve neutral-looking policies that have disadvantageous effects on a particular protected group only because of a host of mediating factors, such as the education levels of a group, its poverty, past injustices towards that group, and so on. So it can look as though the relevant moral difference between direct and indirect discrimination lies in the closeness of the agent to the disadvantage, along the causal chain—or, to borrow a term from tort law, the remoteness of the damage from the agent.

So we might try a third principle.

C. Principle (iii): It is Morally Worse to bring about Harm Directly than it is to bring it about Indirectly through a Causal Chain in which the Harm is More Remotely Connected to the Agent

I have included this alternative in part because the concepts of direct and indirect discrimination seem to invite such an explanation, focussing as they do on the closeness or directness of the agent to the disadvantageous result. But I confess that I find it hard to see how this could be thought of as a defensible moral principle. Why should we think that it is morally worse to bring about harm directly rather than indirectly? Certainly we do not generally suppose that people are *less responsible* for outcomes just because they occur further down the causal chain. If it is my job to take a group of teenagers who have been in trouble with the law onto an island and guard them for a night, and I fall asleep and leave them to their own devices, with the result that they escape, board a boat, drive it recklessly into another boat, and damage that boat, the damage can be laid at my door because, even though there are numerous acts of other agents intervening between my falling asleep and the boat being damaged, this is precisely the sort of eventuality that was reasonably foreseeable and that I had a duty to guard against.[17] Similarly, if I negligently drop a broken bottle in the sand and it is tossed about, carried here and there, and finally washes up on another beach many years later and injures a child, I am morally culpable for this injury in spite of the many factors and the many years intervening between my act and the actual injury—because this is precisely the kind of injury that makes it risky to drop broken bottles on a beach, and so I had a duty not to drop it. It is true that if the causal chain is very long and mediated by many other people's acts, then we do not generally think a particular agent is responsible for the outcome *unless he failed to do something that he had a duty to do*. But this suggests that what is really doing the moral work for us in (iii) is not actually an appeal to the directness or indirectness of the harm or disadvantage, but once again the tacit assumption that we have no duty to prevent disadvantage accruing to the groups marked out by protected characteristics, in cases of indirect discrimination. And this is a problem, for principle (iii) is supposed to explain *why* there might be a moral difference between these two forms of discrimination, and it is supposed to be the *remoteness* of the consequences that does the explanatory work here. It seems that it does not do this work; instead, what does the explanatory work is the claim that agents in cases of indirect discrimination do not have any moral duties to the groups they are disadvantaging.[18]

There is also another difficulty with (iii). The distinction between bringing about harm directly and bringing it about indirectly does not map neatly onto the distinction between direct and indirect discrimination. There are many core cases of direct discrimination where the disadvantage accrues to a particular group only because of many other factors that having nothing to do with the agent. Consider my earlier example of the local club that assigns different access hours to blacks and Latinos in order to reduce racial tensions. This is direct discrimination, and in fact a classic example of it, since it involves racial segregation. But it only disadvantages these groups because of a very complicated history of racial segregation and unequal

[17] See *Dorset Yacht Co Ltd v Home Office* [1970] UKHL 2, [1970] AC 1004.

[18] What about this claim, however? Perhaps *this* is the real reason why indirect discrimination seems less serious to us from a moral standpoint: we are tacitly assuming that agents of indirect discrimination do not stand under any special duties towards members of minority groups. I shall discuss this objection in s IV.

treatment, and the disadvantage results not directly from different opening hours but very indirectly, through people's assumptions about what this segregation stands for, through the symbolic force of segregation, and through all of the many things that different members of these communities and of other communities will do in the face of this new policy of racial segregation in the club. Without all of these mediating acts, the policy of allocating different access hours to different racial groups would impose as little disadvantage on anyone as imposing different access hours for different age groups: babies and pre-schoolers from 9–11am, school-age children from 4–6pm. So even if (iii) were a sound moral principle, it is not clear that it could explain the difference between direct and indirect discrimination.

IV. DIRECT AND INDIRECT DISCRIMINATION AS FORMS OF NEGLIGENCE

I have now tried to show that the most seemingly plausible moral principles that we might invoke to explain why there is a moral difference between direct and indirect discrimination actually fail to explain this. In each case, we saw that either the principle was unsound or it invoked a distinction that did not accurately map onto the distinction between direct and indirect discrimination. This should give us some reason for doubting that the distinction between direct and indirect discrimination has the moral significance that it initially seems to have.

But if we accept that the two forms of discrimination are not so different from a moral standpoint, can we give a unified account of what is morally troubling about them? I think we can, and it is an account that is consistent with a number of different theories that scholars have recently proposed to explain why direct discrimination is unfair. When we looked at examples of indirect and direct discrimination earlier in the chapter, we found that common to all of them was a certain kind of failure to give other people and their interests the kind of moral significance that they should be given in the agent's deliberations. In that sense, it was a failure to think of others as one's equal, and a concomitant failure to treat others as equals through one's actions. I think we can see this as a form of negligence. This sort of negligence mirrors the kind of negligence we recognise as culpable in tort law: though the negligence that discrimination involves is not negligence in the sense of an unreasonable creation of a risk, but negligence in the sense of unreasonably failing to take someone and her interests as seriously as one ought to take them, and then unreasonably failing to act in the way that a person who had taken their interests seriously would have acted.[19]

[19] For a much more detailed account of why we can see both kinds of discrimination as a form of negligence, see my article 'Discrimination as Negligence' (n 15).

I should emphasise here that in suggesting that both direct and indirect discrimination involve a kind of negligence, I am not offering the concept of negligence as a kind of recipe or instruction manual for determining how far an employer or other agent's obligations extend to those who are adversely affected by discrimination. The abstract idea of negligence cannot do that: for that, we need a theory of *when* and *why* it is reasonable for us to take these groups' interests seriously, and of what constitutes taking them seriously in particular circumstances.[20] I think it is helpful for us to think about discrimination as a form of negligence, not because this one idea can specify the full extent of an agent's obligations, but rather because it draws us away from an exclusive and narrow focus on the agent's intentions and aims, and instead broadens our gaze, out towards the many things that the agent has failed to notice and failed to do, and out towards the many effects of his policy on the victims of discrimination, which make the policy into something that the agent ought to have scrutinised further and altered.

There are at least two objections one might make to my suggestion that both direct and indirect discrimination involve negligence. First, one might argue that prohibitions on indirect discrimination are best thought of, not as akin to negligence law, but as a form of strict liability. After all, it is no defence to a claim of indirect discrimination that one took all of the precautions that one reasonably could have taken to avoid disproportionately harming a particular protected group or that one did one's best to look into alternative policies. And presumably, even though in many cases we do think that a reasonable person in the agent's position would have been aware of the disproportionate effects of their policy on a particular group and would have located a viable alternative, nevertheless there will be some cases in which agents, though no fault of their own, fail to notice either the availability of alternative policies or the negative effects of their existing policy. Would we really want to say that these agents are negligent? Wouldn't we want to say, instead, that although they are not negligent and are not in any way at fault, there are nevertheless sound policy reasons for holding that they too should bear the costs of fixing their policies, to eliminate these harmful effects on protected groups?

It is true, of course, that absence of fault is no defence in law to a claim of indirect discrimination, either in the UK or in the United States. But this does not seem to me to show that it is unhelpful to think about the kind of failing that is involved in cases of discrimination as a form of negligence. I think we can view the absence of such a defence as reflecting the diverse nature of the aims of anti-discrimination law. One of the aims of anti-discrimination law is clearly to encourage governments, corporations, employers, providers of goods and services—any agent who is in control of significant resources or is in the position of offering significant opportunities to members of the

[20] See below for further discussion of this, in relation to different theories of discrimination.

public—to consider the impact of his actions on groups that have historically been treated as second-class citizens and significantly disadvantaged. But another aim of anti-discrimination law, and particularly of prohibitions on indirect discrimination, is to try to rectify or reduce some of these disadvantages. In other words, anti-discrimination law focuses not just on the agents of discrimination but on the effects of their policies on protected groups. Presumably, if lack of fault were a defence, this would impede the goal of improving the prospects of these groups. It might also function as a disincentive to employers or other agents of indirect discrimination, who might, under an explicit fault standard, be less likely to stretch themselves, less likely to take that extra step to try to figure out alternatives that would cause less harm to members of protected groups. So we can explain the absence of this defence in a way that is entirely consistent with my theory.

Having said this, I do not think it is true that many *actual* cases of wrongful indirect discrimination have involved agents who made perfectly reasonable assumptions and investigations but were simply unable, through no fault of their own, to grasp that their policies had disproportionate effects on protected groups or to locate better alternatives. We need to remember here who the bearers of a legal duty not to discriminate are. Under the law, these are not ordinary private citizens going about their affairs, but organisations that hold themselves out to the public as providers of goods and services, or bearers of employment opportunities—organisations that in some way act within the public sphere and that are in charge of significant resources and opportunities. As John Gardner has said, describing the role of employers, 'The employer finds himself in a special privileged position in the distributive mechanics of society ... [he will], like a government, determine some of the society's most important distributions.'[21] It seems to me that it is reasonable to expect people in these positions to be aware of the history of social exclusion of minority groups in our society and to be particularly vigilant about the effects of their own policies on these groups. And it seems to me, similarly, that these duty-bearers are likely already to have access to much of the relevant information they need, in order to assess the impact of their policies on these groups. They are a part of many social networks of similar employers or providers of similar goods; and they live in a society in which the media regularly bombard them with information (not all of it accurate, admittedly) about allegations of discrimination made by minority groups in a variety of contexts. The idea that there could, under these circumstances, be many sincere employers who are simply unable to figure out that their tests have unfair adverse effects on ethnic minorities or that their policies unfairly disadvantage women—this seems to me a convenient fiction, one that some agents of indirect discrimination might like us

[21] John Gardner, 'Liberals and Unlawful Discrimination' (1989) 9 *OJLS* 1, 11.

to believe, but not one that has much basis in actual fact. So I think we need to be honest that such cases, if they ever do arise, will arise rarely. When they do, we can say, as I did above, that there are nevertheless sound reasons of distributive justice for holding these agents liable as a matter of law, even if from a moral standpoint we think they are not culpable.

There is also a second objection one might make to my suggestion that both direct and indirect discrimination involve negligence. One might object that it is only negligent to fail to give other people's interests a certain weight in one's own deliberations, and to fail to act accordingly, if we are actually *obliged* to give others' interests that weight. And one might claim that the existence of such obligations is precisely what is contested by at least some of those people who think that indirect discrimination is less morally problematic than direct discrimination. When I have discussed indirect discrimination of the kind that is prohibited by law, I have suggested that the agents ought to make efforts to determine whether there are alternatives to their policies that would disadvantage minority groups to a lesser extent while still serving their overall purpose, and that they are obliged to implement such alternatives if they exist. And I have suggested that those who fail to do this are failing to take other people, and their interests and ambitions, seriously. But some philosophers who theorise about discrimination, such as John Gardner and Richard Arneson, would deny that we stand under *any* such duties towards members of protected groups—at least, not duties that we owe them by virtue of their membership in such groups. These philosophers would argue that the agent who discriminates indirectly does not inappropriately elevate her own interests above theirs because she stands, in the first place, under no obligation to give their interests any particular weight in her own deliberations.[22] Of course, both Gardner and Arneson allow that there could be beneficial effects to prohibiting indirect discrimination that might justify such prohibitions in a legal system: for instance, such prohibitions likely result in a redistribution of opportunities from the privileged to the underprivileged, and this will increase the well-being of underprivileged groups. But these are just beneficial consequences of a certain policy choice; and they do not, for Gardner and Arneson, track any kind of prior moral duty that agents might have to each other. And so agents who fail to give such weight to the interests of disadvantaged groups are not, on their views, negligent.

Neither Gardner nor Arneson gives lengthy arguments for the view that we have no such duties to minority groups. Arneson starts from a principle rather like my principle (ii) in section 2, suggesting that direct discrimination is wrongful because the agent in some way aims at harm or is driven by an unwarranted hatred or prejudice, and then suggests that because

[22] See Richard Arneson, 'What is Wrongful Discrimination? (2006) 43 *San Diego Law Review* 775, and Gardner (n 21).

this motivation is absent in cases of indirect discrimination, we should try instead to explain our legal prohibitions on such cases as driven by policies of bettering the situation of minority groups. I have already argued in section III that most agents of direct discrimination do not aim at harm and are not motivated by unwarranted hatred; and I cannot, in the short space that is left here, offer a full defence of the claim that we do stand under such moral duties. But I do want to note two things. First, it does seem more plausible than not to suppose that we owe some kind of duty to these minority groups, when we consider what all of the groups identified by protected characteristics have in common. I have been silent on this so far in the chapter, and in fact legal discussions of discrimination are often silent on this because we simply take the list of protected characteristics as a given. But of course the kinds of groups that possess these protected traits—racial minorities, women, LGBTQ members, members of religions that have historically faced persecution or that are now regarded as barbaric—all of these groups have suffered social subordination, unjust exclusion, and persistent and severe economic disadvantage. So to suppose that I have a duty, in my deliberations, to give some weight to the disproportionate disadvantage suffered by these groups as a result of my policy is not like supposing that I have a *general* duty to give as much weight to other people's interests in my deliberations as I do to my own. It seems quite plausible that there is some special fact or set of facts concerning the history or situation of these groups and my relationship to them that could ground a duty owed by me to members of these groups, but not to others.

There are many quite different accounts we could give of what these facts are—and this brings me to my second point. The idea that we stand under some such duty is consistent with a number of the theories that are currently being put forward by philosophers who write on discrimination.[23] We could suggest, as Tarun Khaitan has done, that the disadvantages faced by these groups prevent them from accessing some of the basic goods necessary to live a good life, and that this is ultimately what grounds our legal and moral duties towards them.[24] We could adopt a desert-prioritarian account such as Kasper Lippert-Rasmussen's.[25] We could appeal to the importance of

[23] My aim here is simply to suggest that the view that discrimination involves negligence (and thereby involves the violation of a duty to the groups who are directly or indirectly disadvantaged) is consistent with a number of different theories of what makes discrimination unfair. I am not claiming that all of the proponents of these theories would actually endorse my view, but rather that a coherent version of their theory could be constructed that accords with my view. (Also, it is important to note that some of these theorists, such as Hellman, would hold that the relevant duty is a moral duty and a legal duty; others might hold that it is a legal duty but not a moral duty).

[24] Tarun Khaitan, *A Theory of Discrimination Law* (Oxford, Oxford University Press, 2015).

[25] Kasper Lippert-Rasmussen, *Born Free and Equal: A Philosophical Inquiry into the Nature of Discrimination* (Oxford, Oxford University Press, 2014).

preventing the creation and perpetuation of subordinate classes of people, as Owen Fiss did.[26] Or we could instead appeal to Hellman's account of discrimination as problematic insofar as it demeans the groups that are disadvantaged.[27] And I have tried, in other articles, to defend a view of discrimination that grounds our duty not to discriminate upon a right to deliberative freedom,[28] and more recently, a pluralistic view that appeals to a number of these different harmful effects.[29] All of these views offer us potential ways of explaining why, in both cases of direct and cases of indirect discrimination, we can see agents as negligent, as unreasonably failing to give other people and their interests the kind of weight that they should have given to them in their own deliberations.

In this chapter, I began by analysing a number of cases of indirect discrimination that are commonly prohibited by law. I tried to show that they all involve a certain kind of moral failing: a failure to treat others as equals and to give them and their interests due weight in one's deliberations. I then looked at principles that might explain why direct discrimination involves some even greater failing—but I was unable to find any general principle that might satisfactorily explain the difference between cases of direct discrimination and cases of indirect discrimination. Finally, I suggested that rather than assuming that there is a deep moral difference between these forms of discrimination, we might think of both of them as instances of negligence. I have emphasised throughout the chapter that, in focusing on the agents of discrimination and their deliberations, I do not mean to discount the importance of the harms that accrue to victims of discrimination. On the contrary, the negligence of these agents can only be fully explained by appealing to these harmful effects.

[26] Owen Fiss, 'Groups and the Equal Protection Clause' (1976) 5 *Philosophy and Public Affairs* 107.

[27] Deborah Hellman, *When is Discrimination Wrong?* (Cambridge MA, Harvard University Press, 2008). Although Hellman, like Fiss, offers her account as an account of direct discrimination only, it is not clear to me that it is only direct discrimination that demeans people, and not also certain cases of indirect discrimination. I have tried throughout the paper to show that a number of core cases of indirect discrimination can also be understood as demeaning and subordinating. See, for instance, my discussion at the end of Section 2 of the RCMP's Stetson hat policy.

[28] See Sophia Moreau, 'In Defense of a Liberty-Based Account of Discrimination' in Deborah Hellman and Sophia Moreau (eds), *Philosophical Foundations of Discrimination Law* (Oxford, Oxford University Press, 2013) and Moreau (n 8).

[29] Sophia Moreau, 'Equality and Discrimination,' forthcoming in John Tasioulas (ed), *The Cambridge Companion to Philosophy of Law* (Cambridge, Cambridge University Press, 2018).

7

Squaring the Circle: Can an Egalitarian and Individualistic Conception of Freedom of Religion or Belief Co-exist with the Notion of Indirect Discrimination?

RONAN McCREA

IN THIS CHAPTER, I want to look at the complicated relationship between the right to freedom of religion or belief and the prohibition of (unjustified) indirect discrimination on grounds of religion or belief. I will do so in the context of European law which has, in a number of recent cases, brought the tensions between these two principles into focus in a particularly informative way. My main argument goes as follows. The European Court of Human Rights (ECtHR) and EU institutions have been careful to define the fundamental right to freedom of religion or belief as a right that is primarily focused on securing individual autonomy in relation to belief. This is an approach that seeks to ensure that each individual will be entitled to the same degree of liberty to choose and adhere to the beliefs of one's choice (alone or in communion with others). It is egalitarian in the sense that it does not attach greater importance to the right to hold religious rather than non-religious beliefs nor does it give greater protection to orthodox religious beliefs over heterodox or esoteric beliefs. On this approach, religion is not 'special' in the sense of being entitled to protections that are not afforded to other forms of belief and religion is seen primarily as a matter of beliefs to be chosen rather than being a fixed form of identity such as race or gender.

The focus of EU employment legislation, that requires justification of measures that are indirectly discriminatory on grounds of religion or belief, is different. It focuses on the reduction of particular disadvantages faced by identifiable groups defined by their religion or belief. Reducing group disadvantage may have beneficial impacts on the degree of autonomy some individuals have to choose and adhere to particular beliefs but this is not the central focus of rules that seek to restrict measures that are indirectly discriminatory on grounds of religion or belief. Indeed, there is something of a tension between the individualistic and egalitarian focus of the right to freedom of religion and the notions of particular disadvantage and the collective focus seen in relation to indirect discrimination.

This tension picks up the broader tension in the relationship of religion to law that arises from the fact that religion is experienced both as a matter of individual choice and belief (akin to political beliefs) and also as a form of collective identity (that comes through families, which is rarely changeable and which is linked to one's communal identity more like racial or ethnic identity). The fact that religion is experienced in these different ways makes its legal regulation particularly complicated as conceiving of religion as a matter of choice and belief calls for forms of legal regulation that are very different from the forms that appear appropriate when dealing with involuntary features of identity. The right to religious freedom is therefore linked to issues of salient identities and to issues of group rights in a way that other classical liberties such as the right to privacy or free speech are not. Privacy, for example, is a right but there is no identifiable salient identity linked to the status of privacy. There could not, therefore, be a characteristic based on privacy that could form the basis for a status to be protected by anti-discrimination law.

There are two risks arising from a failure to acknowledge adequately the separate nature of the right to religious freedom from the right to require justification of indirectly discriminatory measures. The first is the risk that ideas of 'particular' disadvantage may undermine the egalitarian nature of the interpretation of the right to freedom of religion and belief in favour of a sectarian approach that grants greater religious freedom to established forms of belief (which would be itself discriminatory and would go against the counter-majoritarian aim of the right). The second risk is that viewing indirect discrimination through the lens of the egalitarian and individualistic jurisprudence on freedom of religion may undermine the ability of indirect discrimination to tackle particular disadvantages faced by those with particular religion or belief related identities.

I. EUROPEAN LAW AS AN INSTRUCTIVE EXAMPLE

Pan-European legal norms are the ideal framework in which to analyse this issue. European law covers both the right to freedom of thought, conscience and religion (Article 9 European Convention on Human Rights (ECHR), Article 10 Charter of Fundamental Rights of the European Union (CFREU)) and has legislation in the form of an EU directive (Directive 2000/78) that requires, in the context of employment, justification of measures that are indirectly discriminatory in relation to religion or belief.[1] In addition, pan-European legal norms include a hybrid category that covers fundamental rights and the idea of indirect discrimination which is of most interest for my purposes. Article 14 ECHR has a guarantee of non-discrimination (including in relation to indirect discrimination) but only in relation to the fundamental right guaranteed by the Convention. Therefore, read with Article 9, Article 14 ECHR requires justification of measures that indirectly discriminate in relation to the right to freedom of religion and belief. As this latter right has been interpreted in a way that focuses on individual autonomy and not group rights, this raises the issue of reconciling the idea of particular collective disadvantage with the egalitarian individualistic conception of the right to freedom of religion and belief. I will show that the Court of Human Rights has in fact developed a distinctive individualistic notion of indirect discrimination in relation to a fundamental right that is distinct from the freestanding principle seen in EU legislation.

The chapter proceeds as follows. I will first set out the individualistic, egalitarian and autonomy-focused approach of the ECtHR (and EU institutions) to the right to freedom of religion or belief. I then set out the more collective approach of EU legislation in relation to indirect discrimination in relation to religion or belief showing how its notions of particular disadvantage are in tension with the individualistic approach of Article 9. I will then discuss two cases that highlight the tensions between these approaches, noting how the collective approach inherent in EU indirect discrimination law would undermine valuable features of the current approach to freedom of religion or belief but also how the individualised model of indirect discrimination adopted by the Strasbourg Court in relation to Article 14 cases cannot be extended beyond the fundamental rights context without severely curtailing the aim of reducing group disadvantage that underpins EU legislation.

I will conclude by arguing that an individualistic approach to freedom of religion and belief and a collective approach to indirect discrimination in relation to religion or belief can coexist, but that this requires us to be clear about the differences between them. This means that indirect discrimination in relation to the (necessarily individualistically viewed) Article 9 ECHR will have to be seen as a distinct, individualistic, form of indirect discrimination which differs from the collectively oriented form of indirect discrimination covered by Directive 2000/78. The former, individualised form of indirect discrimination is unlikely to provide significant additional protection to that provided by religious liberty claims made under Article 9 on its own. I will close by highlighting how the tensions between freedom of

[1] Council Directive 2000/78/EC of 27 November 2000 establishing a general framework for equal treatment in employment and occupation, [2000] OJ L303/16.

religion and belief and restrictions of measures that indirectly discriminate on grounds of religion or belief feed into fundamental debates about the relationship between religion, the law and the state in liberal societies.

II. EUROPE'S INDIVIDUALISTIC AND EGALITARIAN APPROACH TO FREEDOM OF RELIGION OR BELIEF

Unlike the First Amendment of the US Constitution which speaks of freedom of religion only, Article 9 of the ECHR covers freedom of 'thought, conscience and religion'.[2] The Court has consistently stated that 'religious freedom is primarily a matter of individual thought and conscience'[3] and that religious beliefs are 'one of the most vital elements that go to make up the identity of believers and their conception of life'.[4] Such an approach is, obviously, not neutral. It is an approach that values religious freedom as one of the ways in which individuals can choose an identity and way of living that is meaningful to them. There will always be world-views with which a meaningful right to religious freedom will conflict. Indeed the protection of a fundamental right to freedom of religion and belief is based on a non-neutral worldview that privileges the idca of human autonomy in matters of belief. Religion is a vast and diverse category that covers a large spectrum of claims and behaviours, some very noble and morally compelling, others quite unworthy or trivial. The task of Courts is not to identify what, as a matter of sociology or theology, falls within the category of religion and to protect that in its entirety, but to identify what it is that is valuable about religious freedom (perhaps on the basis of an ideological preference for liberal values) and to ensure that that is what is protected.

This individualistic and belief-focused approach has been criticised for underplaying ritualistic elements of religion or the idea of religion as a set of embodied practices rather than beliefs.[5] The approach of the ECtHR sees religious freedom as primarily about individual conscience and autonomy and is closer to a Western Protestant view of religion with its emphasis on the individual's relationship with God. However, the preference for a view of religious freedom that favours individual choice in matters of religion over more communal ideas of religion is the inevitable result of the fact that

[2] The equal status of non-religious and religious beliefs is more controversial in First Amendment jurisprudence than it is in European law. See M Schwartzman, 'What if Religion Is Not Special?' (2012) 79 *University of Chicago Law Review* 1351.

[3] *Eweida v United Kingdom* (App no 48420/10) (2013) 57 EHRR 8 [80].

[4] ibid [79].

[5] Carolyn Evans, *Freedom of Religion under the European Convention on Human Rights* (Oxford and New York, Oxford University Press, 2001) 125.

the ECHR is a text committed to the protection of liberal values and that signatory States are committed to being liberal societies that value liberal principles.[6]

This liberal and individualistic approach to Article 9 leads to a second notable feature of the case law in this area: the commitment to the equality of religious and non-religious worldviews. Viewing the right to religious freedom as a means to protect the ability of individuals to hold beliefs of their choosing and to exercise autonomy in their construction of their own identity naturally leads to a view that it is not religion itself but the ability of people to choose and adhere to their beliefs that is the aim of Article 9. The Court has consistently stated that Article 9 'is also a precious asset for atheists, agnostics, sceptics and the unconcerned.'[7] The Court has been willing to recognise atheistic beliefs and other forms of philosophical belief that demonstrate sufficient 'cogency, seriousness, cohesion and importance'[8] as falling within the scope of the protection provided by the Convention. As Dworkin[9] and others have pointed out, the alternative view of freedom of religion and belief, namely that it exists to protect religious belief alone, raises significant issues of discrimination against the non-religious as well as difficult questions relating to the definition of religion.[10]

Although in the past it had sometimes sought to decide for itself what were the requirements of an individual's religion, the European Court of Human Rights now accepts that it is for individuals to determine what their faith requires.[11] The US Supreme Court has a similar approach. Other than assessing the sincerity of a person's belief, it will generally accept an individual's assessment of what their faith requires. The Court has rightly concluded that 'intra-faith differences ... are not uncommon among followers of a particular creed, and the judicial process is singularly ill-equipped to resolve such differences in relation to the Religion Clauses [of the US Constitution] ... Courts are not arbiters of scriptural interpretation'.[12]

6 See R McCrea, 'Religion, Law and State in Contemporary Europe: Key Trends and Dilemmas' in MC Foblets and K Alidadi (eds), *Belief, Law and Politics: What Future for a Secular Europe?* (London, Ashgate, 2014) 91.

7 *Kokkinakis v Greece* Series A no 260-A (1994) 17 EHRR 397; also *Eweida* (n 3) [79].

8 *Bayatyan v Armenia* (App no 23459/03) (2012) 54 EHRR 15, [110]; also *Eweida* (n 3) [81].

9 Ronald Dworkin, *Religion without God* (Cambridge MA, Harvard University Press, 2013).

10 ibid.

11 See for example the summary of applicable principles provided by the Court in *Eweida* (n 3) [82].

12 *Thomas v Review Board of the Indiana Employment Security Division* 450 US 707 (1981).

Refraining from objective assessment of what particular faiths require is the correct approach. After all, if freedom of religion is 'primarily a matter of individual belief' then it follows that the Court should interpret that right so that each person has the same scope to develop and follow those beliefs. This means that, even if we put to one side the enormous difficulties that accompany attempts by judges to decide what a particular faith (to which the judge in question may not even belong) does or does not require, it should still be the case that whether a person's co-religionists share her particular view of what their faith requires, should be irrelevant. The Strasbourg Court has repeatedly stressed that Article 9 equally protects 'atheists, agnostics, skeptics and the unconcerned'.[13] It must also be the case that it provides as much protection to the individual who has a minority interpretation of the requirements of a particular faith.

In adopting this individualistic and egalitarian approach, the ECtHR is very much in line with the approach of the EU. The text of the EU treaties explicitly recognises the equal status of non-religious beliefs.[14] In *Y and Z* the Court of Justice of the European Union (CJEU) explicitly recognised the importance of including non-religious beliefs and the right to abstain from religious practice within the terms of Article 10 of the Charter.[15] A commitment to treating religious and non-religious beliefs equally was also seen in decision of the Grand Chamber in *Achbita* upholding workplace restrictions on religious dress provided that the restrictions covered all visible symbols of religious, political and philosophical belief.[16] Finally, in the context of heated international debate on whether international law ought to recognizse the concept of 'defamation of religion', the Member States of the EU unanimously endorsed in 2013 *Guidelines on the Promotion and Protection of Religion and Belief* in which Member States' governments unanimously set out their commitment to the idea that human rights protect people, not religions, and to the equality of religious and non-religious belief.[17]

III. ANTI-DISCRIMINATION LAW: INDIRECT DISCRIMINATION ON GROUNDS OF RELIGION OR BELIEF

Article 10 of the Charter of Fundamental Rights of the European Union protects the right to freedom of religion and belief in terms that are

[13] *Kokkinakis v Greece* (n 7).

[14] Treaty on the Functioning of the European Union [2012] OJ C326/01, Preamble and Art 17(1).

[15] Joined Cases C-71/11 and C-99/11 *Y and Z v Germany* [2013] 1 CMLR 5.

[16] Case C-157/15 *Achbita v G4S* [2017] IRLR 466 and Case C-188/15 *Asma Bougnaoui and ADDH v Micropole* [2017] IRLR 447.

[17] Council of the European Union, Foreign Affairs Council Meeting (Luxembourg 24 June 2013).

substantially similar to those in Article 9 of the ECHR.[18] However, EU anti-discrimination law is much more expansive than the right to freedom from discrimination under the Convention. Article 14 of the ECHR only covers discrimination in relation to the rights and freedoms protected by the Convention. In contrast, the principle of equal treatment has played a central role in EU law. Not only has non-discrimination been recognised as a general principle of EU law,[19] there is also significant EU legislation in this area. Directive 2000/78 forbids direct discrimination on a range of grounds, including religion or belief, in the area of employment. It also provides that actions that are indirectly discriminatory are to be prohibited unless they are 'objectively justified by a legitimate aim and the means of achieving that aim are appropriate and necessary.'[20]

This means that there is significant scope for differences between EU law and the law of the ECHR in relation to matters of discrimination.[21] This is because there may be some tension between the principles underpinning the right to freedom of religion and belief and those underlying the prohibition of indirect discrimination on grounds of religion or belief. If one views freedom of religion in individualistic and egalitarian terms then, when applying the right to freedom of religion to a particular set of facts, the main objective is to ensure that each person is given the same scope to hold and follow their particular beliefs. The same does not necessarily apply when we are dealing with questions of indirect discrimination on grounds of religion or belief.

Certainly, prohibiting indirect discrimination on this ground can help to ensure that individuals have greater scope to follow their beliefs in situations where workplace rules (such as rules around time off or uniforms) are inconsistent with what an individual regards as the obligations of their faith. However, prohibiting indirect discrimination has other additional purposes. The EU Directive on discrimination in employment provides that, indirect discrimination occurs when, there is 'an apparently neutral provision, criterion or practice [that] would put persons having a particular religion or belief … at a particular disadvantage compared to other persons'.[22]

Two main sets of reasons have underpinned the development of the idea of indirect discrimination. The first set of reasons are heavily influenced by the use of ostensibly neutral rules which were in fact aimed to maintain discrimination against African Americans. From this point of view, rules against indirect discrimination aim at ensuring that the law deals adequately

[18] Charter of Fundamental Rights of the European Union [2007] OJ C303/5 Art 10.

[19] Case C-144/04 *Mangold v Helm* ECR [2005] I-9981.

[20] Equality Directive (n 1) Art 2(2)(b)(i).

[21] See Ronan McCrea 'Singing from the Same Hymn Sheet? What the Differences between Strasbourg and Luxembourg Courts Tell Us about Religious Freedom, Non-Discrimination and the Secular State' (2016) 5(2) *Oxford Journal of Law and Religion* 183.

[22] Equality Directive (n 1) Art 2(2)(b).

with disguised direct discrimination.[23] The second set of reasons come from a recognition that people with particular characteristics (that have salience in a particular society) face structural disadvantages when operating in society.

For indirect discrimination on grounds of religion this recognition comes from the fact that the majority religion in a society will normally have influenced social norms and labour market structures such as holiday times and dress codes to a greater degree than other faiths. This means that those who follow minority religions are more likely than those who follow the majority religion to find themselves in a situation where the requirements of their faith come into conflict with workplace rules and arrangements. Such general workplace rules (which may not relate directly to religion) may therefore place those who belong to minority religions at a particular disadvantage.[24]

On this view, the key issue in relation to indirect discrimination is *group* disadvantage.[25] Rules against indirect discrimination are not focused on ensuring similar treatment of different individuals but are focused on providing a degree of additional protection to compensate groups of people who suffer additional disadvantage related to a salient characteristic that they share. This means that the need to ensure that each person is given the same degree of protection for their individual choices, which the duty to accord equal concern and respect requires in claims of religious freedom, does not apply to the same extent in relation to indirect discrimination on grounds of religion. A collective view of indirect discrimination does not regard it as problematic to give preferential treatment (for example an exemption from compliance with a uniform) to one person (who belongs to a disadvantaged group) and to deny the same advantageous treatment to another person who does not belong to that group. This is because guaranteeing religious freedom and restricting indirect discrimination on grounds

[23] Judges in the UK have disagreed as to the issue of how measures which are facially neutral but where there is an exact correspondence between those who suffer from the disadvantage in question and the protected characteristic. See the discussion in *Bull and Bull v Hall and Preddy* [2013] UKSC 73, [2013] 1 WLR 3741.

[24] See *Griggs v Duke Power Co*, 401 US 424 (1971) where the US Supreme Court found that a measure which had been adopted without any discriminatory intent could never the less be held to be illegal as constituting measures that 'operate as "built-in headwinds" for minority groups'. Interestingly, in relation to religion, majority status can operate as a 'head wind'. Where a majority faith is culturally entrenched it is likely to be difficult to accommodate a worker who wants time off for religious services as the day of such services is likely to be the day on which most people will wish not to work (for example in order to align days off with those of family members) see for example *Mba v London Borough of Merton* [2013] EWCA Civ 1562, [2014] 1 WLR 1501.

[25] For a stimulating discussion of the role of idea of collective disadvantage in discrimination law generally, see Tarunabh Khaitan, *A Theory of Discrimination Law* (Oxford and New York, Oxford University Press, 2015).

of religion have different aims. The goal of one is, amongst other things, to protect individual autonomy by allowing each person to hold and follow the beliefs of their choice. The goal of the other is to reduce some of the disadvantages faced by members of a group whose particular beliefs mean they face particular obstacles not faced by others.[26]

IV. KEY CASES ILLUSTRATING THE TENSIONS

The tension between the individualistic approach towards religion that underpins the interpretation of religious freedom by the ECtHR and the group disadvantage focus of legislation prohibiting indirect discrimination on grounds of religion is highlighted by two cases litigated before the British courts and subsequently before Strasbourg.

The issue of group disadvantage in cases of alleged indirect discrimination brings up complicated questions when a person asserts that a rule or practice at her place of employment puts her individually at a particular disadvantage on grounds of her beliefs but where she cannot show that others who belong to the same religion share her view of what their shared faith requires. This was the scenario in *Eweida v British Airways*,[27] a case decided by the English and Welsh Court of Appeal and which, as *Eweida and Others v UK*,[28] was subsequently the subject of a complaint to the European Court of Human Rights. Ms Eweida worked at British Airways check-in facilities. She was initially refused permission to wear a visible cross over her uniform (though management subsequently reversed this decision). She argued that this initial refusal breached her Article 9 ECHR rights and that it amounted to indirect discrimination on religious grounds contrary to Directive 2000/78 (as implemented in the UK).

Ms Eweida's claim of indirect discrimination was complicated by the fact that she was the only one of many Christians working for British Airways who felt that her faith impelled her to wear a visible cross. Indeed, she herself had at times described her wish to wear a visible cross as a personal choice rather than a religious obligation. Writing for the Court of Appeal Sedley LJ noted that the relevant provision of the Directive and the implementing UK legislation was phrased in the plural ('a provision, criterion or practice ... which puts or would put *persons* of the same religion or belief as [the employee alleging discrimination] at a particular disadvantage

[26] Though see the Opinion of Maduro AG in Case C-303/06 *Coleman v Attridge Law* [2007] IRLR 88, where he argued that freedom of religion be enhanced by measures restricting indirect discrimination on grounds of religion or belief.

[27] *Eweida v British Airways* [2010] EWCA Civ 80, [2010] ICR 890.

[28] *Eweida v UK* (n 3).

compared with other persons').[29] He concluded that this was reflective of the fact that in assessing whether indirect discrimination had taken place

> equality laws on both sides of the Atlantic have, for many years sought to do this by seeing, first, whether an identifiable group is adversely affected, whether actually or potentially, by some ostensibly neutral requirement and then whether the claimant has in fact been disadvantaged by it.[30]

In the view of Sedley LJ, there was 'no indication that the Directive intended either that solitary disadvantage should be sufficient—the use of the plural ("persons") makes such a reading highly problematical—or that any requirement of plural disadvantage must be dropped'.[31] He noted the clearly different wording of legislation prohibiting discrimination on grounds of disability which spoke of an arrangement that 'places the disabled person concerned at a substantial disadvantage'.[32] Thus, he concluded that, in order for indirect discrimination on grounds of religion or belief to be established, 'some identifiable section of the workforce, quite possibly a small one, must be shown to suffer a particular disadvantage which the claimant shares'.[33] He and his colleagues backed the ruling of the Employment Appeal Tribunal which had held that

> in order for indirect discrimination to be established, it must be possible to make some general statements which would be true about a religious group such that an employer ought reasonably be able to appreciate that any particular provision may have a disparate adverse impact on the group.[34]

This approach was confirmed in *Mba v London Borough of Merton* where the Court of Appeal found against a worker seeking exemption from working on Sundays on grounds that, on the facts, her request could not be accommodated without undue hardship being placed on the employer.[35] Although two of the three judges in the case felt that the individualistic approach of Article 9 to religious freedom meant that when the issue of the justification of the employer's refusal to accommodate Ms Mba was being considered, a court should avoid finding that the employee's case for accommodation was weakened by the fact 'that her beliefs are not more widely shared or do not constitute a core belief of any particular religion'.[36] However, the Court was clear that to establish a claim of indirect discrimination in the first place, there was a 'need to establish group disadvantage.'[37]

[29] *Eweida v BA* (n 27) [6].

[30] ibid [13]. Recognising that a group who might potentially be affected is sufficient means that where there is a single victim who can identify others potentially affected, that single victim may be able to show that she is the victim of indirect discrimination.

[31] ibid [15].

[32] ibid

[33] ibid.

[34] ibid [24].

[35] *Mba v Merton* (n 24).

[36] ibid [35]–[42].

[37] ibid [35].

V. THE PROBLEM OF CONFLATION OF RELIGIOUS FREEDOM AND INDIRECT DISCRIMINATION IN RELATION TO RELIGION

This approach to indirect discrimination on grounds of religion has not met with universal approval. Hatzis criticises the approach of the Court of Appeal on the basis that, by looking for evidence of group disadvantage (either that the wearing of the cross was recognised as a requirement of the Christian faith or that there were other Christian workers who had also claimed the right to wear the cross over their uniforms) it 'made the protection of an individual's religious liberty contingent upon official religious doctrine and consensus amongst members of the same religious community as to what the faith requires'.[38] Hatzis goes on to note how, in US freedom of religion case law, the Supreme Court has held that it is ill-equipped to rule on intra-faith disagreements regarding the true content of a faith and accordingly, it is not competent to rule on whether individuals were correct in asserting that a particular act was required by their faith. He presents various scenarios that could have arisen if the Court of Appeal's approach were correct. What, he asks, would have happened if the Court had been faced with clashing evidence from different theologians as to whether or not the wearing of the cross was part of the Christian faith or if Ms Eweida had shown that other Christians did consider it their duty to wear the cross but that the official Church had disagreed with this view? Or, 'what if she were a member of a small religious group without a holy book, clergy and elaborate theological scholarship?'[39] This all leads, in his view, to the conclusion that the Court of Appeal was wrong and ought to have followed the US Supreme Court's injunction to avoid becoming arbiters of scriptural interpretation and recognised that indirect discrimination can occur in relation to a single individual.

Hatzis' critique wrongly conflates the issues of religious freedom and indirect discrimination on grounds of religion. He argues that by requiring evidence of group disadvantage to make out a claim of indirect discrimination, the Court of Appeal 'made the *protection of an individual's religious liberty* contingent upon official religious doctrines' thus misconstruing the claim as one of religious freedom rather than discrimination on grounds of religion.[40] As I have already noted, religious freedom has as a core aim the protection of an individual's right to choose and adhere to beliefs. This right should not depend on whether these beliefs are consistent with the official doctrine of the faith to which the individual belongs. Certainly, anti-discrimination laws have as one of their aims the protection of individual autonomy.[41] But different forms of anti-discrimination norms have

[38] Nicholas Hatzis, 'Personal Religious Beliefs in the Workplace: How Not to Define Indirect Discrimination' (2011) 74(2) *MLR* 287, 290.
[39] ibid 296.
[40] ibid 290 (emphasis added).
[41] See Khaitan (n 25) and *Coleman* (n 26).

different intentions and rules restricting indirect discrimination, as mentioned above, have as one of their key aims reducing the particular discrimination suffered by particular groups. Therefore unlike the prohibition on Direct Discrimination in the Directive which applies 'when one person is treated less favourably than another is, has been or would be treated in a comparable situation',[42] indirect discrimination looks for particular disadvantage in relation to particular characteristics (ie characteristics not shared by all). Thus, the Directive speaks of 'an apparently neutral provision, criterion or practice [that] would put persons having a particular religion or belief ... at a particular disadvantage compared to other persons'.[43]

The key thing to notice here is that the courts have found collective disadvantage to be inherent to claims of indirect discrimination on grounds of religion or belief. It is not necessary that the disadvantage in question be shared by all those who are followers of the faith in question. It would be enough if a small number of one's fellow believers shared this disadvantage (as in the case of a rule disadvantaging the minority of Muslim women who wish to wear face-covering veils), but if only one believer is (or would be) disadvantaged, indirect discrimination has not been established. The courts have been right to rule in this way. The objective of rules against indirect discrimination is to remedy *particular* disadvantage. There are two ways of viewing the term 'particular' in this context. One approach is to see the term 'particular disadvantage' as denoting a disadvantage that is specific to a particular person. A single individual holding particular beliefs may suffer particular disadvantage in that her beliefs mean that she and only she suffers from the disadvantage in question. The other view of the term 'particular' is to see it as denoting disadvantage that is 'exceptional' or 'unusual'. Because the wording of the relevant provisions of Directive 2000/78 is in the plural and in the light of the fact that, historically, measures to combat indirect discrimination developed in order to remedy the 'headwinds' encountered by certain groups, the courts have been right to favour the second option.

This means that, while a person with esoteric religious beliefs may suffer a disadvantage that is particular in so far as no other employee or potential employee is negatively affected as she is by workplace practices that restricts her ability to follow her faith, such a disadvantage is not 'particular' if we see the term as requiring unusual or exceptional disadvantage. No exceptional disadvantage is imposed when a person finds that there is a clash between their beliefs and workplace rules because everyone may find that their beliefs are to some degree, inconsistent with the requirements of

[42] Equality Directive (n 1) Art 2.
[43] ibid.

their employment. The particular—in the sense of unusual or exceptional—disadvantage that is required to activate rules covering indirect discrimination is found only where it is possible for a person to show that the disadvantage from which they suffer is linked to membership of a group that is recognised as facing 'headwinds'[44] which render it unusually (and therefore 'particularly') hard for those belonging to that group to access the degree of autonomy and flourishing enjoyed by others.

This may indeed lead to difficult scenarios under which courts have to engage in inquiries that would be inappropriate in the context of litigation in relation to religious freedom. Particular disadvantage could be shown by showing that the act in question reflects widely accepted conceptions of the requirements of the faith or by showing there are others who share the applicant's beliefs. This kind of second-guessing of individual identity claims is challenging for courts but it is inherent to the idea of indirect discrimination. To take an example, indirect discrimination on grounds of racial or ethnic identity is also covered by UK anti-discrimination law. In a recent UK case, it was held that school rules which prevented students from wearing their hair in a tightly plaited corn-row style were racially discriminatory as they impacted on students from Afro-Caribbean backgrounds for whom such hairstyles were part of their ethnic or racial identity. The Court specifically noted that there was evidence that there were other Afro-Caribbean families who shared the view that the hairstyle in question was part of their culture.[45] If a student in the UK from an Irish cultural background had made a claim that rules preventing him from wearing his hair in that style indirectly discriminated against him on the basis of his ethnic or racial identity would it not be acceptable for the Court to look at evidence from anthropologists or others that corn-row hair was not in fact a widely recognised element of Irish cultural habits? Even if the sincerity of the claim was accepted, I think it would be obvious that some element of further inquiry into whether this was, in fact, a trait linked to an Irish ethnic identity as conceived of by Irish people collectively, would be needed. An entirely idiosyncratic version of Irishness created by one individual that does not share characteristics with any other people claiming an Irish cultural identity cannot be said to be linked to a particular, in the sense of special, disadvantage nor to constitute the kind of 'headwind' that justifies restrictions on indirectly discriminatory measures.

[44] The term comes from the decision in *Griggs Power* (n 24). Khaitan (n 25) argues that all discrimination law (including both rules on indirect and direct discrimination) aims to reduce group disadvantage.

[45] *G (by his litigation friend) v The Head Teacher and Governors of St Gregory's Catholic Science College* [2011] EWHC 1452 (Admin), [2011]. See also: 'School's refusal to let boy wear cornrow braids is ruled racial discrimination' *The Guardian*, 17 June 2011 available at: www.theguardian.com/uk/2011/jun/17/school-ban-cornrow-braids-discrimination.

VI. A HYBRID: INDIRECT DISCRIMINATION IN RELATION TO *FREEDOM* OF RELIGION OR BELIEF AS DISTINCT FROM INDIRECT DISCRIMINATION IN RELATION TO RELIGION OR BELIEF

Sedley LJ was therefore correct to reject Ms Eweida's claim that a rule that restricted her individual religiously-motivated desire to wear a visible cross did not raise the question of indirect discrimination. The ECtHR was given the chance to rule on the issues raised by Ms Eweida in 2013.

The ECtHR found that there had been a violation of Ms Eweida's Article 9 rights. It found that it was not necessary for her to demonstrate that 'she acted in fulfillment of a duty mandated by the religion in question'. Rather, she had to show that there was 'a sufficiently close and direct nexus between the act and the underlying belief.'[46] Because Ms Eweida's Strasbourg claim focused on freedom of religion, rather than indirect discrimination on grounds of religion, the Court was right to avoid the question of whether the Applicant's belief was shared by others with the same religious identity. Freedom of religion or belief, as I have already discussed, is mainly an individual right, not a group-focused right like the right to freedom from indirect discrimination. Although Ms Eweida had lost before the national court and won before the ECtHR does not mean that it follows that the Strasbourg Court's approach to indirect discrimination on grounds of religion or belief is incompatible with the interpretation of Directive 2000/78 given by Sedley LJ in the Court of Appeal. Strasbourg's finding that there had been a violation of Article 9 was both fact-sensitive and, perhaps more importantly for my purposes, did not turn on the issue of discrimination. Five of the seven judges found that insufficient weight had been attached to Ms Eweida's freedom of religion by the national court and went on to conclude that, as a violation of the right to religious freedom had been found, there was no need to proceed to rule on the discrimination elements of Ms Eweida's case.

Ms Eweida's case was heard by the Court alongside three other cases from the UK, including one taken by a registrar employed by a local council who had been fired for refusing, on religious grounds, to register same-sex civil partnerships. Her employer justified the refusal to accommodate the applicant (named Lillian Ladele) on the basis that doing so would violate their internal anti-discrimination policy entitled 'Dignity for All' which required all staff to avoid discriminating on a number of grounds, including sexual orientation. Ms Ladele submitted that the refusal to exempt her from complying with this policy itself amounted to indirect discrimination contrary to Article 14 ECHR read in conjunction with Article 9 ECHR. Thankfully, the Court's decision in respect of Ms Ladele did explicitly address the question of the nature of indirect discrimination in relation to freedom of

[46] *Eweida v UK* (n 3) [82].

religion and belief under the ECHR. Such claims are taken under Article 14 of the Convention which does not provide a freestanding right to be free of discrimination but rather prohibits only discrimination (on grounds including religion) in relation to the rights and freedoms protected by the ECHR. Article 14 cases must, as the Court noted, be pleaded in conjunction with another Article (in this case Article 9). However, it is not necessary to establish a violation of this other article in order to found a claim under Article 14, it is merely necessary to show that 'the facts of the case fall within the ambit of another substantive provision of the Convention.'[47] Addressing Ms Ladele's claim of a violation of Article 14 read with Article 9 the Court stated that 'only differences in treatment based on an identifiable characteristic, or "status", are capable of amounting to discrimination within the meaning of Article 14.'[48] However, it also noted that such discrimination may be found where there is either 'a difference of treatment between persons in relevantly similar positions—or a failure to treat differently persons in relevantly different situations.'[49] In the latter case, a violation will occur where the act complained of 'does not pursue a legitimate aim or if there is not a reasonable relationship of proportionality between the means employed and the aim sought to be realized.'[50]

As noted above, in relation to Ms Eweida's complaint of indirect discrimination on grounds of religion or belief contrary to Directive 2000/78, the English Court of Appeal had attributed considerable importance to the question of whether Ms Eweida's desire to wear a visible cross was shared with others who shared her religious identity. The Strasbourg Court's assessment of whether the refusal of an exemption from a rule requiring Ms Ladele to avoid discriminating on grounds of sexual orientation while working as a registrar had amounted to impermissible indirect discrimination in relation to her Article 9 rights did not see it as necessary to ascertain whether Ms Ladele's desire not to register gay partnerships was one shared by others with the same religious identity. Instead, the Court simply stated that 'the applicant's objection to participating in the creation of same-sex civil partnerships was directly motivated by her religious beliefs. The events in question fell within the ambit of Article 9 and Article 14 is applicable'.[51]

The Court then characterised the question of particular disadvantage in a way that differed notably from the approach taken by the English Court of Appeal to indirect discrimination on grounds of religion or belief under Directive 2000/78. It stated:

> The Court considers that the relevant comparator in this case is a registrar with no religious objection to same-sex unions. It agrees with the applicant's contention

47 ibid [85].
48 ibid [86].
49 ibid [87].
50 ibid [88].
51 ibid [103].

> that the local authority's requirement that all registrars of births, marriages and deaths be designated also as civil partnership registrars had a particularly detrimental impact on her because of her religious beliefs.[52]

It is important to note what is not included in this characterisation of particular disadvantage. There is no reference here to the issue of whether others who shared Ms Ladele's faith also objected to registering same-sex unions or whether such an objection could be seen as characteristic of a particular group. Admittedly, given mainstream Christian teachings in relation to marriage, it may have been easy to find others of Ms Ladele's faith who held a similar view and the judgment did note, in passing, that the Applicant's view that homosexuality and same-sex unions came from 'the orthodox Christian view that marriage is the union of one man and one woman for life.'[53] Nonetheless, this observation was not integrated into the Court's analysis of the requirements for establishing indirect discrimination in relation to the right to freedom of religion under. This analysis treated as irrelevant the issue of whether the disadvantage suffered by Ms Ladele was one that she shared with an identifiable group. Instead it laid out an individualistic conception of indirect discrimination by identifying as the relevant comparator a second hypothetical individual namely 'a registrar with no religious objection to same-sex unions.'[54]

This is a view of indirect discrimination that is notably different to the approach towards indirect discrimination on grounds of religion or belief in Directive 2000/78. There are good reasons for the more individual approach of Strasbourg. As noted above, the right to be free of discrimination granted by Article 14 ECHR is applicable only to discrimination in relation to the protection of the fundamental rights guaranteed by the Convention. It is a right to be free of discrimination in relation to the right to freedom of thought, conscience and religion. This is a different right from the right protected by Directive 2000/78 (in relation to employment) which is the right to be free from discrimination in relation to one's religious identity.

When it addresses the fundamental right to freedom of 'thought, conscience and religion' that Article 9 of the Convention protects, the Strasbourg Court rightly aims to ensure that each person is given the same degree of protection to their right to choose and follow their beliefs. The amount of protection given should not vary according to whether or not the beliefs espoused by an individual are shared by an identifiable group. This means that when it assesses claims of indirect discrimination in relation to this right to freedom of thought, conscience and religion the Court rightly views this kind of indirect discrimination as aiming at protecting individuals

[52] ibid [104].
[53] ibid [102].
[54] ibid [104].

who hold particular beliefs from suffering unjustified disadvantage because of those beliefs. The understanding of indirect discrimination in relation to freedom of religion or belief necessarily reflects the individualistic conception of freedom of religion or belief that we see in the Article 9 case law which has consistently stressed that religious freedom is 'primarily a matter of individual thought and conscience'[55] as well as stressing the equality of religious and non-religious forms of belief.[56] This is not an understanding of indirect discrimination that can be applied to the concept of indirect discrimination on grounds of religion or belief that we see in Directive 2000/78, which, as Sedley LJ rightly noted, is a concept that aims to addressing the 'headwinds' faced by identifiable groups and is consequently less individualistic but which also creates a freestanding requirement that measures that cause particular (in the sense of exceptional or unusual) disadvantage for such groups be justified.[57]

VII. LIMITED IMPACT OF INDIVIDUALISED INDIRECT DISCRIMINATION

What is important to note here is that Strasbourg has come up with a form of indirect discrimination in relation to the right to *freedom* of religion or belief that, in contrast to the concept of indirect discrimination in relation to religion or belief, is individualistic and does not require a link to group disadvantage. However, it is significant that the individualistic form of indirect discrimination so recognised did not actually assist Ms Ladele in winning her case. In finding that the indirectly discriminatory impact on her religious freedom that raised a claim under Article 14 was justified by the need to protect the rights and freedoms of others, the Court did not require any more weighty a justification that it had required to the claims made under Article 9 alone (ie claims that requiring compliance with a non-discrimination policy amounted to an unjustifiable restriction on religious freedom). In both instances the ECtHR judges assessed whether the restriction or discriminatory impact satisfied a proportionality test.[58] It would appear therefore that, while the individualistic understanding of indirect discrimination in relation to freedom of religion or belief that was recognised in Ms Ladele's case makes it easy for an individual (including a solitary believer) to raise a claim of indirect discrimination, raising such a claim

[55] ibid [80].
[56] ibid [79].
[57] It should be noted that the right to freedom of religion belief may benefit indirectly from restricting measures that are indirectly discriminatory on grounds of religion or belief as such restriction may have the effect of reducing the barriers individuals face in following their beliefs.
[58] *Eweida v UK* (n 3) [94], [95], [100], [101], [106], [110].

may be of limited value to applicants. This is because almost all indirectly discriminatory measures will have the effect of restricting religious freedom and the Court has been clear that showing the restriction in question is indirectly discriminatory will not result in the State being required to produce justifications that are more compelling than those that would suffice had the challenge been made on the basis of Article 9 alone. In short, because it has not asked applicants alleging indirect discrimination in relation to Article 9 read with Article 14 to show particular (in the sense of additional or unusual) disadvantage in making their discrimination claim, the Court will not require States to meet an additional or unusual justificatory burden in relation to the challenged measures. This is in contrast to the situation under Directive 2000/78 where individual believers must surmount the hurdle of showing that the disadvantage they suffer is also suffered by others who share their religious identity but once they succeed in so doing, they will be in a stronger position to argue for particular accommodations that may not be given to others who do not share the applicant's religious identity.

This difference between the ECHR and EU anti-discrimination law is appropriate. If one sees individual rights and the right of each individual to equal freedom as the main objective of the right to freedom of religion or belief, then, as Strasbourg's jurisprudence has consistently stated, one cannot characterise religious belief as being entitled to higher levels of protection than non-religious beliefs and philosophies. If we wish to defend individual autonomy and the equal dignity of everyone, it would be highly inappropriate to vary the level of protection given depending on whether the belief the person wishes to follow is religious or non-religious. Such are the requirements of the principle of equal concern and respect. We must defend the right of individuals to choose their beliefs, not their right to choose a favoured form of belief. This view of Article 9 as a right of individual autonomy that applies equally to the religious and non-religious is reinforced by the ruling in *SAS v France*, where the ECtHR ruled on a challenge to the French law forbidding the wearing of face-veils in public.[59] The Grand Chamber's judgment finding no violation of the Convention stated that the applicant's claims under Article 8 (privacy) and Article 10 (freedom of expression) raised the same issues as the claim under Article 9, an approach which appears to regard the claim for autonomy on religious grounds (the fact that the ban interfered with her ability to follow her faith) as being a basis for no greater degree of protection than the claims that it violated other elements of her personal autonomy (her right to construct her own identity under Article 8 or to express herself under Article 10).[60]

[59] *SAS v France* (App no 43835/11) (2015) 60 EHRR 11.

[60] See Ronan McCrea, 'The French Ban on Public Facing Veiling: Enlarging the Margin of Appreciation' *EU Law Analysis* http://eulawanalysis.blogspot.it/2014/07/the-french-ban-on-public-face-veiling.html.

Indeed, the notably individualistic view of religious freedom consistently seen in the case law of the ECtHR is in harmony with the approach to religious freedom unanimously agreed by EU governments in the 2013 EU Guidelines on Freedom of Religion or Belief and the approach of EU institutions in this area, all of which have consistently stressed that non-religious beliefs are entitled to the same degree of protection as religious beliefs.[61]

Therefore, from perspective of those who wish to see the greatest scope for religious expression in areas such as the workplace, the kind of individualised form of indirect discrimination recognised by the Strasbourg Court in relation to Ms Ladele's claim has disadvantages. After all, if disadvantage on the grounds of any form of belief, including beliefs held by only one person, are recognised as forming the grounds for a claim on indirect discrimination, such indirect discrimination is unlikely to be a solid basis to obtain any exemptions or privileges not granted to others. This is because an indirect discrimination claim that is not linked to a broader group disadvantage does not encompass the notion of a 'headwind' or particular (in the sense of exceptional or additional) disadvantage. It is this idea of exceptional disadvantage suffered by identifiable groups that provides the basis for the degree of special treatment involved in granting individuals from a particular group exemptions from norms everyone else has to follow. The idea is that members of such groups face difficulties that others do not in adhering to their religion, therefore they are entitled to some additional degree of protection to enable them to live out their religious identity to the same degree as others.

This kind of particular disadvantage is not present in the case of a solitary believer who finds that her individual beliefs clash with a workplace rule. Everyone has beliefs, which may be deeply held, that can clash with the rules and requirements of our work. Therefore, the individual who finds

[61] However, though courts will defer to an individual's assessment of what her faith requires, it is not obliged to rule that freedom of religion will cover the act in question. The ECtHR has required a 'sufficiently close nexus' between the act and the belief in question. Some American scholars have written in support of such an idea. Geddicks worries about the expansive ideas of complicity with sin raised in cases such as Little Sisters of the Poor in which a claim was made that a law requiring employers to sign an opt-out from providing contraception (thereby activating provision of the contraceptive by a third party) violated religious freedom by making employers complicit in the provision of contraception. He suggests that the term 'substantial burden' on religious freedom caused in the Religious Freedom Restoration Act has to be interpreted objectively by the Court which is not required to defer entirely to what the individual believer regards as a substantial burden. (FM Gedicks, '"Substantial" Burdens', Brigham Young University Law Research Paper 15-18 available at: http://papers.ssrn.com/sol3/papers.cfm?abstract_id=2657733) One can readily imagine how unless this is correct, claims to exemption could become excessive in scope, for example, a petrol station attendant refuse to provide fuel to a taxi driver because she may use the taxi to drive women seeking abortions to a hospital.

that her beliefs are inconsistent with a particular workplace rule is facing a disadvantage that we may all face and so has difficulty in showing why she should not have to follow a rule that everyone else must abide by. If, however, it is possible for an applicant to show that her beliefs are shared with an identifiable group and thus satisfy the test for recognition of indirect discrimination under EU law, then the applicant can argue that the disadvantage faced is indeed particular in the sense of exceptional and additional. She will then have a stronger case for arguing that members of that group have an entitlement to an exemption that others may not be entitled to in order to alleviate this additional disadvantage to which the shared identity of members exposes them.

This approach is consistent with mainstream ideas of indirect discrimination noted by Sedley LJ in his judgment in *Eweida* which regards indirect discrimination norms as means to address particular disadvantages suffered by identifiable groups rather than as a means to safeguard the ability of each individual to express and adhere to their beliefs (this latter aim is much more in line with Strasbourg's individualistic view of the aim of freedom of religion and belief under Article 9).

VIII. BELIEF AND IDENTITY: TWO VIEWS OF RELIGION

The differing views of indirect discrimination seen in the case law of the Strasbourg Court and in applications of EU anti-discrimination law demonstrate how the way in which we characterise religion and the right to freedom of religion can have a major effect on the degree to which restrictions on religious practice and expression are seen as legitimate. Characterising religion as a form of belief means that it will be treated very differently from situations where it is regarded as a form of salient identity.

The difference between the approach of the ECHR and EU law in this area reflects wider debates in the broader issue of the relationship between religion, the state and the law. If we view religion as a form of salient identity and a source of special or additional disadvantage, this makes it easier to argue for exemptions or other special treatment where believers are granted rights not granted to all others. If we view religion as a form of belief, a commitment to treating with equal concern and respect the right of every individual to believe what they wish and follow such beliefs makes it much more difficult to consider exempting believers, but not others, from some rules.

Deciding which way to characterise religion in any particular case is complicated. Two Advocates General of the Court of Justice have taken strikingly different approaches in recent cases on restrictions of the wearing of headscarves at work (though the key disagreement between them was in relation to the issue of direct rather than indirect discrimination which reduces the relevance of the cases somewhat). In *Achbita*,[62] AG Kokott suggested that a:

> requirement of neutrality affects a religious employee in exactly the same way that it affects a confirmed atheist who expresses his anti-religious stance in a clearly visible manner by the way he dresses, or a politically active employee who professes his allegiance to his preferred political party or particular policies through the clothes that he wears (such as symbols, pins or slogans on his shirt, T-shirt or headwear).[63]

She suggested that a distinction could therefore be drawn between:

> immutable physical features or personal characteristics—such as gender, age or sexual orientation—rather than with modes of conduct based on a subjective decision or conviction, such as the wearing or not of a head covering at issue here.[64]

In *Bougnaoi*,[65] on the other hand, AG Sharpston argued that:

> to someone who is an observant member of a faith, religious identity is an integral part of that person's very being. The requirements of one's faith—its discipline and the rules that it lays down for conducting one's life—are not elements that are to be applied when outside work (say, in the evenings and during weekends for those who are in an office job) but that can politely be discarded during working hours. … But it would be entirely wrong to suppose that, whereas one's sex and skin colour accompany one everywhere, somehow one's religion does not.[66]

To some degree the Advocates General were speaking at cross-purposes. As I have written elsewhere in relation to this case:

> It is clear that religion is both identity and belief … What is needed is criteria to work out when it is right to treat religion as belief and when it is right to treat it as identity … Both approaches are appropriate at times. In relation to blasphemy laws, it is probably best to see religion as a form of ideology. In relation to the right to receive service in a shop, it is probably best to see it as a form of identity. The situation of employees is more complicated.[67]

Ultimately, the Court of Justice in these cases held that a policy that restricted the wearing of all visible symbols of religious, political and philosophical belief was indirectly discriminatory and potentially justifiable but that a rule targeting only the headscarf was directly discriminatory and illegal as it could not be seen as reflecting a genuine and determining occupational

[62] *Achbita* (n 16) Opinion of AG Kokott.
[63] ibid [52].
[64] ibid [45].
[65] *Bougnaoui* (n 16), Opinion of AG Sharpston.
[66] ibid [118].
[67] Ronan McCrea, 'Religious Discrimination in the Workplace: Which Approach Should the CJEU Follow?' EU Law Analysis blog, 13 July 2016, available at: http://eulawanalysis.blogspot.co.uk/2016/07/religious-discrimination-in-workplace.html.

requirement. Thus, the Court appeared to follow Kokott AG's characterisation of religion as akin to belief (though it rejected her views on the issue of what constitutes a genuine and determining occupational requirement).

The differences between the Advocates General in this area are seen across a range of debates about different aspects of the relationship between law, religion and the state, including on broader constitutional issues such as symbolic endorsement of religion by the state or the requirement that laws be supported by non-religious 'public reasons'. Such principles are difficult to defend if religion is regarded as simply another form of belief. After all, states regularly endorse controversial symbols (for instance the royal crest in British courtrooms or 'Liberté, Egalité, Fraternité' on French public buildings) and endorse controversial beliefs such as racial or sexual equality. Rules that require the state to avoid endorsing particular religious beliefs (symbolically or otherwise) depend to a great degree on recognising religion as an especially salient (and therefore divisive) form of identity.[68]

IX. CONCLUSION

The fact that the Strasbourg Court has had to come up with its own distinctive form of indirect discrimination in relation to the right to freedom of religion and belief that departs from the collective understanding of indirect discrimination in relation to religion or belief underlines the tensions in the approach of the law to religion. Religion is experienced both as a form of belief, like politics and as a form of individual and collective (often immutable) identity. These different elements of religion call out for very different forms of recognition by the law. Indeed, what is needed to treat religion as a form of belief is often directly in conflict with what is needed to treat religion as a form of collective identity.

In these circumstances, it is important that we maintain the distinction between questions of indirect discrimination and religious freedom. A failure to do so risks either undermining the valuable tradition within European law of granting equal status to all forms of belief (whether religious or not) by requiring individuals to show their beliefs are shared by others or risks undermining the ability of the law to deal with particular collective disadvantage by defining disadvantage in individual terms that preclude granting tailored exemptions to those facing 'head-winds' on account of their salient group identity.

[68] See Ronan McCrea, 'The Consequence of Disaggregation and the Impossibility of a Third Way' in Cecile Laborde and Aurelia Bardon (eds), *Religion in Liberal Political Philosophy* (Oxford, Oxford University Press, 2017).

When the two concepts are merged, as in the *Ladele* case, the solution arrived at by the Strasbourg Court (albeit in a rather under-argued form) is correct. The fundamental incompatibility between the collective orientation of indirect discrimination on grounds of religion or belief as an identity and the egalitarian, individualistic approach of European law to freedom or religion or belief means that a distinct category of indirect discrimination in relation to the right to freedom of belief is necessary. This category has to be individualistic in nature in order to cohere with the deep commitment to treating individuals and their beliefs as equally deserving of concern and respect whether their beliefs are religious or non-religious in nature. This means however that this individualistic form of indirect discrimination is unlikely to add extra protection beyond that provided by the guarantee of freedom of religion or belief in Article 9. This may raise worries for those who are concerned about those who face particular headwinds in asserting their religious freedom on account of their group identity. However, in my view, it is not possible to tackle this problem within the context of the right to freedom of religion and belief without undermining the key idea that liberal fundamental rights must, above all, treat each individual as equally important and deserving of respect. The idea that religion is special in the sense of being entitled to greater protection than other forms of belief or that religion itself, rather than individuals, is the holder of fundamental rights, is a dangerous and in-egalitarian one. Such ideas were at the root of international campaigns to promote highly illiberal ideas such as 'defamation of religion' and the idea that justification of religion for egregious violations of fundamental rights. Collective disadvantage is therefore more appropriately addressed through separate equality rules, such as those in Directive 2000/78, rather than through introducing dangerous in-egalitarian and collectivist elements into fundamental rights principles.

8

Indirect Discrimination, Affirmative Action and Relational Egalitarianism

KASPER LIPPERT-RASMUSSEN*

I. INTRODUCTION

AFFIRMATIVE ACTION HAS been a common feature of admission and employment practices of public institutions and private companies for almost 50 years. Robert Fullinwider describes it as 'positive steps taken to increase the representation of women and minorities in areas of employment, education, and culture from which they have been historically excluded'.[1] Probably, 'positive steps' are steps that go beyond eliminating direct discrimination against these groups that reduces their representation relative to what it would have been in its absence, most notably by also counteracting the effects of *indirect* discrimination.[2]

Fullinwider's characterisation can be improved in various ways. For instance, if we do not use 'exclude' in a very wide sense, in principle at least, there could be areas where, say, women are less well represented than men,

* Previous versions of this chapter were presented at University of Copenhagen, 8 December 2015; the Institute for Futures Studies, Stockholm, 15 December 2015; an Aarhus-Louvain workshop, 8 January 2016; and at Wadham College, University of Oxford, 18 March 2016. I am grateful to Gustaf Arrhenius, David Axelsen, Katharina Berndt Rasmussen, Juliana Bidadanure, Simon Birnbaum, Åsa Carlson, Naima Chahboun, Andreas Christiansen, Hugh Collins, Virginia Mantouvalou, Jens Damgaard Thaysen, Göran Duus-Otterström, Siba Harb, Deborah Hellman, Klemens Kappel, Tarunabh Khaitan, Tim Meijers, Sophia Moreau, Lasse Nielsen, Tom Parr, Hans Ingvar Roth, Julie Suk, Robert Talisse, and Folke Tersman for helpful comments. I owe a special debt to Les Green for a prepared commentary on an earlier version of the chapter.

[1] Robert Fullinwider, 'Affirmative Action' (Stanford Encyclopedia of Philosophy, 2013) available at http://plato.stanford.edu/entries/affirmative-action/; cf Elizabeth Anderson, *The Imperative of Integration* (Princeton, Princeton University Press, 2010) 135; Tarunabh Khaitan, *A Theory of Discrimination Law* (Oxford, Oxford University Press, 2015) 80–87.

[2] cf *Griggs v Duke Power Co*, 401 US 424 (1971); cf Owen M Fiss, 'Groups and the Equal Protection Clause' (1976) 5 *Philosophy & Public Affairs* 107, 141–46. Additionally, affirmative action has also been seen as a means of counteracting the effects of direct discrimination, which is difficult to prove in courts, eg because of the opacity of employers' intentions.

solely because, for unobjectionable reasons, they did not in large numbers form ambitions of entering these areas and where measures to boost their representation, intuitively, should be classified as affirmative action. Also, it is not clear that some steps, eg, quotas, that are known to have the expected consequence of increasing the representation of women and minorities, but are adopted for other reasons, eg, to increase the legitimacy of the institution in question, should not be classified as affirmative action. For present purposes, however, I shall take Fullinwider's characterisation as a point of departure.

At least one important rationale for affirmative action is that it is a way of eliminating or neutralising the adverse effects of rules and practices that amount to indirect discrimination.[3] Like affirmative action, indirect discrimination can be defined in various ways, and again I will rely on a pretty rough characterisation of indirect discrimination:

> Under many legal systems, an act that imposes a disproportionate disadvantage on the members of a certain group can count as discriminatory, even though the agent has no intention to disadvantage the members of the group and no other objectionable mental state, such as indifference or bias, motivating the act.[4]

Three features of this characterisation are striking. First, (in a way which is perfectly legitimate) it does not specify what it is for an act to impose a disproportionate disadvantage—or, to put it differently, to have disparate impact—on different groups. One can determine this relative to different baselines. Suppose a company has 80 male and 20 female workers. It has two and only two options that will enable it to avoid bankruptcy. One involves laying-off 10 workers, all male. The other option involves laying-off 10 workers, eight male and two female workers. Here one could say that since males are already over-represented, the first option does not disproportionately disadvantage men, since even after the lay-off, seven out of nine workers will be men.[5] Alternatively, one could say that the first option imposes disproportionate disadvantages on men, since while they make up 'only' 80 per cent of the present workforce, they make up 100 per cent of

[3] Anderson (n 1) 135–37; Gertrude Ezorsky, *Racism and Justice: The Case for Affirmative Action* (Ithaca, Cornell University Press, 1991); Robert Fullinwider, 'The Life and Death of Racial Preferences' (1997) 85 *Philosophical Studies* 163, 166; James P Sterba, *Affirmative Action for the Future* (Ithaca, Cornell University Press, 2009) 38–53. This is far from the only justification offered in favour of affirmative action. Equally important are justifications in terms of diversity, compensation and social cohesion (Anderson (n 1) 135–54). The first of these additional justifications is not always clearly distinguished from discrimination-related ones, since the intended beneficiaries of increased diversity tend to be groups subjected to discrimination.

[4] Andrew Altman, 'Discrimination' (Stanford Encyclopedia of Philosophy, 2014) available at http://plato.stanford.edu/entries/discrimination/; cf Khaitan (n 1) 73–76, 185.

[5] Indeed, one could say that because men are overrepresented on the job market as such, the first option does not disproportionately disadvantage them.

workers laid-off.[6] My present point is not that one of these views (or, for that matter, some other view) on 'disproportionate disadvantage' is correct, but simply to point out that there is an issue about the baseline relative to which we determine whether something involves disproportionate impact.

Second, suppose we determined that an act imposes a disproportionate disadvantage. That does not imply that it fails the proportionality requirement in a broader sense and, thus, is indirectly discriminatory. Altman's characterisation says that an act *can be* (not: is) indirectly discriminatory if it imposes a disproportionate disadvantage on members of a certain group.[7] Strictly speaking, this does not mean that disproportionate disadvantage is a necessary, but not sufficient, condition of indirect discrimination. However, evidently this is the claim Altman wants to convey and, thus, how I will understand his characterisation. He notes that different jurisdictions differ in relation to which further conditions must be satisfied for an act to qualify as indirectly discrimination. For instance, according to Swedish law, an act which disproportionately disadvantages members of a certain group (without directly discriminating against them) counts as indirectly discriminatory, if it can either not be motivated by a legitimate aim, eg, avoiding bankruptcy, or the means are neither appropriate, nor necessary for achieving the aim.[8]

Third, the wider requirement of non-disproportionality, of which the notion of disproportional disadvantage is one component, can be variously interpreted. I shall assume that disproportionality obtains between, on the one hand, the importance of a certain valuable end being achieved, eg, maximising profitability and/or benefiting protected groups, and, on the other hand, how the relevant act affects different groups in terms of harm and benefits relative to other groups, ie, in terms of disproportional disadvantage.[9] Return to my example of a company that can secure financial survival only

[6] Khaitan (n 1) 75.

[7] cp *Shanaghan v United Kingdom* (App No 37715/97) (2001).

[8] Nina Osin and Dina Porat (eds), *Legislating Against Discrimination: An International Survey of Anti-Discrimination Norms* (Leiden, Martinus Nijhoff, 2005) 864.

[9] cf Sandra Fredman, *Discrimination Law* (Oxford, Oxford University Press, 2015) 179; Kasper Lippert-Rasmussen, 'Indirect Discrimination is Not Necessarily Unjust' (2015) 2 *Journal of Practical Ethics* www.jpe.ox.ac.uk/papers/indirect-discrimination-is-not-necessarily-unjust/. There are other ways to construe the second *relatum* of the disproportionality requirement. However, the comparative conception I expound here is the one usually adopted by friends of indirect discrimination (but see Khaitan (n 1) 34–35, 75; for a reply, see Kasper Lippert-Rasmussen, 'Discrimination, Freedom, and Intentions' (2016) 79 *MLR* 901, 914–15. Note also that an end can be valuable, but not appropriate for a certain agent to pursue, eg, because the agent does not have the authority to pursue this aim. However, the way I am describing indirect discrimination allows that an act may disproportionately disadvantage a group and yet not qualify as indirect discrimination, eg, because it is appropriate and necessary for the agent to achieve the relevant aim in question. This could be the case if all the involved parties have consented in advance to the agent pursuing this aim even when this would involve disproportionate disadvantages for the consenting agents.

by laying off workers. Modify the example such that two available options involve sacking 10 workers, eight of whom are women, or, alternatively, sacking 90 workers, 50 of whom are women. Both options—set aside the baseline issue mentioned above—disproportionately disadvantage women, the former more so than the latter. Nevertheless, it could be the case that the first option, unlike the second, satisfies the non-disproportionality requirement, because the only alternative is laying off a much greater number of workers, including female workers, and avoiding doing so justifies the relevant disproportionate disadvantage for women.

There is much more to be said about Altman's characterisation.[10] What I want to focus on for present purposes is that indirect discrimination is tied by way of its definition to a concern for the distribution of (dis)advantages across groups. The reason I want to focus on this is that, in recent years, a number of so-called social relations egalitarians (henceforth: relational egalitarians), notably Elizabeth Anderson and Samuel Scheffler, have criticised the view that the proper ultimate focus of a theory of justice is distribution. On their view, justice is basically about 'the establishment of a society of equals, a society whose members relate to one another on a footing of equality'.[11] While, typically, achieving this requires the reduction of certain distributive inequalities, eg gross inequalities across racial groups or gender, there is a fairly wide set of possible distributions—including many involving inequality—all of which are compatible with egalitarian social relations and within this set justice is silent on which one we should realise. At first sight, this view of distributive inequality would seem to suggest that from the perspective of social relations egalitarianism indirect discrimination is not unjust and, accordingly, that standard justifications of affirmative action that appeal to how it neutralises the unjust distributive effects of indirectly discriminatory practices fail.

In this chapter, my main aim is not to discuss whether relational egalitarianism is a correct account of justice.[12] However, my main aim is to

[10] Kasper Lippert-Rasmussen, *Born Free and Equal?* (Oxford, Oxford University Press, 2013) 54–78.

[11] Samuel Scheffler, 'The Practice of Equality' in Carina Fourie, Fabian Schuppert and Iwo Walliman-Helmer (eds), *Social Equality* (Oxford, Oxford University Press, 2015) 21; Samuel Scheffler, 'Choice, Circumstance, and the Value of Equality' (2005) 4 *Politics, Philosophy & Economics* 5, 21; Samuel Scheffler, 'What is Egalitarianism?' (2003) 31 *Philosophy & Public Affairs* 5, 23. Fiss (n 2) offers a group-focused, anti-caste account of the Equal Protection Clause in the US constitution, which is congenial to relational egalitarianism. Interestingly, he also makes a number of criticisms of the (then) prevailing anti-discrimination norm, which have some affinity to my claims about the implications of the distributive nature of indirect discrimination below.

[12] Nor shall I discuss whether the concerns of relational egalitarians could be recast as concerns about the distribution of a particular social goods, eg social standing. I have raised such concerns elsewhere Kasper Lippert-Rasmussen, *Luck Egalitarianism* (London, Bloomsbury, 2015) 195–96.

defend two claims about what follows, if it is. First, if relational egalitarianism is the correct theory of justice, indirect discrimination is not unjust as such. Indeed, in principle it could be the case that in certain contexts indirect discrimination *is required* by justice, since it promotes egalitarian social relations. For the sake of clarity about my argumentative aims: I do not think this implication constitutes an objection to relational egalitarianism per se—I myself think that discrimination, indirect and even direct, might sometimes be required by justice—but it is nevertheless a troublesome implication for relational egalitarians for reasons explained two paragraphs below.[13]

My second main claim is this: to the extent that affirmative action is justified from the perspective of relational egalitarianism, it need not be tailored specifically to promoting the interests of disadvantaged groups subjected to indirect discrimination. Justified affirmative action might favour better off non-discriminatees and disfavour worse off discriminatees, when doing so promotes people's relating to one another as equals. People who are unsympathetic to affirmative action for better off non-discriminatees might see these implications as casting doubt on relational egalitarianism.

My two main claims are, I think, interesting in themselves. However, they are also significant because relational egalitarians often contend that their relational ideal of justice, unlike luck egalitarians, who accept a distributive ideal of equality, ie, that justice enjoins a particular distribution, captures the concerns of real-life egalitarians.[14] Anderson, for instance, complains that 'with respect to both the targets of egalitarian concern and their agendas, recent [luck: KLR] egalitarian writing seems strangely detached from existing egalitarian movements'.[15] However, if my two main claims of this chapter—stated in the two previous paragraphs—are correct, the view that relational egalitarians are committed to hold regarding indirect discrimination and affirmative action diverges radically from what most real-life

[13] cf Lippert-Rasmussen (n 10); Lippert-Rasmussen, 'Indirect Discrimination' (n 9).

[14] Admittedly, I do nothing to define a clear concept of 'real-life egalitarians', but simply rely on the few remarks to be found on the matter in the writings of Anderson and Scheffler and on my own preconceptions of who might count as such, eg, labour unions and Social Democrats in a European context. This is a problem. However, I do not think Anderson and Scheffler can point fingers here as they themselves offer little guidance on this matter, though they would seem to count abolitionists, the civil rights movement, disability activism, and at least certain views about how diversity should be accommodated in liberal societies as examples of a real-life egalitarian movements or positions, cp (Elizabeth Anderson, 'What is the Point of Equality?' (1999) 109 *Ethics* 287, 288, 312, 317, 337; Scheffler, 'Egalitarianism?' (n 11) 38). More generally, one might be sceptical of the very notion that a philosophical exploration of the ideal of equality is better to the extent that it coheres well with the concerns of any real-life political movement be it egalitarian or not.

[15] Anderson (n 14) 288; cf Scheffler, 'Practice of Equality' (n 11) 22; Scheffler, 'Egalitarianism?' (n 11) 38.

egalitarians believe.[16] Most real-life egalitarians find indirect discrimination unjust as such and are not indifferent between affirmative action benefiting groups that are worse- and better off in relational terms, respectively. Hence, the two discrepancies noted regarding indirect discrimination and, by implication, indirect discrimination law add an ironic, *ad hominem* twist to the two main lines of argument of this chapter. The complaint about strange detachment from the concerns of real-life egalitarians—whether ultimately forceful or not—can be put forward against relational egalitarianism too—at least when it comes to indirect discrimination.

Section II sets out the relevant parts of the positions of the two leading relational egalitarians, Anderson and Scheffler. Sections III and IV take up the first of my two main questions arguing that both of their views imply that indirect discrimination is not unjust as such. Sections V and VI address the second of my main questions arguing that on both of their views justified forms of affirmative action are quite different from—and sometimes implausibly so—those forms of affirmative action that we know of. Section VII concludes.

II. ANDERSON AND SCHEFFLER

In this section I sketch the anti-distributive views of two of the most prominent relational egalitarians, Anderson and Scheffler, starting with the former. In a much-quoted 1999 *Ethics* article, Anderson launches a staunch criticism of luck egalitarianism and sketches an alternative position, democratic equality.

While her criticism of luck egalitarianism is very rich I will focus on an aspect of it, which, despite Anderson's rather narrow target, applies much more broadly. Contrasting luck egalitarianism and her own view, Anderson writes:

> equality of fortune [ie luck egalitarianism: KLR] regards two people as equal as long as they enjoy equal amounts of some distributable good—income, resources, opportunities for welfare, and so forth. Social relations are largely seen as instrumental to generating such patterns of distribution. By contrast, democratic equality regards two people as equal when each accepts the obligation to justify their actions by principles acceptable to the other, and in which they take mutual

[16] Here I have two different kinds of divergences in mind: that relational egalitarians are committed to views on discrimination and affirmative action that most real-life egalitarians either reject, or alternatively do not accept, because, say, they have never considered possibly marginal or even hypothetical cases, where the relevant views apply. In response, relational egalitarians might contend that there would have been no divergence of either kind, if real-life egalitarians had thought through the issues. However, this response is tricky, because adopting it paves the way for a similar luck egalitarian response to the relational egalitarian challenge that the former's concerns are at odds with those of real-life egalitarians.

> consultation, reciprocation, and recognition for granted. Certain patterns in the distribution of goods may be instrumental to securing such relationships, follow from them, or even be constitutive of them. But democratic egalitarians are fundamentally concerned with the relationships within which goods are distributed, not only with the distribution of goods themselves.[17]

Anderson's point about 'equality of fortune' applies to any view that takes justice to be concerned exclusively and non-instrumentally with the distribution of goods. More specifically, it applies to such views that, unlike luck egalitarianism, ascribes no significance to people's choices or exercise of their responsibility, eg outcome egalitarianism, and it applies, *mutatis mutandis*, to such views that, unlike luck egalitarianism, do not take the relevant distributive pattern sanctioned by justice to be equality, but, say, sufficiency or, like prioritarianism, the maximisation of the overall sum of morally weighted benefits. For instance, according to resource sufficientarians, justice is satisfied when, in a distribution involving two people, both of them have enough resources whether or not they relate to one another as equals. To the extent that luck egalitarianism is incompatible with relational egalitarianism, such a distributive view is too.

Moving on to Anderson's positive ideal—that we relate to one another as equals—it is probably fair to say that she is more detailed in her description of what standing in relations of equality with others is incompatible with—to wit, that distributions matter non-instrumentally and independently of how they are constitutive of social relations—than in her description of what equal social relations amount to, positively speaking. Still, there are various things we can say about what it is for people to relate to one another as equals.

Before setting out the claims, which I take to capture, in part at least, Anderson's ideal of democratic equality, I need to establish a certain claim about how to interpret Anderson's ideal. This claim is not needed per se in an evaluation of indirect discrimination from an Andersonian point of view, but it is needed for determining the content of this ideal. The relevant interpretative point is that the site of Anderson's ideal does not just include individual citizens, but also extends to the state. That is, even if every citizen treated every other citizen as an equal, Anderson's ideal would not be satisfied provided that the state did not treat its citizens as equals. Anderson assumes that a community in which people stand in relations of equality to others, the state (insofar as it exists) acts from principles that express equal respect and concern for all citizens and to the extent that it does not, the ideal of democratic equality is unsatisfied. So, for instance, she thinks that a paternalistic state that makes insurance against various misfortunes mandatory acts disrespectfully by, in effect, acting from principles implying

[17] Anderson (n 14) 313–14.

that citizens are 'too stupid to run their own lives'.[18] Similarly, she thinks that, in recommending not assisting victims of very bad option luck because 'they deserve their misfortune', a luck egalitarian state does not 'treat them with respect'.[19] The interpretative point that I shall rely on is that the features of a relation between the state and its citizens that make it the case that democratic equality is violated are also features that, to the extent that they characterise relations between individual citizens, violate the ideal of democratic equality.

With this interpretative point in mind, I can state the first positive claim about the nature of democratic equality. To the extent that relations between individuals involve paternalistic coercion, contemptuous pity, condescension, envy, demeaning and intrusive judgements of people's capacities to exercise responsibility, or failure to help destitute people on the ground that their situation is their own fault, the relevant community is not one in which people relate to one another as equals.[20] Call this Anderson's *no disrespect requirement*.

Second, a community of equals is incompatible with hierarchies where 'human beings' are 'ranked according to intrinsic worth'.[21] So, most obviously, a community of equals is incompatible with a society where people are ranked in terms of intrinsic worth on the basis of race, sex or gender, and, thus, relations between citizens are relations between 'inferior and superior persons'. An aspect of this is that equality is incompatible with oppression—that is, 'forms of social relationships by which some people dominate, exploit, marginalize, demean, and inflict violence upon others'.[22] Positively, '[the equal moral worth of persons] asserts that all competent adults are equally moral agents; everyone equally has the power to develop and exercise moral responsibility, to cooperate with others according to principles of justice, to share and fulfill a conception of their good'.[23] Hence, every member of the community has a right to take part on an equal footing in the collective self-determination of the community.[24] Call this set of claims the *no-ranking requirement*.

Three, in a society of equals there are certain capabilities—those required for avoiding entanglement in oppressive relationships and those required for

[18] ibid 301.
[19] ibid.
[20] ibid 289, 295, 306–07, 314.
[21] ibid 312.
[22] ibid 313. Anderson says that 'distinct roles in the division of labor' (among other things) never justifies the forms of social relationships involved in oppression (Anderson (n 14) 313). While this does not entail, it certainly suggests, that distinct roles in the division of labour is compatible with Anderson's ideal of democratic equality.
[23] ibid 312.
[24] ibid 313.

participating as an equal citizen in a democratic state and in a democratic civil society—that people 'have access over the course of their whole lives'.[25] Call this the *sufficiency requirement*.[26] This requirement does not support comprehensive equality in the space of capabilities, eg, in the capability for welfare, but it is incompatible with any group of people being 'excluded from or segregated within the institutions of civil society, or subjected to discrimination on the basis of ascribed social identities by institutions of civil society'.[27] Democratic 'equality guarantees all law-abiding citizens effective access to the social conditions of their freedom at all times'.[28] Even setting aside non-law-abiding citizens, this sufficientarian strain in Anderson's thinking suggests that there could be inequalities between groups of people compatible with everyone enjoying the social conditions of their freedom.[29] Indeed, it suggests that there could be inequality of opportunity under democratic equality. I will return to this in section III.

Henceforth, I will take the no-disrespect, no-ranking and the sufficiency requirements to capture Anderson's ideal of democratic equality. While satisfying one of the three requirements might render it more likely that the two other constraints are satisfied, in principle each of them can be satisfied even if none of the other requirements is satisfied. For instance, the sufficiency requirement might be satisfied even if citizens are often disrespectful to one another and even if citizens are ranked in certain ways, eg in terms of looks, that, however, do not affect people's ability to avoid ending up being entangled in oppressive relationships or participating in politics and civil society, eg, while it is *more difficult* for people at the bottom of the hierarchy to do so, they are *able*, expending sufficiently low levels of effort, to do it—it is just that they have to exert themselves more than people higher up the hierarchy have to.

I shall now leave Anderson's views to set out Scheffler's position before, in the next section, returning to the first of my two main questions. In a recent elucidation of the relational egalitarian ideal, Scheffler takes his point of departure in a simple personal relationship between two persons—a marriage—and asks what it is for such a relation to be a relation between equals. One component of such a relationship draws on values other than equality. So, for instance, an egalitarian relation is one in which individuals treat one another with respect and each see the other as a moral agent with the rights and responsibilities accruing to moral agents. Another, and

[25] ibid 314, 316.

[26] This requirement is compatible with Anderson's critique of theories of justice that, at a fundamental level, focus on distributions, since it is rooted in a concern for people relating to one another in an egalitarian manner.

[27] Anderson (n 14) 317.

[28] ibid 289.

[29] cf ibid 326.

distinctively egalitarian component, is what Scheffler dubs the *egalitarian deliberative constraint*:

> If you and I have an egalitarian relationship, then I have a standing disposition to treat your strong interests [understood broadly to include the person's needs, values, and preferences] as playing just as significant a role as mine in constraining our decisions and influencing what we do. And you have a reciprocal disposition with regard to my interests. In addition, both of us normally act on these dispositions.[30]

Scheffler explicitly notes that satisfying the constraint is compatible with reaching decisions that do not leave the parties, who relate to one another as equals, equally well off.[31] Indeed, he thinks that it is unlikely that participants in egalitarian personal relationships will 'attempt to satisfy the [deliberative] constraint through the self-conscious application of a fixed distributive formula', though the constraint will 'exert pressure in the direction of egalitarian distribution'.[32] Conversely, even if a strict distributive formula of equality was continuously satisfied, the ideal of relating to one another as equals could fail to be satisfied if one of the parties to the relationship continuously flouted the deliberative constraint. This connects with a more general point that he makes: that equality, as he construes it, is 'a form of practice rather than a normative pattern of distribution'.[33] Hence, we cannot helpfully define a certain good, say, social standing, as something that, all other things being equal, two people have equal amounts of if, and only if, they relate to one another as equals and one has more of than the other to the extent that the former relates to the latter as superior and the latter relates to the former as inferior.[34] Doing so would simply leave out the 'deliberative and practical dimensions' of relational equality. More generally, it shows that there is a deep and genuine difference between distributive views of equality and those subscribed to by relational egalitarians.

What can we learn about a society of equals from this characterisation of a two-person egalitarian relationship? Very much, Scheffler thinks. The deliberative constraint applies to a society of equals as well:

> each member accepts that every other member's equally important interests should play an equally significant role in influencing the decisions made on behalf of the society as a whole. Moreover, each member has a normally effective disposition to treat the interests of others accordingly.[35]

So, for instance, in a society of equals, gay marriage laws would be decided on the basis that the interests of gay persons in being able to marry is just

[30] Scheffler, 'Practice of Equality' (n 11) 25.
[31] ibid 28–29.
[32] ibid 33, 34.
[33] ibid 31.
[34] Lippert-Rasmussen (n 12) 195.
[35] Scheffler, 'Practice of Equality' (n 11) 35.

as strong as the interests of heterosexuals and everyone being disposed to treat these interests equally. While the deliberative constraint exerts a strong pressure in direction of social and political equality, eg, it seems incompatible with the huge inequalities generated under laissez-faire, this pressure can give way to other considerations such that it does not issue in a fixed distributive formula, even when interpreted against the broader background of the ideal of relating to one another as equals.[36]

Before exploring how Anderson's and Scheffler's views bear on indirect discrimination, let me briefly comment on whether Anderson's three requirements follow from Scheffler's deliberative constraint, or vice versa. First, the satisfaction of the deliberative constraint does not imply the satisfaction of Anderson's three requirements. Citizens can comply with the deliberative constraint even if not everyone, perhaps not anyone, has enough to participate as an equal in a democratic state or in civil society, eg, because there is extreme scarcity. Perhaps the constraint could even be satisfied in the presence of ranking of people, eg, in a scenario where we take turns being nobles and undoing the relevant changing-places hierarchy would be bad for all concerned. Lastly, it seems citizens might comply with the deliberative constraint and still be motivated in part by attitudes, eg, pity, that clash with Anderson's no-disrespect requirement. More generally, Scheffler's deliberative constraint is not concerned with what principles or acting from certain principles expresses.[37]

Second, the satisfaction of Anderson's three requirements does not imply the satisfaction of the deliberative constraint. Suppose everyone has a sufficient set of freedoms such that Anderson's sufficiency requirement is satisfied. Suppose, moreover, that people subscribe to laissez-faire, whenever everyone is above the required minimum. They do not take any disrespectful attitudes towards one another or act from principles that express disrespect but simply disregard the interests of others in such cases, except to the extent that not doing so is instrumental from the point of view of promoting their own interests. (I am assuming with Anderson that indifference to the interests of someone above the minimum threshold is not disrespectful.) Lastly, the no ranking requirement is satisfied because, let us suppose, it alternates who is harmed by the fact that no one satisfies the deliberative constraint, ie (roughly) of each of us it is true that sometimes we gain and sometimes we lose. We can infer that while Anderson and Scheffler might share certain views about the flaws of distributive conceptions of justice, their positive ideals of relating to one another as equals are quite different. This warrants treating their views separately in what follows.

[36] ibid 40.

[37] Scheffler's deliberative constraint is merely a central component in his ideal of relating to one another as equals and what I say here leaves open that the less central components of his ideal imply the satisfaction of Anderson's three requirements.

III. RELATIONAL EGALITARIANS ON THE INJUSTICE OF INDIRECT DISCRIMINATION: ANDERSON

Is indirect discrimination unjust per se on either of the two relational egalitarian views laid out in section II? Again, I will start with Anderson's view.

Initially, I should repeat that I am focusing on indirect discrimination. By the definition I adopted, the indirect discriminator 'has no intention to disadvantage the members of the group and no other objectionable mental state, such as indifference or bias, motivating the act'. Hence, while there might be many forms of direct discrimination which *are* incompatible with people relating to one another as equals—eg, it might be incompatible with employers refusing to hire applicants on account of their race, gender or sexuality—because these forms of discrimination violate the no-disrespect requirement, that incompatibility is not relevant to the current issue. Our exclusive focus here is on indirect discrimination, where such objectionable mental states are absent.[38] Undoubtedly, many actual forms of direct discrimination involve people relating to one another as *un*equals, eg old-style racial or sex discrimination. However, our question is whether indirect discrimination is compatible with people relating to one another as equals and whether its absence could even contribute to people not relating to one another as equals.

So, return to my question about democratic equality and indirect discrimination. I shall assume that if indirect discrimination can co-exist with the joint satisfaction of all three requirements identified in the previous section, relational egalitarianism is compatible, at least in principle, with indirect discrimination. This leaves open that, as a matter of fact, many forms of indirect discrimination are incompatible with people relating to one another as equals, because they tend to lead to the violation of either one or more of the three requirements of democratic equality. However, this is analogous to how many forms of distributive inequality as a matter of fact are incompatible with egalitarian social relations—something which Anderson and Scheffler both agree but which nevertheless does not prevent them from thinking that they disagree with proponents of the distributive view.

Consider first the no-disrespect requirement. While some forms of indirect discrimination might embody, express or promote disrespect, indirect discrimination need not do so. Suppose that university admissions are based on the score obtained by applicants in a certain test. Suppose that this practice disadvantages a certain racial group disproportionately, although it does

[38] Moreover, whether or not they involve objectionable mental states many forms of direct discrimination might be compatible with standing in relations to one another as equals. Suppose the police spend more resources on screening and surveillance of young males in relation to sexual violence than on elderly women on the basis of perfectly reliable crime statistics. Presumably, this is direct discrimination against young men. Yet, it would not seem treating young males as not being equals with elderly women or anyone else for that matter.

not reflect any form of direct discrimination. In using the test, a university neither must be acting from a principle that expresses contempt for people doing less well in the test, nor need leave anyone very badly off (applicants not admitted might have reasonably good alternatives to the relevant study programe), nor act from paternalistic motives etc. Indeed, it might be the case that the university is innocently unaware of the disproportionate under-representation of certain groups that results from using the test, eg because many applicants reject the idea of race-classification.

Consider next the no-ranking requirement. Indirect discrimination is compatible with the satisfaction of this requirement as well. Surely, in using the relevant test described in the previous paragraph the university does not posit a 'hierarchy of human beings' or deny the 'equal moral worth of persons'. Indeed, it could be true that it would stick to the test if it produced the same disproportional representation but across different racial groups. Similarly, it need not deny that we each have an obligation to justify our actions by principles acceptable to others.[39]

Some might suggest that if the university is aware of how using the test negatively affects the interests of a certain group and nevertheless persists in using it, then the indifference to the interests of the members of this group amounts to denying them 'equal moral worth'. Nothing prevents me from accepting this point, since, as suggested above, it suffices for my argumentative purposes that the university *could* innocently be unaware of the relevant consequences. But even setting aside this fact, the present suggestion is no threat to my line of argument. In general we can display considerable blindness to the interests of others without in any way coming close to denying the 'equal moral worth of persons' in the way that racists or believers in caste societies deny this ideal. For instance, I am aware that most of the money I spend would have satisfied much greater needs of others had I donated them to, say, Oxfam's activities in Ethiopia instead and even if my not doing so is morally wrong, most would not suppose that my consumption pattern expresses my denial that Ethiopians and I have an equal moral status. For instance, unlike racists I would think no differently of rich Ethiopians, who in a hypothetical situation ignored the plight of impoverished Danes, myself included, and I would deem actively harming, as opposed to not helping, Ethiopians morally equivalent to harming Danes, myself included. If so, might the university not, on similar grounds, argue that its admission test does not express a denial of the equal moral worth of persons? It seems that to answer this question negatively, we would have to adopt a very broad view of what it is to deny the equal moral worth of persons. The downside to this argumentative move is that it now becomes very controversial whether acting in such a way that one expresses a denial

[39] cf Anderson (n 14) 313.

of the equal moral worth of persons is morally impermissible. Hence, for many interlocutors appealing to this broad understanding of equal moral worth will cut little argumentative ice.

One way to see this is to recall Anderson's positive description of what it means for persons to have equal moral worth. Surely, her otherwise forceful examples of a luck egalitarian state that abandons victims of very bad option luck or compensates victims of very bad brute luck in no way expresses a denial that all adults are moral agents. Indeed, as regards the former case, it is the very way in which victims of bad option luck exercised their moral agency that motivates their abandonment. As regards the latter case, one can exercise responsibility, cooperate, and hold and fulfil a conception of the good even if one is (labelled) a victim of bad brute luck. In fact, many forms of bad brute luck would not qualify as such, or qualify as such to a much lesser extent, if the victim did not have a conception of the good, eg, if the 'ugly and socially awkward' did not see having a partner as part of his or her plan of life. I conclude that indirect discrimination per se does not violate the no-ranking requirement either.

Consider, finally, Anderson's sufficientarian requirement. According to Anderson once 'all citizens enjoy a decent set of freedoms, sufficient for functioning as an equal in society, income inequalities beyond that point do not seem so troubling in themselves'.[40] Hence, my example of an indirectly discriminating university admission test is compatible with the satisfaction of the sufficiency requirement. Anderson writes: 'Democratic equality does not object if not everyone knows a foreign language, and only few have a PhD-level training in literature'.[41] Assuming this is right, would things be any different if the reason that differential knowledge of foreign languages or differential access to PhD-level training in literature reflects indirect discrimination, eg, that the particular foreign languages in which instruction is offered or the curricula used in PhD literature training programmes disproportionately favour some (non-protected) groups over others (who do constitute protected groups in the eyes of discrimination law)? I do not see how they could be. Surely, whether one enjoys a decent set of freedoms in the present sense depends on what this set of freedoms enables one to do and not on the way in which one came to enjoy this set of freedoms (and others came to enjoy their set of freedoms).

One might deny this claim by arguing that some sort of requirement of equality of opportunity is built into the notion of having a set of freedoms sufficient for functioning as an equal in society—recall Anderson's remark in the second paragraph of section II above to the effect that certain distributions might be constitutive of egalitarian social relations—and that

[40] ibid 326. Her formulation suggests that these inequalities are *somewhat* objectionable. It is not clear however, that the source of this objectionableness lies in democratic equality.

[41] ibid 318–19.

indirect discrimination necessarily is conducive to inequality of opportunity in which case the sufficiency requirement might after all be incompatible with indirect discrimination. For instance, it might be argued that to have a sufficient set of freedoms to function as an equal in the political sphere, it is necessary that one's set of freedoms in terms of being able to influence political outcomes is no better, no worse, than the comparable sets of freedoms of others. An additional attractive feature of this move is that relational egalitarians claim that their ideal captures what real-life egalitarians care about and since real-life egalitarians do care about equality of opportunity—in fact, more or less everyone cares about equality of opportunity in some form or other—this particular claim becomes more credible.

Whatever the merits of this move are when considered in isolation, there are several reasons why, given the wider context, it is unattractive for relational egalitarians to endorse it. First, as we have seen, relational egalitarians criticise luck egalitarians for their focus on distributions as opposed to social relations. However, if it turns out that the relevant kind of egalitarian social relations only obtain provided that a certain distributive requirement is met, to wit, that equality of opportunity is satisfied, then the satisfaction of certain distributive requirements is part and parcel of the ideal of relating to one another as equals and, accordingly, the distance to the distributive paradigm becomes much smaller.[42]

Second, it is implausible to claim that strict equality of opportunity is part of what it is for people to relate as equals given how relational egalitarians characterise the latter ideal. One important distinction that needs to be made here is between people actually having equal opportunities (which does not seem to be a matter of social relations in the relevant sense), on the one hand, and people believing (truly or not) that they have equal opportunities and acting in ways informed by this belief, on the other. Suppose men and women believe that, overall, they have equal opportunities, but as a matter of fact men have somewhat better opportunities than women have. In this scenario, one's gender in no way carries any message about one's ranking in any hierarchy and members of different sexes in no way relate to one another in disrespectful ways on the basis of their gender. Indeed, we can imagine situations where, as a matter of fact, members of one gender need to have better opportunities than members of another gender, if the two are to be generally believed to have equal opportunities and if one's gender is to have no hierarchical symbolic content, eg, if the representation of members of one gender for some reason is more salient than the equal representation of members of the other gender.[43] If, in addition to that, the

[42] This distance is not reduced to zero, since relational egalitarians might still give a different account of why it is valuable that the distribution takes a certain form, to wit, that it enables the realisation of a certain kind of social relations.

[43] Similarly, there might be cases where minorities need to enjoy indirect discrimination in their favour in order not be seen as invisible and inferior.

sufficiency requirement is met, it is hard to see why such a society might not fully meet Anderson's standards of democratic equality.

Third, in any case indirect discrimination could exist together with global equality of opportunity. That is, it could be the case that, in relation to one set of jobs, women are disadvantaged by indirect discrimination. However, if that is perfectly counterbalanced by how men are disadvantaged by indirect discrimination in relation to another set of jobs (or, for that matter, in relation to opportunities other than opportunities for jobs), there need not be any morally objectionable inequality of opportunity between men and women. Admittedly, there might be local inequalities of opportunities, but, generally, it is global equality of opportunity that, morally speaking, people care about.[44] I conclude that indirect discrimination per se can coexist with the satisfaction of the three Andersonian requirements. Hence, indirect discrimination is not unjust as such according to democratic equality.

IV. RELATIONAL EGALITARIANS ON THE INJUSTICE OF INDIRECT DISCRIMINATION: SCHEFFLER

So let us take a look at Scheffler's deliberative constraint and its relation to indirect discrimination. The crucial question is whether there could be forms of indirect discrimination among individuals all of whom comply with the deliberative constraint. This seems quite possible. Consider a situation in which there is a choice between two different hiring policies: one will result in a much greater percentage of men than women being hired, while the other policy will result in an equal distribution across gender, albeit, for some reason, fewer people will be hired such that on the second policy there will be hired fewer women than on the first policy. This would appear to be one of the cases where the pull towards equality exerted by Scheffler's deliberative constraint is resisted. That is, since there would be no relevant conflict between the individuals' interests, ex ante everyone's interests would be better promoted by the former hiring policy, individuals reasoning in compliance with Scheffler's constraint might well favour the first policy.[45] Yet, it might amount to a form of indirect discrimination. Whether it does depends on whether the disproportionate disadvantage to women of that policy violates the non-proportionality requirement (see the Introduction to this chapter). Assuming that the relevant disproportionate disadvantage is comparative—ie it is a matter of how much women are

[44] cf Lippert-Rasmussen, 'Indirect Discrimination' (n 9). This point is perfectly consistent with the view that the legal ideal of equal opportunities informing law of indirect discrimination concerns local inequalities in opportunities, eg, opportunities for jobs in general or opportunities for particular categories of jobs.

[45] Alternatively we can suppose that any person employed under the second policy would also be hired under the first policy.

underrepresented relative to men—it could violate the non-disproportionality requirement in that the moral gain achieved through hiring more people does not justify the disparate impact on women, eg, hiring an additional 10 workers might not outweigh the badness of having a workforce of which almost 60 per cent is men instead of a workforce that is perfectly gender-balanced.[46] Hence, it seems that not only is indirect discrimination logically consistent with full compliance with Scheffler's deliberative constraint, there are possible situations in which agents, who comply with this constraint, favour a scheme which is indirectly discriminatory in comparison to a scheme which is not.[47] The wider upshot of this section, thus, is that both Anderson's and Scheffler's ideal of social relations egalitarianism can be realised despite the existence of indirect discrimination and non-existence of rules disallowing it. Indeed, in some situations schemes that are indirectly discriminatory might be preferred to schemes that are not (cf my example immediately above in this paragraph, footnote 45, and my third response to the inbuilt-equality-of-opportunity-requirement-response).

V. RELATIONAL EGALITARIANS ON JUSTIFIED FORMS OF AFFIRMATIVE ACTION: ANDERSON

Which forms of affirmative action, if any, are justified on either of the two relational egalitarian views laid out in section II? I start with Anderson's view.

One of the more persistent objections to many kinds of affirmative action is that they stigmatise the intended beneficiaries as inferior. Here is what Carl Cohen, a fierce opponent of affirmative action, claims:

> Preference puts distinguished minority achievement under a cloud. It imposes upon every member of the preferred minority the demeaning burden of presumed inferiority. Preference creates that burden; it *makes* a stigma of the race of those who are preferred by race. An ethnic group given special favor by the community is *marked* as needing special favor—and the mark is borne by every one of its members.[48]

It is difficult not to be struck by the parallels between Cohen's stigma objection to affirmative action and Anderson's objection to luck egalitarian

[46] cf Lippert-Rasmussen, 'Indirect Discrimination' (n 9). I am not contending that such a policy *does* violate the non-disproportionality requirement. It all depends on how one weighs the disvalue of avoiding disparate impact on women against the value of employing more people, including more women.

[47] Admittedly, the present point presupposes that for something to qualify as indirect discrimination, it is necessary that it is not the case that it benefits those, who are harmed comparatively speaking, absolutely speaking and harms no one absolutely speaking.

[48] Carl Cohen and James Sterba, *Affirmative Action and Racial Preference* (New York, Oxford University Press, 2003) 110.

compensation to those who suffer very bad brute luck, eg, those who are very unattractive or very untalented. This is one prima facie reason for thinking that affirmative action, or at least some forms of it, are incompatible with Anderson's no-disrespect requirement.

Anderson also offers another criticism of luck egalitarianism, which seems to apply, *mutatis mutandis*, to some forms of affirmative action. She argues that the compensation for bad brute luck justified by luck egalitarianism, if implemented, give

> individuals an *incentive to deny personal responsibility for their problems*, and to represent their situation as one in which they were helpless before uncontrollable forces. Better social conditions for fostering the spread of a passive whining victim's mentality could hardly be constructed.[49]

It is not entirely clear whether Anderson regards these claims as objections to luck egalitarianism, eg, because she thinks that because acting on luck egalitarian principles creates incentives for representing oneself as inferior, these principles do not express equal respect and concern for all citizens. Alternatively, she might regard them as observations about the loss in terms of other values resulting from acting on luck egalitarian principles that do not tell us anything about the validity of these principles themselves. In any case, it is difficult not to see the parallels to similar criticisms, justified or not, of affirmative action, ie that affirmative action creates incentives for individuals to deny personal responsibility for their problems and creates a similar diversion of 'self-seeking energies' away from 'productive work' into lobbying for affirmative action schemes benefiting one's group.

Anderson mentions discrimination among the relatively privileged and contends in this connection that 'egalitarians aim at enabling all citizens to stand as equals to one another in civil society, and this requires that careers be open to talents'.[50] There are different ways of understanding what it is for careers to be open to talents, but if it simply refers to the 'aspiration to establish a world where government posts go to the most qualified and economic opportunities may be seized by anyone independently of whether or not one's parents are of noble blood or cronies of the king' etc, then again affirmative action that seeks to adjust requirements in the light of the fact that members of different groups had differential access to acquire the relevant qualifications appears incompatible with democratic equality as she understands the ideal.[51]

[49] Anderson (n 14) 311. For a related, though not entirely identical, point about the perverse incentives created by affirmative action, see Glen C Loury, *The Anatomy of Racial Inequality* (Cambridge MA, Harvard University Press, 2002) 32–33.

[50] Anderson (n 14) 317.

[51] Richard Arneson, 'Equality of opportunity' (Stanford Encyclopaedia of Philosophy, 2015) available at http://plato.stanford.edu/entries/equal-opportunity/.

However, Anderson favours affirmative action. In a recent book, she discusses four models of affirmative action.[52] She endorses two of the four models: the discrimination-blocking model and the integrative model. I will now consider them in turn. The discrimination-blocking model

> focuses on the practical difficulties of stopping current discrimination in a world saturated with stigmatizing stereotypes of disadvantaged groups and structured by entrenched habits that favor advantaged groups. To remedy this problem, merely passing antidiscrimination laws is insufficient to stop discrimination. Affirmative action is needed.[53]

Anderson does not explicitly state whether the relevant kind of discrimination that the discrimination-blocking model concerns is direct discrimination only, or includes indirect discrimination as well.[54] If the latter, then it is surprising that she considers this model 'indispensable' on the assumption that indirect discrimination can co-exist with the satisfaction of the ideal of democratic equality.[55] It is surprising because, presumably, the source of this indispensability is not democratic equality but some other moral ideal and, at least in the case of indirect discrimination, the relevant ideal is some form of distributive ideal, to wit, distributive equality across groups. To the extent that Anderson's discrimination-blocking ideal pertains to direct discrimination only, it does not modify the previous prima facie affirmative action sceptical claims.

Turning now to the integrative model of racially-focused affirmative action, this model begins with the observation that

> De facto racial segregation unjustly impedes socioeconomic opportunities for disadvantaged groups, causes racial stigmatization and discrimination, and is inconsistent with a fully democratic society. To remedy these problems, we need to practice racial integration.[56]

Affirmative action for racial minorities should be seen 'as a means to racially integrate the main institutions of civil society'.[57] Before I explain how the integrative model justifies unusual forms of affirmative action, let me first note the somewhat surprising 'and' in the previous Anderson quote.

[52] It is unclear what exactly the relevant models are models of. It seems clear, though, that they are at one and the same time explanatory models of what causes or caused the relevant disparity, which affirmative action is a means to eliminate, and models of what, as a matter of fact, justifies affirmative action (or what is the justification of affirmative action normally offered).

[53] Anderson (n 1) 144.

[54] While most of the examples of discrimination she offers involve direct discrimination, one of them does not, ie, the advertising of 'job openings through word-of-mouth to a racially homogeneous, segregated workforce' (ibid 145).

[55] ibid 148.

[56] ibid 148.

[57] ibid 136.

One would have thought that according to a champion of democratic equality the reason why impeding the socioeconomic opportunities for disadvantaged groups is objectionable *is* that this is incompatible with a fully democratic society. But the most natural reading of this passage is that Anderson sees this as a list of distinct problems and that the two first items on the list are problems independently of how they might contribute to the incomplete realisation of democratic equality. In that case, she does have some non-derivative concerns about distribution, to wit, the distribution of opportunities. Setting this possible inconsistency aside, I will now note some ways in which the integrative model justifies forms of affirmative action that are not exactly standard.

Consider first affirmative action for better off non-discriminatees.[58] Suppose men are under-represented in professions such as nurses, teachers and social workers. Suppose that while this feeds into social hierarchy in the sense that women are associated with providing care and providing care is generally undervalued in society with the effect that women earn less than men and have fewer and worse career opportunities, this does not imply that Anderson's sufficient requirement is unsatisfied. Typically, affirmative action measures taken to address such disparities are measures seeking to encourage women to apply for high-pay, prestigious jobs. However, from the point of view of democratic equality, all other things being equal, it is just as good to make, say, it more attractive for men to become nurses.[59]

Some would object that this would be doubly unjust. Not only are men already over-represented within the most well-paid jobs, they are also being given additional benefits if they apply for low paid jobs in the care sectors increasing overall distributive inequality between men and women. This objection, however, is not one that relational egalitarians can mount. If the two forms of affirmative action involve equally effective ways of attacking

[58] Strictly speaking, many such schemes might not qualify as affirmative action on Fullinwider's characterisation (cp section I). Note also that my characterisation is compatible with the view that any affirmative action measure must be 'designed to benefit members of *protected groups*' (Khaitan (n 1) 238), since the ultimate aim behind measures to increase the representation of men etc in, say, less well paid professions might be to benefit protected groups through the elimination of stigmatic harm etc, which they endure. I disregard this terminological point. The schemes I have in mind are similar to those aiming at increasing the representation of women and minorities, except for the fact that they aim at increasing the representation of men and the majority in less attractive positions in which, historically, they have been less well represented. If you do not want to call such measures 'affirmative action', I can accommodate you by reformulating my point as follows: in a range of cases relational egalitarians are indifferent between affirmative action and otherwise similar schemes aimed at boosting the representation of men and the majority in less attractive jobs etc.

[59] The editors of this volume suggested to me that there are grounds other than sex, eg, race and religion, for which the present point is less relevant than it is to gender groups. But, first, even if so, this is consistent with my main claim here. Second, while the editors' point might be well-taken, when it comes to religious groups in many Western societies today, jobs can be racialised in roughly the same way as they can be gendered.

gender stereotypes and hierarchy, we should, from the point of view of democratic equality, be indifferent between them. Indeed, if affirmative action for men is the more effective means, we should prefer it from that point of view assuming we cannot have both. As Anderson puts it: the integrative model 'identifies the proper targets of affirmative action as those who can function as agents of integration and destigmatization'.[60] She also acknowledges that nothing in the integrative model rules out affirmative action that benefits better off individuals within disadvantaged groups.[61] I am simply extrapolating this claim to better off groups, or worse off individuals within better off groups.

Consider next distributive inequalities, the existence of which very few people are aware of and which do not directly affect how people relate to one another as equals. On the distributive paradigm, but not according to relational egalitarianism, there can still be good reason for affirmative action in this case. Suppose that, as a matter of fact, the expected lifetime differs across two ethnic groups—say, Swedes and Finns living in Sweden—such that Swedes live on average five years longer than Finns. On a distributive paradigm, this might well motivate some kind of affirmative action programme in health care intended to increase the life span of Finns.[62] However, on the ideal of democratic equality no such thing is desirable. Indeed, we can imagine that because of the fact that Swedes, on average, live longer and, on average, older people have a worse health than young people, Swedes are stigmatised as having bad health. For some reason, it is impossible to do anything about the stigmatisation of people perceived as having bad health, but we can through spending more health care resources on Swedes than on Finns eliminate this particular stigma, thus, enabling Swedes and Finns to relate to one another as equals and further increasing the gap between Swedes and Finns in terms of expected life span. From the point of view of democratic equality, there would seem to be no reason not to do so. I contend that few friends of affirmative action would be particularly favourably inclined towards such an affirmative action scheme, which, like the previous one, is affirmative action favouring already better off groups.

VI. RELATIONAL EGALITARIANS ON JUSTIFIED FORMS OF AFFIRMATIVE ACTION: SCHEFFLER

Consider next Scheffler's deliberative constraint and affirmative action. A set of people, who all comply with it, might reject standard forms of

60 Anderson (n 1) 150.

61 ibid 151.

62 For a discussion of affirmative action in health, see Shlomi Segall, *Equality and Opportunity* (Oxford, Oxford University Press, 2014) 193–206. It is an interesting question what makes relational egalitarianism insensitive to differences in length of life as such.

affirmative action and, in certain contexts, favour non-standard forms of the sort I described above. In defence of the former possibility, suppose that a certain group of people adhere to strong meritocratic values, which lead them to reject any measure of affirmative action—even affirmative action that benefits groups that have historically been excluded from certain areas. In doing so they might all act on their disposition to treat the 'strong interests'—where interests includes values—of those who would have benefited from affirmative action as 'playing just as significant a role' as their own strong interests in 'constraining' any decision about whether to adopt or reject the relevant affirmative action schemes.[63]

Similarly, a group of people might comply with the deliberative egalitarian constraint in endorsing affirmative action schemes for the better off when doing so is a way of counteracting stigma and hierarchy and those who are stigmatised and at the bottom of the relevant hierarchies have a strong preference for not being so and affirmative action measures targeting the privileged is the best way of satisfying this preference.

Scheffler might offer three responses to these points. First, he might revise his claim that interests include people's actual values and instead suggest that they include the values people would hold if they were better informed. He might add that merit, correctly understood, takes account of the fact that people do not face equally good opportunities for realising talents and, accordingly, that, in my example of a community of people who reject affirmative action measures, these would not conflict with the view of merit that members of this community would hold if they were better informed.[64]

In response, I contend that, whatever the overall merits of such a position are, it involves a view which is hard to reconcile with other parts of what Scheffler (and Anderson) has to say about what it is to treat one another as equals. Relational egalitarians condemn what they see as the paternalistic impulse underpinning certain luck egalitarian schemes of compensation—giving equal weight not to people's actual values, but to the values (one believes) they would hold if they were better informed is different from, but still very much akin to, paternalism in that it clashes with a requirement of (expressing) respect that both Scheffler (and Anderson) subscribe to.[65]

Second, Scheffler might remind us that the deliberative constraint is just a central component of the ideal of relating to one another as equals.

[63] Scheffler, 'Practice of Equality' (n 11) 25.

[64] cf Andrew Mason, *Levelling the Playing Field* (Oxford, Oxford University Press, 2006) 39–67.

[65] I concede though that there is a sense in which a set of agents who give exactly the same weight to the values they believe that others would hold if they were better informed as they do to the values that they believe they themselves would hold if they were better informed (probably the values that they actually hold) and accept that others do the same in relation to them are treating one another as equals. Hence, a focus on the values etc. that people would hold if they were better informed in itself is compatible with treating one another as equals.

However, the ideal has other components and perhaps some of these imply a more standard view of affirmative action than the deliberative constraints does in itself. So, for instance, if there are two affirmative schemes both of which weaken a certain stigma attaching to one group and one does it by way of benefiting a worse off group and the other does it by benefiting a better off group, the former might be preferable from the point of view of Scheffler's ideal of relating to one another as equals as such even if both schemes could be endorsed by a set of people complying with the deliberative constraint.

In response, I concede that this is a possibility. However, the burden of proof rests on proponents of relational egalitarianism to identify such components. Moreover, I conjecture any strong contender would involve some sort of distributive concern along the lines of Anderson's suggestion that certain distributions might be partly constitutive of what it is for people to relate to one another as equals and I have already expressed reservations about this view.

Third, Scheffler might concede that, given certain assumptions, the ideal of relating to one another as equals warrants affirmative action for advantaged groups and does not justify standard forms of affirmative action. However, this is not a problem, because, first, the way in which we have to imagine the world to be like for such implications to follow is quite different from what the world is actually like and if it were really like that, the relevant implications would not be embarrassing. Second, the concerns of real life egalitarians, whom relational egalitarians claim to be better in tune with than luck egalitarians are, reflect what the world is actually like.

There is some force to the first point—we should be open to non-standard forms of affirmative action being justified. However, as I noted in the introduction my main concern in this chapter is not to assess the plausibility of relational egalitarianism, but to explore its implications for (indirect discrimination and) affirmative action and, accordingly, the relevant Schefflerian reply is compatible with my main thesis in this chapter.[66]

As regards the second point, it is well taken. However, given the dialectical context it is problematic for relational egalitarians to use it. If they can use it, so can distributive egalitarians. That is, distributive egalitarians can contend that their concerns might legitimately diverge from the concerns of real-life egalitarians, since, for good reason, their concerns are shaped by how the world actually works, whereas the concerns of the former is the ideal of equality and exploring an ideal requires exploring what this ideal would imply under counterfactual circumstances.[67] If this view is

[66] For the record: I do think affirmative action for worse off people is preferable to affirmative action for better off people even when the two promote the ideal of relational egalitarianism to an equal extent and everything else is equal.

[67] cf GA Cohen, *Rescuing Justice and Equality* (Cambridge MA, Harvard University Press, 2008) 268–72, 365–67; Lippert-Rasmussen (n 10) 4–6.

admissible, then one of the main complaints relational egalitarians direct against luck egalitarians, eg, how they are obsessed with the question of whether people with exotic, expensive tastes should receive compensation and similar questions alien to the agenda of real-life egalitarians, is not a complaint relational egalitarians are entitled to make.

VII. CONCLUSION

In this chapter, I have argued that the two main versions of relational egalitarianism on offer have implications regarding the injustice of indirect discrimination and the justifiability of affirmative action that are out of tune with those held by most real-life egalitarians. The general view of egalitarians is that indirect discrimination is not unjust per se and that affirmative action favouring privileged people might be unjustified when there are alternative affirmative action schemes that are better in achieving the relevant desirable aims, eg, egalitarian social relations, and favour worse off people. My main concern has not been to argue that these conflicts amount to objections to relational egalitarianism as such, though I do think the latter of the two implications is unattractive and that relational egalitarianism gives the wrong sort of explanation of why some forms of indirect discrimination are not unjust per se. However, both implications amount to objections to how relational egalitarians conceive of themselves, ie as proponents of a theory that captures the concerns of real life egalitarians.

Could there be forms of relational egalitarianism other than Anderson's and Scheffler's that, in relation to indirect discrimination and affirmative action, are more in tune with the concerns of real life egalitarians? I have not argued that there could not be, but for what it is worth I suspect that such forms would have to incorporate some kind of distributive concern as being constitutive of egalitarian relations. Not only would such a move amount to a revisionist account of what it is to treat one another as equals, but it also reduces the distance between distributive and relational egalitarians significantly. For instance, according to such a version of relational egalitarianism, in part, 'equality is an essentially distributive value' and relational egalitarians should be much exercised by the question of what the proper 'currency' of egalitarian justice is—a question which, generally, they tend to think of as misconceived or peripheral.[68] A more promising alternative to explore is a form of pluralist egalitarianism that is concern with social relations as well as distributions.[69]

[68] Scheffler, 'Practice of Equality' (n 11) 21.
[69] Lippert-Rasmussen (n 12).

9

Wrongs, Group Disadvantage and the Legitimacy of Indirect Discrimination Law

TARUNABH KHAITAN AND SANDY STEEL*

I. INTRODUCTION

IS INDIRECT DISCRIMINATION liability akin to an affirmative action programme or more like the tort of negligence?[1] Is it a redistributive measure or a corrective one?[2] Is it best characterised as 'public law' or 'private law'? Does it seek to protect groups or individuals? In this chapter, we will argue that liability for indirect discrimination occupies a middle ground between these supposedly settled legal categories, combining features of both items in each dichotomy. It is this seemingly unstable and somewhat unfamiliar middle position that partially explains the persisting doubts expressed regarding the legitimacy of indirect discrimination liability.[3]

An act, policy or practice that—while facially neutral—nonetheless has a disproportionate impact on a group protected by discrimination law

* We thank the participants at the Oxford workshop on indirect discrimination law and theory, and several other seminars and workshops were this paper was discussed. Special thanks to David Edmonds, Barbara Havelkova, Deborah Hellman, Colin Campbell, Sophia Moreau, Denise Reaume, Samuel Bagenstos and Hugh Collins. Thanks also to Ira Chadha-Sridhar for excellent research support.

[1] On indirect discrimination as affirmative action, see Justice Scalia's concurring opinion in *Ricci v DeStefano* 557 US 557 (2009) 594 which stated that 'disparate-impact provisions place a racial thumb on the scales, often requiring employers to evaluate the racial outcomes of their policies, and to make decisions based on (because of) those racial outcomes'. See also Benjamin Eidelson, *Discrimination and Disrespect* (Oxford, Oxford University Press, 2015) 39. On indirect discrimination as akin to tort, see Denise Réaume, 'Harm and Fault in Discrimination Law' (2001) 2 *Theoretical Inquiries in Law* and Sophia Moreau, 'Discrimination as Negligence' (2013) 40 *Canadian Journal of Philosophy* 123.

[2] See John Gardner, 'Discrimination as Injustice' (1996) 16 *OJLS* 353.

[3] *Ricci* (n 1), *Home Office (UK Border Agency) v Essop* [2015] EWCA Civ 609, [2016] 3 All ER 137.

(such as blacks or women) is prima facie indirectly discriminatory.[4] Once a claimant establishes prima facie indirect discrimination, the law allows the defendant an opportunity to *justify* her conduct, typically by showing that it is a proportionate means to achieve a legitimate objective. If the defendant fails to do so, the law typically grants declaratory, recommendatory and (sometimes) injunctive relief, but damages are allowed in extremely rare cases of indirect discrimination.[5]

In a previous work, one of us had argued that discriminatory acts (including indirectly discriminatory acts) are 'doubly wrongful', inasmuch as they have a *systemic* impact of exacerbating relative group disadvantage and a *particular* impact of making those subject to it suffer because of their normatively irrelevant (or, in some cases, normatively valuable) group membership.[6] It was suggested that discrimination law's systemic concern of eliminating relative group disadvantage (of a substantial, abiding and pervasive kind) was its overall point and purpose—the very raison d'être of discrimination law. But, such an overall purpose is compatible with many different implementation designs that could achieve it. The design of choice for discrimination law—or, the manner in which discrimination law distributes its rights and duties to achieve its overall purpose—is a personal-wrongs based approach, where certain acts by specified duty-bearers trigger the legal liability.[7]

In a generous and sympathetic review of this earlier work, Sophia Moreau admits that it is indeed a feature of discrimination law that it pulls in these two opposite directions: that, on the one hand, it cares about 'bettering the situation of these underprivileged groups', but at the same time its duties are mediated by 'personal wrongs', ie 'a personal duty upon the discriminator, a duty toward the particular person who is, for instance at risk of not being hired, or not being promoted because of an apparently discriminatory policy.'[8] She complains, however, that 'Khaitan does not himself explain how the two accounts fit together ... Why should we suppose that both are always necessary, and that neither is ever independently sufficient.'[9]

In this chapter, we will show that the *personal wrongs* approach to indirect discrimination liability in Anglo-American jurisprudence needs the

[4] *Griggs v Duke Power Co* 401 US 424 (1971). On indirect discrimination more generally, see T Khaitan, 'Indirect Discrimination' in K Lippert-Rasmussen (ed), *The Routledge Handbook of the Ethics of Discrimination* (Abingdon, Routledge, 2017) 30.

[5] Equality Act 2010 s 124(4) and (5).

[6] Tarunabh Khaitan, *A Theory of Discrimination Law* (Oxford, Oxford University Press, 2015) 168.

[7] ibid 10.

[8] Sophia Moreau, 'Discrimination Law and the Freedom to Live a Good Life' (2016) 35 *Law and Philosophy* 511, 525. See also Colm O'Cinneide, 'Justifying Discrimination Law' (2016) 36 *OJLS* 909, 916.

[9] Moreau, ibid.

systemic functional goal of reducing relative group disadvantage in order to be legitimate. It is possible that that systemic goal may be achievable through other tools too (progressive taxation or social insurance, for example), but we make no claims with regard to those alternative possibilities in this paper, except to point out that law's reliance on personal wrongs as a distributional strategy when allocating rights and liabilities is ubiquitous in other contexts too. In section II, we will identify the two distinct duties—one general and the other particular—that underpin indirect discrimination. In section III, we will provide a conceptual restatement of British indirect discrimination law and identify the general and particular dimensions of this liability. This section will outline how the particular duty in indirect discrimination diverges from traditional causation-demanding private law liability for the tort of negligence, and how these divergences are justified given social realities and the general/distributive dimension of indirect discrimination liability. Section IV will show that despite the indirect discrimination liability being technically strict, it is to some degree avoidable, and at any rate, not unfair.

II. INDIRECT DISCRIMINATION AS DOUBLY WRONGFUL

Suppose that Garfner, who is a Sagittarian, loses out on several job offers because facially neutral selection criteria somehow disadvantage him on account of his zodiac sign.[10] Plausibly, this is unjust. Garfner is disadvantaged in virtue of a normatively irrelevant characteristic. We can call the moral duty not to disadvantage others on the basis of normatively irrelevant characteristics a *particular* duty owed to specific persons such as Garfner, who are wronged by its breach.

Compare Garfner with Ifemelu, who is black. If Ifemelu is disadvantaged by (facially neutral) selection criteria in virtue of her being black, she will be the victim of a breach of the particular duty. However, the agent who breaches this particular duty may breach a further duty. If Ifemelu belongs to a group which is severely disadvantaged vis-à-vis other groups, then the agent may also have contributed to the disadvantage of the group. This, in

[10] There is some evidence that suggests that school admissions that determine the class a child will be admitted to based on the month s/he was born in disadvantages children towards the lower end of the age spectrum in their class. S Weale, 'Are Children Born in the Summer Really at a Big Disadvantage?' *Guardian* (London, 14 October 2016) www.theguardian.com/world/2016/oct/14/what-happened-to-allowing-children-born-in-summer-to-start-school-later. So, it is plausible, that a 31 August cut-off would have a disparate impact on children with the star sign Leo. We are assuming, for the purposes of this example, that age is a facially neutral criterion—most jurisdictions that treat age as a protected characteristic are likely to see this as a case of direct age discrimination.

turn, may contribute to making members of Ifemelu's group less free.[11] We can call breach of this further duty not to contribute to relative group disadvantage the *general* duty owed not to anyone in particular, but generally to the group in question, or even to one's society—a duty whose breach is *wrongful* even if it wrongs no particular person.

As this comparison shows, while breach of the particular duty may entail breach of the general duty, this is not always the case. The logical space between these duties arises because the particular duty is insensitive to the distributive position of the victim, while a breach of the general duty is wrongful precisely in virtue of its contribution to unjust distributions. In the rest of this chapter, we will show that this doubly-wrongful nature of indirect discrimination is essential to our understanding of the general and particular duties it enforces.

A. Particular and General Duties in British Indirect Discrimination Law

Indirect discrimination is listed as a 'Prohibited Conduct' under the UK Equality Act 2010 and is defined under section 19(2) of that Act:

> a provision, criterion or practice is discriminatory in relation to a relevant protected characteristic of B's if—
>
> (a) A applies, or would apply, it to persons with whom B does not share the characteristic,
> (b) it puts, or would put, persons with whom B shares the characteristic at a particular disadvantage when compared with persons with whom B does not share it,
> (c) it puts, or would put, B at that disadvantage, and
> (d) A cannot show it to be a proportionate means of achieving a legitimate aim.

Read alongside judicial pronouncements on indirect discrimination liability, clause (a) can be taken to establish the requirement that the provision, criterion or practice ('act', for short) is facially neutral, ie it is applied to all persons regardless of their race, sex or other protected characteristic (hereinafter, 'grounds'). Implicit in this clause is the requirement that the act must not intentionally be based on any of these grounds. Any discriminatory animus will make a case one of *direct* discrimination.[12]

In the complicated section 19(2)(b), notice first that the word 'puts' establishes a causation requirement: the act in question *puts* (or would *put*) the relevant persons at a particular disadvantage.

[11] For a full account of how membership of relatively disadvantaged groups affects the freedom of its members, see Khaitan (n 6) chs 4, 5.

[12] Case C-83/14 *CHEZ Razpredelenie Bulgaria AD v Komisia za zashtita ot diskriminatsia* [2016] 1 CMLR 14, [75]–[76], [95].

Next, if the relevant ground is race, 'persons with whom B shares the characteristic' could be black people, white people, non-whites (section 9(4)), South Asians, Poles (section 9(1)(b)), or any other racial group (section 9(2)(b) Equality Act 2010). The 'disadvantage' suffered by the group must be comparative: 'when compared with persons with whom B does not share [the characteristic]'. The comparison required is between two groups defined by the same protected characteristic: whites and Asians, Jews and non-Jews, men and women, wheelchair users and non-users, and so on.

Finally, the provision requires proof of 'particular' disadvantage. The term is borrowed from EU law (Article 2(2)(b) Framework Directive 2000/78/EC), and was intended as a claimant-friendly change from the original language requiring *disproportionate* impact (used, for example, in section 1(1)(b)(i) Race Relations Act 1976). As the Supreme Court has recognised:

> [T]he new formulation was not intended to make it more difficult to establish indirect discrimination: quite the reverse ... It was intended to do away with the need for statistical comparisons where no statistics might exist. It was intended to do away with the complexities involved in identifying those who could comply and those who could not and how great the disparity had to be.[13]

Whether framed as 'disproportionate impact' or comparative 'particular disadvantage', the requirement is essentially one of correlation. When those disadvantaged by an act *disproportionately* or *particularly* belong to a protected group (say women), clause (b) has been satisfied. It is also worth pointing out that if everyone disadvantaged by an act belongs to one protected group (women) and everyone advantaged or not affected by the same act belongs to another protected group defined by the same ground (here, men), British law treats the act as directly discriminatory, irrespective of whether there was any intention involved.[14] However, if all members of the disadvantaged group suffer, but so do some members of its cognate group, the discrimination is still *in*direct, albeit 'a form of indirect discrimination which comes as close as it can to direct discrimination'.[15] The law, therefore, recognises that indirect discrimination liability admits to degrees of severity—the greater the correspondence between the two sets of groups (those disadvantaged and advantaged by the act and those belonging to a protected group and its corresponding comparator group), the more disapproving is the law of the conduct in question.

[13] *Homer v Chief Constable of West Yorkshire Police* [2012] UKSC 15, [2012] 3 All ER 1287 [14].

[14] *Bull and Bull v Hall and Preddy* [2013] UKSC 73, [2013] 1 WLR 3741 [19]: 'I take there to be direct discrimination when the category of those receiving a certain advantage and the category of those suffering a correlative disadvantage coincide exactly with the respective categories of persons distinguished only by applying a prohibited classification.'

[15] *Rodriguez v Minister of Housing* [2009] UKPC 52; [2010] UKHRR 144 [19].

To summarise, prima facie indirect discrimination in British law occurs when the following two requirements are satisfied:

— a causal connection between the defendant's facially neutral act and some adversity suffered by a set of persons;
— a significant correlation between membership of this set of adversely affected persons and membership of a *group* protected by discrimination law.

Our claim in this section is that prima facie indirect discrimination, in archetypal—but not necessarily all—cases, amounts to the breach of the general duty and the particular duty. To recap, the general duty is characterised as the duty to refrain from causing adversity to relatively disadvantaged (protected) groups.[16] The particular duty, we will claim, is the duty to refrain from causing disadvantage to a person because of her membership of that group, where such membership is morally permitted.

Before we clarify these duties, let us consider an example in order to understand the relationship between correlation and causation in this area of law. We choose as our exemplar case one where there is clear evidence of a significant correlation between group membership and the disadvantage, but no direct causal explanation.[17] We exclude cases where there exists a direct causal explanation—eg between a turban ban's impact on Sikhs or an inflexible working hours policy's impact on women—because they are theoretically easier to defend. This correlative—but not self-evidently causal—relationship is key to understanding the two duties. Imagine a facially neutral test, passing which is a prerequisite for a job, one that is not designed or administered with any discriminatory animus. In the first scenario, no particular racial group disproportionately fails the test, that is, the chances of one's passing the test do not correlate with her race in this case. In the second scenario, black candidates are only 25 per cent as likely as their white counterparts to pass the test, and this difference between the two groups is statistically significant. Technically, an outcome is 'significant' if it is improbable that it occurred by chance. Imagine also a black candidate, Ifemelu, who fails the test in both scenarios. We will look into when and why Ifemelu ought to be able to bring a claim when discussing the particular duty. For now, it suffices to notice that Ifemelu (or anyone else, for that matter) will have an indirect discrimination claim only in the second scenario.

[16] Most of the discussion in this paper is in relation to protected groups that suffer abiding, pervasive and substantial disadvantage in their societies. We take these to include women, racial minorities, gays and lesbians, transpersons, and disabled persons, among others. Whether, and when, socially dominant groups should be protected requires a separate argument: one of us has provided one such argument at Khaitan (n 6) 171–80.

[17] This closely tracks the facts of *Essop v Home Office* [2017] UKSC 27, [2017] 1 WLR 1343. See also, T Khaitan, 'Indirect Discrimination Law: Causation, Explanation and Coat-Tailers' (2016) 132 *LQR* 35.

Our first scenario is what statisticians call the 'null hypothesis'—all else being equal, this is what one would expect. In our second scenario, the null hypothesis is disproved. In other words, the finding of a statistically significant difference between the two racial groups makes it improbable that the difference is down to chance or luck. The term 'improbable' is used advisedly. A finding of statistical 'significance', absent an explanation, cannot rule out chance, it can only make it highly improbable. This should not bother lawyers, who are used to working with proof on balance of probabilities. A significant correlation therefore points to *some* non-random cause of the disparity between the groups.

It is true that the law no longer requires a strict proof of statistical significance. But legal truths cannot be (and ought not to be) as fine-grained as scientific truths. Meeting scientific standards of truth imposes significant costs, both on adjudicatory institutions and on the parties (especially on the party that bears the burden of proof). To keep these costs manageable, law has to make a judgment about the probability and moral tolerability of false positives vis-à-vis false negatives. In criminal law, for example, false positives are anathema, and rightly so. It is morally much worse to convict someone who is innocent that to acquit someone who is guilty. This is why the burden of proof is typically on the prosecution and the standard of proof is very high.

In discrimination law, litigation takes place under conditions of significant resource and information asymmetry in favour of the defendant. The legal shift from the requirement of 'disproportionality' to that of 'particular disadvantage' is in light of the recognition of this asymmetry. The law no longer requires the claimant to prove statistical significance of the differential impact. But the claimant still needs to make a plausible prima facie case that the difference is unlikely to be random in order to establish *particular disadvantage*. It remains open to the defendant to rebut this prima facie case by showing that the disparity is indeed down to chance. The divergence from the exemplar case is down to how litigation operates in the real world. But this divergence does not take away the explanatory force of that case. Even the rule of thumb inquiry that the law now permits is still asking the same question: is the difference between the groups likely to be down to chance or not? This departure becomes more palatable because the typical claimant against indirect discrimination is expected to be a member of a relatively disadvantaged group. Thus, the systemic purpose of discrimination law supports the legal requirements for showing the breach of the particular duty.

Once chance is ruled out and the existence of *some* non-random cause of the disparity is established as a legal fact, discrimination law is best understood as *presuming* two causal claims:

(i) the defendant's act *caused* a particular disadvantage to blacks as a group (i.e. the general duty was breached), and

(ii) the claimant suffered some adversity *because of* her membership of her racial group (i.e. the particular duty was breached).[18]

Note that these are background presumptions that *we* are attributing to law, in order to put it in its best light. The doctrinal requirements for proving indirect discrimination that the law insists upon have already been outlined earlier in this section. The legal duty is unitary—do not discriminate indirectly without justification. The general and particular duties that we identify are two—related—moral duties that underpin the single legal duty. The law relies on the breach of the general duty to assume the breach of the particular duty as well. In other words, so long as the claimant is a typical member of the group, the second causal claim is entailed in the first. If the first claim is established, at least some members of the group suffered adversity because of their membership of the relevant group: the only remaining question is whether the claimant is one such member.

B. The General Duty

Before we make the entailment of (ii) in (i) clearer, a few further comments on the legal presumption in (i) are merited. We have seen that law's move from statistical proof to the rule-of-thumb standard of 'particular disadvantage' was justifiable because of the civil nature of the liability in discrimination law, and because of the information asymmetry that usually afflicts these cases. Such inferential reasoning, after all, is not unknown to tort law.[19] But there are other reasons too, which further support this legal presumption.

One of them is that the presumptions are rebuttable by the information-rich defendant.[20] It remains open to the defendant to show that despite the extant significant correlation, there is no 'particular *disadvantage*' caused to the group. In the example we are working with, assume that the defendant in question is an affirmative action employer who especially encourages black candidates to apply for the concerned job. If this is the case, it is plausible that more under-qualified black candidates end up applying

[18] These presumptions are made explicit in the Equality Act 2010 s 136(2): 'If there are facts from which the court could decide, in the absence of any other explanation, that a person (A) contravened the provision concerned, the court must hold that the contravention occurred.' On shifting of the burden of proof to the defendant, see also *Hoogendijk v Netherlands (Admissibility)* (App no 58641/00) (2005) 40 EHRR SE22.

[19] See Sandy Steel, *Proof of Causation in Tort Law* (Cambridge, Cambridge University Press, 2015) ch 2.

[20] Equality Act 2010 s 138(4) recognises this information asymmetry by allowing a court to draw adverse inferences from a defendant's refusal to answer a question, or from his or her providing an evasive or equivocal answer.

for the job than under-qualified white candidates. This is likely to result in the correlation that we noticed. If the defendant can demonstrate any such benign explanation for the correlation, there is no *disadvantage* caused to the group. Then, the presumption of 'particular disadvantage' to the group will be rebutted.

The defendant can also challenge the finding of '*particular* disadvantage' by denying its particularity, despite the existence of significant correlation. She can do so, for example, in cases where the statistical outcomes are subject to the Simpson's Paradox. This Paradox was observed in graduate admissions at the University of California, Berkeley in 1973. Although the aggregate data did show a statistically significant bias against women candidates, closer inspection of the data revealed that women were much more likely to apply to departments which were more difficult to get into (for persons of either sex).[21] In such cases, the defendant can effectively show that by moving the analysis to a more specific level, the correlation demonstrating particular disadvantage disappears. There may be other similar avenues available to the defendant to challenge the prima facie case of particular disadvantage.

As soon as the defendant rebuts the first causal claim, the second—entailed—causal presumption is automatically rebutted. If the defendant fails to offer any such rebuttal, it seems fair to draw the most plausible conclusion from the correlation established by the claimant: that the defendant's act caused particular disadvantage to the group in question. This is because we already have very good reasons to rule out chance. If there is a benign explanation for the correlation, the defendant is best placed to offer it. If no such exculpatory explanation is forthcoming from the defendant, the weight of evidence implicates her. In such circumstances, to demand that the claimant prove not merely the correlation (and the consequent causation), but also explain the cause,[22] is asking for too much.

Furthermore, even after all this is established, the defendant still has the opportunity to *justify* her act under section 19(2)(d) by showing that it is a proportionate means of achieving a legitimate objective. Even if an employer's act is found to amount to unintentional indirect discrimination, declaration and recommendation are the preferred remedies under section 124 of the Equality Act, with damages permitted only exceptionally. The recommendation is likely to ask the defendant to change her discriminatory and unjustified policy so that it becomes non-discriminatory, or, if discriminatory, is a proportionate response to her legitimate objectives. The multiple legal presumptions against the defendant seem a lot less worrying when judged alongside a remarkably light-touch remedial scheme.

[21] P Bickel, E Hammel and J O'Connell, 'Sex Bias in Graduate Admissions: Data from Berkeley' (1975) 187 *Science* 398.

[22] As the Court of Appeal did in *Essop* CA (n 3) (later overruled by the Supreme Court).

We can now examine how the first causal claim relates to the general duty. What has been established in law is that the defendant's act caused a particular disadvantage to the relevant group qua group. In the second scenario, therefore, Ifemelu's group—blacks—was adversely affected *as a group*. The essential feature of the general duty breached by indirectly discriminatory conduct is that it adversely affects a group that is protected by discrimination law, qua its being a group and is wrongful for that reason. This claim assumes a direct correspondence between adverse effect on a sub-set of a group and on the group as a whole. The extent of adversity on the group because of an act of indirect discrimination may be trivial, or significant. An employer with a small workforce is likely to make only a minuscule impact on women as a group through indirect sex discrimination. But an indirectly discriminatory law of general application (say, the criminalisation of sodomy) could have pervasive and serious impact on the entire group (in this case, gay men).[23] We take the assumption that there is some knock-on effect on the group as a whole to hold in most, if not all, cases. This will suffice in order to justify the *general* claim that indirect discrimination breaches the general duty.

C. The Particular Duty

Now we can move to the particular duty entailed in the general duty. A discriminator [X] *wrongs* a particular person subject to indirect discrimination [Y] because X makes Y suffer some adversity because of her (morally permitted) membership of a protected group.[24] This is exactly what happens when the second causal claim—the claimant suffered adversity *because of* her membership of her group—is satisfied. The phrase 'because of' one's race etc is ubiquitous in discrimination law, and has given rise to much controversy.[25] Most of this controversy arises as 'these phrases can refer either to a) the reasons that guide the acts of agents or to b) factors that do not guide agents but do help explain why the disadvantageous outcomes of

[23] Oran Doyle, 'Direct Discrimination, Indirect Discrimination and Autonomy' (2007) 27 *OJLS* 537–53.

[24] Whether a person is allowed to bring a claim of indirect discrimination is related to, but not determined by, whether they suffered a relational wrong. There may be good institutional reasons for extending standing to those who did not suffer such wrong, or restricting it to a sub-group of those thus wronged, or allowing a regulator to bring a claim. See *CHEZ* (n 12). Indeed, the fact that most jurisdictions allow regulators and even third parties to bring antidiscrimination claims is a nod to our claim that a simple corrective justice framework that does not acknowledge its distributive impulses cannot fully explain the law.

[25] John Gardner, 'On the Ground of Her Sex(uality)' (1998) 18 *OJLS* 167; John Finnis, 'Directly Discriminatory Decisions: A Missed Opportunity' (2010) 126 *LQR* 491.

certain acts and policies fall disproportionately on certain salient groups.'[26] To be sure, the law does not require proof of a causal connection between the adversity suffered and the protected characteristic as a doctrinal matter: as the UK Supreme Court clarified in *Essop*, doctrinally the claimant only needs to prove a causal connection between the adversity suffered and the policy/criterion/practice in question.[27] The point we are making is a conceptual one—even when the law does not impose it as a causal requirement, it is best understood as assuming some such background connection.[28]

This second causal claim is entailed in the first for a simple reason. If the defendant caused some adversity to a group qua group, then it follows (short of any separate reason to believe otherwise)[29] that affected members of that group suffered because of their group membership. Indirect discrimination breaches a particular duty, inasmuch as it entails a *wrong* to these particular members of the group. In our first scenario, although Ifemelu herself failed the test, her group (blacks) had not suffered particular disadvantage as a group. For this reason, her failure could not be connected with her group membership. In the second scenario, however, Ifemelu fails as a member of a particularly disadvantaged group. Unless there is any reason to believe that she is an atypical member of the group, her failure can normally be attributed to her group membership. *In most cases*, therefore, we can infer that Ifemelu suffered because of her race. This causal presumption in the particular duty, it should be obvious, hangs on the prior breach of the general duty.

One might object to this claim by suggesting that Ifemelu suffers not *because of* her race, but because she is poor/less well-educated/less experienced/not mentored or coached for the test etc.[30] On the face of it, this objection seems plausible. On closer analysis, however, it fails. Consider first a different set of cases: say, a Sikh man is fired because he wears a turban, or a black woman is not hired because of her cornrows. In such cases, we would readily admit that they suffered because of their religion/race. This will be the case even if the employer would happily retain the Sikh man if he removed his turban, or hire the black woman if she straightened her hair. The immediate cause is proximate enough to the protected characteristic to

[26] A Altman, 'Discrimination' (Stanford Encyclopaedia of Philosophy, 2016) available at https://plato.stanford.edu/cgi-bin/encyclopedia/archinfo.cgi?entry=discrimination. See further K Lippert-Rasmussen, *Born Free and Equal? A Philosophical Inquiry into the Nature of Discrimination* (Oxford, Oxford University Press, 2014) 36–40.

[27] *Essop* UKSC (n 17).

[28] ibid 26.

[29] As the Supreme Court held in *Essop* UKSC (n 17) 32 'It [is] permissible for an employer to show that an employee has not suffered harm as a result of the [policy] in question.'

[30] We are grateful to Debbie Hellman for this objection, and to Denise Reaume for framing the response. See also Benjamin Eidelson, *Discrimination and Disrespect* (Oxford, Oxford University Press, 2015) 53f.

help us see the connection clearly. Our hesitation in cases where such a clear, single factorial, connection is absent is akin to the 'remoteness problem' that tort lawyers are familiar with: the underlying assumption behind the objection must be that the connection between poverty and race is somehow not close enough to establish a chain of causation, in the way that hair style and race might be. There is no conceptual distinction—other than remoteness—between the types of features (dress, hair-type, religious observance) that are readily admitted as racial and those (such as poverty, poor education, lack of influential connections and other social capital) that are not. It is not, for example, the case that one category is 'natural' and the other 'cultural' or 'chosen'. The impoverishing impact of salient characteristics such as race and caste is well-documented. We are not claiming that race is the only cause in this case; Ifemelu's poverty and poorer education may also have caused her failure, and are indeed likely to be a more proximate explanation of her failure than her race. That does not mean that race cannot be located lower down the chain of causes that led to her failure. Given the disproportionate rate at which black candidates failed the test, it is in fact very likely that race contributed to their failure in most cases. What is more, it is not even obvious that the connection between one's poverty and one's race is necessarily more remote than between a person's dress or hair-style and race. In fact, some scholars argue that the (material, social, political and educational) disadvantage faced by a group is part of the *requirement* a personal characteristic needs to satisfy in order to qualify for the protection of discrimination law.[31]

Another objection might be that the facts at hand are not sufficient to get to the second presumption that the claimant suffered some adversity because of her membership of her racial group.[32] All we know about the scenario under consideration is that black candidates are only 25 per cent as likely as their white counterparts to pass the test, that this difference between the two groups is statistically significant, and that Ifemelu is a black applicant who failed the test. The objection is that Ifemelu might have failed the test anyway, even in this second scenario. This would especially be the case if the pass rate (for everyone) is quite low: say, the ratio between the applicants to available places is rather large. At least in such cases, it may be argued, one cannot say that Ifemelu suffered *because of* her race.

The objection is a good one, but is based on the (mistaken) presumption that the only relevant adversity that Ifemelu suffers is actually failing the test.[33] Let us try to get inside Ifemelu's mind to see if she suffers in the

[31] Khaitan (n 6) ch 2; Owen Fiss, 'Groups and the Equal Protection Clause' (1976) 5 *Philosophy and Public Affairs* 107–77.

[32] We are grateful to David Edmonds for pressing this objection.

[33] Here, we diverge from the law, which acknowledges the difference between potential and actual disadvantage, but treats them—for pragmatic doctrinal reasons—as ultimately the same disadvantage, *Essop* UKSC (n 17).

case at hand because of her race. To avoid any suggestion that this thought experiment imports subjective feelings into indirect discrimination analysis, let us ask not what Ifemelu is *likely* to think or *actually* thinks, but what would be *reasonable* for her to think. Let us also go back in time when our reasonable Ifemelu is considering whether to apply for the job in question. As a reasonable person who does not much fancy wasting her time, she is likely to apply only if she considers her chances of getting the job to be at least plausible. If she knows that as a black person, the chances of her getting the job are 25 per cent lower than if she were white, this is sufficient for her to reasonably think that the likelihood of her getting the job depends, to some extent, upon her race. It is true that the plausibility of her getting this job will also depend, in addition to her race, on the overall success rate. Even so, a lower overall success rate in fact makes it *more* likely that Ifemelu, as a black applicant, won't get the job. If the job had a high success rate, Ifemelu's application may be plausible despite the statistical significance of race. However, the same significance in a job with a very low success rate is likely to lead Ifemelu to conclude that even making the application would be a waste of her time. This type of reasoning also explains that a lower success rate for vulnerable groups has a chilling effect on applications from its members, thereby frustrating the systemic objective of discrimination law to reduce relative group disadvantage. At any rate, whether, for that reason, Ifemelu chooses not to make the application at all, or whether, having made the application, she fails, she would have suffered (in part) because of her race.[34]

On this view Ifemelu suffers because of her race not in virtue, necessarily, of her not getting the job, but rather because her chances of obtaining the job have been significantly reduced. Although the absolute level of her chance of the job was already low, it is made even less likely by the policy in question. The disadvantage that Ifemelu suffers here can be conceptualised in at least two ways. Following Moreau's earlier work, we might conceive of it as an interference with Ifemelu's deliberative freedom.[35] Since Ifemelu's race affects her probability of success, it thereby becomes rationally salient in her deliberations. This analysis plausibly identifies a disadvantage in cases where the victim is aware of the effect her race has on her chances of obtaining the job. We are less persuaded of the force of the analysis where the victim is unaware. This is not because we believe one cannot suffer disadvantage without being aware of it. It is rather because the focus upon the victim's hypothetical deliberations, or the deliberative perspective of a rational or reasonable victim, in cases where the victim is not aware of the

[34] In fact, on this account, she suffers even if she eventually gets the job. That the law does not give her standing to bring a claim in such cases is a distinct policy choice.

[35] Sophia Moreau, 'What is Discrimination?' (2010) 38 *Philosophy and Public Affairs* 143–79. Moreau presents a different, if compatible, explanation in her contribution to this volume—our criticism is directed only at the earlier work cited here.

probabilities ex ante, seems somewhat to deflect from a more basic way in which the victim suffers disadvantage in these cases. Disadvantage is suffered in virtue of the fact that one of the victim's opportunities becomes rationally less attractive and so less valuable to her. Since autonomy requires the possession of a wide set of valuable options, the diminishment in the value of an option has an impact on an agent's autonomy. It seems clear that one's autonomy can be diminished without one's knowledge: if the conference organisers lock us in the room, without our knowledge, we have been deprived of our freedom to leave, even if this remains unknown to us.[36] Even if this loss to particular individuals may be small in some cases, the systemic effect on the group, many of whose members do not even apply, is often significant.

We have therefore seen that, for most claimants, breach of the particular duty is entailed in the general one. Furthermore, several features of the law's regulation of indirect discrimination are in fact explained and justified because of the relationship between the two (moral) duties.

III. CULPABILITY IN INDIRECT DISCRIMINATION

In this part of the chapter we shift attention to another feature of indirect discrimination liability, namely, that indirect discrimination liability is strict. We argue that this strict liability in respect of indirect discrimination can be justified and that part of the justification lies in the doubly wrongful nature of indirect discrimination: the fact that particular acts of indirect discrimination typically involve the violation not only of the particular duty, but also the general duty, and more generally, the aim of reducing relative group disadvantage. The argument proceeds in three stages. First, we establish that indirect discrimination liability is indeed strict. Second, we address, and aim to refute, the objection that, if indirect discrimination liability is strict, it cannot be justified by the moral wrongs we claimed to underlie particular acts of indirect discrimination since moral wrongdoing requires culpability. Third, we set out positive justifications for strict indirect discrimination liability.

A. Strict Liability for Indirect Discrimination

In UK law, the indirect discrimination duty (section 19) is framed without an explicit culpability requirement: it requires no (potentially) blameworthy

[36] There may yet be a still more basic sense in which Ifemelu is harmed. It is at least arguable that merely being at risk of disadvantage is itself a form of disadvantage: see Sandy Steel, *Proof of Causation in Tort Law* (Cambridge, Cambridge University Press, 2015) ch 6. See, on the link between risk and autonomy, John Oberdiek, *Imposing Risk* (Oxford, Oxford University Press, 2017).

mental state such as intention or recklessness, nor is there an explicit negligence requirement.

The indirect discrimination duty appears, then, to be a *strict* duty. A strict duty is a duty whose breach is not contingent upon the prohibited conduct being done with fault. That is: it is liability which attaches to an agent, A, for X-ing regardless of any steps A took or could have taken to avoid X-ing and regardless of whether A knew or had reason to know whether A would X.[37]

It might be questioned whether section 19(2)(d) has the effect of introducing culpability considerations into the question of whether a person breaches their indirect discrimination duty or into the question of whether a person can justify or excuse their breach of that duty. If A could avoid being liable by demonstrating that A 'reasonably believed' that the means adopted were proportionate to achieving a legitimate aim, then it would follow that the absence of culpability would act as a valid excusatory condition. But demonstrating a reasonable belief in the proportionality of the means is clearly insufficient for it to be the case that A can show it to be a proportionate means. Showing that it *is* proportionate is obviously different from showing that one had a *reasonable belief* that it was proportionate.[38]

An objection to this view might be that the defendant's failure to *justify* a prima facie act of indirect discrimination makes her act culpable in the relevant sense. It is true that liability for indirect discrimination does not arise unless the defendant has failed to show that the act in question was a proportionate means of achieving a legitimate aim (or some such means-end justification). The absence of such justification may indeed point to the fact that the defendant might have been negligent or reckless. This is not, however, necessarily the case. The justification test is an objective means-end inquiry, and does not seek to smoke out any subjective mental state of the defendant. It is quite possible for a prima facie act of indirect discrimination to be unjustified and yet remain non-culpable.

B. Strict Liability and Non-culpable Wrongdoing

The valid point thus remains that the indirect discrimination duty can be breached *without any* fault. This may seem to challenge our view that the indirect discrimination duty is justified by the moral wrongs involved in particular acts of indirect discrimination: is it intelligible to say that a person

37 This definition is drawn from J Gardner, 'Some Rule-of-Law Anxieties about Strict Liability in Private Law' in L Austin and D Klimchuk (eds), *Private Law and the Rule of Law* (Oxford, Oxford University Press, 2014).

38 Although some earlier decisions did appear to incorporate a reasonable belief limitation here, see: S Fredman, *Discrimination Law* 2nd edn (Oxford, Oxford University Press, 2011) 193–96.

is a wrongdoer though they were not at fault in committing the wrong? In this part of the paper, we argue that plausible accounts of at least some moral wrongs do not, on analysis, embed a fault requirement. It does not, of course, follow that the law ought always to enforce these strict moral duties directly, without the interposition of a fault requirement.

It will be useful to set out here three different ways in which it might be claimed that considerations of culpability figure in the moral wrong of indirect discrimination.

(i) *Culpability as constituent of the wrong*. On this view, culpability is an essential part of the primary moral indirect discrimination *duty*; there could be no wrong of indirect discrimination without culpable conduct. Compare the moral wrong of negligence. On one view of this wrong, or of one species of it, it specifies a duty to have a certain attitude of care towards the interests of others. On that understanding, the wrongness of negligence cannot be specified independently of culpability. This view seeks to cast indirect discrimination liability as a classic private law wrong like the tort of negligence.

(ii) *Culpability as necessary for responsibility for a wrong*. On this view, while culpability may not figure in the existence of a primary moral duty to not commit indirect discrimination, it is essential in order to hold someone morally *responsible* for its breach. It may be, for example, that the insane are capable of breaching serious moral duties (not to kill, for example) and yet are not morally responsible for those breaches.

(iii) *Absence of culpability as an excusatory condition*. On this view, culpability does not figure in the primary moral indirect discrimination duty, but rather is relevant to whether the wrong was *excused*. A person can be morally responsible for a wrong despite being excused for it. For instance, a person might be excused for acting in the face of extreme provocation (in response, say, to domestic violence) and yet be morally responsible for their wrongdoing.[39]

i. Culpability as Constituent of the Wrong

Suppose A promises to have goods delivered to B by next Monday morning. A's supplier, C, who has always been reliable in the past, notifies A on Sunday evening that C will not be able to deliver the goods to B.

[39] A further role for culpability is: *Culpability as an aggravating feature of the wrong*. On this view, there can be non-culpable wrongs of indirect discrimination, but culpability enhances the blameworthiness of the wrong, perhaps rendering the wrongdoer liable to different normative consequences to non-culpable indirect-discrimination-feasors. This is less important to our present discussion which focuses on the legitimacy of liability *without* fault.

By breaching A's promise, A wrongs B. Plausibly A's wrong is non-culpable.[40] The idea that we can be under duties simply (not) to produce certain outcomes is morally intelligible, as Gardner explains, in virtue of the fact that our primary reasons are reasons *to succeed*. We have reasons to try not to run people over because we have reasons not to run people over. If we can have reasons to succeed in producing certain outcomes, why not *obligations* to succeed in producing certain outcomes?[41] The idea that one could have a moral duty to succeed in not disadvantaging others due to normatively irrelevant characteristics thus seems, in principle, morally intelligible.

It is also the case that, despite first appearances, prominent accounts of the moral wrong of indirect discrimination are compatible with its being a strict liability wrong. Consider, in this regard, what we can call the 'reasons-based' account of the indirect discrimination wrong, which endorses the first of the two interpretations of the 'because of' requirement that Altman identified: as indicating 'the reasons that guide the acts of agents'.[42] One version of this view states that wrongful indirect discrimination consists (partly) in an agent's causing relative disadvantage by *acting on* an illegitimate reason—a reason which bears some relation to a prohibited ground, such as race. Suppose that a university decides to accept applicants only from local regions because they sincerely believe this reduces the complexity of their admissions procedures. Suppose further that this has a disparate impact on racial minorities. Holmes, followed here by Fishkin, claims that, if this is a wrongful act of discrimination, it can be explained as such by conceiving of the policy (P) as a 'proxy' criterion for race: adopting P-like policies is likely to have a disparate impact on racial minorities.[43] Acting on reasons which bear a proxy relation to race-based reasons partakes of the illegitimacy of acting on the race-based reasons.

Whatever one thinks of the plausibility of this manoeuvre, it very significantly expands the concept of 'acting on a prohibited/illegitimate reason'. In particular, it seems that one can 'act on an illegitimate reason' on this view even where the ultimate reason why the proxy reason is illegitimate plays no causal role in the explanation of why one took the action. So even if the university would have adopted the same policy had the racial composition of the surrounding area been entirely different, it still seems to be the case, on this view, that it has acted on a prohibited reason here. Further, this account

[40] See further S Shiffrin, 'Enhancing Moral Relationships through Strict Liability' (2016) 66 *University of Toronto Law Journal* 353.

[41] See, in detail, J Gardner, 'Obligations and Outcomes in the Law of Torts' in P Cane and J Gardner (eds), *Relating to Responsibility: Essays for Tony Honoré* (Oxford, Hart Publishing, 2001).

[42] Altman (n 26).

[43] E Holmes, 'Anti-discrimination Rights without Equality' (2005) 68 *Modern Law Review* 175, 184; J Fishkin, *Bottlenecks: A New Theory of Equality of Opportunity* (Oxford, Oxford University Press, 2014) 247.

requires no awareness of the relationship the proxy reason bears to the illegitimate reason—in short it requires no subjective or constructive knowledge as to why the proxy reason is indeed a proxy. As such, this divorces the reasons-account from any notion of culpability since it requires no awareness (or objective ability to be aware) of the wrong-making features of the act (namely, its connection to the effects on racial minorities in this example). Even expressive accounts which locate the wrongness of (some) acts of indirect discrimination in the, say, demeaning message communicated by acts of discrimination can accept that what is communicated by an action in a certain community could be wholly unknown to the communicator, who is reasonably unaware of the relevant linguistic or social conventions.

Moreau's earlier analysis of the wrong of discrimination might seem to imply a culpability requirement.[44] On her view, discrimination is wrongful in so far as it denies to a person their entitlement to certain deliberative freedoms, in particular freedoms to decide about aspects of one's life without pressure from one's normatively irrelevant characteristics. She describes the wrong as 'tort-like' and, more specifically, as 'akin to the tort of negligence'.[45] She denies that our entitlement is to suffer no adverse effects because of a normatively irrelevant characteristic. Instead, it is rather to suffer no adverse effects because of such characteristics *to the extent this can be reasonably demanded against others* who cause such effects:

> Adverse effect discrimination is not an act or practice that has the effect of excluding someone on the basis of a prohibited ground, but rather an act that excludes someone in circumstances where there is some reasonable way of accommodating this person short of undue hardship.[46]

Here, then, like the move to read culpability in the absence of justification, the primary indirect discrimination duty is one of reasonable accommodation. When an employer argues that its policy is justified on grounds of business necessity, it does not justify or excuse a wrong, but rather disputes its existence entirely.[47] While Moreau establishes wrongfulness, nothing here imports a requirement of culpability. An act is unreasonable (and, therefore, wrongful) on this view if it does not instantiate the right balance between the (legitimate) interests of the discriminator and the deliberative freedoms

[44] Moreau (n 35). For an earlier analysis along similar lines, but without the focus on deliberative freedoms in particular: D Reaume, 'Harm and Fault in Discrimination Law: The Transition from Intentional to Adverse Effect Discrimination' (2001) 2 *Theoretical Inquiries in Law* 349.

[45] Moreau (n 1) 130.

[46] ibid, 134.

[47] Sometimes, though, Moreau seems to speak of the interference with (certain) deliberative freedoms as itself an infringement of a right without the need any balancing exercise, which suggests the balancing is best understood as a defence to the wrong, rather than a constituent element: see ibid 139, cf 140.

of the victim. But whether the economic interests of the business owner are more important than the deliberative freedoms of the victim is an objective question which holds independently of anyone's attitudes or knowledge. It is not surprising that Moreau is conscious of the need to allay concerns that her account involves strict liability. It does.[48]

In sum, then, since it seems unlikely that we should believe (i) in relation to indirect discrimination, (i) gives us no reason to conclude that the law departs from a plausible moral conception of the wrong of indirect discrimination.

ii. Culpability as Necessary for Responsibility for a Wrong

What about (ii) (ie culpability as necessary for *responsibility* for a wrong)? As a general matter, moral responsibility, at least in one important sense, can diverge from culpability. We can be morally responsible for our wrongful acts even though it would be inappropriate to *blame* us (and even though the act may itself not be *blameworthy*). Consider cases of agents who commit justified wrongs. If, in order to save the lives of passengers, the captain of a ship anchors the ship to a dock owned by another person without that person's consent during a storm, damaging the dock, the captain wrongs the dock owner, and is responsible for the wrong, but she is in no other way culpable.[49] Claim (ii) therefore seems generally untrue. It is also untrue as an explanation of indirect discrimination liability, as the law does not require proof of culpability as a precondition for making the defendant responsible for her actions.

iii. Absence of Culpability as an Excusatory Condition

Most, perhaps all, excuses involve denials that the (wrongful) act in question was blameworthy.[50] More specifically, excuses concede *responsibility* for the wrong, but deny that the wrong reflects badly, in some sense, upon the agent.[51] So when a person points to the fact that they committed a

[48] Even if, as Moreau suggests at one point, the causation requirement in indirect discrimination will involve considerations of foreseeability, this only goes to show that some degree of avoidability might be built into the indirect discrimination-wrong. But this need not imply that the agent was culpable. See the next section for the divergence between avoidability and culpability.

[49] cf *Vincent v Lake Erie Transportation Co* 109 Minn 456 (1910).

[50] Though some believe that blameworthiness is defined in terms of absence of excuse rather than the other way around. But see A Simester, 'A Disintegrated Theory of Culpability' in D Baker and J Horder (eds), *The Sanctity of Life and the Criminal Law* (Cambridge, Cambridge University Press, 2013) 183.

[51] See J Gardner, *Offences and Defences: Selected Essays in the Philosophy of Criminal Law* (Oxford, Oxford University Press, 2007) ch 6.

wrong because another threatened them with violence, they do not, or need not, deny that the wrong was their doing and that they can be called to account for it, but they do deny that they should be blamed for it. Similarly, if the next time I type 't' on the screen, due to some bizarre chain of causation an earthquake is caused, it would be inappropriate to *blame* me for this—I had no reason whatsoever to believe that this consequence would result. However, that one is excused only blocks an inference from *wrongdoing* to *blameworthiness*. It does not follow that one is relieved of any moral obligations arising out of one's wrong. In other words, only certain kinds of responses to one's wrongdoing are ruled out by the absence of culpability. For instance, it seems plausible that one could still be under moral obligations of repair. If this is so, as the law, at any rate, holds, in the case of the justified wrongdoer in tort law (the example of the sea captain), *a fortiori* in the case of the excused wrongdoer. Consequently, since the legal responses to the breaches of the indirect discrimination duty are not necessarily responses which express blame or which trace their rational source to blaming, the law need not be at variance with morality here. This would only be so if the legal responses to indirect discrimination necessarily communicated blame in circumstances where they have a genuine excuse. Although we do not deal with the question of justification, it may well be that the absence of culpability is a necessary condition for justifying indirect discrimination in law.[52]

C. Justifying Liability in the Absence of Culpability

Even if there can be moral responsibility without culpability, and even if the absence of culpability does not entail the absence of normative consequences for one's wrongdoing, strict legal liability for indirect discrimination still calls for justification.

This is for two reasons. First, there is a concern of fairness that agents should not be subject to legal liabilities for wrongs which they cannot avoid committing at the time of acting. If liability is imposed, as it is for indirect discrimination, without a requirement that it be reasonably foreseeable at the time of A's acting (at the time of breach of the duty) that the 'provision, criterion, or practice' puts (or would put) persons sharing B's characteristic at a disadvantage, then they are subject to liabilities which they may have no reason to believe will arise when they acted. Second, the ideal of the rule of law seems also to demand that people be able to assure themselves at the

[52] In fact, Canadian law has an explicit 'good faith' requirement as part of the justification exercise.

time of acting that their acts will not lead to legal liability.[53] In short, the ability to avoid the commission of a wrong seems to be required both by considerations of fairness and the ideal of the rule of law.

These are important concerns to which we offer two immediate responses. First, it might be said that a person *can* avoid breaching an indirect discrimination duty by avoiding entering into one of the legally recognised roles/statuses (such as that of an employer, a landlord and so on) to which the indirect discrimination duty attaches. So long as these roles are clearly identified and relatively limited in number, there is a degree of avoidability. It is true that liability will attach even in cases where there is no foreseeability of the likelihood that the practice in question will produce a disparate impact. But there is general knowledge that one of the abstract risks of setting criteria for the allocation of valuable resources is that the criteria one selects could produce a disparate impact. Although this avoidability comes at immense personal costs (entailed in avoiding otherwise legitimate occupations), and cannot seriously be recommended to anyone, this is still at considerable remove from holding a person responsible for the destruction of a plane which, by some miraculous causal path, happens when they pick up a lettuce in the supermarket. The risk of disparate impact is a known risk which attaches to the setting of criteria for the allocation of resources. The imposition of this risk will seem less unfair if we note that the duty-bearers in discrimination law (employers, landlords, retailers, service-providers) tend to be gatekeepers of valuable opportunities in our societies, and also usually the stronger party in the equation (in relation to their employees, tenants, consumers).[54]

Second, the degree to which avoidability considerations should be taken into account either within the legal definition of the indirect discrimination duty or as a matter of a defence to the breach of that duty is partly a function of the kind of consequences which attach to the breach. Obviously, if persons who breached the indirect discrimination duty were subject to *punishment*, there would be a need to provide a much greater degree of avoidability than the current law allows, and thus a much greater role for considerations of culpability within the definition of the wrong or defences to the wrong. But, as we have already observed, the current law does not even provide compensation as of right for unjustified breaches. An employer who innocently breaches their indirect discrimination duty is likely only to be subject to a declaration of breach and a recommendation to alter their policy so as to conform to their initial primary duty.[55]

[53] See J Gardner, 'Some Rule-of-Law Anxieties about Strict Liability in Private Law' in L Austin and D Klimchuk (eds), *Private Law and the Rule of Law* (Oxford, Oxford University Press, 2014).

[54] See Khaitan (n 6) ch 7 on duty bearers.

[55] See Equality Act 2010 s 124(5).

Apart from the possibility of avoidability and the fact that the degree of avoidability required is a function of the severity of the consequences imposed for the breach of a duty, there are three further reasons for believing that the imposition of strict liability for the breach of the indirect discrimination duty can be justified to persons subject to the duty, all things considered.

First, alongside the indirect discrimination duty, the law imposes other duties which help to mollify the strict liability nature of the indirect discrimination duty. Section 149(1) of the Equality Act 2010 imposes an obligation on public authorities to 'have due regard to the need to', inter alia, 'eliminate discrimination, harassment, victimisation and any other conduct that is prohibited by or under this Act'.[56] If an authority is to have 'due regard' to this need, this may require, or at least encourage, the authority to gather information about the potential effects of common policies or practices upon protected groups. This helps to establish a body of information about the likely effects of certain practices which others, including private individuals subject to the indirect discrimination duty, could potentially draw upon in making their own decisions. By improving the state of knowledge about the effects of certain policies on protected groups, this reduces the possibility that persons subject to the indirect discrimination duty will be caught off guard by its strict liability effect. At the very least, it seems inconsistent with obligation to 'have due regard' not to investigate further incipient signs of disparate impact.[57] Even if diligent information gathering prior to the adoption of a practice, criterion or policy fails to highlight potential disparate impact, reliable data should be available *after* such policy has been implemented. Furthermore, assuming that any claimant is likely to seek internal remedies in the first instance before going to the courts, *legal* liability for future breaches is almost always avoidable. Here, then, the broader goal of indirect discrimination law of reducing group disadvantage—expressed here in the section 149 duty—helps to justify the imposition of a strict liability in respect of the indirect discrimination duty.

Second, the strictness of the indirect discrimination duty provides incentives for duty-bearers to invest in information gathering to avoid liability. If the duty were limited to cases of reasonably foreseeable effects, duty-bearers would have less incentives to invest in information since they could avoid liability by showing that the information was not available to the

[56] Equality Act 2010 s 149(1)(a).

[57] cf *The Queen on the Application of Bapio Action Ltd v Royal College of General Practitioners, General Medical Council* [2014] EWHC 1416: 'Section 149 does not permit a person exercising public functions to identify the need to eliminate discrimination in one of the public functions it exercises and then do nothing about it', [31] (Mittering J). See further S Fredman, 'Addressing Disparate Impact: Indirect Discrimination and the Public Sector Equality Duty' (2014) 43 *Industrial Law Journal* 349.

reasonable person. Of course, given the minimal remedial regime, the extra incentive provided is likely to be a relatively weak one. A finding of unjustified discrimination does have stigmatising implications for the defendant, and is not inconsequential. Even so, the law keeps the big guns locked up when it comes to deciding upon the appropriate remedy for indirect discrimination law, in part to mitigate the strictness of the duty. In fact, as our societies become more educated about indirect discrimination, a more robust remedial approach may well be legitimate at least in cases where the discrimination was reasonably foreseeable.

Third, defining the duty in a culpability-free manner, while taking considerations of culpability into account at the remedial stage, allows the law to provide clear guidance to duty-bearers, while also accommodating considerations of fairness to the latter.[58] Incorporating, for instance, a reasonableness standard into the definition of the primary duty would cloud the clarity of the law's message. It might be objected here that strict liability nature of the duty could cloud the law's message in a different way. It might lead to the impression that indirect discrimination is wrongful only in a technical, purely legal, sense.[59] This concern seems unjustified for two reasons. First, by associating culpable breaches of the indirect discrimination duty with potential (albeit unlikely) compensatory liability, the law still sends the message that breach of the indirect discrimination duty is a serious matter. Second, the strict liability nature of the wrong might actually signify how serious the interest in non-discrimination is to the law. In tort law, our most fundamental interests in bodily integrity and liberty are often protected by strict liability wrongs (eg in trespass to the person and false imprisonment). The fact that non-culpable infringements of these interests are *wrongful* is a reflection of the law's commitment to stringent protection of these interests, and especially to its systemic goal of eliminating abiding, pervasive and substantial relative group disadvantage.

In sum, then, the absence of culpability in the definition of the primary duty is defensible. Culpability is not required in order for the law to map onto the moral duty of refraining from committing indirect discrimination (i). Moral responsibility for a wrong does not entail culpability either (ii). To the extent that considerations of avoidability are relevant, there are opportunities to avoid breach of the strict indirect discrimination duty and, in any event, the level of avoidability required for responsibility varies with

[58] cf M Dan Cohen, 'Decision Rules and Conduct Rules: On Acoustic Separation in the Criminal Law' (1983) 97 *Harvard Law Review* 625.

[59] cf P Shin, 'Liability for Unconscious Discrimination: A Thought-experiment in the Theory of Employment Discrimination Law' (NELLCO Legal Scholarship Repository) available at http://lsr.nellco.org/cgi/viewcontent.cgi?article=1070&context=suffolk_fp, 42 on unconscious bias, suggesting that recognition of liability for unconscious bias discrimination might have a negative effect on the law's message or perceptions thereof.

the harshness of the consequences attached to breach. Absence of culpability is not formally recognised as an excusatory condition (iii), but this is one way of understanding the general absence of significant normative consequences for the innocent breach. It may be noted that we have addressed unfairness concerns largely within the parameters of corrective justice. In doing so, we do not intend to deny the possibility that the distributive justice goals of indirect discrimination liability may, independently, offer sufficient justification for the imposition of this liability. In other words, an indirect discrimination regime that takes a more robust approach to damages may, nonetheless, be fair.

IV. CONCLUSION: WHY INDIRECT DISCRIMINATION LAW NEEDS THE SYSTEMIC ANALYSIS

In the preceding sections, we have seen that although the liability for indirect discrimination is comparable to a personal wrong, like the tort of negligence, there are important differences. Unlike negligence, where the law insists upon the proof of causation in every particular case, indirect discrimination presupposes such causation to exist in most cases and does not burden the claimant with establishing that her disadvantage was *because of* her group membership. Even when it comes to establishing that the group itself has suffered particular disadvantage, the law has relaxed the demanding statistical standards and settled for rule-of-thumb evidence as sufficient. Furthermore, unlike negligence law with a strict proximity requirement, the proximity of the claimant's race etc as at least a contributory cause is usually presumed. Even when the claimant suffers nominal harm, it is understood that the adverse effect on the group might still be significant: discrimination law therefore has no *de minimis* threshold. Further still, the tort of negligence can be established only after the claimant has proved that the defendant's conduct would, from the perspective of a reasonable person, foreseeably lead to the type of injury she has suffered. In indirect discrimination liability, although in many cases the disparate impact on the claimant's group would be foreseeable, this is not always the case, and is not something the claimant must establish in order to succeed. Indirect discrimination liability is strict and arises even when the defendant is not culpable. Finally, while the typical remedy in tort law is damages, this is not the case with indirect discrimination liability.

These differences suggest that indirect discrimination law employs a rule-of-thumb approach for determining liability, bearing in mind societal realities, especially the usually different status of the parties (including their differential access to relevant information), but tempers this rough justice approach with weak remedies. However, this rough justice approach in individual cases cannot be legitimate unless it was in service of some broader purpose, which we identify as the need to reduce and eliminate substantial, abiding and pervasive advantage gaps between groups defined by normatively irrelevant personal characteristics. The approach to causation provides a clear illustration. The fact that a statistically significant correlation triggers a rebuttable presumption that the practice is causally connected to group disadvantage goes beyond the causal presumptions normally applied by the common law of torts. Statistically significant correlation itself is not usually enough to establish general causation—that the agent in question *could* cause the harmful outcome in question. If indirect discrimination were simply concerned with correcting, or marking, the breach of the particular duty, it would be difficult to understand why it would not also follow the general approach in tort law. However, this becomes intelligible once indirect discrimination law's broader aim of reducing relative group disadvantage is borne in mind.

The bottomline is this: a false negative in indirect discrimination law (failing to detect wrongful indirect discrimination where it exists) is not simply a failure to correct an interpersonal wrong, it is potentially a failure to address a causal source of relative group disadvantage. In short, there can usually be presumed to be more at stake. It is the systemic purpose of discrimination law, which is ultimately geared towards securing to us certain key freedoms, that motivates the law's strong aversion to false negatives, even as it uses a personal-wrongs based approach to seek its systemic goal of eliminating relative group disadvantage.

This response was motivated by Moreau's challenge that the corrective justice dimension of discrimination law could bear all the justificatory burden of indirect discrimination liability. We have therefore shown how this cannot be, and that the distributive justice dimension is necessary. One might be tempted to provide the opposite critique—that distributive justice can do all the heavy lifting. They will also be wrong. Distributive justice cannot explain why the liability is interpersonal, attaches only to certain persons who are somehow implicated in the disparate impact their actions (are taken to) cause. A purely distributive justice approach would also lose out on the importance that we attach to fixing *moral responsibility* for acts of indirect discrimination by particular persons. Indirect discrimination liability draws upon both corrective and distributive justice requirements, and mimics aspects of private as well as public law. This, in itself, is no bad thing.

10

Anti-discrimination Law and the Duty to Integrate

JULIE C SUK

IN RECENT YEARS, a new indirect discrimination doctrine has emerged in European Court of Human Rights (ECtHR) cases alleging discrimination in the exercise of the right to education. The ECtHR has found violations in a series of cases challenging national education systems' practices contributing to the separation and diminished opportunities of Roma children. Since the 2007 Grand Chamber judgment in *DH and Others v Czech Republic*, NGOs monitoring the implementation of the judgment have argued that, despite some reforms undertaken by the governments in attempts to comply with these judgments, de facto segregation is continuing in the Czech Republic, and thus Convention rights are still being violated. Indeed, the European Court of Human Rights' formulation of indirect discrimination theory articulates a positive duty to integrate Roma children into mainstream public schools. This chapter further develops the normative underpinnings of the democratic state's duty to integrate children of different backgrounds in public education, in light of patterns of resegregation in the United States, even after anti-discrimination law was deployed to undo segregation.

Commentators have called *DH and Others* the 'Brown v Board of Education of Europe.'[1] But the understanding of Roma segregation as indirect discrimination departs significantly from current American understandings of segregation as intentional discrimination and disparate impact (the American analogue to indirect discrimination) as an unworkable framework for Equal Protection adjudication. The European Court of Human Rights has made the absence of integration both a necessary and sufficient condition of racial discrimination in education. By contrast, the US Supreme Court's equal protection education jurisprudence evolved to reject disparate impact or indirect discrimination theories, distinguishing between non-discrimination and integration, and declining to impose a duty of integration.

[1] See, eg, J Greenberg, 'Report on Roma Education Today: From Slavery to Segregation And Beyond' (2010) 110 *Columbia Law Review* 919; M Minow, 'Brown v. Board in the World: How the Global Turn Matters for School Reform, Human Rights, and Legal Knowledge' (2013) 50 *San Diego Law Review* 1.

This chapter develops two theoretical insights, one normative and one descriptive, emerging from the contrast between the European Court of Human Rights and the US Supreme Court's approaches to indirect discrimination and the duty of integration. First, as a normative matter, the duty to integrate is a moral imperative of democracy which foregrounds state liability for indirect discrimination in education. If taken seriously, the European Court of Human Rights' duty to integrate would create a sense of moral and legal urgency about the patterns of resegregation in American public education, and call into question many accepted practices in American public education. Second, as a descriptive matter, a court's inclination to recognise indirect discrimination and the duty to integrate is facilitated by its reluctance to impose specific effective remedies. Thus, the ECtHR's indirect discrimination doctrine is bringing about reform indirectly, not through strong legal remedies, but by giving a robust moral legal language to NGOs nudging legislative action. In the United States, by contrast, judges' fears of backlash against strong remedies have led courts to abandon the moral-legal language of integration, making it difficult for other actors to frame current patterns of intense racial separation and education disparities as unlawful discrimination.

I. *DH AND OTHERS v CZECH REPUBLIC*: A NEW INDIRECT DISCRIMINATION FRAMEWORK

None of the states subject to ECtHR judgments on Roma segregation had official policies segregating or otherwise classifying pupils because they were Roma. Unlike the explicit American state laws, sometimes enshrined in constitutions, which officially required black and white children to be educated in separate schools before *Brown v Board of Education*, the education systems that are under review in these cases are facially neutral with regard to race or ethnicity. However, in many Eastern European countries, schools and educational programmes came to be known informally as 'Roma only' as a consequence of the education system's attempt to classify students by ability and disability. The complaints brought before the European Court of Human Rights alleged that Roma children were frequently misdiagnosed as disabled and then placed into programmes intended for mentally disabled students. In *DH v Czech Republic*, and in the Roma school segregation cases subsequently decided by the European Court of Human Rights, the Court relied on the concept of indirect discrimination to invalidate a wide range of practices that resulted in the separation of Romani children from non-Romani children in various educational settings. These decisions have been premised on Article 14 taken with Article 2 of Protocol 1 of the European Convention on Human Rights. Article 14 provides:

> The enjoyment of the rights and freedoms set forth in this Convention shall be secured without discrimination on any ground such as sex, race, colour, language,

> religion, political or other opinion, national or social origin, association with a national minority, property, birth or other status.[2]

Article 2 of Protocol 1 guarantees the right to education:

> No person shall be denied the right to education. In the exercise of any functions which it assumes in relation to education and to teaching, the State shall respect the right of parents to ensure such education and teaching in conformity with their own religious and philosophical convictions.[3]

In finding the Czech education system to be in violation of these provisions, the Court's description of the problematic educational practices reveals the normative underpinnings of its indirect discrimination doctrine.

In *DH*, the Czech education system included special schools for children with special needs, including those suffering from a mental or social handicap.[4] Before 1989, most Roma children attended these special schools. Placement was determined by teachers on the basis of intelligence tests and parental consent. The *DH* litigation was brought to challenge the segregation by way of special schools in the town of Ostrava. The following statistics regarding Ostrava when the litigation commenced was noted by the Court in *DH*. There were 33,372 primary-school pupils in Ostrava, of which 2.26 per cent were Roma. However, of the 1,360 students placed in Ostrava's special schools, 56 per cent were Roma. Only 1.8 per cent of non-Roma pupils were placed in special schools, whereas 50.3 per cent of Roma children were placed in these schools. On the basis of these disparities, documented in official statistics, the ECtHR shifted the burden of justification to the Czech Government.

There were other facts that the Court highlighted, including how these placements came about, particularly for the claimants in this litigation. The claimants had been evaluated in an educational psychology centre, in accordance with the statute governing the special schools. A psychologist had recommended placement for these students in special schools, and in each instance, the parents of the children had accepted and thereby consented to the placements. The statute does not require the automatic or compulsory testing of every pupil entering the public school system. Teachers generally make recommendations as to who gets tested, 'either when the child first enrolled at the school or if difficulties were noted in its ordinary primary-school education—or by pediatricians.'[5] The psychology centres tended to administer variants of the Wechsler Intelligence Scale for Children and the Stanford-Binet intelligence test.[6] The litigants called into question the

[2] European Convention on Human Rights, art 14.
[3] European Convention on Human Rights, Protocol 1, art 2.
[4] *DH and Others v Czech Republic* (App no 57325/00) (2008) 47 EHRR 3, [15].
[5] ibid [39].
[6] Wechsler and Stanford-Binet are also the tests upon which the tests used for admission by selective and highly regarded private schools and public gifted programmes and schools in New York City.

legitimacy of these tests as measures of mental disability, because 'they had been devised solely for Czech children, and had not recently been standardized or approved for use with Roma children.'[7] It was also noted that 'no measures had been taken to enable Roma children to overcome their cultural and linguistic disadvantages in the tests.'[8]

In *DH*, the ECtHR developed a flexible and pluralistic approach to proving discrimination. Rejecting 'predetermined formulae' for the assessment of evidence in favour of 'free evaluation of all evidence', the court noted that, in some cases, it might be appropriate for the defendant state to bear the burden of proving the absence of discrimination, even where a prima facie case (which they simultaneously refuse to define) is not made.[9] Citing precedent, the Court determined that 'in the legal systems of many countries proof of the discriminatory effect of a policy, decision or practice would dispense with the need to prove intent in respect of alleged discrimination in employment or in the provision of services.'[10] Thus, when applicants 'alleged a difference in the effect of a general measure or de facto situation' in a discrimination claim, 'the Court relied extensively on statistics produced by the parties to establish a difference in treatment between two groups ... in similar situations.'[11] If 'undisputed official statistics' are presented, the statistics alone raise the inference that 'a specific rule—although formulated in a neutral manner—in fact affects a clearly higher percentage' of one group than another and this shifts the burden to the government 'to show that this is the result of objective factors unrelated to any discrimination' on the prohibited grounds.

What this means is that a statistical disparity—such as the disproportionately high numbers of Roma children in special schools relative to their share of the pupil populations—raises the inference that 'a specific rule' is causing it. But it is not the claimant's duty to name and prove which specific rule or practice is causing the disparity. Instead, the burden gets shifted to the defendant. Because claimants are not required to pinpoint specific practices, the Government's response tends to cover a broad range of explanations and observations regarding the statistical disparity.[12] Indeed, there are many practices contributing to racial stratification in the Czech education system, and changing any of them could potentially remedy the stratification.

[7] *DH* (n 4) [40].
[8] ibid.
[9] ibid [178].
[10] ibid [179].
[11] ibid [180].
[12] I have compared this framework to the US framework, which imposes a duty on plaintiffs to point to a specific practice. See JC Suk, 'Disparate Impact Abroad' in S Bagenstos and E Katz (eds), *A Nation of Widening Opportunities? The Civil Rights Act at 50* (Ann Arbor, University of Michigan Press, 2016).

Which specific rule or practice should a court's finding of indirect discrimination lead to changing? If a specific practice is not identified, a specific remedy cannot be imposed. Consider the wide range of possible changes in policy that might correct the statistical disparities being complained of in this case. Perhaps the real problem is the existence of separate schools for the mildly mentally disabled, in which case the solution produced by this litigation should be the abolition of these schools. Perhaps it is not the existence of special schools, but the tests administered to determine placement, which lead to misdiagnosis of mental disabilities. If the tests are problematic, the solution produced by the litigation should be to adopt better placement tests. Perhaps the problem is not the test, but the bias of teachers and psychologists in selecting the students for testing and administering the tests? In that case, the solution would be training and opportunities to challenge the test results. Finally, is the true cause of Roma separation the consent of Roma parents to the placement of their children in special schools? If so, perhaps parental consent should be disregarded or eliminated as a feature of the placement scheme. Each one of these practices is arguably what causes the disproportionate separation of Roma children, and making a major change to any one of these practices might be sufficient to end the separation. On the other hand, if all these practices were abolished but the racial stratification continued through other practices, the question arises as to whether the scenario should be regarded as a continuing manifestation of indirect discrimination. Nonetheless, the indirect discrimination framework adopted by the Court does not put the burden on the claimants to identify specific practices and prove that they (as opposed to other factors) have caused the disproportionate impact. In statutory employment discrimination disparate impact claims, US courts, by contrast, do require the plaintiff to show that a specific practice (or set of practices) caused the disparate impact before the defendant is required to articulate a legitimate nondiscriminatory justification for those practices.[13]

The Czech government defended the continued existence of special schools, arguing that they were needed to serve mentally disabled children who are entitled to special education services. The government also claimed that it was the parents' consent, rather than the government's acts of testing and proposing placement in special schools, that ultimately caused Roma children to be placed in special schools. In finding a violation of Article 14 taken with Article 2 of Protocol 1, the Court does not give much guidance as to which practice is problematic and required to be changed under its ruling:

> The facts of the instant case indicate that the schooling arrangements for Roma children were not attended by safeguards (see paragraph 28 above) that would

[13] See *Watson v Fort Worth Bank & Trust* 487 US 977, 994 (1988); *Wards Cove Packing Co Inc v Atonio* 490 US 642, 656 (1989).

> ensure that, in the exercise of its margin of appreciation in the education sphere, the State took into account their special needs as members of a disadvantaged class ... Furthermore, as a result of the arrangements the applicants were placed in schools for children with mental disabilities where a more basic curriculum was followed than in ordinary schools and where they were isolated from pupils from the wider population. As a result, they received an education that compounded their difficulties and compromised their subsequent personal development instead of tackling their real problems or helping them to integrate into the ordinary schools and develop the skills that would facilitate life among the majority population.[14]

In this extremely significant paragraph elaborating its conclusion that there has been a violation of Article 14, the Court refers here to 'safeguards (see paragraph 28 above)' that might have saved the legitimacy of the education regime being condemned by bringing it within the state's 'margin of appreciation'. Yet, 'paragraph 28 above' does not spell out those safeguards, but simply recounts the Czech Constitutional Court's rejection of the claimants' constitutional claims on both procedural and substantive grounds. Within Paragraph 207 as quoted above, one safeguard that the Court mentions which was missing in the facts here was any effort by the state to consider the 'special needs' of the Roma as a 'disadvantaged class', presumably in designing the psychological tests that determined their school placement. Had the state designed a test that was consciously sensitive to Roma children's linguistic disadvantages, for example, perhaps the disproportionate placement of Roma children in special schools would not be quite as problematic.

The Court is not explicit about what would have saved the special education scheme, and instead engages in the rhetoric of integration. The provision is violated because the Roma children were 'isolated from pupils from the wider population' and the special school was not 'tackling their real problems or helping them integrate into the ordinary schools and develop the skills that would facilitate life among the majority population.'[15] Implicit in all these remarks is the assumption that the prohibition of discrimination requires the state to make efforts to integrate disadvantaged populations into the mainstream institutions, particularly public schools, with an awareness of the special needs of these groups related to their disadvantage. Special treatment, and perhaps even temporary separation to meet the special needs of disadvantaged pupils, if utilised, must aim towards integration, and actually achieve it eventually. The absence of discrimination is equivalent to the presence of integration.

This normative account of indirect discrimination in violation of Article 14 taken with Article 2 of Protocol No 1 is more fully articulated in the European Court's subsequent Roma education cases. In *Sampanis v Greece*,[16]

[14] *DH* (n 4) [207].
[15] ibid.
[16] *Sampanis and Others v Greece* (App no 32526/05) (ECHR, 5 June 2008).

the ECtHR found Greece in violation of the same two articles (non-discrimination and right to education) based on the following facts: Romani parents attempted to enroll their children at a school in Aspropyrgos, near the Psari Roma camp. The teachers refused to enroll the students. The students were assisted by NGOs and the Ombudsmen's Office, and eventually some of these children were enrolled. On the first day of school, many non-Roma parents and children blockaded the school and harassed the Romani children who attempted to enter.[17] Similar incidents and a boycott by the non-Romani parents continued through the month. In October, the Romani children were placed in a separate building for almost two years. These children, prior to enrollment at the school, had not previously been educated. The declared objective of placement in separate 'preparatory classes', which consisted exclusively of Romani children, was to enable these children to work towards the level of education necessary to enter the ordinary classes. However, there was no evidence suggesting that the preparatory classes facilitated the Romani children's eventual integration.

Because the racist incidents preventing Romani children's access to the school occurred shortly before the government's decision to place the Romani students in preparatory classes in a separate building, the Court did not use an indirect discrimination theory to shift the burden of proof to the Greek government. The Greek government attempted to justify the placement of the children in preparatory classes on grounds of the affected children's special educational needs. Even though the government showed that 90 per cent of the pupils in these classes were deficient in reading and writing the Greek language, the Court noted that the children were tested after they were placed in these classes, not before. This raised the inference that the placement was motivated by an intent to treat differently based on race or ethnicity. But more importantly, the Court suggests that even when students show a lower aptitude, when those students belong to a disfavoured ethnic minority, the Government should do what it can to integrate them into ordinary classes so that they can integrate eventually into local society.[18] When subject to blatant racial hatred and harassment, as the claimants in this case were, the Court determined that their placement in separate classes, even if pedagogically justified, would reasonably be understood as intending to segregate.[19] Therefore, meeting their special educational needs through separate educational facilities was incompatible with the Convention rights in question. These facts were the subject of two subsequent judgments finding Greece in violation of Article 14 and Article 2 of Protocol 1 in 2012[20] and 2013.[21]

[17] ibid [18]–[23].
[18] ibid [92].
[19] ibid.
[20] *Sampanis* (n 16).
[21] *Lavida and Others v Greece* (App no 7973/10) [2013] ECHR 488.

Similarly, in *Oršuš v Croatia*, the Government of Croatia claimed that Roma children who were placed in predominantly Roma classes had a special need for extra language instruction and support. In the *Oršuš* case, the ECtHR elaborated upon its theory of indirect discrimination introduced in *DH*. In *Oršuš*, the ECtHR determined that 'indirect discrimination may be proved without statistical evidence', citing *DH*. Here, the Court identified a 'difference in treatment' by pointing out that the only children who were placed in separate classes due to their lack of Croatian language skills were Roma. The difference in treatment is not 'direct' discrimination because it was premised on Croatian language ability rather than race. When there exists no non-Roma child who meets the criterion, the requirement becomes 'indirectly' discriminatory against the Roma, without statistics. This analysis was sufficient to require a justification by the state, to be scrutinised.

The Government claimed that these children of Roma origin had been grouped together 'not because of their ethnic origin, but rather because they were often not proficient in Croatian and it took more exercises and repetitions for them to master the subjects taught.'[22] The purpose of these classes was to provide extra instruction in Croatian, and to eliminate the consequences of prior social disadvantage, including the consequences of not having attended preschool prior to entry into elementary school.[23] Here, the European Court of Human Rights established that the determination as to whether there was a violation turned on the following question: 'whether adequate steps were taken by the school authorities to ensure the applicants' speedy progress in acquiring adequate command of Croatian and, once this was achieved, their immediate integration into mixed classes.'[24]

On the one hand, the Court said that

> temporary placement of children in a separate class on the ground that they lack an adequate command of language is not, as such, automatically contrary to Article 14 of the Convention. It might be said that in certain circumstances such placement would pursue the legitimate aim of adapting the education system to the specific needs of the children.[25]

While recognising the legitimacy of the goal of separating students to fulfil their special needs, the Court then noted that this goal must be pursued 'with safeguards' when the students affected are 'members of a specific ethnic group'.[26] In scrutinising the experience of the students who were placed in these special programs, the Court found that they were subject to a curriculum reduced by 30 per cent which did not include means of addressing the students' Croatian-language deficiencies. The Court, invoking the principle

[22] *Oršuš v Croatia* (App no 15766/03) (2009) 49 EHRR 26) [55].
[23] ibid [74].
[24] ibid [145].
[25] ibid [157].
[26] ibid.

of proportionality, determined that there was no 'reasonable relationship of proportionality between the means used and the legitimate aim said to be pursued', and therefore the placement of children in classes that became Roma-only lacked an objective and reasonable justification. Here, the Court scrutinises the educational programme, not to show that anti-Roma hostility drove the placements (as in the *Sampanis* case), but to unearth a duty of integration. The Court makes clear that the Government does not usually have a duty to be efficient in achieving its stated goal, but when pursuit of that stated goal adversely affects integration, the state is obligated to pursue its goal in alternative ways.

Finally, in *Horvath & Kiss v Hungary*, the Court found Hungary to be in violation of Articles 14 and Article 2 of Protocol 1 for the disproportionate placement of Romani children in separate education programmes for the mentally disabled. In that case, once the disproportionate over-representation of Roma students in these programmes was established, the Government had the burden of justification. The Hungarian Government argued that there was a 'high occurrence of disadvantageous social background among the Roma',[27] and this explained why the Roma children performed poorly on the placement tests. In the *Horvath & Kiss* case, the applicants attacked the IQ tests that had been used to place children into special schools, arguing that they did not measure intelligence. The Government defended the test in the following manner:

> What they did measure was the effect of cultural deprivation or insufficient cultural stimuli in early childhood on the mental development of children, irrespective of their ethnic origin. Disproportionate representation of Roma children in special education was explained by their disproportionate representation in the group deprived of the beneficial effects of modernization on the mental development of children.[28]

The Hungarian Government argued that there was no discrimination because the tests measured the children's readiness to learn, which was inevitably affected by their social disadvantage. According to the Government, these tests helped the schools make determinations about the speed and curriculum that a child should be subject to, and therefore were justified.

The ECtHR rejected the Government's submissions. While it accepted 'that the Government's position to retain the system of special schools/classes has been motivated by the desire to find a solution for children with special educational needs', the Court was troubled by the 'more basic curriculum' given to these children, and 'in particular, the segregation which the system causes.'[29] Thus, due to the segregation caused by the testing system,

[27] *Horváth and Kiss v Hungary* (App no 11146/11) (2013) 57 EHRR 31, [110].
[28] ibid, [96].
[29] ibid [113].

the indirect discrimination framework imposed a duty on the Government to prove that 'the tests and their application were capable of determining fairly and objectively the school aptitude and mental capacity of the applicants.'[30] On the one hand, the Court acknowledged that 'it is not its role to judge the validity of such tests, or to identify the state-of-the-art, least culturally biased test of educational aptitude.'[31] Rather, the Court had to enforce the state's obligation to put safeguards in place against misdiagnosis, not as a general matter, but because the obligation followed from 'the positive obligations incumbent on the State in a situation where there is a history of discrimination against ethnic minority children.'[32]

The Court recognised the 'positive obligations of the State to undo a history of racial segregation in special schools.' The system found to violate the Convention is problematic because '[t]he education provided might have compounded their difficulties and compromised their subsequent personal development instead of helping them to integrate into the ordinary schools and develop the skills that would facilitate life among the majority population.'[33] Here, the Court is quite explicit that its enforcement of Article 14 in conjunction with Article 2 of Protocol 1 serves to nudge states to achieve real integration of the Roma. The state is obligated to refrain from distributing special education in a way that hampers Roma children's eventual endeavours in living 'among the majority populations.'[34]

In *DH*, *Oršuš* and *Horvath*, the ECtHR rejected justifications given by government defendants to explain why Roma children had ended up in separate classes or schools that were premised on the alleged educational needs of the children themselves. In *DH* in particular, Judge Jungwiert, the Czech judge, dissented on the understanding that the special education framework was in fact an attempt by the Czech government to promote equal educational opportunities through affirmative action; it had the 'positive aim' 'to get children to attend school in order to have a chance to succeed through positive discrimination in favour of a disadvantaged population.'[35] Nonetheless, the Court seems to think that even a good-faith effort to equalise educational opportunities through special education supports is misguided and problematic if it results in racial separation with no plan to eventually integrate the disadvantaged group into mainstream society. It appears that the violation occurs not in the measures that produced racial separation, but in the racial separation itself, regardless of its cause. The separation harms the prospects for eventual integration of a disadvantaged group.

[30] ibid [117].
[31] ibid [119].
[32] ibid [119].
[33] ibid [127].
[34] ibid [207].
[35] *DH* (n 4), Dissenting Opinion of Judge Jungwiert, 81.

II. THE DUTY TO INTEGRATE

At the same time, the Court does not explicitly develop the normative account of integration independently of equal opportunity. In the education context, the equal opportunity to receive an adequate education has been at the centre of enforcing anti-discrimination norms. In *A Theory of Discrimination Law*, Tarunabh Khaitan argues that the goal of anti-discrimination law is to secure persons' access to three basic goods necessary to live a good life: negative freedom, an adequate range of valuable opportunities and self-respect.[36] Thus, the prohibition of discrimination in education can be understood to secure every person's access to valuable opportunities. Education is a precondition for the pursuit of most valuable opportunities in modern societies. If equal educational opportunity is understood as a precondition of meaningful freedom, and anti-discrimination law protects individuals' exercise of meaningful freedom, then the duty of integration has its moral underpinnings in an autonomy-based account of equal educational opportunity.

The right to equal educational opportunity does not capture everything that is at stake when the Court uses indirect discrimination theory to invalidate educational practices that lead to Roma separation. In these cases, the government claimed that special education for socially disadvantaged children best met their educational needs. In addition to Judge Jungwiert's view of Czech 'special schools' as positive action for a severely disadvantaged group, the Croatian government claimed in *Oršuš* that the students in special schools, due to their linguistic and socioeconomic disadvantages, required additional support that only separate classes could provide. The suggestion here is that children who actually need special education will fare worse if placed in a regular classroom, because their disadvantages prevent them from meeting the higher expectations of regular school. In justifying their scrutiny of such purported justifications, the ECtHR pointed out that none of these programmes were eventually integrating the Roma children with alleged special needs into majority classes or mainstream society. The absence of integration raises an inference that discrimination is occurring, regardless of a distributive justice-based account of equal educational opportunity that is purportedly realised when children's special needs are addressed.

The US Supreme Court in *Brown v Board of Education* declared that 'separate education facilities are inherently unequal.'[37] In *Brown*, the Court relied on psychologists' accounts of harm to black children's ability to learn and develop as a result of being placed in segregated schools that were

[36] T Khaitan, *A Theory of Discrimination Law* (Oxford, Oxford University Press, 2015).
[37] *Brown v Board of Education* 347 US 483 (1957).

intended to denote their inferiority. This emphasis on the black children's ability to learn conflated the quest for equal educational opportunity with integration.

In the Roma indirect discrimination/segregation cases, the ECtHR similarly assumes that the ability of Roma children to learn is hampered by their placement in schools that are disproportionately Roma. The problem is not the clear message of inferiority that can be imputed to an official state policy of racial segregation, as in *Brown*, but the culture of low academic expectations and the teaching of a reduced curriculum in the predominantly Roma schools and classrooms. The reduced curriculum makes it highly unlikely, if not impossible, for students in these schools or programmes to proceed to high school and university, and this lack of educational attainment is obviously correlated with low rates of employment and high rates of poverty among Roma in Europe.[38]

The autonomy-based right to equal opportunity assumes that the state owes a duty to integrate only to the disadvantaged groups whose educational opportunities might be harmed by segregation. A white or non-Roma Czech citizen has no interest in integration, on this account, and in fact, whites and non-Roma Czech citizens have interests that are adverse to integration. They, too, have rights as individuals to an adequate range of valuable opportunities. In the United States, white parents today resist policy changes that would achieve socioeconomic and racial integration in schools, not because they oppose integration as such, but because they fear that the influx of poor and academically under-prepared children in their schools will compromise the high educational standards and curriculum necessary for their own children to have access to an adequate range of valuable opportunities. Thus, anti-discrimination law becomes a mechanism by which the interests of racial minorities in integration are pitted against the interest of racial majorities in quality education. Both groups are struggling for access to educational opportunities.

But the right to integration, and the state's corresponding duty, can also be understood to create the same interest for members of both advantaged and disadvantaged groups. Integration is not merely a means of promoting disadvantaged groups' access to meaningful opportunities to exercise autonomy. Integration defines the social relations of equality necessary for legitimate decision-making in a democracy. Elizabeth Anderson develops this account of the democratic normative foundations of integration in *The Imperative of Integration*. Democracy is a membership organisation, a mode of government and a culture.[39] Anderson focuses on the cultural dimension

[38] See *DH* (n 4) [50] (citing Commissioner for Human Rights report linking special schools to diminished future employment prospects for Roma children).

[39] E Anderson, *The Imperative of Integration* (Princeton, Princeton University Press, 2010) 89.

of democracy. On the one hand, democracy requires certain legal rules and institutions, such as a universal franchise, elections and transparency rules. But democracy also requires the citizens to interact with each other in such a manner that the outcomes arrived at are accepted by all as legitimate. Locating this conception of democracy in the political philosophy of the Radical Republicans in proposing Equal Protection, Anderson notes that, in a democracy, 'citizens from all walks of life discuss matters of public interest together, as equals.'[40] The dialogical nature of the democracy's vision of the public interest, as distinct from a vision that aggregates the opinions of all, makes a difference to producing the consent of the governed.[41] When the most advantaged members of a democratic society live and work in complete isolation from the least advantaged members, they lack the information and experience to make legitimate decisions that determine the fate of everyone. When the governing elites in a democracy are typically educated in private schools, and/or in public schools only attended by the most advantaged members of society, they have not been socialised properly for democratic citizenship or legitimate leadership. Thus, failure to integrate harms the health and legitimacy of democracy itself, in which advantaged and disadvantaged people have the same interest as citizens.

When anti-discrimination law is understood to be primarily concerned with integration as a precondition of democracy, the goal is not to maximise the opportunities of individuals to live autonomous lives, but to achieve the social relations of equality and mutual respect that make it possible for democracies to engage in legitimate self-government. When we try to focus on equality of educational opportunity, the individuals who are claiming it as a matter of right have an interest in maximising the good of education. Thus, we recognise an injury with regard to this right when any individual's interest in an educational opportunity is adversely affected. This is why it becomes conceptually coherent within existing anti-discrimination law for a white person to claim that her right to equal educational opportunity was violated when she was denied admission to school under a race-based affirmative action scheme.[42] The white person did not get an educational opportunity which she might have otherwise gotten had race not been taken into account.

Alternatively, when we conceptualise democracy as the normative foundation of equality and non-discrimination, the individual's right to equality is not dependent on the individual's interest in the good whose equalisation is sought. Rather, all members of a democratic polity have a right to the social relations of equality that sustain and legitimise democratic

[40] ibid at 92.
[41] ibid.
[42] See, eg, *Fisher v University of Texas* 133 S Ct 2198 (2016); 133 S Ct 2411 (2013).

will-formation in the public interest. Thus understood, the 'reverse' discrimination claim that challenges an integration programme becomes incoherent. Members of all groups share an interest in the same set of social relations. By contrast, under the equal opportunity model, members of the majority race have an enforceable interest in the optimisation of their opportunities, which conflict with the enforceable interest that members of the minority race have in the optimisation of their opportunities.

III. THE DUTY TO INTEGRATE IN THE NARRATIVES OF FAILED IMPLEMENTATION

Reports by human rights NGOs and the Council of Europe monitoring the implementation of the *DH* judgment in the Czech Republic suggest that, although many of the practices that were thought to contribute to Roma separation have been repealed or changed, the isolation of Roma children in the education system continues. According to these reports, the changes are insufficient to remedy the violation that was found in the *DH* judgment. It is assumed that the violation will not be remedied until the statistical disparities indicating de facto segregation are reduced, if not eradicated.

In March 2015, the European Roma Rights Centre, Amnesty International, Open Society Fund Prague, and Czech Society for Inclusive Education issued a joint statement on implementing the *DH* ruling. It noted, 'Piecemeal measures post 2007 failed to eliminate discrimination.' It also noted, 'Despite the reforms adopted in the past, Romani children continue to be overrepresented in schools and classes for pupils with mild mental disabilities and segregated in Roma-only schools and classes.' These groups have called for a comprehensive desegregation plan, involving support measures for pupils with special educational needs, compulsory pre-school education for all pupils, and the abolition of the educational programme for pupils with mild mental disabilities.[43] These groups, having brought the *DH* litigation, succeeded in persuading the European Commission to initiate, in 2014, infringement proceedings against the Czech republic for education practices in breach of the EU race equality directive. Council Directive 2000/43/EC of 29 June 2000 Article 2 prohibits direct and indirect discrimination on grounds of racial or ethnic origin, and Article 3(1) makes clear that the equal treatment obligation applies to states in the provision of education. The Commission also invoked Article 21(1) of the Charter of Fundamental Rights of the EU, which prohibits discrimination on various

[43] Joint statement of the European Roma Rights Centre, Amnesty International, Open Society Fund Prague, and Czech Society for Inclusive Education (13 November 2015) available at www.errc.org/article/czech-republic-eight-years-after-the-dh-judgement-a-comprehensive-desegregation-of-schools-must-take-place/4431.

grounds including race. An October 2014 European Commission Report on the discrimination of Roma children in education noted, 'no tangible progress has been made at dismantling the segregation of Romani children in schools with substandard education.'[44]

What has changed with regard to the assignment of Romani children to special schools in the Czech Republic? And what does it mean to say that these changes have changed nothing? It is widely acknowledged that the percentage of Romani children in special schools, reported at over 50 per cent in the *DH* opinion in 2007, has now decreased to around 35 per cent. That is still disproportionately high, in light of Romani children making up only one to two per cent of the students in Ostrava. In a 2013 report alleging that Czech education practices continued to violate the Convention and the EU race equality directive, Amnesty International noted that the 'special' schools that were repudiated by the *DH* judgment were now called 'practical schools', and Romani pupils were over-represented in 'practical' schools. More importantly, the report noted that, while reforms have enabled some Romani pupils to be assigned to 'mainstream' elementary schools, there is segregation within mainstream schools as Roma children tend to be tracked into classes with a reduced curriculum.[45]

The most recent Council of Europe progress report on the implementation of *DH* notes the following developments: after the *DH* judgment, the Czech legislature adopted a new framework that provides that pupils with a 'social disadvantage' can no longer be educated in a class for pupils with 'mild mental disabilities'.[46] The psychological tests used to determine whether a child belongs in a class for pupils with 'mild mental disabilities' have also been reformed. There have been new trainings for psychologists administering these tests. Parents are given information and advice before consenting to their child being tested, and they have the right to request re-testing by a different counselling centre. In addition, the school placement remains valid for only one year, and any pupil diagnosed with a 'mild mental disability' must be re-tested annually. Compensatory and support measures have been put in place for pupils with special needs, with the goal of preparing these pupils to attend mainstream schools.

[44] Lilla Farkas, *Report on the discrimination of Roma children in education* (European Commission—Directorate General for Justice, October 2014) http://ec.europa.eu/justice/discrimination/files/roma_childdiscrimination_en.pdf at 20.

[45] Amnesty International, European Institutions Office, *The Czech Republic's Discriminatory Treatment of Roma Breaches EU Race Directive* (2013) available at www.amnesty.eu/en/news/statements-reports/eu/human-rights-in-the-eu/the-czech-republic-s-discriminatory-treatment-of-roma-breaches-eu-race-directive-0686/#.WXX_CIjyvIU, 4.

[46] See Department for the Execution of Judgments of the European Court of Human Rights, *Memorandum on General Measures for the execution of judgments of the European Court of Human Rights on DH and others against Czech Republic* (March 2015, H/Exec 2015(8)) at 4 (citing Decree No 73/2005).

So far, however, Roma pupils are still over-represented in schools for students with 'mild mental disability' in the Czech Republic. In 2013–14, for instance, Roma children were 32 per cent of the pupils in programmes for students with 'mild mental disability', while Roma constitute 1.4 to 2.8 per cent of the Czech population.[47] While it is more common than it was before for students to transfer from special classes to mainstream education (3,638 students from 2013 to 2015), Roma transferees (440) still made up a very small proportion.[48] It appears, then, that whenever separate schools or separate classes with reduced curricula are maintained, Roma are over-represented in them, perhaps due to the 'prejudice that continues to course through much of the Czech educational system.'[49] Thus, the NGOs advocating for Roma integration have called for the phasing out of educational programmes for pupils with mild mental disabilities. They have also called for compulsory preschool, and objected to the Czech government's maintenance of 'preparatory classes' for students who require extra support, and in which Roma are disproportionately placed within mainstream schools. The preparatory classes were allegedly created to give students with 'social disadvantage' more attention, but Roma advocacy groups have viewed them as a new mechanism of segregation. Socially disadvantaged students, and students with special needs, under the new statute effective September 2016,[50] will receive extra support within integrated classrooms.

According to a 2015 report by Amnesty International, the segregation of Roma children is now occurring within mainstream schools as well. There is a dynamic similar to 'white flight' in the United States. Non-Roma parents tend to remove their children from a school once they feel there are too many Roma children. The report describes another public school which contains a regular primary school as well as a 'selective' primary school. 90 per cent of the students in the regular primary school are Roma, and the curriculum is tailored to them as children of a 'socially disadvantaged background'. In the selective school within the same building, by contrast, there are only two or three Roma children in each class. The selective school was created recently to retain the non-Roma pupils whose parents were concerned about the academic level of the school and its ability to prepare the children for secondary education. The selective school offers business and administration classes, and children are tested upon entry to qualify for the programme. Roma parents have been told that the selective school is for smarter children, and that the regular school is a slow school.[51]

[47] See Amnesty International, *Czech Republic: Roma Progress Report* (August 2016) available at www.amnesty.org/en/latest/campaigns/2016/08/czech-republic-roma-progress-report/.

[48] ibid at 6.

[49] See Joint Statement (n 43).

[50] Amendment to Czech Schools Act, March 2015.

[51] Amnesty International, *Ethnic Discrimination of Romani Children in Czech Schools* (April 2015).

The report details another school, which presents itself as an open and diverse institution aiming to provide education tailored to diverse children's needs. The school includes the history of Roma in its curriculum, and was created when a special school merged with a regular school in 2004.[52] However, it is reported that almost half of the non-Roma children left the school after the merger. School directors are now wary of enrolling too many Romani students in an integrated school, for fear of departure by non-Roma parents,[53] which will then result in the same situation of separation between Roma and non-Roma pupils. The concentration of Roma students in separate classes triggers an inference of indirect discrimination. These dynamics of 'white flight' are familiar from the US experience. The exercise of parental choice by non-Romani parents leads to the re-emergence of schools that are predominantly Roma. In addition, Roma children report that they have experienced bullying and violence when they attend integrated schools. Safety concerns then lead Roma parents to select schools that are predominantly Roma.

If indirect discrimination law enforces the state's positive and continuing duty to integrate, the state has a duty to disrupt the dynamics of white flight, and bullying. Perhaps the state needs to rethink its school system entirely, so that parental choices are more restricted, and bullying of Roma children in schools is adequately remedied and prevented. Although the European Court of Human Rights lacks the remedial power or practice of ordering such detailed or expansive remedies, the duty of integration embedded into the indirect discrimination judgments suggest that the Czech Republic will continue to be in violation until education is fully integrated.

IV. THE AMERICAN JUDICIAL DISAGGREGATION OF DESEGREGATION AND INTEGRATION

Anderson has noted that integration takes place in four stages: (1) formal desegregation, (2) spatial integration, (3) formal social integration, and (4) informal social integration.[54] Anderson's framework is helpful for comparing the Roma situation in Europe with the racial disparities that persist in American public education. The ECtHR's Roma education judgments reflect a normative commitment to at least the first three stages, if not also the fourth. In the United States, by contrast, the Supreme Court has defined the American constitutional commitment to equal protection as requiring nothing beyond the first stage. In fact, the Supreme Court's recent case law appears to prohibit attempts to move to the second and third stages.

52 ibid at 33.
53 ibid at 35.
54 Anderson (n 39) 115.

The understanding that equal protection imposed an imperative to integrate public schools permeated *Brown v Board of Education* and the US Supreme Court's initial school desegregation cases, but it eroded in the early 1970s. The cases which distinguished desegregation from integration, thereby stopping equal protection at stage 1 of Anderson's breakdown, began a normative discourse that continued in the US Supreme Court's rejection of disparate impact as a constitutional Equal Protection standard. While *Brown v Board of Education* famously declared that separate education for black and white children was 'inherently unequal', it postponed the determination of appropriate remedies, such as integration. Indeed, integration emerged as a remedy for segregation, and not as an independent moral imperative. In *Brown II*, the Supreme Court equated desegregation with integration initially. In that decision, lower courts were instructed to adopt measures that were 'necessary and proper to admit to public schools on a racially nondiscriminatory basis with all deliberate speed the parties to these cases.'[55]

In *Cooper v Aaron*, responding to violent resistance to integration, the Court upheld a school board's desegregation efforts citing 'the right of a student not to be segregated on racial grounds.'[56] The duty to end unconstitutional segregation could not, in *Griffin v County School Board of Prince Edward County*, be met by a state by simply closing down its public schools.[57] Nor could a state fulfil its duty to desegregate by allowing white and black pupils to choose which school to attend post-segregation.[58] In observing that no white child had chosen to attend a former black school in the 'freedom of choice' plan, the Court noted that its inquiry was 'whether the Board has taken steps adequate to abolish its dual, segregated system.'[59] In that case, the Court declared that school authorities are 'clearly charged with the affirmative duty to take whatever steps might be necessary to convert to a unitary system in which racial discrimination would be eliminated root and branch.'[60] In the context of past segregation by the state, there was a duty to remedy the situation through integration. In *Alexander v Holmes County Board of Education*,[61] the Court reiterated that 'the obligation of every school district is to terminate dual school systems at once and to operate now and hereafter only unitary schools.' In these formulations of the late 1960s, the duty to desegregate seems equivalent to the duty to operate an integrated school system.

[55] *Brown v Board of Education of Topeka* 349 US 294 (1955) ('Brown II').
[56] *Cooper v Aaron* 358 US 1, 19 (1958).
[57] *Griffin v County School Board of Prince Edward County* 377 US 218, 234 (1964).
[58] *Green v County School Bd of New Kent County* 391 US 430, 437 (1968).
[59] ibid.
[60] ibid at 437–38.
[61] *Alexander v Holmes County Board of Education* 319 US 19, 20 (1969).

Yet, by 1971, the Court began to distinguish between the duty to desegregate and the duty to integrate. In *Swann v Charlotte-Mecklenburg Board of Education*, the Court held that states that had maintained separate schools based on race as a governmental policy had to desegregate. Title IV had defined 'desegregation' as 'the assignment of students to public schools and within such schools without regard to their race, color, religion, or national origin, but "desegregation" shall not mean the assignment of students to public schools in order to overcome racial imbalance.'[62] The Court also declared,

> We are concerned in these cases with the elimination of the discrimination inherent in the dual school systems, not with myriad factors of human existence which can cause discrimination in a multitude of ways on racial, religious, or ethnic grounds ... The elimination of racial discrimination in public schools is a large task and one that should not be retarded by efforts to achieve broader purposes lying beyond the jurisdiction of school authorities.[63]

Thus, the Court 'does not and cannot embrace all the problems of racial prejudice, even when those problems contribute to disproportionate racial concentrations in some schools.'[64] The Court explicitly noted that 'the existence of some small number of one-race, or virtually one-race, schools within a school district is not in and of itself the mark of a system that still practices segregation by law.'[65]

In 1973, the Supreme Court decided a pair of cases that implicitly rejected disparate impact theory and declined to impose a duty to integrate. Argued on the same day, both *Keyes v School District No 1* and *San Antonio v Rodriguez* challenged apparently neutral practices—the maintenance of 'neighbourhood' schools and the use of local property taxes to fund public schools—which caused high concentrations of minority students in some schools.[66] *Keyes* authorised judges to scrutinise schools that were disproportionately one race when they were part of a school district that had intentionally segregated some of its schools in the past, but affirmed the distinction between desegregation and integration.[67] Only desegregation was legally required, and could only be obligatory if the racial separation was the consequence of official segregation.

Without using the language of disparate impact or indirect discrimination, the trial court in Rodriguez had invalidated a neutrally formulated

62 *Swann v Charlotte-Mecklenburg Board of Education* 402 US 15, 17 (1971) (citing Title IV).
63 ibid at 22–23.
64 ibid at 23.
65 ibid at 26.
66 The plaintiffs noted in their briefs that 90 per cent of the students in the poor school district in which plaintiffs resided were Mexican American, and that Texas had a history of maintaining separate schools for Mexican Americans. See Brief for Appellees, *San Antonio Independent School District v Rodriguez* (1971) WL 134333, at 16.
67 *Keyes v School District No 1* 413 US 189 (1973).

practice (use of property tax base to partially fund public schools) based on its disparate impact on minorities. It noted, 'As might be expected, those districts most rich in property also have the highest median family income and the lowest percentage of minority pupils, while the poor property districts are poor in income and predominately minority in composition.'[68] But the Supreme Court reversed this decision, and held that, as education was not a constitutionally guaranteed right, and the classification at issue here was wealth and not race, courts should not strictly scrutinise such practices. The Supreme Court's reluctance to follow the logic of disparate impact to find a duty to do something about one-race schools preceded its more explicit rejection of disparate impact as a constitutional standard three years later in *Washington v Davis*.[69]

The distinction between desegregation and integration became extremely salient from the 1990s to the present, when the Supreme Court struck down several attempts to desegregate, holding that they engaged in integration beyond what was required to remedy the wrong of segregation. In *Freeman v Pitts*, for instance, the Court noted, 'Where resegregation is a product not of state action but of private choices, it does not have constitutional implications.'[70] Again, the Court observed that it was 'beyond the practical ability of the federal courts to try to counteract these kinds of continuous and massive demographic shifts.'[71] In 2007, the Supreme Court invalidated efforts of two public school districts to achieve racial integration, holding that there was no compelling governmental interest in racially balanced primary and secondary schools.[72] The US Supreme Court has consolidated the wedge between desegregation and integration by replacing the morally infused term, 'integration', with the morally empty 'racial balance for its own sake.'

V. COURTS' REMEDIAL POWERS IN INDIRECT DISCRIMINATION THEORY

In all of the judgments finding a violation of Article 14 and Article 2 of Protocol 1, the ECtHR determined that a wide range of practices that contributed to Roma children's placement in predominantly Roma schools and classes constituted discrimination, typically under an indirect discrimination framework. As is typical when the ECtHR finds a violation, it did not issue

[68] *San Antonio Independent School District v Rodriguez* 337 F Supp 280, 282 (WD Tex 1971).

[69] See *Washington v Davis* 426 US 229, 241 (1976).

[70] *Freeman v Pitts* 503 US 467 (1992).

[71] ibid at 495.

[72] See *Parents Involved in Community Schools v Seattle School District No 1* 551 US 701, 729 (2007).

a specific remedy to correct the violations it declared. In most of these judgments, the Court required the state to pay damages between €1,000 and €8,000 per complainant to compensate non-pecuniary harms. In *DH*, the Court restated the standard obligations of states subject to its judgments under Article 46 of the Convention:

> [T]hat a judgment in which the Court finds a breach imposes on the respondent State a legal obligation not just to pay those concerned the sums awarded by way of just satisfaction under Article 41, but also to select, subject to supervision by the Committee of Ministers, the general and/or, if appropriate, individual measures to be adopted in their domestic legal order to put an end to the violation found by the Court and to redress so far as possible the effects.[73]

In general, the European Court of Human Rights provides declaratory relief when it finds a violation of the Convention, but it does not typically specify the measures that the state must take to remedy the violations found. States are given a margin of appreciation to identify the appropriate measures to remedy the violation.[74]

In the most recent case of *Lavida and Others v Greece*, the claimants specifically asked the Court to require the Government to

> adopt a national plan of action to (1) make segregation of the Roma disappear progressively and (2) to proceed to a new distribution of students in the public schools of Sofades [the district at issue] in a manner that reflects the diversity of the population of that district.[75]

The Court rejected this proposal, reiterating that it was for the state subject to the judgment to choose the measures required to implement the judgment within their internal legal order, and to eliminate all eventual obstacles to the adequate redress of the complainant's situation in view of the conclusions arrived at in the Court's judgment.[76] The ECtHR's lack of involvement in fashioning specific measures to remedy the violation liberates the European human rights judge to develop a robust *theory* of indirect discrimination that is uncontaminated by anxieties about the practical difficulties of discharging the duty to integrate, in light of past and potential resistance on the ground.

By contrast, American judges have exercised expansive powers to order busing and other specific plans to integrate schools. Judges' exercise of these powers, and their frustrations with the resistance to integration orders, have influenced the way they have formulated substantive anti-discrimination doctrine. The distinction between the duty to desegregate and the duty to

[73] ibid at [216].

[74] See Council of Europe, Supervision of the execution of judgments and decisions of the European Court of Human Rights, available at www.coe.int/t/dghl/monitoring/execution/Presentation/Pres_Exec_en.asp.

[75] *Lavida* (n 21) [79].

[76] ibid [82].

integrate was articulated in the same breath as the Court's acknowledgment of the practical difficulties encountered in the implementation of Brown. Consider this passage from *Swann*:

> Over the 16 years since *Brown II*, many difficulties were encountered in implementation of the basic constitutional requirement that the State not discriminate between public school children on the basis of their race. Nothing in our national experience prior to 1955 prepared anyone for dealing with changes and adjustments of the magnitude and complexity encountered since then. Deliberate resistance of some of the Court's mandates has impeded good-faith efforts of others to bring school systems into compliance. The detail and nature of these dilatory tactics have been noted frequently by this Court and other courts.[77]

The conceptual wedge between desegregation and integration is driven by the judicial consciousness of political resistance to desegregation when it means integration. Because judges have the authority to order a range of specific remedies to integrate schools, they need to justify their decision not to use them. Resistance to integration orders challenges the legitimacy of courts, and judges have an interest in preserving their own legitimacy and authority. Thus, desegregation begins to mean something less than integration. The absence of integration—for instance, a school where a large majority of the students are of the same race—is only pronounced wrong by courts if it can be traced to a state policy of racial separation.

The Supreme Court's implicit rejection of the disparate impact theory to integrate Texas schools in *San Antonio v Rodriguez* was partially driven by the acknowledgment, as in *Swann*, of likely resistance to implementation:

> It cannot be questioned that the constitutional judgment reached by the District Court [striking down Texas's policy of tying school funding to local property tax] and approved by our dissenting Brothers today would occasion in Texas and elsewhere an unprecedented upheaval in public education.[78]

Finding a constitutional violation in this education scheme due to its segregative effects would lead to 'massive change in the financing and control of public education.'[79] At the same time, the Court insisted that '[t]hese practical considerations, of course, play no role in the adjudication of the constitutional issues presented here.'[80]

In *From Jim Crow to Civil Rights*, Michael Klarman surmises that *Brown v Board of Education* did not directly produce school desegregation. Many school districts were already in the process of ending segregation before the litigation was brought. In the South, courts were cautious about requiring

[77] *Swann* (n 62) 13.
[78] *San Antonio Independent School District v Rodriguez* 411 US 1, 54 (1973).
[79] ibid at 58.
[80] ibid.

integration, aware of the potential for resistance and violence. Throughout the 1970s, the Supreme Court rejected disparate impact theory as an Equal Protection standard. The US disparate impact theory, shaped by a strong requirement for plaintiffs to demonstrate that a specific practice produced the disparate impact, seems to reflect the Court's concern with its own legitimacy and the judicial branch's ability to issue remedies that are actually followed by other branches of government and complied with by businesses. Many lower courts adhered to the view that *Brown* and its progeny required formal desegregation without requiring integration.[81] In the United States, it is widely acknowledged that, while courts ordered integration to remedy the constitutional violation of segregation, courts' influence on actual integration was largely indirect.[82] Litigation served as a catalyst for legislative processes that implemented the constitutional norm. Over six decades later, neither judicial nor legislative attempts have produced real integration in many American cities.

As the aftermath of both *Brown* and *DH* illustrate overwhelmingly, real racial integration in public education is very difficult and still rare. Examples of success, even in 2016, are few and far between. In the United States, recent patterns of resegregation are well-documented, but they are not discussed as a problem of discrimination. Recent reports suggest that black children in the American South are twice as likely today than they were 40 years ago to attend a school in which in which at least nine out of 10 students are racial minorities.[83] A 2014 study of New York City schools by the UCLA Civil Rights Project declared it 'home to the largest and one of the most segregated public school systems in the nation.'[84] In New York City, a third of public schools serve more than 80 per cent white students, and another third serves less than 40 per cent white students. 90 per cent of black students in New York attended majority-minority schools in 2010, that is, schools with 50 per cent or greater minority students. A majority of these students (75 per cent) attended schools with 90 per cent or greater minority students.

The ECtHR's indirect discrimination doctrine would facilitate a framing of the patterns of resegregation in the United States as human rights violations. In 2011, although black and Latino students made up 70 per cent of students in the New York City school system, 73 per cent of kindergarteners

[81] M Klarman, *From Jim Crow to Civil Rights: The Supreme Court and the Struggle for Racial Equality* (Oxford, Oxford University Press, 2004) 357.

[82] See ibid; G Rosenberg, *The Hollow Hope: Can Courts Bring About Social Change?* (Chicago, University of Chicago Press, 1991) 449.

[83] Nikole Hannah-Jones, 'Segregation Now' (*The Atlantic Monthly*, May 2014) available at www.theatlantic.com/magazine/archive/2014/05/segregation-now/359813/.

[84] UCLA Civil Rights Project, *New York State's Extreme School Segregation* (March 2014) available at www.civilrightsproject.ucla.edu/research/k-12-education/integration-and-diversity/ny-norflet-report-placeholder.

placed in gifted and talented classrooms were white and Asian.[85] Similar to the current situation in Czech schools, racial segregation occurs in New York City within a school as well as between schools. A disproportionately large percentage of students in a regular 'general education' class is Black and Latino, whereas a disproportionately large percentage of students in the 'gifted and talented' class in the same school are white and Asian. Similar to the situation in the Czech Republic, the assignment of students to one ability track versus the other is dependent on a standardised IQ test which is administered at the government's expense at the parent's request. An attempt was made in 2012 to reform the test, but it has not changed the admission numbers,[86] and some reports suggest that the new test exacerbated segregation.[87] While some have called for the abolition of gifted programmes due to their racially segregative tendencies, government officials have promoted these programmes upon the belief that white middle-class families would abandon the public school system altogether, potentially making segregation more salient.[88] Should the government's maintenance of a gifted-and-talented programme be challenged as indirectly discriminatory? Or should the government be required to show that the tests it administers to four-year-old children (and the public expenditures to administer the tests) are justified? If justifiable, by what standard? Must the government show a correlation between superior performance on these IQ tests at the age of four and academic achievement in secondary and higher education? Or must the justification be tied to the goal of integration and other demonstrable public goods? If the latter, the government would have to show that the early identification and separation of 'gifted and talented' children ultimately helped rather than hindered the integration of disadvantaged minorities into mainstream society.

While there is increased attention by education reform organisations and social scientists to the problem of de facto resegregation in the United States, it is generally assumed that these problems are beyond the scope of current US anti-discrimination law, largely because judges stopped short of reading this body of law as imposing a duty of integration. They did so because of their dual consciousness of (1) their official equitable power to issue specific

[85] New York Appleseed, *Within Our Reach: Segregation in NYC District Elementary Schools and What We Can Do About It: Addressing Internal Segregation and Harnessing the Educational Benefits of Diversity* (2014) available at www.appleseednetwork.org/wp-content/uploads/2014/02/Within-Our-Reach-2nd-Brief-February-2014-FINAL.pdf.

[86] See Geoff Decker, 'More Children Passing the Gifted Exam, But Not in Poorer Districts' (Chalkbeat, April 2012) available at www.chalkbeat.org/posts/ny/2012/04/13/more-children-passing-the-gifted-exam-but-not-in-poorer-districts/.

[87] Philissa Cramer, 'Inequities Grew After City Fixed Pearson's G&T screening errors' (Chalkbeat, May 2013) available at www.chalkbeat.org/posts/ny/2013/05/01/inequities-grew-after-city-fixed-pearsons-gt-screening-errors/.

[88] Appleseed Report (n 85) 7.

injunctions for integration, such as busing, as well as (2) widespread resistance to the imposition of power, which would undermine the legitimacy of their rulings. Thus, the theory of indirect discrimination was rejected as a constitutional standard, and articulated in the statutory context in a way that did not require interventions that would be resisted. By contrast, in observing similar dynamics of white flight and resegregation in the Czech Republic, NGOs and the Council of Europe committee monitoring the implementation of the *DH* judgment explicitly frame these dynamics as discrimination in violation of the Convention.

VI. CONCLUSION

The main difference between segregation in Europe and in the United States is that the theory of indirect discrimination in the United States reflects an understanding of what is politically possible, even while disavowing such considerations, and the European Court has pronounced an ambitious and idealistic duty of integration, even while its implementation in Central and Eastern Europe remains far-fetched politically. Ironically, the European Court of Human Rights' lack of remedial powers seems to enable it to articulate a more robust end goal of integration for antidiscrimination law, free from the messy business of reforming institutions. By design, indirect discrimination law can only indirectly reform institutional practices. The integration framing of anti-discrimination law makes the lack of integration the most salient feature of wrongful discrimination. If the absence of integration is necessary *and* sufficient to establish indirect discrimination, this framework makes it more difficult for remedial orders or injunctions to identify specific practices to change, even assuming a court that has the legal authority and inclination to do so. That work is then left to NGOs and legislatures. Nonetheless, this division of labour between courts and other institutions may enable courts to better articulate the normative foundations of anti-discrimination law.

11

Justice for Foxes: Fundamental Rights and Justification of Indirect Discrimination

HUGH COLLINS

TO SAY THAT discrimination on forbidden grounds such as sex and race can be justified may seem odd. The substantial reduction of discrimination against women, racial minorities and other protected groups has been steered by robust legal prohibitions against discrimination. Devices and excuses that attempt to justify the avoidance of those laws have generally been blocked. Admittedly, some possibilities for justification of otherwise discriminatory action have always been present in the law of discrimination. For example, in order to create a fair playing field in sports, where appropriate, teams and competitions can be segregated on grounds of sex or disability (though not race). Necessary occupational requirements such as specifications of the sex of an actor for reasons of authenticity are also usually permitted. But these closely circumscribed instances where justification of discrimination is allowed in the law are usually regarded as narrowly drawn exceptions to deal with a few anomalous cases. Yet the prediction that any justification of discrimination is unlikely to be available in the law to any great extent must account for the fact that one major part of the law of discrimination includes a broad-ranging idea of justification as one of its central features. Although direct discrimination cannot usually be justified, the law of indirect discrimination or, as it is called in the USA, disparate impact, requires that a justification for this kind of alleged discriminatory behaviour should always be possible. In every instance of alleged indirect discrimination, the question must be considered whether the conduct of the defendant can be justified. In the fable of the fox and the stork, where the fox serves soup on a flat plate that prevents the stork from eating, if the fox is accused of indirect discrimination, it should be open to the fox to try to justify its conduct. If the conduct can be justified, there is no unlawful discrimination.

This chapter seeks to understand the moral reasons for the presence of this key element of justification in the law of indirect discrimination. In so doing, it must consider a number of connected issues. One question is why does the law apparently differ between direct and indirect discrimination with respect to the availability of a general possibility of justifying discrimination, or is that interpretation of the law a misapprehension? Another fundamental question that must be tackled is whether the presence of the possibility of a justification for some instances of discrimination can be explained by reference to the general aim of laws against discrimination or whether the moral foundations for the justification element in the law of discrimination derive from different moral principles. In tackling these questions, though it is not assumed that anti-discrimination law exactly tracks a coherent moral justification, it is expected that the main provisions of the legislation can be broadly justified by reference to a coherent moral position.

Having briefly described the legal framework with respect to justification in indirect discrimination, section I of the chapter sets out what I will call a standard explanation of why a broad ground of justification is permitted in indirect discrimination, but not typically in direct discrimination. That standard explanation advances a proposition that indirect discrimination is not a moral wrong in the same way or to the same extent as direct discrimination. The chapter then proceeds in section II to itemise a number of doubts and queries regarding the adequacy of that standard explanation for the presence of a broad-ranging justification element in the law of indirect discrimination. That critical analysis leads to several, perhaps controversial, conclusions. It is contended that direct and indirect discrimination are not so very different with respect to the element of justification found in discrimination law. It is further argued that the justification element in discrimination law should be regarded as an intrinsic part of the constitution of the moral wrong of discrimination rather than a separate defence or a kind of exception to the law. In other words, it is suggested that discrimination is never wrong unless it is unjustified. Yet, it will then be argued that, although the justification element in discrimination law is constitutive of the wrong of discrimination, the moral principles that underpin the justification element are not the same as those that account for the aim or central values of the law, whether those values be described in terms of equality, liberty or social policy. The justification element in the law of discrimination must be derived, it is argued, from a different moral principle.

Section III proceeds to offer such an explanation of the function and moral foundations of the element of justification in the laws against discrimination. This explanation focusses on the point that discrimination laws interfere with the freedom of the alleged discriminator. It argues that the justification element usually protects the alleged discriminator such as an employer against disproportionate interference with its liberty and other rights. In most instances, it will be claimed, we can best understand the function of the justification element in discrimination laws as seeking to create a balance between the fundamental rights of the parties. In other words, the justification element in the law of discrimination ensures that the fox is treated justly despite the alleged discrimination against the stork. That interpretation of the moral foundations of the law regarding justification in discrimination law tends to confirm the earlier hypothesis that the element of justification is a vital and constitutive moral and legal ingredient in both direct and indirect discrimination.

I. JUSTIFICATION IN THE LAW OF INDIRECT DISCRIMINATION

What explains the presence in the law of indirect discrimination of provisions that permit this kind of discrimination to be justified on broad grounds? A typical case of a claim for indirect discrimination might involve a challenge to an employer's requirement that all employees should have a particular educational qualification. On its face, this requirement does not discriminate on a forbidden ground such as sex or race. Yet if this qualification happens to be a requirement that many fewer people from a minority black racial group than the majority white group can satisfy, with the consequence that few, if any, members of that racial minority can obtain a job from that employer, this adverse effect on the racial minority group could be challenged. Even though the employer's requirement does not apparently discriminate between racial groups, the law of indirect discrimination states that such a requirement would be unlawful owing to its adverse impact on a racial minority in the job market, unless the employer's educational requirement can be justified. The employer might be able to demonstrate, for instance, that without the formal educational qualification, employees would not be able to perform the job to the necessary standard, and on that ground the discriminatory adverse effect on a racial minority would probably be justifiable. The possibility of justifying the use of rules and practices that tend to have a discriminatory effect whilst being neutral on their face is a core feature of the legal framework of the law of indirect discrimination. The focus of this paper is on the question of how this broad scope for justification in the law of indirect discrimination can be morally justified. In short, the main question is: in the law of indirect discrimination, what justifies the presence of the element of justification?

Ever since the idea of adverse impact or indirect discrimination was adopted by the law, it has contained this key element of justification. Whereas intentional, explicit or direct discrimination on grounds of race, sex and other protected characteristics, as for example defined in UK law,[1] could not usually be justified in law at all, it was always possible for employers, governments and other defendants to put forward a justification of their neutral rule or practice that might be held to negate a finding of discrimination. In *Griggs v Duke Power*, the US Supreme Court recognised that an apparently neutral qualification for a job could have the effect (and quite possibly the covert purpose) of excluding in practice most, if not all, members of a minority from that job, so the Court decided that it would be appropriate to infer discrimination from that adverse effect unless the requirement of that particular qualification could satisfy a test of 'business necessity'.[2] When the similar concept of indirect discrimination was later formulated in UK and EU law, it invariably included a general justification defence to enable defendants to demonstrate the need and appropriateness of their neutral requirement or condition, though the precise formulation of this justification element has evolved over the years. As a consequence of the application of EU law to nearly all aspects of anti-discrimination law, currently the governing formulation of the test of justification is a test of proportionality. In accordance with EU law, section 19 Equality Act 2010 in the UK states that indirect discrimination comprises a provision, criterion or practice that is generally applied by its user to applicants for jobs, tenancies, etc, but which puts applicants with one of the protected characteristics such as race or sex at a particular disadvantage, and the user cannot show that the provision, criterion or practice is a proportionate means of achieving a legitimate aim.[3] The final phrase of this definition includes a test of proportionality.

[1] Equality Act 2010, s 13(1) 'A person (A) discriminates against another (B) if, because of a protected characteristic, A treats B less favourably than A treats or would treat others.' In EU law the formula is: '(a) direct discrimination shall be taken to occur where one person is treated less favourably than another is, has been or would be treated in a comparable situation on grounds of racial or ethnic origin' (Council Directive 2000/78/EC of 27 November 2000 establishing a general framework for equal treatment in employment and occupation, [2000] OJ L303/16, Art 2.2).

[2] *Griggs v Duke Power* Co, 401 US 424 (1971), now contained in 42 USC § 2000e-2(k).

[3] Equality Act 2010, s 19(1) 'A person (A) discriminates against another (B) if A applies to B a provision, criterion or practice which is discriminatory in relation to a relevant protected characteristic of B's.

> (2) For the purposes of subsection (1), a provision, criterion or practice is discriminatory in relation to a relevant protected characteristic of B's if—
>
> (a) A applies, or would apply, it to persons with whom B does not share the characteristic,
> (b) it puts, or would put, persons with whom B shares the characteristic at a particular disadvantage when compared with persons with whom B does not share it,
> (c) it puts, or would put, B at that disadvantage, and
> (d) A cannot show it to be a proportionate means of achieving a legitimate aim.'

Much the same test applies in EU law: '(b) indirect discrimination shall be taken to occur where an apparently neutral provision, criterion or practice would put persons of a racial or ethnic origin at a particular disadvantage compared with other persons, unless that provision, criterion or practice is objectively justified by a legitimate aim and the means of achieving that aim are appropriate and necessary.' (Directive 2000/43/EC, Art 2.2).

The statutory definition of indirect discrimination therefore constructs the possibility of justifying this kind of discrimination. It indicates that a rule or practice that on its face does not explicitly impose a disadvantage on a protected group, but which in practice has a particular adverse effect on this group, may be justified on the ground that it serves a legitimate aim in a proportionate manner. The test of proportionality often includes the additional element that the rule will not be justified if there were other ways of achieving the same aim that would have had a lesser adverse impact on a disadvantaged group.[4]

The inclusion of the possibility of justification either by reference to a test of proportionality or business necessity or some other balancing mechanism is generally regarded as a hallmark of the legal concept of indirect discrimination. Indeed, in many accounts of the law of discrimination, the presence of the possibility of avoiding a finding of discrimination by advancing a justification is regarded as a key distinguishing feature between the legal conceptions of direct and indirect discrimination. 'The main difference between them [ie direct and indirect discrimination] is that direct discrimination cannot be justified. Indirect discrimination can be justified if it is a proportionate means of achieving a legitimate aim …'[5] In contrast, as we have noted, leaving aside some specific exceptions mentioned in the legislation such as a necessary occupational qualification for a job, justification for direct discrimination is not generally permitted by the law. How is this difference between direct and indirect discrimination with respect to justification normally explained?

At first sight, there does seem to be a plausible explanation of this difference with respect to justification. I will refer to this explanation as the 'standard account', though it is a blend of a number of accounts that are similar to the extent that the idea of equality in the sense of equal treatment is a core idea, though within that framework significant differences emerge. In these varieties of the standard account, the moral wrong of discrimination is viewed as not treating people as morally equal, or not with equal respect, or not treating people with dignity or as an individual, or as meting out demeaning treatment, or some other reason that suggests a suspect prejudicial reason for the action.[6] Given this view of the purpose

[4] Case C-170/84 *Bilka-Kaufhaus GmbH v Weber von Hartz* [1986] ECR 1607; *Homer v Chief Constable of West Yorkshire Police* [2012] UKSC 15, [2012] 3 All ER 1287, [25] (Baroness Hale); and *Griggs* (n 2), now 42 USC § 2000e-2(k)(1)(A)(ii).

[5] *Regina (E) v Governing Body of JFS and another (United Synagogue and others intervening)* [2009] UKSC 15, [2010] 2 AC 728, [57] (Baroness Hale).

[6] Examples of these kinds of accounts of moral principle underlying discrimination law include: Larry Alexander, 'What Makes Wrongful Discrimination Wrong?' (1992) 141 *University of Pennsylvania Law Review* 149 (disrespect for equal worth); Deborah Hellman, 'When is Discrimination Wrong?' (Cambridge MA, Harvard University Press, 2008) (demeaning treatment); Benjamin Eidelson, 'Treating People as Individuals' in Deborah Hellman and Sophia Moreau (eds), *Philosophical Foundations of Discrimination Law* (Oxford, Oxford

and application of the law of discrimination, it seems unlikely that any deliberate adverse discrimination or prejudice could ever be justified or excused in a liberal society that is committed to equal respect for its citizens. But when that moral reasoning with regard to the wrongfulness of discrimination is applied to indirect discrimination, the moral condemnation seems to be much weaker, if it even exists at all. If the rule is neutral on its face and therefore bears no obvious sign of treating one group of people with less than equal respect, it is not a clear breach of the moral standard of treating people as equals or with dignity. Even if the rule or practice turns out in practice to have a disproportionate adverse impact on a protected group, it is still hard to infer any morally questionable reason for the use of the rule and it is therefore not apparently morally wrongful. Where, however, the facially neutral rule does not appear to serve any legitimate purpose such as improving the efficiency of the business or the effectiveness of a service, it may be regarded with a suspicion that it conceals prejudicial action behind a facially neutral rule. If the rule serves a legitimate purpose such as requiring an educational qualification that is essential for successful performance of a job, however, the concern about respect for the equality of others does not appear to be engaged by the neutral rule. Even the cynical preservation of the system of segregated jobs in *Griggs v Duke Power* would have survived judicial scrutiny if the employers had applied a rule or aptitude test that was defensible because it genuinely identified necessary skills and other requirements for a job. On this standard account, the moral wrong of discrimination, viewed as a denial of equal respect or a similar denigration of individual dignity, simply may not arise in the case of a facially neutral rule or practice.

Furthermore, even if the rule or practice does not pass the test of serving a legitimate purpose or satisfying a business necessity, it is possible that it may not have been motivated by any kind of disrespect or unequal treatment. The rule or practice might be followed as a matter of custom, a mistaken belief in its necessity or rationality, or some other innocent explanation. Thus, even where the rule with an adverse impact on a particular minority cannot be justified by reference to a strict test of proportionality or necessity to achieve a legitimate purpose, it seems probable that any moral condemnation of the use of the rule from the perspective of equal respect is likely be much weaker than for cases of deliberate discrimination. The neutral rule, even though not justifiable, does not merit the same condemnation as a rule that is deliberately discriminatory on a ground such as race. It is true,

University Press, 2013) 203 (treat a person with respect). I am not including as examples of the standard account those theories of the wrongfulness of discrimination that emphasise liberty or autonomy as the foundational value of the law: eg Sophia Moreau, 'What is Discrimination?' (2010) 38 *Philosophy & Public Affairs* 143; Tarunabh Khaitan, *A Theory of Discrimination Law* (Oxford, Oxford University Press, 2015).

of course, that once a claimant has established the fact of adverse impact on a protected group, the defendant has become aware that it is causing this detriment to a protected group, but even so it is hard to attribute to the defendant an initial intention to commit the wrong of treating individuals with less than equal respect. This lower degree of moral condemnation may well explain why in some jurisdictions the legal remedy for indirect discrimination has sometimes been confined to a requirement to change the rule rather than to pay compensation to anyone who was disadvantaged.[7]

We can now sum up some of the features of the application of the standard account of discrimination law based upon respect for equality or dignity to the legal structures of the law of indirect discrimination. On this standard account of the moral wrong of discrimination that underlies the law in terms of dignity, equality or equal respect, the wrongfulness of an indirectly discriminatory rule is significantly less serious than a deliberately discriminatory rule or practice. A neutral rule does not apparently breach the moral standard that requires equal treatment regardless of sex, race, etc. Even where the rule is successfully challenged as perhaps representing a disguised form of deliberate discrimination or at least a rule that has adverse effects on a protected group, the standard account seems likely to endorse the view that a justification defence should be readily available and easily obtained because the moral wrongfulness of the facially neutral rule is doubtful. The principal role of the justification defence on this standard account seems to be one of rebutting the suspicion of disguised intentional discrimination by the ability to point to a legitimate purpose such as the need for a particular required qualification in order to perform the job. In contrast, where there is direct discrimination, a justification defence should normally fail, because the wrong of disrespect will normally be present because of the use of the suspect classification (except perhaps in cases of positive action in favour of a minority).

II. QUESTIONING THE STANDARD ACCOUNT

This standard account of the presence of a justification element in indirect discrimination and its absence in direct discrimination may well account historically for the origins of this division. The idea that blatant sex and race discrimination could ever be justified was certainly unattractive to legislators. The extension of the law to catch indirect discrimination could be supported if it caught surreptitious acts of discrimination, which may have

[7] The original position in the UK Sex Discrimination Act 1975 ss 65(1)(b) and 66(3); and Race Relations Act 1976 ss 56(1)(b) and 57(3). In the USA, the Civil Rights Act 1964 s 706(g) and Civil Rights Act 1991 s 101 focus on the award of generous damages and possible reinstatement to a job in the case of intentional discrimination.

been the original purpose of the US adverse impact approach. It could also be supported if it tackled structural barriers to social mobility for disadvantaged groups. But on the standard account, the moral condemnation of neutral rules that had such adverse effects on disadvantaged groups had to be qualified by the possibility that any suggestion of wrongful discrimination could be rebutted by a demonstration that the impugned neutral rule or practice satisfied a rational purpose that was not itself discriminatory.

Yet there remain some nagging questions about this standard account of the moral soundness of this distinctive presence and extent of the element of justification in the law of indirect discrimination. In my view, these problems lead us eventually to reject the standard account of the presence of a general justification element in the law of indirect discrimination.

A. Tracking the Moral Wrong of Discrimination

An initial problem with the standard account is that the categories of direct and indirect discrimination do not always map tightly onto the moral wrong of disrespect for the equality of citizens in the way that has just been described.

If we examine first the law of direct discrimination, as it has been interpreted in some jurisdictions such as the UK, it does not always require proof of disrespect or conduct that is calculated to demean another's protected characteristic such as sex or race. The law simply requires the use of the protected characteristic as a ground for the decision or the adoption of a rule under which 100 per cent of those with the protected characteristic are disadvantaged. Recall, for instance, the finding of direct discrimination on the ground of sex in the case where entrance to a leisure facility was granted at a concessionary rate to persons over the state pension age, which at the time meant that women but not men aged 61 could benefit from the concession.[8] Moreover, the use of gender or race as a criterion of decision-making might also be motivated by benign reasons such as a desire to help a disadvantaged group without disrespecting anyone, but that would still amount to direct discrimination under the law, even if the moral wrong seems to be absent. If the standard account were correct, we might expect a fairly broad possibility for justification in direct discrimination on the ground that the admittedly suspect classification of race or sex had in fact been used for benign reasons, but that possibility of lawful positive action has generally been foreclosed.

On the other side of the coin, if we examine the law of indirect discrimination, not everyone accepts that the moral wrong is absent when a neutral

[8] *James v Eastleigh Borough Council* [1990] 2 AC 751 (HL).

rule with adverse effects on a protected group is employed. For example, as Sophia Moreau argues forcefully in her contribution to this volume, indirect discrimination is not necessarily free of the moral wrong of disrespect for the equality of citizens or some other kind of morally wrongful conduct. Moreau points out that, at least in some instances of indirect discrimination, such as the aerobic and physical tests that in practice excluded nearly all women in British Columbia from jobs such as being a firefighter,[9] the unlawful rule or practice may be maintained as a result of a failure to consider fairly the interests of a disadvantaged group; a failure that is likely to be influenced by a potentially demeaning stereotypical view of that minority such as regarding women as weak and timid. If correct, that argument casts doubt on the assumption of the standard account that indirect discrimination, unlike direct discrimination, should always in principle be justifiable because it is quite possibly innocent of any moral wrongdoing. At the very least, this argument—that there is an inherent wrongfulness in indirectly discriminatory rules because they signify a failure to regard the interests of others with sufficient care—points to the need for a narrower scope for justification of indirectly discriminatory rules and practices that may end up not so different from the tailored exceptions to direct discrimination claims.

Therefore, it seems too crude to say, as the standard account does, that the justification defence should never be available in instances of direct discrimination for the reason that such conduct always involves the moral wrong of treating others as less than moral equals, whereas that moral condemnation does not arise in cases of indirect discrimination. The law plainly does not track precisely the standard account's view of the moral wrong of discrimination and there are reasons to question the view that neutral rules cannot be impugned on the ground that they commit the moral wrong of treating others as less than moral equals.

B. Defence or Ingredient?

A second potential difficulty with the standard explanation of the element of justification present in the law of indirect discrimination is that in one respect it seems to be incoherent. In common with typical legal analyses, the standard explanation appears to treat justification as a form of defence to a claim for indirect discrimination, rather than an essential element in the wrong that has to be established. To draw an analogy with criminal law, we might ask whether the justification element in indirect discrimination is like a requirement of 'mens rea' in a criminal offence, which is usually regarded

[9] *British Columbia (Public Service Employee Relations Commission) v British Columbia Government Service Employees' Union* [1999] 3 SCR 3.

as an essential ingredient of the offence that has to be established and without which there can be no wrong and no crime, or is the justification element a kind of defence, like self-defence, which is only invoked when all the other essential ingredients of the wrong have been proven.

In the case of direct discrimination, the standard explanation can without much difficulty treat the use of an exception as a defence in this latter sense like self-defence. For instance, an employer's claim that sex was a necessary occupational qualification for this particular position for reasons of authenticity or decency can be treated as a defence. The employer's directly discriminatory choice based upon sex does appear to be a prima facie wrong, since it violates the principle of equal treatment and equal opportunity, and therefore satisfies the normal ingredients of the moral wrong of direct discrimination. Nevertheless, if the employer can successfully rely on the response that sex was a genuine occupational qualification, it has a complete defence to allegation of wrongful discrimination. In the context of direct discrimination, therefore, the standard account seems to be on solid ground when it treats the permitted justifications of direct discrimination as defences.

But does the same approach work in the context of indirect discrimination? Can the justification element be regarded as a defence to a wrongful act? Typical accounts of the law of indirect discrimination often describe the element of justification as a defence in that sense and that account is sometimes used by the standard moral account of the law of indirect discrimination. But that approach creates a problem of inconsistency or incoherence, for, on the one hand, the standard moral account of the law of discrimination explains the existence of a broad justification element in the law of indirect discrimination (and its absence in direct discrimination) on the ground that the application of a neutral rule cannot be inherently wrongful, but, on the other hand, if that judgement is correct, the justification element cannot be providing a defence in the sense of a defence to an acknowledged prima facie wrong, because on the standard moral account there is no moral wrong in using a neutral rule. In effect the standard account, as described above, seems to be saying both that there is no moral wrong in the use of facially neutral rules, so there is no moral wrong at least until the rules are shown to be irrational or illegitimate, and at the same time, inconsistently, it seems to tacitly endorse the view that there is a wrong arising from the use of a facially neutral rule, though this wrong can be rebutted by the defence of justification.

To regard the justification element in indirect discrimination as a defence therefore necessitates the formation of a view, apparently contrary to the standard moral account, that the use of a neutral rule that has in fact a disproportionate adverse impact on a protected group is itself a moral wrong. Such a view seems to be supported, for instance, by Tarun Khaitan and Sandy Steel in their chapter in this volume. They argue that the fact of adverse impact on a protected group is itself a breach of duty, which is described as a 'duty to refrain from causing adversity to a relatively disadvantaged protected group.' But that seems to be a very broad and sweeping moral duty, if it can be broken by the adoption of facially neutral rules. Although Khaitan and Steel may be right that there is a general duty to refrain from causing adversity to protected groups where the result is intended, it seems to me unlikely that such a general duty extends to a prohibition of the adoption of facially neutral rules that may cause adversity to a protected group. In the absence of a covert prejudicial intention or the presence of an inevitable and significant adverse impact on a protected group, the adoption of a neutral rule on its own does not seem to me to amount to breach of any kind of moral duty at all. To become a moral wrong, in my view, it would require at least an additional element of fault of the kind that Moreau seeks to propose with her analogy to the law of negligence.

In my view, therefore, it is incorrect to regard the justification element in the law of indirect discrimination as a kind of defence. Instead, it should be understood as an essential ingredient of the wrong, not a separate defence. It is like the requirement of 'mens rea' in criminal law, a vital ingredient of the wrong, rather than a possible exceptional defence to a crime like the defence of self-defence. There is in my view only a breach of a moral (and legal) duty if the use of a facially neutral rule that has an adverse impact on a protected group cannot be justified. My view is to that extent consistent with the standard moral account described above that views the moral wrong of indirect discrimination as not being established until at the very least it is determined that the rule has no legitimate purpose or when the legitimate purpose is insufficiently important to provide a reason for using it when it has those adverse effects.

Consider, for instance, a requirement of an employer that new recruits to management trainee positions should have the qualification of an upper second class degree (or some other minimum standard of university education). Suppose that it could be demonstrated as well that certain racial and ethnic minorities in the labour market are statistically much less likely to be able to comply with this rule, so that in practice disproportionately few apply for or obtain these positions. Is this fact of disproportionate adverse impact on some minorities in itself evidence of prima facie wrongfulness or a breach of duty, which needs to be justified, or is this evidence of merely one necessary ingredient of wrongfulness that, standing alone, however, is not in itself wrongful at all? In my account of the justification element in the law of indirect discrimination, it is only when the employer is unable to demonstrate the relevance of the university qualification to the ability to perform a managerial job that the essential elements of the wrong represented by indirect discrimination can be said to be in place. If an employer's requirement of having an upper second class degree were to be regarded as a moral wrong in itself in a country where minorities were less likely to obtain university places, as in the UK at present, that view would imply, for instance, that all law firms that require such a qualification for a training contract and all universities that require such a qualification to be admitted to a Masters programme would be committing a moral wrong by adopting this rule. Although the courts would no doubt say in all these cases that the requirement or condition was justified and so there would be no legal liability, those who view the justification element as a kind of defence would necessarily be committed to the view that even so the law firms and the universities had all committed a moral wrong or a breach of duty. Since I doubt that few would agree with that analysis of the moral position, it seems to me more convincing and in line with most people's moral intuitions to support the proposition that far from being a defence, the element of justification should be regarded as an essential ingredient in identifying the wrong of indirect discrimination. This contention that insists that the element of justification in indirect discrimination is not a defence but rather an essential ingredient in the wrong seems to be hard for lawyers to accept owing to two features of the law.

First, lawyers may tend to think of the justification element in indirect discrimination as a defence because of the analogy that was drawn above with respect to the exceptions to direct discrimination. In cases of direct discrimination, the unequal treatment is normally regarded as wrongful in itself. If one of the exceptions is successfully invoked, such as the exception of a genuine need for an occupational qualification, those exceptions seem to be properly classified as defences to a wrong. The argument of the theatre producer who insists upon hiring a man to play the part of Prince Hamlet for reasons of authenticity is that, though it is usually wrong to engage in direct sex discrimination, on this particular occasion there is a very powerful justification for making an exception. In disability law, where justification is possible in connection with direct discrimination, again the argument seems to be that although it is wrong in general to disadvantage disabled workers, the adverse treatment in this particular case was justifiable (though regrettable) because the worker was physically or mentally unable to perform the job even with reasonable adjustments by the employer. Below we will cast doubt on aspects of this analysis of the justification element in direct discrimination. But even if it is correct to argue that when justifications are made in connection with direct discrimination that those justifications function as a defence, it does not follow necessarily that the justifying element in connection with indirect discrimination is a defence also.

Second, lawyers may also tend to speak of the justification element in indirect discrimination as a defence because typically the burden of proof is allocated to the defendant. A court will say that it is up to the defendant employer to demonstrate that an educational requirement serves a necessary or at least a legitimate purpose (though of course the claimant may contest and rebut that argument). That allocation of the burden of proof is partly based on the pragmatic ground that only the employer is likely to be in possession of some of the material evidence such as the comparative standards of job performance of those employees with and without the educational qualification. In the Article 14 jurisprudence of the European Court of Human Rights, for example, the way indirect discrimination is presented is a matter of proof—the statistics that establish disproportionate disadvantage for a protected group establish a prima facie case of discrimination (perhaps unconscious rather than intentional), and then the alleged perpetrator of the discrimination has to justify its formally neutral rule. So there is a switch in the burden of proof, which tends to confirm the impression that the justification defence is a separate requirement.

> [W]here an applicant is able to show, on the basis of undisputed official statistics, the existence of a prima facie indication that a specific rule—although formulated in a neutral manner—in fact affects a clearly higher percentage of women than men, it is for the respondent Government to show that this is the result of objective factors unrelated to any discrimination on grounds of sex. If the onus of demonstrating that a difference in impact for men and women is not in practice discriminatory does not shift to the respondent Government, it will be in practice extremely difficult for applicants to prove indirect discrimination.[10]

But this reversal of the burden of proof, (which is a common practice throughout the law of discrimination owing to the difficulty of ever proving intentional discrimination),[11] should not lead us necessarily to classify the element of justification as a defence. Although it is true in general that defendants carry the burden of proof in order to establish defences, the corollary is untrue: it is incorrect that wherever a burden of proof is allocated onto a defendant, the legal issue must concern a defendant raising a defence. Placing the evidential burden on the person in possession of the facts explains the burden of proof in discrimination law without implying necessarily that the justification element is properly classified as a defence.

The UK legislation, as set out above,[12] lists four ingredients for the wrong of indirect discrimination. Each of these ingredients is necessary and is presented as constitutive of the legal wrong. No doubt it assists the legal process to consider each element in turn, and if there is no disproportionate adverse impact on a protected group at all, there is certainly little point in considering the possibility of justification. Yet the practical convenience of that linear legal process should not lead us into the error of thinking that the element of justification in indirect discrimination is a defence as opposed to one of the vital ingredients of the claim or 'offence'. Justification, or

[10] *Hoogendijk v Netherlands (Admissibility)* (App no 58641/00) (2005) 40 EHRR SE22 approved in *DH and Others v Czech Republic* (App no 57325/00) (2008) 47 EHRR 3.

[11] Equality Act 2010, s 136.

[12] Above n 3.

rather the absence thereof, is better regarded as a constitutive element of the wrong of indirect discrimination. There is no wrong until it has been established that there is both a neutral rule that causes adverse effects to a disadvantaged group and that the rule lacks a rational purpose and is therefore unjustified. 'There is no finding of unlawful discrimination until all four elements of the definition are met.'[13] The proof of the rational purpose of the rule is not a defence to a wrong but rather negates one of the constitutive elements of the wrong. The full implications of that point will be considered after we revisit the question of whether a crucial difference between direct and indirect discrimination concerns the availability of a general defence of justification only in connection with indirect discrimination. For the present, we can merely conclude that in so far as the standard account treats the justification element in indirect discrimination as a defence, it is incoherent.

C. Justification in Direct Discrimination

A third nagging question about the characterisation of indirect discrimination as the unique site of a general justification element is whether that accounts sufficiently for the presence of elements of justification in relation to direct discrimination. In other words, is an element of justification not also an intrinsic part of direct discrimination? It is true that UK law, reflecting EU law,[14] frames the issue of justification differently in the law of direct discrimination, at least in some contexts. With regard to exceptions such as occupational qualifications and single sex associations, the UK legislation seems to be precise and detailed on the scope of such exceptions rather than permitting the courts to apply a general justification standard for such exceptions. This specificity in the legislation may reflect a legislative choice strictly to control the extent to which courts might be tempted to discover reasons for justifying discrimination on grounds of sex and race rather than the absence of the possibility of justification of direct discrimination. Is it possible therefore to argue that the difference between direct and indirect discrimination is more a matter of the form of the legislation than the substance of the underlying principle of justification?

How far is it possible to insist that the proportionality test of justification used in connection with indirect discrimination also lies at the core of many of the provisions applicable to direct discrimination? When we look closely, indeed, the proportionality test of justification is lurking throughout the law

[13] *Essop v Home Office (UK Border Agency)* [2017] UKSC 27, [2017] 1 WLR 1343, [29] Lady Hale.

[14] Directive 2006/54/EC of the European Parliament and of the Council of 5 July 2006 on the implementation of the principle of equal opportunities and equal treatment of men and women in matters of employment and occupation [2006] OJ L204/23, Art 2.

of direct discrimination. For instance, under UK law, the general exception for occupational requirements only applies if it is a proportionate means of achieving a legitimate aim.[15] The same proportionality test is applied to the requirement for a person to hold particular religious beliefs as a member or employee of a faith organisation such as a church.[16] Moreover it should be recalled that, in connection with some protected characteristics, the law of direct discrimination does permit a general justification defence that is similar to that used in connection with indirect discrimination. In relation to disability, for instance, the discriminator avoids liability by showing that the unfavourable treatment is a proportionate means of achieving a legitimate aim.[17] Similarly, 'if the protected characteristic is age, A does not discriminate against B if A can show A's treatment of B to be a proportionate means of achieving a legitimate aim.'[18]

These examples demonstrate that the claim that a general justification defence only applies in indirect discrimination is not strictly speaking accurate. Not only can the general justification defence be used in relation to certain kinds of protected characteristics, but it is evident that some general defences such as an occupational requirement embody a particularised statement of the test of proportionality. Given all these examples of the presence of a test of proportionality for a justification in connection with direct discrimination, the better view appears to be that the difference between direct and indirect discrimination with respect to a general justification element is more a matter of the form of the legislation than a matter of substance in the applicable law and underlying principle.

If it is correct that a justification element using a test of proportionality applies throughout the law of discrimination, albeit using different modes of expression, what implications might that view have for the standard explanation that we have been considering? It seems to undermine its explanation of why a general justification defence is not permitted in connection with direct discrimination on the ground that the wrong of unequal treatment is too severe to be justifiable except in rare exceptional circumstances. If one accepts that a justification element is present throughout the law against discrimination, it seems to follow that the standard explanation is trying to account for something that does not exist, namely the exclusion of a general justification defence in direct discrimination. Furthermore, subject to the point above regarding the mismatch between the law and the moral wrong of disrespect, the standard account of the general aim of discrimination law in terms of the denial of equal treatment and respect also appears

[15] Equality Act 2010, Sched 9, Part 1, para 1. See also Art 14, Directive 2006/54/EC on equal treatment between men and women.

[16] Equality Act 2010, Sched 9, Part 1, para 3. See also para 4 for the test of proportionality applied to the aim of combat effectiveness for the armed forces.

[17] Equality Act 2010, s 15(1)(b).

[18] Equality Act 2010, s 13(2).

to be undermined, for one of its apparent strengths was its ability to explain why no justification defence could be available to the moral wrong of direct discrimination because it involved disrespect. If in fact there is a justification defence to direct discrimination, though formulated more cautiously in many contexts, it may follow that the general aim of the law is not best described as combatting conduct that treats others as inferiors or less than equal.

D. The General Justifying Aim

All the above points are troubling for the standard explanation of the existence of a general justification element in the law of indirect discrimination, but they are for the most part raising internal questions about the coherence of that account of the law. It is also possible to question the standard explanation by advancing more radical challenges. The standard account assumes that both direct and indirect discrimination pursue the same general aim, and that the general aim is best described in terms of treating people with equal respect or a similar principle. Both of these contentions could be challenged and of course have been. It could be argued by a 'dualist' that laws against direct and indirect discrimination pursue different goals, and that therefore it is the difference in goals that explains the presence or absence of a general justification element. Alternatively, it might be accepted by a 'monist' that although laws against direct and indirect discrimination pursue the same general aim, the aim has little to do with equality and respect, as maintained in the standard explanation, and that this alternative aim can explain the incidence and formulation of the general justification element in discrimination law. Although we cannot explore these possibilities in detail in the space available here, we can illustrate the potential implications of the dualist and monist approaches for accounts of the justification element in the law of indirect discrimination (and possibly direct discrimination as well).

It is possible to advance a dualist theory that indirect discrimination pursues a different goal from direct discrimination. It is sometimes said, for instance, that direct discrimination is concerned with equal respect whereas indirect discrimination is targeted at more substantive egalitarian concerns. In this vein, Lady Hale has observed that

> The rule against direct discrimination aims to achieve formal equality of treatment: there must be no less favourable treatment between otherwise similarly situated people on grounds of colour, race, nationality or ethnic or national origins. Indirect discrimination looks beyond formal equality towards a more substantive equality of results: criteria which appear neutral on their face may have a disproportionately adverse impact upon people of a particular colour, race, nationality or ethnic or national origins.[19]

[19] *R v JFS* (n 5) [56].

If there is such a difference in the general aims of direct and indirect discrimination law, the standard explanation of the general justification element in the law of indirect discrimination would need to be reconsidered. In the standard account where the moral justification for direct and indirect discrimination is the same, the presence of a justification defence for indirect discrimination can only be explained by an argument that the conduct labelled as indirect discrimination is not seriously wrongful at all. But if the law of indirect discrimination is linked to some other general aim such as substantive equality or social inclusion, the reason for having a justification element might differ considerably.

Consider, for instance, the potential explanation of the justification element in the law of indirect discrimination that might be supplied by a theory that holds that the principal aim of the law of indirect discrimination is to reduce social exclusion.[20] On this account, the prohibition of indirect discrimination fits into the frameworks of welfare provision that are supposed to reduce social exclusion such as free schools and health care, progressive taxation, support for people on low incomes through the social security system, and the need to prevent gross inequalities from undermining social cohesion and provoking disorder in poor neighbourhoods. From this perspective, the law of indirect discrimination is concerned about rules and practices that appear to present structural obstacles to social mobility, or about the achievement of access to goods that help well-being, or to social inclusion. It performs a function similar to that achieved by free education by enabling everyone to develop their abilities and function successfully in our society. On this view, neutral rules and practices that disproportionately exclude members of disadvantaged groups are not in themselves evidence of a moral wrong, but to the extent that those rules and practices operate to obstruct social mobility and exacerbate social exclusion, they are likely to be regarded as rules and practices that should be discouraged and if possible, at reasonable cost, eliminated. From this social justice perspective, the target of the law of indirect discrimination is not morally blameworthy conduct but rather social and institutional structures that have, whether wittingly or accidentally, an undesirable or unfair exclusionary effect. When explaining the presence of the general justification element in the law of indirect discrimination from this perspective, we might say that although the contested rule or practice contributes to social exclusion and therefore is rightly targeted by discrimination law, its removal or amendment in this particular instance will not be required if either the removal would not contribute to social inclusion or it would cause unreasonable costs to the defendant. The test of proportionality would be understood on this view to amount to an assessment of the costs and benefits of the removal of this structural obstacle to social inclusion. Whilst this chapter cannot delve any

[20] H Collins, 'Discrimination, Equality and Social Inclusion' (2003) 66 *MLR* 16.

further into the moral justifications for direct and indirect discrimination, if we want to understand the moral reason for the justification element in indirect discrimination, we need to be alert to the point that, if the general aim or combination of aims of law of indirect discrimination is significantly different from that underpinning direct discrimination, the element of justification may perform a rather different role and rest on a different moral justification from that provided by the standard account.

Equally, we need to be alert to the possibility that the standard explanation is wedded to a particular monist account of all the laws against discrimination, both direct and indirect, that is flawed or at least can be improved upon. For instance, Tarunabh Khaitan,[21] following a line of argument first suggested by John Gardner,[22] advances the theory that the principal purpose of discrimination law is to protect individual autonomy in the sense of trying to ensure that everyone has access to valuable options so that they enjoy the freedom to develop and fulfil their own life plans. On this view of the purpose of the law of discrimination, rules and practices that block people from taking up valuable opportunities are likely to inhibit individual autonomy and are therefore at least prima facie wrongful or at least undesirable. For instance, if a rule has the effect of excluding non-graduates from managerial training positions and this has a disproportionate adverse impact on members of a black minority group, we can argue that their autonomy (or at least those who applied or might have applied for the position) has been restricted by the rule. This general aim regarding the enhancement of autonomy provides a persuasive account of the prohibition of indirect discrimination.[23] That general aim might also throw some light on the purpose of the justification element in the law of indirect discrimination by indicating that justified rules might be ones that do not block people from opportunities from which they might be able to benefit in practice.[24] For instance, if the rule is one that requires a medical qualification to become a hospital nurse, the justification for the rule, even if it has discriminatory effects on minority groups, would be that the opportunity to be a nurse without that relevant body of knowledge would place the person in a very difficult position, dangerous not only to the patients but also potentially extremely distressing for the nurse.

[21] T Khaitan, *A Theory of Discrimination Law* (Oxford, Oxford University Press, 2015).

[22] J Gardner, 'On the Ground of her Sex(uality)' (1998) 18 *OJLS* 167.

[23] Unlike Khaitan, Gardner does not appear to see a moral wrong arising from the fact that the neutral rule obstructs valuable opportunities, but describes indirect discrimination as providing positive duties to attend to discriminatory side effects in order to make the law more effective. J Gardner, 'On the Ground of her Sex(uality)' (1998) 18 *OJLS* 167, 182. This position is criticised in O Doyle, 'Direct Discrimination, Indirect Discrimination and Autonomy' (2007) 27 *OJLS* 537, 548–50.

[24] Khaitan does not accept this implication about the element of justification of his view of the purpose of the law of discrimination since he accepts in outline at least the contrary view that is endorsed in the next section.

These points demonstrate that rival theories about the general aim of laws against discrimination, whether monist, dualist or indeed pluralist, might well provide rather different explanations of the presence of a justification element in indirect discrimination from that supplied by the standard account. In particular, if the laws against discrimination are regarded as having at least in part a distributive justice aim, such as a more equitable distribution of worthwhile opportunities or the reduction of social exclusion, a general element of justification that tests whether a change in the rules or practices would in fact serve those goals (or would only do so only at disproportionate cost) would fit coherently into this account of the law. This account might explain both why a justification element is present in both direct and indirect discrimination, and furthermore it might illuminate the meaning and application of the test of proportionality as a mechanism for assessing the costs and benefits of the pursuit of a distributive aim.

E. The Need for a Separate Foundation for Justification

As attractive as the arguments in the previous section appear to be, ultimately in my view they point in the wrong direction. The above points about how rival theories about the general aim of the law of discrimination might be linked to different accounts of the justification element all make the assumption that there must be a link between the justification element and the general aim (or aims) of the law against discrimination. It is both a parsimonious and plausible assumption, and for that reason attractive. Indeed, if my arguments above to the effect that the justification element is a constituent element of indirect discrimination and that there is no radical difference in this respect between direct and indirect discrimination are correct, that seems to strengthen the argument for viewing the justification element as closely related to or derived from the general justifying aim of the law. In particular, if the justification element is not a defence at all, it is much less likely that it has a separate and independent moral justification from the purpose of discrimination law.

Nevertheless, the remainder of this chapter will argue for the opposite proposition. It holds that the justification element in discrimination law has its own independent moral foundation. Whilst it is possible to concede that the precise formulation of the justification element in discrimination law may be influenced by the general aim of the law (and other considerations perhaps as well), my main argument is that the justification element represents, at base, a value that stands in opposition to a comprehensive and fully effective law against discrimination. This value concerns the freedom or liberty of the alleged discriminator.

Why must the justification element in the law of discrimination rest on a separate foundation from the general aim of the law? My claim is that the justification element, though not properly regarded as a defence, nevertheless introduces an independent set of values into the law of discrimination. In that sense, it has a separate foundation that can enter into opposition with the pursuit of the values of the law of discrimination. The justification element does not derive from the general aim of the law, for if it did, it should never obstruct the achievement of the goals of the law. Yet, it is evident that the justification element can so restrict the worthy goals pursued by the law. The law of indirect discrimination may identify a rule that seriously disadvantages women or a minority. Yet the justification element may endorse the legitimacy of the rule even though the goal of the law would be better secured by invalidating the rule. In other words, the structure of law of discrimination includes the justification element because it needs to embrace this other foundational value, even though it can anticipate that in balancing these competing values the justification element may sometimes seriously obstruct the goals of anti-discrimination law. The effect of this abstract argument becomes clearer below once it is appreciated that the competing values at stake are the classic liberal values of equality (in many of its manifestations) embraced by the aims of laws against discrimination and of liberty that provides the foundation for the ever-present justification element in the law of discrimination.

That structural argument for an independent foundational value lying underneath the element of justification in the law of discrimination is, however, compatible with a weaker contention that the general aim of the law against discrimination may help to shape the detailed content of the justification element and its application in particular instances. This shaping of the details of the element of justification does not demonstrate that it is derived from the general aim of the laws against discrimination. The point is rather that as the independent element of justification interacts with the remainder of the law of discrimination, which will be determined at least to some extent by the general aim of the law, that interaction is likely to be coloured by understandings of the goal of the law against discrimination. The justification element, though based on its own independent value, is likely to be influenced by its interaction with the details of the law of discrimination and its underlying purposes and values. The flash points raised by the element of justification and the details of the mechanism by which the justification element is weighed in the legal analysis are likely to be influenced by views about the general aims of the law against discrimination. Even so, it is my contention that the justification element has an independent foundational value that requires its presence in the law, though its mode of expression may be influenced by the claims that it may seek to resist.

The standard account of the element of justification in the law of indirect discrimination has been assessed in this section and found wanting.

Although its coherence and ability to explain important features of the law have been the focus of the challenge, it is this last point that is in fact the one that must be fatal to the standard account of the justification element in the law of discrimination and indeed undermines other theories that try to derive an account of the justification element from views about the general aim of discrimination laws. The main reason why the standard account lapses into incoherence is, in my view, that it attempts to explain the presence or absence of the justification element in laws against discrimination by reference to its conception of the general aim of the law as being connected to the idea of formal equality or equal respect. The mistake is to assume that there must be a connection between the general aim and the presence of the element of justification, so that one is derived from the former. Once that assumption is dropped and it is accepted that the justification element rests on a separate foundation, we can brush aside the debris of the standard account and start afresh with a better framework in which the justification element in indirect discrimination (and direct discrimination) rests on an independent moral foundation.

III. BALANCING RIGHTS IN INDIRECT DISCRIMINATION

The law of discrimination restricts the liberty of individuals with respect to the choice of contractual partners and freedom of association. However, there are several aspects of the law of discrimination that seek to avoid too great an interference with the liberty of individuals. The law does not attempt to control a person's choice of friends, a consumer's choice of retailer or contractor, a worker's choice of employer, or a tenant's choice of landlord. Whether or not we should be so very concerned about the freedom of the individual in all these circumstances may these days be controversial, but it is plainly a structural feature of the law of discrimination that it uses exclusions from the coverage of the law to protect individuals from having their preferences and tastes impugned by the legal system. My argument is that the same concern for the liberty of the individual also explains the presence, formulation, and scope of the element of justification in the law of discrimination.

But in this context of the justification element, the concern from liberty is not solely about negative liberty or freedom from restrictions. Its function consists of a more nuanced protection of the interests of the alleged discriminator. This function can be better expressed as the protection of the fundamental rights of the alleged discriminator against those of the alleged victim or claimant. The right of the claimant such as an employee, tenant or student is to be treated equally or with equal respect by private actors with regard to important aspects of well-being that are often articulated in the form of social and economic rights such as the rights to work,[25] to education, to shelter and to subsistence. The opposing right of the employer, the landlord, the educational institution or the shopkeeper or other kind of defendant is a general liberty, which may include freedom of contract, and more particularly the freedom to conduct a business.[26] As we shall see below, in any particular case, various additional fundamental rights may be at stake on both sides of the argument. My claim is that the function of a justification defence is to balance these rights against each other. Usually both parties have rights and the question posed by the issue of justification in indirect discrimination law is whose rights should prevail in the circumstances.

A. Double Proportionality

The answer provided to that question by the law of indirect discrimination proceeds in a number of steps. In the first place, the claimant has to establish the disadvantage produced by a rule or practice that affects members of the protected class and that the claimant in fact suffered that disadvantage. The point of that stage in the analysis is to establish that indeed that has been an interference with the right of the claimant, such as the right to work of an applicant for a job, and that the criterion used for selection can be impugned for its discriminatory effects. The defendant employer is then permitted to establish that the purpose of the rule or practice was to pursue a legitimate goal, such as the selection of applicants for a job on the ground of competence, aptitude and merit, and that the value or strength of the employer's right to use that rule or practice exceeds the value to be attached to any unavoidable interference with the rights of the claimant. In a case of indirect discrimination where an employer applies a rule to select applicants that has an adverse impact in practice, the employer's defence should succeed if the rule is genuinely relevant to the needs of the business to select appropriate staff. Provided its rule and practices stick close to the needs of the business and serve that goal, an employer maintains its right to manage its business and to choose its contractual partners. To use different language, the supervision of a private employer's personnel practices by the courts through the mechanism of the laws against discrimination should never be so invasive as to destroy the employer's right to manage its business for legitimate purposes. If protected groups cannot pass the employer's test or meet the required qualifications, provided the rules are appropriate and necessary to fulfil the employer's purpose, there may be a misfortune for the applicants,

[25] Charter of Fundamental Rights of the European Union [2007] OJ C303/5, Art 15(1): 'Everyone has the right to engage in work and to pursue a freely chosen of accepted occupation.'
[26] EU Charter of Fundamental Rights, ibid, Art 16.

but there is no wrongful interference with their rights. The justification element in the law of indirect discrimination provides the moment when the alleged discriminator's rights are brought into the equation to ensure that those rights are not unnecessarily eviscerated.

If it is correct that the underlying purpose of the justification element in the law of indirect discrimination is best understood as the balancing of the rights of the parties, the structure of the legal enquiry turns out to be similar to that employed by the courts sometimes in the context of applying the law of human rights in the private sphere. For example, in the case of a newspaper that wants to publicise the non-marital sexual activities of a politician or a footballer, the newspaper undoubtedly benefits from the right to freedom of expression and freedom of the press, but the politician or footballer benefits from a right to privacy. In determining whether the newspaper should be permitted to publish its titillating story, a court has to balance these competing rights against each other. In such cases, the courts have recognised that the correct approach is that the interference with both rights should be minimised as far as possible without totally eliminating respect for the rights of each party.[27] The correct method, which is sometimes called 'the ultimate balancing test', should be to apply a test of proportionality to both rights. In other words, the question should be whether the interference with one right, such as freedom of the press, is necessary and appropriate in pursuit of a legitimate aim, namely to preserve some element of privacy for the politician. The same question then should be posed with respect to restrictions on the right to privacy. The aim of this 'double proportionality' enquiry is to protect as much of each party's right as may be possible without tolerating a disproportionate interference with the right of the other party.

Although the test of justification in the law of indirect discrimination is not expressly formulated by the law in terms of a test of double proportionality, my argument is that the element of justification performs this function and this role casts light on some of its controversial applications. When applying the element of justification, the critical, though not always fully acknowledged question, is whether a finding of indirect discrimination would involve a disproportionate interference with the fundamental rights of the defendant to the extent of removing most of the substance of that right. If the employer's rule or practice is necessary for the operation of the business and there is no alternative that avoids discriminatory impact, the rule or practice must be upheld as valid, for otherwise the defendant or employer's right will become empty of content.

[27] *Re S (Identity Restrictions on Publication)* [2004] UKHL 47, [2005] 1 AC 593, [17]; *A Local Authority v W* [2005] EWHC 1564 (Fam). cf Hugh Collins, 'On the (In)compatibility of Human Rights Discourse and Private Law' in Hans-W Micklitz (ed), *Constitutionalization of European Private Law* (Oxford, Oxford University Press, 2014) 26, 49–51.

Once the justification element in the law of indirect discrimination is understood as an application of the double proportionality test used in the law of human rights, some of the difficulties that were experienced initially in formulating the appropriate legal test become understandable. When the courts in the UK originally described the process as one of balancing the rights of the parties against one another,[28] though open to the criticism that it was too lax, that description was correct at an abstract level. It was true that the right of the employer to conduct its business had not been eliminated wherever that conduct might have a discriminatory adverse impact on a protected group. That right has to be respected and balanced against the rights of the employees or claimants. Nevertheless, the correct way to manage that balancing process has to involve a double proportionality test, so that interference with the rights of both parties is minimised and satisfies a test of necessity along the lines of the test of proportionality. What is not always appreciated is that the proportionality test is not only being applied to the rights of the employer but also the rights of the employee or claimant. Where the employer's rule or practice is regarded as justifiable, in effect the court has determined that the interference with the worker's right to work or with their right to equal respect is proportionate. In other words, it is right that the courts should apply a balancing test as they initially stated, but it is also right that the balancing test should involve a test of proportionality in order to minimise interference with both parties' rights. That is why courts often frame the final stage of the enquiry of the element of justification to be a requirement to assess whether the measures were a proportionate balancing of the real needs of the employer against the effect of the rules and practices on the affected employees. To achieve that minimum interference with both parties' rights, it is necessary to apply a double proportionality test.

B. Direct Discrimination

A further and perhaps striking implication of this characterisation of the justification element in indirect discrimination as a mechanism for the balancing of the rights of the parties according to a test of double proportionality is that this mechanism should logically be replicated in the law of direct discrimination. It must follow from my argument in connection with indirect discrimination that the law of direct discrimination needs a mechanism for ensuring that it does not disproportionately interfere with the fundamental rights of the alleged discriminator. The advent of direct discrimination law

[28] *Hampson v Department of Education and Science* [1989] ICR 179 (CA) per Balcome LJ; approved by the House of Lords in *Webb v Emo Air Cargo Ltd* [1993] ICR 175, 183.

in effect ensured that an employer's and a landlord's rights to liberty and freedom to choose a contractual partner did not automatically extend (as they had previously)[29] to intentional discrimination on one of the prohibited grounds such as sex and race. The law of direct discrimination altered the legal balance of the rights, placing much greater weight on the right of employees and tenants to be treated with equal respect and regarding intentional discrimination as an abuse of rights. Nevertheless, the law of direct discrimination had to be structured so as to protect the fundamental interests or rights of alleged discriminators where the law of direct discrimination might impose a disproportionate interference. Instead of permitting judges to decide where there was a disproportionate interference on a case by case basis, the early legislation in the UK on sex and race discrimination tried to anticipate every issue in advance with detailed rules that carved out narrow exceptions regarding, for example, occupational requirements. Recognising the complexity of the task, however, the subsequent UK legislation on disability and age discrimination introduced the same proportionality defence of justification in connection with allegations of direct discrimination.[30]

C. Multiple Rights

It is important to note that in some cases involving either direct or indirect discrimination several different fundamental rights or interests may be at stake and will therefore have to be accounted for in the process of balancing rights. For instance, one party may invoke the right to manifest a religion or to freedom of expression as a further ground for justifying direct or indirect discrimination. In some instances that additional right will outweigh the right to be treated with equal respect. For instance, churches are permitted to discriminate against women and on the ground of sexual orientation if that is a tenet of their doctrines that has to be manifested by such practices. Khaitan calls this 'permitted' discrimination,[31] as opposed to justified discrimination. This label seems to acknowledge that rights such as the right to manifest a religion are at stake in these cases, not merely business goals and efficiency considerations. Nevertheless, on my analysis these cases merely exemplify a particularly complex application of the test of double proportionality caused by the presence of the invocation of a plurality of fundamental rights.

A case that illustrates both the application of a plurality of rights and the application of a general justification defence to direct discrimination

[29] *Scala Ballroom (Wolverhampton) Ltd v Ratcliffe* [1958] 1 WLR 1057 (CA) legal to bar non-whites from the ballroom.

[30] Equality Act 2010, s 13(2) (age); s 15 (disability).

[31] Khaitan (n 6) 181.

framed in terms of fundamental rights is *Bull and Bull v Hall and Preddy*.[32] In accordance with their religious faith, the owners of a small hotel refused to permit unmarried guests to occupy rooms with a double bed. On arrival at the hotel, Mr Hall and Mr Preddy, a gay couple who were in a civil partnership, were denied the double-bedded accommodation that they had booked by phone. The legal institution of civil partnership, which in virtually every respect is the same as marriage, is only available to gay and lesbian couples, whereas at that time only heterosexual couples could marry.[33] The impugned action of the hoteliers could therefore be described as using a rule that excluded from double-bedded accommodation either couples in civil partnerships or non-married couples. On behalf of a majority of the court, Lady Hale held that the conduct could be classified as both direct and indirect discrimination. It was direct discrimination on the ground of sexual orientation in so far as civil partners were not treated the same as married partners, but indirect discrimination in so far as only married couples would be allocated a double bed, because that rule would also disadvantage some unmarried heterosexuals.

Lady Hale (speaking for the whole court) held that the indirect discrimination was not justified because the aim sought by the hoteliers, which was to prevent sexual intercourse between persons of the same sex in their bedrooms, directly contradicted the aim of the institution of civil partnership and the law against discrimination on grounds of sexual orientation and therefore could not be a legitimate aim and therefore justify the indirectly discriminatory rule. In accordance with the theory being advanced here, this argument is stating that if such discrimination with regard to double-bedded rooms were to be permitted, it would deprive the claimants of the very essence of their right to be treated equally with respect to their sexual orientation.

With respect to direct discrimination, though the law did not expressly include a justification defence to direct discrimination, the application of the Human Rights Act 1998 required the court to consider whether a finding of direct discrimination was compatible with proper respect for the rights of the hoteliers to manifest their religion. On this point, Lady Hale concluded that any interference with the right of the hoteliers was done for the legitimate aim of upholding the legal rights of Hall and Preddy, as defined by Parliament, and, perhaps crucially, including their right for respect for

[32] *Bull and Bull v Hall and Preddy* [2013] UKSC 73, [2013] 1 WLR 3741. The case was decided under the Equality Act (Sexual Orientation) Regulations 2007, which have since been subsumed within the Equality Act 2010; the standard distinction between direct and indirect discrimination is present in Regulation 3, though the defence of justification is not expressed in terms of proportionality but in Regulation 3(3)(d) as the application of a rule or practice that the user 'cannot reasonably justify'.

[33] Changed by s 1 of the Marriage (Same Sex Couples) Act 2013.

their sexual orientation as a core component of a person's identity under Article 8 of the European Convention on Human Rights (ECHR). Lady Hale quoted the European Court of Human Rights (ECtHR) to the effect that the Convention requires 'very weighty reasons' to justify discrimination on the ground of sexual orientation, and clearly the court regarded the interest of hoteliers in discriminating against homosexuals for religious reasons as far from being sufficiently weighty. Notice that the insertion of the Human Rights Act 1998 and the ECHR at this point in the reasoning requires a court to consider whether a finding of direct discrimination is consistent with Convention rights, which poses a question of justification within direct discrimination, though one that is turned around to ask whether the legislative prohibition of direct discrimination rather than the conduct of the defendant is justifiable.

D. Legislative Discrimination

The contention that the justification element in discrimination law concerns the need to protect the fundamental rights of the alleged discriminator receives some support from an unexpected direction. This balancing of fundamental rights must only apply logically where the defendant (as well as the claimant) possesses relevant fundamental rights. Where the legislature or government authority is in effect the defendant to a claim of indirect discrimination, the state may not be able to rely upon fundamental rights in the same way as private actors. Where the state is legislating or implementing democratically chosen policies, it cannot invoke as a justification for its actions its own fundamental rights. Therefore the test of justification on these occasions cannot be the normal balancing mechanism provided by the test of proportionality. The resulting divergence in the meaning of the justification test in the law of indirect discrimination therefore tends to support the contention that in the normal case of the application of the justification element, the task presented to the court is ultimately one of balancing competing rights.

This expected divergence is confirmed in the judicial interpretations of the test of justification with respect to indirect discrimination. In cases where legislation is itself challenged on the ground that it has indirect discriminatory effects, instead of applying the normal test of proportionality the courts substitute a deferential test. For instance, one controversial topic in UK employment law concerns the rule that employees have to serve a lengthy qualifying period before they become entitled to protection against unfair dismissal. A lengthy service requirement is likely from a statistical point of view to affect women adversely because they tend to have more career breaks and shorter tenure of jobs than men. Furthermore, the legitimate aim claimed by government, such as the aim of increasing levels of employment for women, has never been shown to have been achieved by a lengthy qualifying period. Nevertheless, the government's defence of justification for the qualifying period is invariably successful despite the inadequately justified indirect sex discrimination embedded in the law. The main reason why this legislation escapes judicial censure is due to the loose test of justification applied in such cases by the Court of Justice of the European Union, as in the following quotation.

> [I]f a considerably smaller percentage of women than men is capable of fulfilling the requirement ... imposed by the disputed rule, it is for the Member State, as the author of the allegedly discriminatory rule, to show that the said rule reflects a legitimate aim of its social policy, that that aim is unrelated to any discrimination based on sex, and that it could reasonably consider that the means chosen were suitable for attaining that aim.[34]

In this test, a legal rule or a government regulation with a discriminatory impact on a protected group can be justified if the government or Parliament reasonably thought it was justified. It was recognised by the UK courts in this case that the normal test of proportionality was 'too stringent'.[35] In truth this reasonableness test is really no more than an irrationality test, so that governments will be able to maintain rules with indirectly discriminatory adverse effects on protected groups unless those rules seem arbitrary or capricious. The same deference occurs in the context of claims under the European Convention of Human Rights. When applicants seek to challenge welfare provisions and other democratically chosen laws on taxation and benefits, the ECtHR employs a 'manifestly without reasonable foundation' test.[36] Although this test preserves the possibility of challenging arbitrary, capricious and irrational regulations, in general government policies will escape the strict scrutiny of the normal test of proportionality.

In other contexts, where the government is performing actions that could be carried out by private actors, such as being an employer or a landlord, the normal stricter test of proportionality will be applied to claims of indirect dis-

[34] Case C-167/97 *Regina v Secretary of State for Employment, ex parte Nicole Seymour-Smith and Laura Perez* [1999] ECR I-00623, [77]. A slightly different formulation is used in other cases: Case 171/99 *Rinner-Kuhn v FWW Spezial-Gebaudereinigung GmbH* [1989] ECR 2743: 'if the Member State can show that the means chosen meet a necessary aim of its social policy and that they are suitable and requisite for attaining that aim, the mere fact that the provision affects a much greater number of female workers than male workers cannot be regarded as constituting an infringement ...'. See also for a loose test of proportionality: Case 317/93 *Nolte v Landesversicherungsanatalt Hannover* [199] ECR I-4625.

[35] Lord Nicholls in *R v Secretary of State for Employment ex parte Seymour-Smith and Perez* [2000] 1 WLR 435 (HL).

[36] *James v United Kingdom* (App no 8793/79) (1986) 8 EHRR 123, [46]; *National & Provincial Building Society v United Kingdom* (App no 21319/93) (1997) 25 EHRR 127, [80]; *Carson v. United Kingdom* (App. no 42184/05) (2010) 51 EHRR 13, [61]. This approach was followed in *R (RJM) v Secretary of State for Work and Pensions* [2008] UKHL 63, [2009] 1 AC 311; and *Humphreys v Revenue and Customs* [2012] UKSC 18, [2012] 1 WLR 1545.

crimination. For instance, in *London Underground Ltd v Edwards (No 2)*,[37] a new shift system for underground train drivers introduced by a collective agreement made it hard for single parents to manage their child care arrangements in the morning before school, though in fact this problem only seems to have affected Ms Edwards. Having concluded that this adverse effect on single parents disproportionately affected women, the tribunal held that it would have been possible for the employer to have introduced an exception to the new roster for single parents, so the rule could not pass a strict test of justification. Indeed, the employer had initially proposed this exception on a temporary basis, to which the trade union seems to have objected, so in effect the employer had admitted that the alternative rule would have been appropriate to achieve its legitimate purpose.

Although the division of cases for the application of different standards of justification between legislative acts and ordinary contractual cases is usually clear, there can be hybrid cases where the state is both acting as an employer and at the same time trying to implement democratically chosen policies through its terms of employment. In such a case, when applying the test of justification for indirect discrimination a court is apparently required both to apply a strict test of necessity and to defer to the policy choice of the democratically accountable body. The decision in *Ladele v Islington*[38] illustrates this conundrum, for Islington's equality policy of serving all its constituents regardless of their possessing one of the protected characteristics was a policy choice that could not easily be impugned by the court because it had been democratically adopted by the local authority and it was not irrational. Despite the fact that the Council acted in a rather heavy-handed manner and refused to create any exceptions to its requirement that Registrars of marriages should also conduct civil partnership ceremonies, its arguably disproportionate interference with the freedom of its employee to manifest her religion was not a policy choice that the court was willing to question.[39]

IV. CONCLUSION

Although many queries remain and many controversial points have been ventured without adequate support, my tentative general answer to the question of what justifies justification in indirect discrimination law is that

[37] *London Underground Ltd v Edwards (No 2)* [1997] IRLR 157 (EAT).

[38] *Ladele v London Borough of Islington* [2009] EWCA Civ 1357, [2010] ICR 532; *Eweida v United Kingdom* (App no 48420/10) (2013) 57 EHRR 8.

[39] Similarly a Parliamentary scheme for early retirement in the police service could not be challenged by individual officers under a strict test of proportionality: *Chief Constable of West Midlands Police v Harrod* UKEAT/189/14, [2015] ICR 1311 (EAT).

this provision in the law should be regarded as an application in this context of a broader approach to balancing competing rights of private actors that is found in human rights law. Under this ultimate balancing test, a court is required to apply a double proportionality test in order to minimise any interference with the rights of both parties. Normally a court should avoid a conclusion that eliminates the essence of the rights of one party altogether. For this reason, indirect discrimination must include a justification element for otherwise landlords and employers would not in some instances be able to run their enterprises effectively. For instance, hoteliers must be able to restrict entry to those who can afford to pay the charges, even if their prices have a disparate adverse impact on some protected groups. Similarly, employers must be able to insist upon job-related qualifications in order to ensure competence and efficiency in the workplace. The justification element protects the rights of hoteliers, employers and other duty holders where necessary, though in a way that involves minimising the harm to the rights of others. Foxes have rights too.

Index

www.ingramcontent.com/pod-product-compliance
Ingram Content Group UK Ltd.
Pitfield, Milton Keynes, MK11 3LW, UK
UKHW020244290926
15470UKWH00002B/732

9 781509 912544